HQ:SB

The Complete Frankie Howerd

FRANKIE HOWERD

The Complete Frankie Howerd

ROBERT ROSS

Reynolds & Hearn Ltd
London

Dedicated to that 'lovely boy'
Gunner Parkin: Christopher Mitchell
(1948-2001), a dear, valued friend, a
fine actor and a much-missed part of
my life. God bless, old pal.

First published in 2001 by
Reynolds & Hearn Ltd
61a Priory Road
Kew Gardens
Richmond
Surrey TW9 3DH

© Robert Ross 2001

A CIP catalogue record for this book is
available from the British Library.

ISBN 1 903111 08 0

Designed by Kate Pankhurst.

Printed and bound in Great Britain by Biddles
Ltd, Guildford, Surrey.

Contents

Acknowledgments

My thanks to those who worked with
and knew the great man: Ian Carmichael,
Barry Cryer, Jim Dale, Yolande Donlan,
Dave Freeman, Ray Galton, Val Guest,
Norman Mitchell, Caroline Munro,
Peter Rogers. Alan Simpson, Joan Sims and
Kathy Staff.

Many thanks once again to Marcus Hearn
and Richard Reynolds, for allowing me
another wallow in the countless delights of
my favourite British comedy.

My gratitude, also, to
Charlie Baker, Jeremy Bentham,
Rick and Christine Blackman,
Michael Cofer, Ian Crane,
the Joel Finler Collection,
the ever-dependable John Herron,
the eternally helpful Tessa Le Bars,
Kate Pankhurst for a truly excellent
job of design, Professor Tony Williams
(Area Head of Film Studies, Southern
Illinois University), the British Film Institute's
Special Materials Unit, Colindale Newspaper
Library, Hammer Film Productions, the
gang at Pinewood Studios and…
last but not least… my good pal Alan Coles
for absolutely nothing this time round!

Hats off, too, to the ever-resourceful
Adrian Rigelsford. And a special thank you
to Jonathan Rigby, whose invaluable help
made all the difference.

And a final toast to the main man himself –
the late, much-loved and much-missed
Frankie Howerd.

And just to clear up any confusion in advance:
throughout, I've referred to the TV *Up
Pompeii!* with an exclamation mark at the end,
as it was habitually billed in *Radio Times* and
on the end credits of the programmes
themselves. The film of *Up Pompeii* doesn't get
one, however – those granite credit titles never
found room for one!

Foreword

Val Guest and his wife, actress Yolande Donlan, pictured in 1957. Val directed Frankie in the feature films *The Runaway Bus* (1953) and *Further Up the Creek* (1958).

There are comedians and comedians and then there was our chum Frankie Howerd. Frankie was king of British comics, his appeal stretching from the beer-drinking workers to the champagne-toting aristocracy. And, like a king, he was completely at ease in either strata of society.

What most people don't know about Frankie is that he had an amazing, childlike curiosity about our world and the people in it. Which, through reading and researching, made him an intelligent, self-educated man and a great conversationalist who could, and did, hold his own with the intellectuals. It also kept him up to date in his dialogue, which was possibly why he was able to make so many comebacks, being aware of the issues, political and mystical, that interested each generation. In fact, about these subjects, Frankie was so genuinely witty he could have written all his own material had he had the confidence to do so.

Unlike other comics, so often wrapped up in themselves, Frankie was interested in you as a person and your day-to-day problems. More than that, he was there to help when you needed him. On top of which, he was intensely loyal to his friends and family. Whenever we invited him to our parties he always asked 'Can I bring Betty?' Betty was his sister whom he cosseted like a doting father.

However, although he entertained generously, his only selfish quirk was when Betty made her famous Golden Pudding. Frankie would scoop all the best gooey treacle off the top onto his own plate before passing the rest around. Of course, when we chided him about this he merely let out one of his 'Ooh-errs'.

We also recall one day on the Côte d'Azur, on the dining terrace of Beaulieu's Metropole Hôtel, when Frankie warned the waiters that he was 'the biggest demi-pensione on the French Riviera' so he'd like 'a bit more of their Fruit Compost.' Then there was the time at London's Caprice when he started nibbling the marzipan sails of the decorative boat tray in which the petit-fours were served. The waiters were in a panic. But when admonished by one of them, Frankie bristled, 'So why did you make the boat edible if you didn't want me to eat it? Ooh-err!' We all agreed.

But the best thing about Frankie was that he was very aware of the human condition and its fears and frailties. If it bores you to learn that at heart he was a wonderful human being then, as Frankie would say, 'Bore ye not – ooh-err!' Because he was.

He's now up there past the clouds, probably making jokes about those American tourist billionaires whirling around him in spaceships. And the other angels are hooting with laughter.

Ooh-err, Frankie, you were a person worth loving.

Val Guest and Yolande Donlan
Palm Springs
May 2001

The Prologue

'Every time you go on stage it's an audition!'
Frankie Howerd

t was a warm, pleasant night. Ironically, the throng of expectant audience members were excitedly preparing to rejoice in being told that 'It's bitter out!' The loyal crowd clutched their tickets and eagerly took their seats in the splendour of the Garrick Theatre in London's West End. We had happily forked out for the cheap and cheerful (black-and-white-with-a-splash-of-red) programmes, detailing the life and times of the man we had come to see. The huge photographs of our hero loomed up out of the pages, that hound-dog expression with impossibly bushy eyebrows and heavy jowls revealing scarcely a glimpse of the real man behind them, the man who had served his humour-hungry public for almost half a century.

We had gathered in the foyer, studied the posters and chuckled at the promise of 'scintillating wit!' from this one-man joke factory. We had already released the moths from our student grant-starved wallets to pick up an audio tape or two, a 'Titter Ye Not' T-shirt or even a drink from the typically expensive bar. None of us had tuned into the man's initial broadcasts on *Variety Bandbox*; few had even heard of them, never mind heard them. We hadn't seen his greatest 1960s West End triumph in *A Funny Thing Happened on the Way to the Forum*, we hadn't seen his films at the cinema, we hadn't even seen his finest contribution to the small screen, *Up Pompeii!*, on its first outrageous broadcast. But somehow we knew the man.

He was an ever-recurring figure from our collective, television-obsessed childhood. A wicked, larger-than-life demon who talked about sex, forbidden pleasures and having a good time while making no secret of his inner uncertainty and uneasy position as the ultimate fairy at the top of the comedy Christmas tree. Here was a man born to be Queen. The chief miner at the quip quippery. The King of smutty comedy. A man who looked more at ease in a toga than a crumpled stage suit. A naughty man with a naughty style. A beloved uncle figure who, somehow, always seemed to tell us the truth. We were happy in his company and happy in the knowledge that we knew the jokes to come. We knew the shambling, stuttering stage persona. We knew this was *the* man. At the start of the Naughty Nineties, we needed a saucy elder statesman to make sense of things. A comedian who related jokes so old they had telegrams from Her Majesty, performing in front of an audience just about coming to grips with what life was all about.

We were the ever-cheering, ever-faithful and ever-amused 'Frankie Pankies'. He was Frankie Howerd.

The truly great comedians have a uniqueness which sets them apart from the crowd of average gag tellers. Indeed, perhaps the very finest aren't really gag tellers at all. They are observers of life's little trials and tribulations. Half-baked political satire or outrageous innuendo – it doesn't matter what the material may be, some performers need an audience merely to listen to their inner thoughts in order to charm, entertain and amuse. Frankie Howerd is arguably the ultimate example of this. For nearly 50 years he toured the country – indeed, the world – with the same well-worn, well-honed collection of rambling short stories, biting commentary and ruthlessly corny one-liners.

Ready for his close-up in a 1970 studio portrait.

The material, for much of his television work, was never more than workmanlike. It didn't need to be. Frankie Howerd could get away with anything. In the autumn of his days, when the Monkhouses, the Hills, the Tarbucks and the Forsyths were continually mocked as the ageing dinosaurs of British comedy, Frankie was somehow immune from the brickbats. This was, after all, a man who had cavorted with scantily clad glamour girls on our screens and tossed in politically unfashionable gags as a matter of course. He was a survivor. With monumental comebacks from the brink of total career failure, he was the Frank Sinatra of British comedy. No performer, before or since, has reached the top so quickly and faced the bottom so radically as did Frankie.

Even in the ultra-cynical environment of the early 1990s, the nation continued to warm to a gentle comedian who tried to be hard-nosed and cruel but always seemed to be apologising for any offence he may have caused. In retrospect, Frankie's outrageous humour seemed to be the perfect antidote to the 'greed is good' mentality of Thatcher's Britain. A generation earlier, Max Miller had inspired the same unadulterated, unconditional love from his audiences. Frankie Howerd was the natural successor. Indeed, Frankie is quite simply the finest post-war, front-cloth comedian of all, a man who muttered and spluttered his way through almost 50 rocky years. Throughout his reign as the King of Innuendo, Frankie delighted in the corniest, cheapest japes and most obvious, painful puns. The act hardly altered at all. From his earliest days, wowing the battle-weary Home Service audiences with his nervous stage patter, until his very last days of remorseless touring, there was seldom anything other than relentlessly strung-out shaggy dog stories, pained looks of pleading disdain to his audience and a torrent of over-used, over-familiar and over-precious catchphrases. 'Titter ye not!' was assured an audience reaction on a par with 'To be or not to be' at the National.

Everything he did was peppered with a never-ending line of painstakingly scripted and remorselessly rehearsed 'Oohs', 'Ahhs', 'No Missus', 'Not on your nellie', 'Shut your face'

business which could grip an audience for two hours and reduce them to a quivering, insanely smiling jelly. He was the master of droll patter. A comedian who could get a crowd laughing the moment he wandered onto the stage to the child-like theme of 'Happy Days Are Here Again'. An ill-fitting suit, an ill-fitting toupée and a collection of tailor-made anecdotes that had been nipped, tucked and embellished over the years by the finest crop of scriptwriters in the business. Johnny Speight, Barry Took, Marty Feldman, Ray Galton, Alan Simpson, Eric Sykes, Barry Cryer, Dick Vosburgh, Peter Cook: all of them were convinced that Frankie owed them money from almost every gig he performed. The material was stored in that colossal bundle of pent-up angst and nervous energy that was Frankie Howerd.

Few could explain why this shaggy mammoth from a distant age was suddenly the hippest comedian in the country. A contemporary of the relentlessly working Ken Dodd and Max Bygraves, Frankie seemed to wipe the dust of decades from his shoes, sidestep the 'oh, what a lovely war!' jamboree aimed at audiences of his own age and speak instead to the university generation. He didn't so much reinvent himself as reinvent the teenager. He had done it once before during the early 1960s and, in the late 1980s, he did it once again with pretty much the same material and the same crumpled suit. For the last three or four years of his life he became the darling of the younger set, delighting in the adoration, applause and appreciation of his beloved Frankie Pankies.

Po-faced journalists tried to dismiss it as the fresh-faced student brigade adopting this veteran titter-monger in an ironic way. It was suggested that Frankie was packing out theatres because the show was so bad it was good. In fact, the complete opposite is true. The show was good. Very, very good. I know because I was there. Quite a lot, as it happens. I was mighty proud to be one of the switched-on groupies for the grand old man of corn and prouder still, at the very last show I saw Frankie give, to be individually dubbed 'a Basingstoke beastie!' You don't forget a personal touch like that from your all-time favourite stand-up in a hurry!

Strangely, his genius is less celebrated today. There is a warm and misty-eyed love for his innuendo-encrusted prologues to *Up Pompeii!* and almost the entire population cites him as a legendary Carry On star, although he only appeared in two of those illustrious films. It seems that, like Kenneth Williams, it takes the barrel-scraping wit of screenwriter Talbot Rothwell to keep the Howerd legend in the limelight. But Frankie's huge back-catalogue is rarely screened on TV. The tip of the iceberg is joyous, of course, but the bit beneath the surface is packed with treasures.

Along the way Frankie dominated the airwaves with vivacious tales of bizarre happenings, recorded hit records with June Whitfield and Margaret Rutherford and became (albeit for just a few years) the major comedy box-office draw in British cinemas. Through the decades he was championed by powerful movers and shakers, from Peter Cook and Ned Sherrin to Jonathan Ross, and continually played the fame game on his own, very personal terms. He remorselessly trod the boards, facing the all-consuming nerves of live performance to enchant crowds from lowly working men's clubs to the London Palladium. He rejoiced in countless charity and troop shows, bewitched children in pantomime performances and became one of the nation's favourite small screen comedy actors with credits ranging from the eponymous *Frankie Howerd Show* to the initially untransmitted *Then Churchill Said To Me*. He even broke through into Hollywood with a cameo role in *Sgt. Pepper's Lonely Hearts Club Band*, starred in a pop video and recorded a rap record without a 'c'!

As in my book dedicated to Sid James, this celebration of Frankie Howerd is not intended to be a definitive biography of the great man – others have gone that route before – but instead a thorough investigation of a captivating career on radio, film, television, record and stage. Hopefully, the result will rekindle the readers' pleasure in the comic greatness of Frankie Howerd, a droll clown who, unlike any of his beloved and brilliant contemporaries – whether it be Eric Morecambe, Tony Hancock, Peter Sellers or Tommy Cooper – ended his days safe in the knowledge that he was at the very top: a cult star, worshipped by a new breed of fan and still adored by his faithful followers from the past.●

It's not what I say, but what you think I say – Frankie pleads innocent in the 1970 film version of *Up Pompeii*.

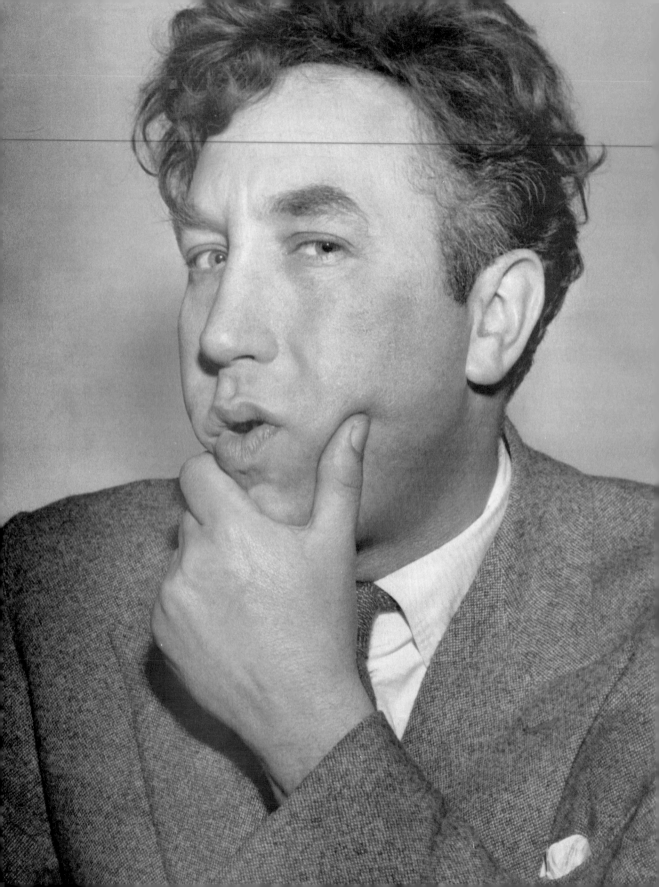

CHAPTER

1

The Boy From York
FRANKIE'S EARLY YEARS

'I learned through failure!'

Frankie Howerd

Above the unassuming stage door of the Grand Opera House York is a rather ambiguous blue plaque from Comic Heritage. It reads simply 'Frankie Howerd – Son of York'. There is no mention of his innuendo-mongering genius, his toga-wearing flamboyance or even his date of birth. However, what that plaque does illustrate is that, far from being a born-and-bred London comedian as many assume, the young Frankie was a Yorkshire lad and proud of it.

He was born plain old Francis Alick Howard at York's City Hospital on 6 March 1917. Later, for official public disclosure and his *Who's Who* entry, that date would be amended to 6 March 1922 and contribute to a thousand incorrect reference book entries which remained incorrect until his real date of birth was released after his death. Indeed, almost all the newspaper obituaries in April 1992 got the all-important birth date incorrect by that precious five years. One can imagine Frankie's smirk of satisfaction.

The family lived at 53 Hartoft Street. Frankie's father, Frank Alfred William Howard, was a respected regular private solider in the 1st Royal Dragoons, while his mother, Edith Florence née Morrison, was a Presbyterian Scot who worked in the local Rowntree chocolate factory. With the young Francis barely three years old and the First World War just ended, Frank Senior was transferred to the Royal Artillery at Woolwich Barracks, promoted to sergeant and forced to relocate to London. The soldier and his family moved to 19 Arbroath Road, Eltham, South London. Although still unknown, Leslie Towns Hope, a son of Eltham, would become one of Hollywood's top comedians in the late 1930s by changing his name to Bob Hope. The little local theatre that Frankie knew as a boy has since been rechristened the Bob Hope Theatre and, indeed, Frankie is seen visiting the newly christened venue in the *Omnibus* programme, *Titter Ye Not! The Frankie Howerd Story*.

Settled in their new home, the family was extended with a brother for Francis, Sidney, and a sister, Bettina, commonly known by family and friends as simply Betty. However, the move didn't prove a success. Frank Senior was invalided out of service and had to face a new career as an academic trainer of soldiers in the Army Education Corps. Like Benny Hill's father, Frankie's parental influence appears to have been strict and unemotional. He died in 1934 when Frankie was still a teenager. Interviewed in *TV Times* 35 years

A pensive publicity shot from 1958

later, Frankie commented that his father 'was *all right*. He was away a lot. Look, I didn't let you in here to ask me Freudian questions.'

The acting bug can be traced back to Frankie's very first experience of a theatre. As with most of us, it was a pantomime and the sheer delight of the brightly coloured scenery and tune-filled wonderland never left him. It was Boxing Day 1925 when the young Frankie first stepped foot in Woolwich's Royal Artillery Theatre to relish a performance of *Cinderella*. The family had queued patiently for two hours for the start of the 8.00 pm performance to gaze on Nora Delaney as Prince Charming. Almost three decades later, Frankie himself performed on that very stage and revelled in the memories of the show that sealed his fate. Frankie's Mum, an equally besotted lover of theatre and show business, would often scrape together some precious housekeeping money and treat the family to a rare and greatly anticipated trip to the local music hall. Besides that, the Boxing Day pantomime trip became an annual traditional treat for the Howard family. Francis was so entranced by the magic of play-acting that he created his very own home stage out of a tea tray. He cut out characters from the pages of *Film Fun* and often entertained his family with impromptu performances of the pantomime classics.

Ultimately, this home-made exercise developed further and, roping in the girl next door, Ivy Smith, for moral support, Francis became the youngest theatrical entrepreneur in South London by staging his own concert parties at the bottom of the girl's garden. Ever the bright spark, Francis even managed to make the local kids part with the princely sum of a farthing in order to enter the garden and enjoy the show. His mother was furious at this outrageous behaviour and made the heartbroken boy give all the money back. In his 1976 autobiography, *On the Way I Lost It*, Frankie dismissed the incident by grandly proclaiming that 'I assumed that if I charged a farthing and kids paid I just had to be worth it!'

However, the incident clearly turned him off performing for a while. Indeed, life wasn't easy for Frankie and this innocent form of expression had been an attempt to find an escape route from his South London environment, an increasingly distant father and a growing sense of uncertainty. Indeed, on the Pinewood set of *Carry On Doctor* in late 1967, Frankie opened his heart to an interviewer, explaining that 'It's a fear of rejection really. I suppose it really came from my unhappy childhood and all the failure I had when I was trying to make it as a comedian ... That insecure feeling is something I've never lost ... For me there was a great deal of loneliness and sadness in being young. I wasn't wanted.'

With show business apparently ruled out, Francis turned to the church for comfort and direction. Naturally, his mother was keen to encourage this ambition and the lonely schoolboy found solace in his religious pursuits. Indeed, his mother saw a bright future for her eldest son even at the tender age of nine. He was to have a career as a respected clergyman. In later years Frankie elaborated on this and was convinced that he himself had his sights set on something much higher. 'I decided to become a Saint!'

Enrolled in the Church of St Barnabus Sunday School, Frankie also joined the Band of Hope and the Society for the Propagation of the Gospel, not to mention the more restrained pleasures of the Cub Scouts. The gangly Francis Alick Howard also attended the Gordon Elementary School, then, from the age of 11, the Woolwich County School For Boys. He later won a London County Council scholarship to Shooter's Hill Grammar School. There, he developed an excellent grasp of mathematics, a complete inability to comprehend geography and a rather cavalier delight in the game of cricket.

Shooter's Hill Grammar also saw Frankie's interest in performing re-emerge. He joined the school's amateur dramatic classes and stepped onto a stage for the first time when performing in a talent competition at the Eltham Parish Hall (ironically the very venue later named after Eltham's most famous export, Bob Hope). Talking in 1990, Frankie recalled those fledgling days with a mixture of dismay and nostalgia. 'I was very naïve –

stupid is another word for it!' For he returned proudly to his local amateur dramatics pursuits and eagerly unveiled his very own play, *Lord Halliday's Birthday Party*, which he intended to be staged as the official school play. Rupert Affleck, the dour headmaster, had other ideas and Frankie's hour-long, ramshackle 'masterpiece' was unceremoniously banned!

Though a shy boy, the young Francis was seemingly bubbling over with belief in his own talent. Undaunted, he rejoiced in his nickname of 'the actor' and carried on writing plays. Obsessed with murder mysteries until his very last days, Frankie wrote pseudo-Agatha Christie pieces and later admitted that these plays were 'bits of all the books I'd ever read!' But a fertile imagination was quite clearly at work. The result was another self-penned play, *Sweet Fanny Adams*, and after that the school 'never put on another masterpiece I wrote!' Instead, he found a new avenue for his writing and this would drag him down the path of corny humour and slightly ribald observations that would prove his stock in trade.

In the early 1930s Frankie was merrily writing for the school magazine, the *Ship*, an annual, end-of-term publication. This allowed the future comedian to amuse his undiscerning readers with a regular 'Frank's Howlers' section full of typically corny blunders, including a definition of Ali Baba as 'being somewhere else when the crime was committed'. With the corniest of jokes becoming his forte it was perhaps surprising that, at the age of 13, Frankie was invited by the Reverend Jonathan Chisholm to become a Sunday School teacher. Combining the traditional tales of Biblical heroes with his own imaginative flights focused on pirates, detectives and historical characters like Robin Hood, these slightly unorthodox teaching sessions proved hugely popular. Frankie was a hit with pupils and staff alike and was encouraged to join the Church Dramatic Society.

He may have been the school's most popular teacher but he was not a confident actor. According to Frankie himself, 'I was all stutter and gabble.' Indeed, his audition for the part of Tilly's father in the old Ian Hay comedy

Butter wouldn't melt – the young Francis Howard stands behind his younger brother Sidney and sister Betty in this late 1920s family portrait.

warhorse, *Tilly of Bloomsbury*, was replete with stammered nervousness. However, the producer, Winifred Young, saw potential in the young man's performance and admired his convincing ability to play old age. After all, here was a mere teenager in a white beard playing a 65-year-old. Winifred Young kindly set aside extra time twice a week to tutor the young man on his performance and technique.

The effort paid off. Following the hugely successful first night performance, a verger warmly congratulated Frankie and blurted out, 'You should be an actor!' Frankie agreed! With very good reviews from the *South London Press*, who wouldn't? He was determined to continue with amateur dramatics and now, in stark contrast to her horror at the back garden concerts, Frankie's mother was very supportive. Indeed, so supportive was she that she endorsed his decision to try for a full-time acting career and sent her younger children, Sidney and Betty, out to work from the age of 14, while Francis concentrated on acting lessons.

At 16 he began evening classes in acting with the London County Council. One of his teachers was the experienced actress Mary Hope who coached Frankie for his audition for the Royal Academy of Dramatic Art. With nerves at breaking point and equipped with a bag of cheese sandwiches lovingly prepared by his mother, Frankie arrived at Holborn Station and slowly made his way to the RADA headquarters at 62 Gower Street. He stammered his way through his well-practised set-pieces, finally crumbling as he muttered one of Hamlet's soliloquies. Not surprisingly the jury failed the young hopeful and with heavy heart he returned home. A mere two hours after the humiliating rejection he was strolling through the fields in Eltham, a lonely and reflective figure. However, this was the major turning point. According to Frankie mythology and, indeed, the great man's memoirs, he concluded that if he couldn't make a success as a straight Shakespearean actor then his future lay in comedy.

It is unlikely, however, that Frankie, notoriously indecisive at the best of times, could have bounced back so quickly. He returned to grammar school and the calmer, more receptive waters of amateur dramatics. With his father in poor health, the family were struggling and Frankie's mother became the housekeeper for a wealthy family in Eltham. The desire to tread the boards didn't leave Frankie and he teamed up with his sister Betty for a number of local charity concerts. Largely based around short pieces that Frankie wrote himself, the duo would sing, dance and do almost anything to raise a smile from the audience. Boosted by the popularity of these undemanding pieces, Frankie was welcomed back to the Church Dramatic Society and the Shooter's Hill Old Boys' Dramatic Society.

After the RADA disaster, *Hamlet* was

clearly never going to be his forte but he was frequently reminded of his rave reviews for *Tilly of Bloomsbury* – a comedy piece. A reflective (and unpublished) comment from a 1978 interview is probably the nearest we will ever get to hearing the truth about Frankie's motivation from the horse's mouth. He recalled that 'When I was very young I originally wanted to be an actor but I had a speech impediment and used to stutter. My voice used to go and I got very frightened. I joined amateur dramatics societies and enrolled in London County Council Drama School to become an actor. Then, because we were poor, I applied for a scholarship at the Royal Academy of Dramatic Art. But I failed at the audition because I started stuttering and became afraid so they threw me out.

'Then I thought that if I can't be a straight actor I'll become a comedian and concentrate on being funny. So I did patter acts and jokes of my own at concert parties, entertained at hospitals, scout halls, church halls, amateur talent competitions, anywhere that would have me. When I went into the army I entertained soldiers but not as a professional. I just did it as a hobby. That's how I learned what little I knew about show business – by just standing up and talking.' That 'just standing up and talking' would become an art form.

Although he was saddled with a job as filing clerk for Henry A Lane of Shooter's Hill, and subsequently a position at the firm's Southwark office (37-45 Tooley Street), during his spare evenings Frankie would perform anywhere, be it a Sunday School in Herne Bay or an Old Folks' Home. With renewed confidence, Frankie started performing his own revues, featuring self-penned gags and a vast array of comic characters. He toured with the Gertchers Concert Party and, ultimately, the eponymous Frank Howard's Knock Out Concert Party. Revelling in the exposure and happily seizing the lion's share of the laughs, Frankie appeared in all but one of the show's 22 revue sketches and, speaking to *Radio Times* in 1955, recalled that 'I always cast myself as a bumbling, stupid fellow – a sort of village idiot with a London accent.' Writing in

1976, Frankie admitted that 'the ego was in full flight. The 22nd [item] was given over to a girl singer and I've often wondered why I never made it a duet.'

In 1940 Frankie had braved air-raids to see Max Miller and Vera Lynn in the Holborn Empire revue *Apple Sauce*, and the following year he caught Leslie Henson, Cyril Ritchard, Stanley Holloway and Binnie Hale in *Up and Doing* at the Saville Theatre. On both occasions air-raid warnings forced performers and punters to stay put in the auditorium until the small hours and on both occasions Frankie shied away from an impromptu rendition of 'Three Little Fishes'. 'They asked for volunteers to go on stage and "do something",' Frankie explained. 'I said to myself, "At least you'll have what might be your one and only opportunity to appear on a West End stage" – but every time I started to get up, shyness forced me back into my seat.' Ironically, both shows contained future co-stars of Frankie's: Holloway, Hale and, as Max Miller's stooge in *Apple Sauce*, the young Jean Kent.

It was around this time that the young comedian suddenly and inexplicably changed his name from Frank Howard to the 'irresistible star quality' of Ronnie Ordex. It was only for a very brief period, but for a handful of rather lowly and potentially damaging appearances in South London, Frankie submerged himself in this alter ego for the same old pot-pourri of comic monologues, humorous vignettes and uproarious music hall songs. Needless to say, Frankie quickly reverted to his own name and it was as the relatively plain-sounding Frank Howard that he performed at talent nights in music halls throughout London.

One particular appearance clearly sticks out as a nightmarish situation. It was at the Lewisham Hippodrome. Jack Payne and his Orchestra, with whom Frankie would appear at the London Palladium some 20 years later, were in residence. Frankie's future *Variety Bandbox* sparring partner, Derek Roy, was performing, as was the truly legendary Jimmy James. Frankie was totally overawed by the great man's prowess and ability to charm his audience. To make matters worse, Frankie was due to follow James on the bill. A severe sense of inferiority succeeded in knocking Frankie's comic timing for six. Even at the height of his powers there could be few worse or more embarrassingly shambolic clowns than Frankie when his timing had gone. Thankfully it happened all too rarely but this important revue with important colleagues was not the ideal moment.

As with Benny Hill and Peter Sellers, younger comedians who would make it in Frankie's wake, the majority of Frankie's comic patter was based around workmanlike impressions of the great and good of film and stage. He would impersonate the staccato energy of James Cagney, the delicious clipped tones of Noël Coward, the Gallic charisma of Maurice Chevalier and the multi-faceted grotesquerie of Charles Laughton. He might have fallen back on the stock hunchback performance one too many times but at least they were self-contained, self-written comic interludes for the characters to inhabit, not simply impressions for impressions' sake. We are denied a record of Frankie's impersonation skills, although he had a keen ear for dialogue and was a self-confessed movie buff. His favourite film, *Kiss of Death*, the 1947 thriller that made a star of Richard Widmark, provided him with his favourite off-duty impression, that of Widmark's distinctive, chilling chuckle. Those who heard it were amazed by its uncanny accuracy.

Regardless of Frankie's ability to regurgitate chunks of *Private Lives* in a uniquely comic style, the Lewisham gig wasn't going down very well at all. After one stumble and stutter too many, the frustrated musical director bellowed 'Do something or get off!' The distraught comedian did the latter and even 30 years later seemed to shudder as he recalled the walk of shame. 'I stumbled off in tears.' From showbiz dream to stammering wreck seemed to be the norm for Frankie's fledgling attempts at stage comedy. He had survived initial put-downs, a RADA failure and four rejections from the all-powerful Carrol Levis. Auditioning for the Canadian talent scout, he

A 1954 recording of *The Frankie Howerd Show* at the Camden Theatre with one of Frankie's all-time comedy heroes, Jimmy James.

had tried elaborate shaggy dog stories at the Lewisham Hippodrome and colourful impersonations at the New Cross Empire, but both acts failed and Frankie was a mightily dejected wannabe clown. 'I was the most undiscovered discovery of my day!' he told *Radio Times* in 1955.

Half-hearted, he continued to perform at church halls while secretly believing that his future was more than likely to rest in the job he had secured in an insurance firm. Then came 3 September 1939, the day war broke out. It was, as Frankie often mentioned in his stand-up performances, a very important date. Without the German invasion of Poland and Chamberlain's stance against Adolf Hitler, the face of popular entertainment from the late 1940s might have been totally different. A whole catalogue of prime performers emerged from the army, navy and RAF and, for a short

but potent time, Frankie Howerd was the biggest of the lot.

With the war in Europe Frankie's thoughts of show business were put on the back-burner – for a short while, anyway. Besides, his country had other plans. In February 1940 Howard F A was called up to serve with his father's old mob, the Royal Artillery, and posted to Shoeburyness near Southend-on-Sea. Hardly making the most impressive of starts, Frankie was dubbed 'the unknown quantity' by the outfit's ruthless sergeant major, Alfred Tonks. The loud-mouthed authority figure had been at the receiving end of one of Frankie's off-the-cuff moments of cheek when he muttered 'Speak up!' on the parade ground.

Soldiering was hardly the major thing on Frankie's mind. He continued to write songs during his army days and it is even alleged that he started to rewrite and restructure his vintage play, *Sweet Fanny Adams*, which had been performed at his grammar school, as a new musical. With conscripted professional musicians in tow, he would write, produce and star in the shows *Fine Goings On* (later the title for his first star vehicle on radio), *Talk About Laugh* and *Rise and Shine*. Whatever his extracurricular activities, the business of preparing for battle continued unabated and, following basic training, Frankie decamped to another part of the Shoeburyness barracks. It was here, towards the end of 1940, that Frankie's ambition could be suppressed no longer. He applied for a transfer to the Entertainment National Services Association.

It wasn't long before that cockney wag Tommy Trinder rechristened ENSA as 'Every Night Something Awful'. Awful or not, for the 23-year-old Francis Howard it was yet another failure. His much-anticipated audition at the Theatre Royal Drury Lane failed to land him a place with ENSA and it was back to square one. He was still not beaten, however. The YMCA, one of the very few entertainment ports of call for servicemen, held Sunday night camp concerts in the mess and literally anybody willing to have a bash could climb up for his three or four minutes in the spotlight. That 'anybody' happened to include Francis Howard. His material was pretty nondescript stuff and, in common with nine out of ten comedians trying to win the admiration of the troops, the majority of it was borrowed (or rearranged) Max Miller. However, at least one copper-bottomed Howerdism shone through and, in fact, he considered it the first successful gag he ever told professionally. It concerned a beautiful girl being walked home after a dance by a charming chap on the make. She's carrying two ducks and he ponders how to make love to her. The solution? She lets *him* hold them! It was the perfect humorous fare for blokes stationed miles from their loved ones.

The other crucial feature of Frankie's first Sunday garrison concert appearance related to his name. The army barracks were hives of good-natured familiarity and the announcer thought nothing of introducing the latest turn as Gunner Frankie Howard of B Battery. At first, Frankie disliked 'Frankie' intensely and to his dying day his closest friends always called him Frank. However, the young servicemen seemed to warm to it and so it stuck.

The 'oohs' and 'ahhs' weren't far behind. Initially they were simply part of the stammering, nerve-wracked Frankie persona but the audiences laughed and the more they laughed the more Frankie enjoyed it. The dazed looks, pregnant pauses and garbled phrases would cover dialogue fluffs and forgotten lines throughout his career but the majority were scripted, beautifully crafted and perfectly timed.

However, the rising star was going nowhere in particular while the war raged on. Indeed, in 1940 there was an invasion scare on the Home Front and at one stage, according to Frankie, our hapless hero was 'almost single-handedly' defending Wakering and Southend-on-Sea before returning to Shoeburyness. Over the months, Frankie rose to the top of the bill in the lowly camp concerts. In these dimly lit halls, the immortal Frankie style was fashioned. Surrounded by struggling singers and magicians, continually fighting attacks of nerves, hitting on the notion of dubbing all hated authority figures as 'them!' and injecting that immortal, laughter-inducing stammer into a torrent of silly shaggy dog stories, Frankie was emerging as something of a star.

Together with Betty, Frankie laboured at improving his performances and the two hit upon the idea of Frankie singing the alphabet to himself to improve his voice and prepare for a stint on stage. The patter, the uncertain style and the ever-so-slightly rude comic observations proved irresistible. And then there was that ever-celebrated favourite: female impersonation. Frankie, together with two other guys, all dressed as ATS girls, would entertain the troops as Miss Twillow, Miss True and Miss Twist. This unique slice of fun became so popular that it was incorporated into a civilian outfit and toured the Southend area in a van. The glamour of showbiz! As

The ultimate accolade – Frankie features as a radio celebrity on this Turf cigarette card from 1950.

"TURF" CIGARETTES

FRANKIE HOWERD

50 RADIO CELEBRITIES Nº 25

been a hit for Max Miller, so why not borrow it? Frankie would also 'borrow' a couple of young ladies who made his acquaintance during the war years. Vere Roper and Blanche Moore would both, many years later, become elderly and apparently deaf matrons stationed at the piano as Frankie bellowed his front-cloth patter.

Frankie's beloved stage persona was beginning to take on a life of its own. The oft-heard early catchphrase, 'I'll just make myself comfy!', originated during the wartime concerts. In 1942 Frankie had been posted to the Army Experimental Station near Swansea. The experience left an indelible mark on him. Interviewed in 1955 he commented, 'Whenever I am in South Wales I always go back to visit the old derelict huts where I was stationed in the army. Although they're all overgrown and completely deserted I walk around wondering where my old comrades have gone and what they're doing now.'

In 1944 Frankie was transferred to Plymouth for the Allied invasion of France. Despite making something of a name for himself as a stand-up comedian, he had auditioned unsuccessfully for the coveted Stars in Battledress no fewer than four times. These so-called auditions usually took place in a cold and humourless cookhouse in front of just one cold and humourless officer. At the end of the audition the officer's reaction was simply 'Very good, Howard' and the young comedian heard nothing more. Frankie needed an audience for his particular brand of comic magic to fully come together.

Promoted to sergeant, he was then stationed in Brussels, closer to enemy action than he had ever been before. Indeed, he regaled dinner parties forever more with his comically tinged tale of bobbing in the waters during the D-Day landings and somehow got away with it. The shortage of talent towards the end of the war saw our man in Brussels become almost a one-man show. He poured his time and effort into organising unofficial concert parties in Hanover to keep the British troops, still stationed in the defeated Germany, amused. Talking to *TV Times* in 1969, Frankie reflected

often as not borrowing uniforms from personnel stationed at the bases where they were performing and leaving many an ATS girl freezing in the wings, it was as a direct result of these performances that Frankie was promoted to the rank of bombardier and joined the concert party in Westcliff.

One particular talent night at the Palace Theatre is celebrated for Frankie standing erect and proud and warbling the tasty little ditty, 'She Sits Among the Cabbages… and Peas!' After much indignation from the wings he was ordered off the stage. Never one to leave good material out of his act, this loud barracking from behind the curtain was later toned down to nothing more than imaginary heckles from the manager and milked by Frankie for all its worth. Besides, the whole 'threat from the management' routine had that 'As a sergeant I was quite ready to be out in front of a crowd of people and I lost a good deal of my nervousness and shyness.'

Frankie tried for yet another audition in Nienburg and this one seemed to hold more promise. The showbiz-orientated officer in charge was the much respected Major (later Colonel) Richard Stone. His number two was none other than Captain Ian Carmichael. 'We had broken for lunch after the morning auditions,' Carmichael recalls, 'and the bombardier came up to us as we were leaving and said, "Can I do an audition for you?" Richard Stone said, "No, I'm the Officer in charge of the lads who've come from my unit." He eventually auditioned for us with a song called 'A Tisket a Tasket' which he interspersed with jokes. When he finished Richard said to me, "What do you think?" I said, "Oh no, no, he's too raw, with no timing, and I don't think he's particularly funny." Richard said, "I think you're got it wrong. I'm going to book him for one of our shows" – and that was Frankie Howerd!'

The talent-spotting duo had been instrumental in selecting Benny Hill for concert party prominence and it was at this time that Frankie and Benny first met – the eternal pessimist finally rubbing shoulders with the eternal optimist. Stone was suitably impressed and immediately put Frankie in charge of a concert party touring North West Germany. Finally making headway, Frankie's moment of glory lasted just three months before the inevitable demob. After six years of service he returned home to Great Britain 'with less than £100, a chalk-striped suit and a pork pie hat!' He also had a one-page reference from Richard Stone.

The first thing on every comedian's mind on returning home was to get an agent and quickly. Thus it was that Frankie made long and fruitless trawls through Soho, where the majority of influential agents were based, desperately looking for the latest clue to success or a lead to regular stage work. Eventually he was tempted back to Germany to perform in more troop shows before officially being demobbed and returning to his

long search for an agent in England. The agent Robert Layton tried to keep Frankie's confidence alive but it was another agent, Harry Lowe, who, having declined the chance to represent him, advised him to perform at the Stage Door Canteen in Piccadilly Circus.

It was hardly the most profitable of starts. There was absolutely no payment for the performers and the top of the bill spot was by invitation only – both Bing Crosby and, ironically, Eltham's very own Bob Hope had appeared. The major advantage, as far as Frankie was concerned, was that you didn't need to be represented by an agent to get a gig at the establishment. You did, however, have to be a serviceman. Donning his recently relinquished uniform and heading for yet another audition, 'Sergeant Howard' was successful in landing a brief spot at the venue and eagerly invited Harry Lowe to witness his triumph. Sadly, after an extraordinarily successful spot, Frankie discovered to his horror that the agent hadn't shown up. However, the management were impressed and Frankie was invited to fill a gap on the bill for the following Friday night.

He was initially reluctant, feeling that the fates never played fair with him, allowing him to give of his best when the audience was completely devoid of worthwhile contacts. However, his mother thought another bash at the Stage Door was a good idea and dutifully Frankie agreed. His performance went down a storm once again and this time an agent, or at least someone with a bit of clout, was in the house. This was Stanley Dale. Known as Scruffy, Dale was a booker for the Jack Payne Organisation and arranged a meeting between Frankie and senior Payne representative, Frank Barnard. Quite naturally intimidated by the high-pressure audition, Frankie succeeded in doing just enough to impress the hard-to-please Barnard. The top man encouraged Payne himself to see Frankie entertain an audience and luckily the performance was a hilarious one. Payne signed Frankie on the spot and booked him for the touring revue, *For the Fun of It*. The year was 1946 and Frankie Howerd was a professional comedian.●

CHAPTER

Happy Days are Here Again

FRANKIE ON STAGE

'The easiest thing by far is the stage … because you have a live audience in front of you and you know exactly what you're doing.' **Frankie Howerd**

Frankie's stage work comprised many diverse, challenging and sometimes downright ill-conceived productions. The stage afforded him the opportunity to dip his toes into the waters of classical acting and, more to the point, presented him with the toga-clad role which would rocket him to smutty stardom and remain the most potent of all his comedy personae.

The 1940s

Prior to Frankie's major launch with a featured turn in *For the Fun of It*, it is suggested that he worked for a brief time as a Butlins 'red coat' in Filey, Yorkshire where he was denounced as 'disgusting filth'. This doesn't seem particularly likely and, as far as being a totally professional comedian is concerned, the Frankie story really kicks off with his work under the watchful eye of Jack Payne. Despite the fact that Frankie didn't exactly feel very professional – he maintained that *For the Fun of It* showcased him as a 'timid Max Miller' – the production certainly made waves around the country. It was the summer of 1946 and the tour marked the birth of Frankie Howerd, quite literally.

The story of how Frankie Howard became Frankie Howerd is one of those showbiz legends that has been blown out of all proportion. Some claim that the change occurred during the run of *For the Fun of It*, others that it came even earlier, during the wartime troop shows, when a careless poster designer replaced the 'a' with an 'e' by mistake. The gig went so well that Frankie superstitiously retained it from that point on. The other, more reasonable tale is that the idea to change the surname – albeit only slightly – was Frankie's own. He imagined people catching the name by accident on a poster, doing a double-take at the unusual spelling and remembering the name.

Whatever the reason, Frankie's lukewarm Max Miller-isms and, more significantly, his fledgling attempts at rambling comic stories were proving popular with audiences. The headlining act for the touring revue was stylish singer Donald Peers with the elegant Ernie Ponticelli at the piano, while the broad and warmly funny Nosmo King was the star comedian. The young Frankie (weekly wage: £13 10s) was unceremoniously positioned at the bottom of the bill in a little interlude showcasing new talent.

He's got my part! Frankie visits New York to see Zero Mostel in the original Broadway production of *A Funny Thing Happened on the Way to the Forum*, May 1963.

Entitled, rather provocatively, 'They're Out', he shared the limelight with contortionist Pam Denton and a laid-back comic-cum-crooner called Max Bygraves. The show was produced by Bill Lyon-Shaw who, only a few years later, would be put in charge of Frankie's first television series, *The Howerd Crowd*.

Fittingly, Frankie's first professional engagement was in his native Yorkshire. *For the Fun of It* opened at the Empire Theatre Sheffield on 31 July 1946. His act was, by all accounts, quite extraordinary. Billing himself as 'Frankie Howerd: The Borderline Case', he was granted eight minutes in which to impress the audience. This vignette included a batch of typically long-drawn-out funnies and the already familiar (having featured in his pre-war and conflict performances) treatment of the beloved children's song of mass marine destruction, 'Three Little Fishes', which would splash adoring audiences for almost half a century.

Frankie's sister Betty, demobbed from the ATS, acted as Frankie's unofficial and, as often as not, unpaid stage manager. She would study the auditorium before Frankie's appearances and religiously move around it, from circle to stalls to gallery, in order to gauge the resonance of the place. Frankie would practise his comic patter and Betty would instruct him if his jokes couldn't be heard in certain parts of the theatre.

A stickler for detail even at this early stage, Frankie opted for minimal make-up, like his hero Max Miller, and simply used a lot of blue around his eyelids 'to help the eyes sparkle'. The dress code, stuck to rigorously throughout his stage career, was to wear 'warm colours' in order to endear him to his audience straight away – usually brown or a certain shade of blue. To Frankie's mind, these were friendly colours. The comic element would be heightened by the fact that the brown or blue lounge suit would have a less-than-immaculate appearance. In the days before radio made him a household name, Frankie wanted to win over audiences who had never heard of him before by coming across as part of the crowd, one of 'us', the ordinary sort of bloke you could chat to down the pub. His observations on life were no more funny or revealing than anybody else's, but the way he projected them was all his own. He wanted ordinariness with an edge.

To this end he cross-fertilised the cheeky, near-the-knuckle cosiness of Max Miller with the more acrid tone of another of his great heroes, the legendary W C Fields. As the years went on, this mixture would mellow into Frankie's own unique persona but, for the time being, he was trying to introduce a dangerous element and, like everybody else in the late 1940s, looked to Sid Field for further inspiration. Indeed, in Field's second and final star vehicle for the big screen, *Cardboard Cavalier*, the great man, in petulant, frustrated mood, mutters, 'How very, very dare you!' Frankie would adopt this and other such cries of mock-outrage for his legion of catchphrases.

For the Fun of It ran for nine months and was, as Frankie recalled, 'our tour of the Empire … the Empire Sheffield, Wigan, Huddersfield, Glasgow…' Before the dreaded Glasgow dates, which in fact went extremely well, the show also took in Liverpool, Manchester, Newcastle and Sunderland, usually taking residence for six nights with performances 'twice nightly'. There followed a ten-week variety tour and an audition for one of the string of BBC Radio variety shows at the Aeolian Hall, Mayfair.

Before long Frankie was a rising star on radio's *Variety Bandbox*, and was in need of winning material. Friend and co-star on film and television, Norman Mitchell, remembers Frankie's early desperation to get fresh pieces for his act, a desperation that never subsided. 'Frankie would often come up to me and say, "Hey Norman, if you've any jokes I'll buy them off you! It's all right for you, you just say what's given to you, but I have to practise seven hours for five minutes ad-lib!" He explained to me once that, "The first joke I bought was about an elephant. This Maharishi sent me a white elephant and as we were going round the Cape of Good Hope and across the Bay of Biscay it got chronic diarrhoea. No listen! So when I got it to my house in Napier Street I rang the vet and said, I've got this

elephant with acute diarrhoea – what shall I give it? He said, Give it plenty of room!" Frankie was a lovely man. A great comedian, but so sad. Like Hancock, he was a depressive person who couldn't see how funny he was.'

One fellow comedian who was fully aware of how funny Frankie was, was Eric Sykes. Having been principal comedian in one touring troop show during the war while Frankie had been principal comedian in another, the two budding performers had seen each other work but barely met. While Frankie was principal comic in *The Waggoners*, Sykes had been principal comic in *Strictly Off the*

Record. With an all-consuming passion to get more and better material for his act, Frankie was desperate to track down Sykes and buy the patter he had been performing during the war years.

In 1947 Sykes was earning a meagre living with the Accrington Rep so was more than happy to accept Frankie's offer. Frankie, meanwhile, having enjoyed a successful summer season in sunny Clacton, was appearing at Christmas 1947 in his first pantomime, as Simple Simon in *Jack and the Beanstalk* at the Lyceum Sheffield with Bunny Doyle and Marion Gordon. Luckily, Eric and

Young hopefuls make a hair-raising start to their professional careers as Frankie and Max Bygraves clown just *For the Fun of It* in 1946.

Frankie found each other and a meeting was arranged in Frankie's Sheffield dressing room. The pair gelled perfectly, with Sykes injecting bizarre flights of fancy into Frankie's slightly confused ramblings.

As a thank you to the Stage Door Canteen where it all started, Frankie would return to the venue for variety appearances. Interviewed by John Morrish in 1990, Frankie commented that 'I was considered to be very much the alternative comedian at that time. I was different to everybody else: my attitude was different. Somebody once described me as being 'theatrically untheatrical'. I did things differently technically, on stage: I was very ordinary … I looked as if I'd walked in from the street.'

Eric Sykes was by now firmly established as Frankie's regular scriptwriter, while Spike Milligan was also penning one or two items for his stage routine. With Frankie's fame reaching fever-pitch in 1948, Jack Payne was quick to utilise his bright young find, while audiences were falling over themselves to see what this frantic young comedian looked like in the flesh. Ominously, however, the Jack Payne Organisation constructed an all-encompassing personal management contract, allowing them a bigger slice of the cake than the accepted ten per cent and a five-year agreement which reaped them well over a third of Frankie's earnings during his initial, meteoric rise.

Frankie's rise continued with the risqué touring revue *Ta-Ra-Ra-Boom-De-Ay*. Billed as 'Professor Howerd of *Variety Bandbox*' and revelling in the freedom and flexibility that huge public awareness had brought him, Frankie told reporters that 'I'm on my own so I do more or less what I want!' And at the end of 1948, he was booked to play Buttons in *Cinderella* at Wimbledon, a role he would reprise on three further occasions, the last – in 1980 – at the same theatre.

Living in a rented flat owned by comedian Ben Warriss (6 Holland Villas Road), Frankie seemed unstoppable. 1949 saw Jack Payne further exploit Frankie's *Variety Bandbox* success in a touring showcase called, aptly enough, *Ladies and Gentle-men*. And on Monday 11 April 1949, when the show hit the Shepherd's Bush Empire, Londoners flocked to see the top-billed Frankie Howerd 'in a speedy, all-laughter, musical and dancing roadshow'. The bill of fare was a mouthwatering one all round…

Jack Payne presents
Ladies and Gentle-men

1 – The Hooper Sisters (moving in artistic circles)
2 – The Three Robertis (the Continent's speediest acrobats)
3 – Charlie Clapham (the BBC's No-Consequential Comedian)
4 – Pop, White and Stagger (half dancers-half crackers)
5 – Peggy Cochrane (with her piano, violin and songs)

Intermission – Jack Robson and his Orchestra

6 – The Hooper Sisters dance for your pleasure again
7 – The Henderson Twins (Triss and Wyn, from BBC Variety Bandbox)
8 – Frankie Howerd (resident comedian from BBC Variety Bandbox)
9 – Lotus and José (a Mexican novelty)

Frankie's technique was more akin to his radio style than his later 1970s approach: faster, slicker and more off-the-wall. He was a young man whose inner turmoil and nervousness was masked with bubbling energy. The act was dangerous, at times even sinister. One famous performance, at the Wood Green Empire, saw Frankie wax lyrical on the love of his life – an innocent young girlfriend by the name of Deirdre Cuttlebunt. ('What a pretty name!') For many the humour was halted when Frankie revealed that the poor girl had killed herself. Full of remorse, Frankie plunged into a self-pitying, agonised rant of 'I'm going to throw myself into the river…'

The river, for dramatic effect, was the theatre's inviting orchestra pit. The piece went on for an age and reached emotional heights before Frankie pleaded with his audience, 'Shall I throw myself into the river? Shall I do it?' and waited for his planted stooge to yell out 'Yes!' before muttering, 'What, for you lot? Not bloody likely!' For an audience who could expect nothing more sophisticated than a 'knock-knock' gag or tried-and-tested cross-talk, this ability to paint pictures with words and puncture humour with elongated vowels and manic hair-tussling was refreshing, even radical, stuff.

1949's summer season was spent alongside Ted and Barbara Andrews, parents of Julie, at the Blackpool Central. 'Julie was about 12 years old at the time,' Frankie maintained, 'and 20 years later in Hollywood she still remembered my rendering (or should it be rending?) of 'Three Little Fishes'.' The end of that year saw Frankie heading the cast of *Puss in Boots* at the Liverpool Empire with George Bolton, Sunny Rogers and Paula Grey – and also appearing at Buckingham Palace alongside 'deaf' pianist Madame Vere-Roper, ventriloquist-cum-MC Peter Brough, impressionist Florence Desmond and moustachioed wit Jimmy Edwards.

As Frankie put it, 'My act was, as always, an intimate gossip with the audience … This made it very tricky – it's a bit terrifying to talk to the King and Queen in terms of: "No, listen, missus! No… No, don't laugh, moosh! There are those among us today whom I shall do-o-o," etc, but if I didn't say such things then I wasn't doing my act. It was very fraught.' Thankfully, the Royals lapped it up. 'To coin a phrase, my flabber was never so gasted.'

The 1950s

By 1950, Frankie was the hottest and best-paid comedian in the country. He reigned supreme during the summer at Great Yarmouth's Britannia Theatre with Sonny Jenks, John Hanson and Bonnie Downs, and later made his professional West End début in fine style, commanding the top-of-the-bill spot in Val Parnell's dazzling revue, *Out of This World*, which opened at the London Palladium on 17

October. On that day, Frankie recalled, 'I went to Leicester Square to look at the huge posters advertising the show, and as I gazed at them I was emotional almost to the point of tears … I stood looking at my name for so long I was nearly arrested for loitering with intent!'

Out of This World

presented by Val Parnell at the London Palladium from 17 October to 16 December 1950
The Company: Frankie Howerd, Binnie Hale, Nat Jackley, Jerry Desmonde, Sheila Mathews, Maureen Sims, Ed Hoffman, the Ben Yost Royal Guards, Denis Murray, Freddie Vale, Sammy Curtis, Gloria 'Australia' Williams, Madame

Frankie receives a request to open a charity fête and shows his mother, Edith, the letter. This picture was taken in Frankie's dressing room at the London Palladium during rehearsals for Out of This World, September 1950.

Violette de Saxe, Warren Latona & Sparks, Angela Barrie, Russell Joudreau, the Trio Gipsys, Show Ladies, Dancing Débutantes, Mayfair Revellers, the John Tiller Girls, plus the Sky Rocket Orchestra under the direction of Woolf Phillips

Producers: Alec Shanks and Joan Davis; Dances and musical numbers arranged by Joan Davis; Décor: Erté, Alec Shanks, Edward Delaney, Berkeley Sutcliffe; Costumes: Josephine Clinch, Alec Shanks, Erté; Musical arrangements by Ronnie Hanmer and Bobby Howell; Songs by Hamish Menzies and Gordon Humphries, Phil Park, Bob Hilliard and Dave Mann; 'Down to Earth' by Con West with additional dialogue by

Talbot Rothwell; 'Meet the Authors' by Jerome Chodorov; Additional dialogue by Frankie Howerd, Eric Sykes, Con West, Jackie Marks, Talbot Rothwell

With Frankie partnered by the evergreen comedy star Binnie Hale, up-and-coming droll Nat Jackley and Sid Field's supercilious former stooge Jerry Desmonde, the show was a surefire success, clocking up 112 performances, twice nightly with a matinée added on Wednesdays. Frankie was given two stand-up spots either side of the intermission (accompanied by Madame Violette de Saxe in the latter) and appeared as Dr Drawbridge in

Richard Hearne as the Captain, Sonnie Hale as Cook and Frankie as Idle Jack pictured during dress rehearsals for *Dick Whittington* in December 1952.

the Jerome Chodorov sketch 'Meet the Authors'. With Nat Jackley he was a government worker in the Second Act sketch 'No 10 Downing Street' (with Jerry Desmonde improbably cast as a GI) and, in the musical medley closing the first half, 'The Realm of Romance', he offered a comic rendition of 'Come Dance With Me'.

The show also prompted Frankie's first of many appearances at the Royal Command Performance. Val Parnell was producing the Palladium-based regal bash that year and naturally wanted to promote his own Frankie-led Palladium extravaganza at the same time. On 13 November, the Royal show was preceded by a press lunch at the swanky Café de Paris and was performed in front of Queen Elizabeth and King George VI. The nervous Frankie joined an astonishing bill that included Gracie Fields, Max Miller, Frankie's *For the Fun of It* pal Max Bygraves, Max Wall, the Crazy Gang, Tommy Trinder, Donald Peers, Dinah Shore and Jack Benny.

Unfortunately for Frankie, he went on directly after a barnstorming session from the Billy Cotton Band Show and, feeling outshone in advance, his performance was nervous, shambolic and mis-timed. In fact, he considered his career to be over. However, Frankie would be a regular on subsequent shows until 1978 and become one of the most eagerly awaited performers in the line-up, whether billed as the headlining comedy attraction or stumbling on in 1953 to help out Joan Sims in the 'Shop Girl Princess' number from the West End musical *High Spirits*.

When *Out of This World* drew to a close, Frankie starred in *Babes in the Wood* with Marjorie Browne, Jack Stanford and Erica Yorke at the Birmingham Royal. The show continued into 1951, a year that was to prove a turning point in many ways, marking the end of Frankie's regular association with *Variety Bandbox* and the beginning of a sticky disassociation from Jack Payne. During the run of *Out of This World*, he had discovered that 'while I was being paid £600 a week (of which Jack got £300, less my basic salary), he'd made a separate contract with Val Parnell

whereby he got an extra £300 for himself.' With Payne in breach of contract, Frankie was reluctantly forced to initiate legal proceedings, so that 'by the time the case opened on 15 March 1953, I was up to my eyes in 'sue-age'.'

Perhaps predictably, the hearing was not without its lighter moments. Upon learning that Frankie was earning a whopping £900 a week, Mr Justice Hilbery asked, 'Do they pay £900 a week for one artist at the Palladium?' Gilbert Beyfus, Frankie's QC, replied, 'Yes. Why do we practise at the bar?' Retorted the judge: 'I suppose it is because you cannot give that other type of performance.'

Frankie was compensated for misdirected funds, but the situation had already led to the establishment, in February 1951, of Frankie Howerd Ltd. The company was designed to gauge and balance Frankie's earnings and its directors were Frankie himself, Stanley Dale and Frankie's mother, E F Howard. Situated

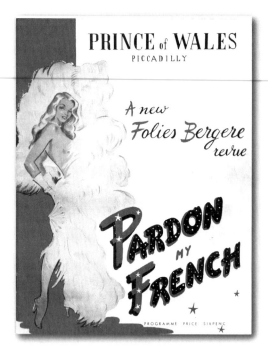

PRINCE of WALES
PICCADILLY

A new
Folies Bergère
revue

PARDON MY FRENCH

PROGRAMME PRICE SIXPENCE

at 130 Uxbridge Road W12, the parent company was soon joined by Frankie Howerd (Scripts) Ltd, which again boasted Frankie and Dale as co-directors, with Eric Sykes also on board. This organisation became Associated London Scripts on 1 September 1956 and served as a mecca for the likes of Spike Milligan, Tony Hancock, Ray Galton, Alan Simpson, Johnny Speight and Terry Nation.

In 1952 Frankie played the Swindon Empire and ventured into the world's war zones when he did a tour of benefit shows for troops in Korea, performing some 14 shows in just one week in Hong Kong. And in December he starred as Idle Jack in 'Val Parnell's Fifth Magnificent Pantomime, *Dick Whittington*' at the London Palladium. Vanessa Lee played the title role, Sonnie Hale (brother of Frankie's *Out of This World* co-star, Binnie) was Daphne Dumpling, Richard Hearne (aka Mr Pastry) was the Mate and the young Warren Mitchell clowned around as the Chef. 'Specialities' included Knie's Chimpanzees (trained and presented by Captain A Smith), Rob Murray, Eliane & Rodolph, the Seven Volants, the George Mitchell Singers, the Aida Foster Babes, the Pauline Grant Ballet and the

Sky Rocket Orchestra (under the direction of Woolf Phillips). The book was written by Barbara Gordon and Basil Thomas ('additional dialogue,' noted the programme tellingly, 'by Eric Sykes') and the whole thing was staged by Charles Henry. Told in 16 eye-catching scenes, the show clocked up 105 performances between 23 December and 28 February 1953.

1953 saw TV work, the legal wrangle with Jack Payne and Frankie's film début taking up much of his time, but on 20 August he began rehearsals for a new West End show. The result opened on 24 September and was the smash-hit revue *Pardon My French*. Presented by Russian-born impresario Bernard Delfont at the Prince of Wales Theatre, the cast included Frankie's long-time friends Lee Young and Sunny Rogers plus popular pianist Winifred Atwell. Frankie was fool enough, on the first night, to agree to 'some bright spark's suggestion that I should make my entrance by parachute' but sensibly walked on in the normal way throughout the remainder of the run.

Pardon My French
presented by Val Parnell and Bernard Delfont at the Prince of Wales Theatre London, 24 September 1953 to 11 December 1954. The Company: Frankie Howerd, Winifred Atwell, Cecile Tchernova, Anny Berryer, Sunny Rogers, Los Likajos, Trio Lanos, the Four Congaroos, Ted & George Durante, Stanley Robinson, Lee Young, Helen Davis, Rita Keane, Tony Hulley, Bobby Trantor, Peter Brichta, Kenneth Birrell Producer: Dick Hurran; Stage director: Fred Gray; Designers: Charles Reading, Tod Kingman; Costumes: R St John Roper; Choreography: Hazel Gee; Ballet mistress: Thelma Bentley; Masks: Stagecraft, John Lee

A Folies Bergère-style extravaganza, *Pardon My French* numbered among its more prominent attractions numerous topless showgirls, required by law to remain absolutely still at all times. On New Year's Eve the traditional arm-linking chorus of 'Auld Lang Syne' induced audience hilarity when the slightly tipsy chorus line linked arms too and started bouncing all over the place. 'Okay, so it's pretty tame stuff compared with today,' Frankie later pointed out, 'but in 1953 it could have had us all arrested.'

Early in the run, Frankie was honoured once again to appear at the Royal Command Performance in November, performing a musical interlude with Joan Sims and the legendary Jack Buchanan. It was also at this time that Frankie first met Johnny Speight, who would later construct the lion's share of Frankie's *That Was The Week That Was* revival and add a cosy but deadly edge of political observation to his humour. Stiff-necked during the run of *Pardon My French*, Frankie had

been introduced to Speight by his masseur.

Pardon My French eventually clocked up (twice nightly) 758 performances, after which Frankie headlined a roadshow version of it. Throughout 1955, Frankie was touring Britain's variety theatres with *The Howerd Crowd*, featuring his regular radio cohort Lee Young. It was during this run that he met another significant collaborator – fellow comedian and subsequent scriptwriter Barry Took. Took stooged for Frankie when the show hit the Congress Theatre Eastbourne and again, a week later, when the show stopped off in Taunton. Another young comedian was acting as warm-up man for Frankie's stage

Frankie and Gwyn Panter get stuck into rehearsals for *Pardon My French*, Prince of Wales Theatre, 20 September 1953.

performances. As Jim Dale explains, 'Yes, can you believe that? I shared Frankie's agent, Stanley Dale. In fact, that's how I got my name. I was born Jim Smith. So I actually did a couple of shows at army camps in England. I mean, warming the audience up for Frankie Howerd! I wouldn't say it was a difficult job but everyone to a man just wanted me off. I got the biggest cheer when I left the stage!'

However, Frankie was restless with continually touring the same old material. He had a desire to flex his acting muscles on stage and to that end he accepted an offer to star as Lord Fancourt Babberley in an H M Tennent revival of Brandon Thomas' comic classic of 1892, *Charley's Aunt*.

Charley's Aunt

by Brandon Thomas
presented by H M Tennent Ltd at the Globe Theatre Shaftesbury Avenue, 22 December 1955 to 17 March 1956
Cast: Frankie Howerd (Lord Fancourt Babberley), Gerald Harper (Jack Chesney), Richard Waring (Charley Wykeham), Wensley Pithey (Stephen Spettigue), Joy Rodgers (Amy Spettigue), Wendy Williams (Kitty Verdun), Jane Downs (Ela Delahay), Marjorie Stewart (Donna Lucia d'Alvadorez), Charles Cullum (Sir Francis Chesney), A J Brown (Brasset)
Director: William Chappell; Décor: Motley

Directed by William Chappell, the show opened on 22 December 1955 at the Globe Theatre and a three-month run of 102 performances was followed by a nationwide tour. The play had last occupied the West End as recently as February 1954, in a glamorous production directed by John Gielgud and starring John Mills as Babberley. The Frankie Howerd version shared design team Motley and ingenue Joy Rodgers with the Gielgud model but was otherwise very different. As the *Observer* put it, 'An historic stroke of miscasting has produced a performance which could (and should) run for several years.'

Indeed, in *Plays and Players* Raymond Marriott devoted his entire review to an enthusiastic account of Frankie's performance.

'Frankie Howerd's Aunt in William Chappell's quick, gay production of our funniest farce,' Marriott wrote, 'is a brilliant performance, thoroughly alive, witty, vigorous in attack yet never clumsy, and bristling with the best of the comic invention Mr Howerd has learned in variety. He creates the part on the lines of a pantomime Dame, but never so much as to put a scene out of balance, and it is remarkable how well he sustains the impersonation when so unaccustomed to the legitimate stage. When he has to revert to being Lord Fancourt Babberley we notice very much his lack of style and poise, but as this occupies only a few minutes of the play, it does not matter much. There is humour in the way he swishes his skirts; the cigar scene and the tea-pouring really do have people shouting with laughter; the assignations with the elderly gentlemen can rarely have been presented in such a brightly ludicrous spirit.'

For Frankie, the only drawback to playing *Charley's Aunt* was a corpsing problem he traced to fellow actor Richard Waring. Waring's undisguised hilarity over everything Frankie did was contagious and reduced the performance on 26 December to 'a complete shambles'. 'After London,' Frankie noted, '*Charley's Aunt* went on tour, and Waring was agony to play with. I don't know what it was about me that so tickled him ... He'd have been a godsend in the audience, but was absolute murder on stage.'

Following the tour, Frankie reverted to stand-up performance for a brace of service shows in Nicosia, leaving on 5 May with co-stars Blanchie Moore, Clarry Ashton, Barbara Leigh and Alma Warren. He then starred in the Will Evans and Valentine farce *Tons of Money* at the New Theatre Bromley. Having already appeared in the play for the Shooter's Hill Old Boys' Dramatic Society – and also done a TV version of it – Frankie was at ease with the piece. Back in 1922, the play, complete with the legendary triumvirate of Ralph Lynn, Tom Walls and Robertson Hare, had succeeded in kick-starting the legendary Aldwych farces despite the historical accident that it opened at the Shaftesbury.

Frankie as Lord Fancourt Babberley in *Charley's Aunt*, which opened at the Globe on 22 December 1955.

Tons of Money

*by Will Evans and Valentine
New Theatre Bromley, 17 to
29 September 1956*

*Cast: Frankie Howerd (Aubrey Henry Maitland
Allington), Sheila Hancock (Louise Allington),
Robert Lankesheer (Sprules, a butler), Ursula
Curtis (Simpson, a parlourmaid), Judith Gick
(Miss Benita Mullett), Arnold Fry (Giles, a
gardener), Louis Haslar (James Chesterman,
solicitor), Joy Wood (Jean Everard), Ivor Salter
(Henery), Nigel Hawthorne (George Maitland)
Director: David Poulson; Décor: Henry
Graveney*

'Frankie Howerd, in the first week of his
fortnight's run of *Tons of Money* with the
Bromley repertory company,' reported the
Stage, 'smashed the record for the highest
takings at the theatre in straight plays by more
than £100. As the theatre has been running
continuously since December 1947, and has up
to the present time produced 366 plays, this
achievement is no small affair. It was also a
happy gesture that the [theatre's] directors,
Peter Goss and David Poulson, secured their
former leading lady, Sheila Hancock, to return
to play opposite Mr Howerd ... As Aubrey
Allington, Mr Howerd ... gives a clever
impersonation, carried through with most
natural humour, and though there are many of
his now familiar touches, he keeps well in the
picture ... The company play together with the
serious efficiency which makes farce doubly
worthwhile, and they fully deserve their share
of the success attained.'

Frankie was happy with the production and
remounted it himself at the Nottingham
Empire for the 1956 Christmas season, with
much of the original cast, plus Jeanne
Mockford, still in tow. It was the first time
Frankie had met and worked with Mockford,
later to appear as the soothsayer in *Up
Pompeii!*, and an instant friendship was born.
Also in 1956, she joined Frankie for a charity
performance of extracts from *Charley's Aunt*
in Carlisle.

But *Tons of Money* was even more
significant for a bit of 'absolute heresy', as

Frankie called it, that he committed during the
run – a heresy that casts doubt on the *Stage*'s
opinion that he kept 'well in the picture'. 'On
the first night of *Tons of Money* at the New
Theatre Bromley,' Sheila Hancock recalled,
'we legits, Nigel Hawthorne and I, were
astounded when Frank came on in best
Ralph Lynn manner to deliver the first
scripted line: "Good morning all, good
morning fish, good morning rolls, good night
bills, good morning Auntie Ben." No laugh. So
he turned balefully to the audience and said,
"What a load of old rubbish." From then on,
every time I tried to keep to the script –
particularly if I got a laugh – Frank would
interrupt with something like: "No, don't laugh
– she's from the RADA you know
[pronounced radar]. No, no, she doesn't like it.
Have a bit of respect. Poor soul."'

Frankie himself placed this crucial moment
during the Nottingham rather than Bromley
run of the play, and pointed out that 'Since the
audience liked it I went on to elaborate the
technique of 'coming out' of the play and
addressing remarks to the audience until it
included the entire cast and then the very play
itself ... Yet it was a style I never really
developed as an integral part of a show until
Up Pompeii!.' In a funny sort of way, it was a
style not a million miles removed from the
theories of that apostle of theatrical
'alienation', Bertold Brecht. 'Where,' asked
theatre critic Michael Billington in 1973, 'in
the modern theatre does one find any
evidence of the acceptability of the Brechtian
approach? The first and most obvious place to
look is the world of the music hall ... A
British vaudevillian like Frankie Howerd ...
constantly steps outside the frame of the
action to show us what he thinks of the script,
the director and even his fellow actors ...
He is arguably the most Brechtian actor
in Britain.'

Brechtian or not, stage farces were proving
successful for Frankie but many felt that he
was losing sight of his loyal audience and the
very essence of that 'ordinary' quality which
he had striven for. A lifeline was offered by
Bernard Delfont, who was keen to cast

Frankie in another colourful revue, *Plaisirs de Paris*, but Frankie (who would have preferred Delfont to restage *Tons of Money* in the West End) turned down the top-billing slot. When the show opened at the Prince of Wales on 20 April 1957, Dickie Henderson headed a cast that included Noelle Adam, Sabrina and the Bernard Brothers – and Frankie later described his decision as 'the worst error of judgment I was to make in my entire professional life.'

Suffering from nervous exhaustion, Frankie took solace in his friends and faithful boxer dog, Red. But he was still determined to 'find art' and improve his standing as an actor. After a June concert party tour in Cyprus, he had his chance in July. Having worked with the legendary Alec Guinness in Ealing's *The Ladykillers*, Frankie tried to emulate the actor by taking on a role made famous by Guinness at the Winter Garden the previous year.

Hotel Paradiso

by Georges Feydeau and Maurice Desvallieres, adapted by Peter Glenville
Streatham Hill Theatre July 1957, then tour
Cast: Frankie Howerd (Boniface), Phyllis Montefiore (Angelique), Heather Chasen (Marcelle), Michael Logan (Cot), Michael Danvers Walker (Maxime), Margo Jenkins (Victoire), Peter Stephens (Martin), Ernest Woodford (first porter), Peter Lamsley (second porter), Patrick Newell (third porter), Anthony Selby (fourth porter), Thomas Elliott (fifth porter), Mary Richards (Violette), Angela Crow (Marguerite), Ann Beach (Paquerette), Peggy Ann Taylor (Pervenche), John Gordon (Anniello), Anthony Selby (Georges), Rose Power (a lady), Patrick Newell (a Duke), Peter Lamsley (Tabu), Patrick Newell (Inspector Bouchard), Thomas Elliott, Peter Lamsley, Ernest Woodford (policemen)
Director: William Chappell; Settings and costumes: Osbert Lancaster

Georges Feydeau's famous farce of 1899, *L'Hôtel du libre échange*, had been adapted by actor/director Peter Glenville as *Hotel Paradiso* and proved extremely successful

when it opened in May 1956. The 1957 tour in which Frankie headlined was less so, though it reunited him with his *Charley's Aunt* director, William Chappell, and featured future sitcom stars Tony Selby and (in her professional début) Ann Beach. 'After Guinness,' Frankie conceded, 'the public must have thought me pretty flat beer – and were probably right! We didn't do brilliant business. Part of the problem was that the shrinking audiences who were still interested in me expected the "Ladies and Gentle-*men*" Frankie Howerd, and didn't altogether take to me as a would-be comic actor. But I battered on – determined to persevere with this new image.'

The opportunity to do so, and in the poshest surroundings possible, came at the end of the year when, much to his amazement, Frankie was cast as Bottom in Shakespeare's *A Midsummer Night's Dream* at the Old Vic. 'I nearly had a heart attack when I learned the salary was £30 a week (including matinées),' Frankie remarked.

A Midsummer Night's Dream

by William Shakespeare
Old Vic Theatre London from 23 December 1957
Cast in order of speaking: Jack Gwillim (Theseus), Margaret Courtenay (Hippolyta), Harold Innocent (Philostrate), David Waller (Egeus), Rosemary Webster (Hermia), John Humphry (Demetrius), Richard Gale (Lysander), Coral Browne (Helena), Paul Daneman (Quince), Frankie Howerd (Bottom), Ronald Fraser (Flute), Daniel Thorndike (Starveling), Derek Francis (Snout), James Culliford (Snug), Adrienne Hill, Barbara Leigh-Hunt, Barrie Ingham, Michael Culver (Attendants), Keith Taylor (Puck), Judi Dench (First Fairy), Derek Godfrey (Oberon), Joyce Redman (Titania), Juliet Cooke (Second Fairy), Bridget Wood (Peaseblossom), Gillian Bosworth (Cobweb), Stella Orton (Moth), Valerie Gibson (Mustardseed), Jean Atkinson, Nancy Kwan (other fairies)
Director: Michael Benthall; Décor and costumes: James Bailey; Music by Mendelssohn, arranged by Gordon Jacob

Nobody sleeps while I'm on … but Joyce Redman dozes as Frankie runs through his Bottom with Daniel Thorndike, Derek Francis, James Culliford, Paul Daneman and Ronald Fraser in *A Midsummer Night's Dream*, 23 December 1957.

Though describing the play (after its protagonists, Titania and Bottom) as 'The Tit and Bum Show', director Michael Benthall was quick to point out that 'This is Shakespeare. You can't Howerdise it. You can't alter the text.' Frankie was well aware of the fact ('Not one "Ooh" or "Aah",' he mockingly complained) and mined the action instead for visual gags, pointing out that 'Bottom's great play scene … [is] very much like a music hall sketch, as the Crazy Gang demonstrated when they did it.'

Shakespeare himself, of course, had his own resident 'low' comedian in the person of Will Kempe, but the announcement that Frankie was entering the hallowed portals of the Old

Vic still brought forth predictable sniffs of highbrow distaste. And, at first, Frankie himself admitted to being 'twitchy' about the whole enterprise. 'I have problems learning lines at the best of times,' he complained, 'but to have to memorise Ye Olde Englishe was sheer murder. It was a foreign language to me.' He also admitted that 'At the beginning of rehearsals I was incredibly shy at having to mix with distinguished Shakespearean performers.' But the company – which included Coral Browne, Paul Daneman, Joyce Redman, Frankie's future *Whoops Baghdad* co-star Derek Francis and even rising stars like Judi Dench and Nancy Kwan – were very welcoming and so were the critics when opening night came around on 23 December.

'As Michael Benthall must know,' commented *Plays and Players* editor Peter Roberts, 'there is nothing we find more exhilarating than a little bit of unconventional casting. Although I suppose we can never hope for the exciting experiment of an Arthur Askey Lear or a Joyce Grenfell Lady Macbeth, to be going along with it was a real Christmas treat to find Frankie Howerd at the Old Vic. There may perhaps have been more Widow Twankey than Bully Bottom about Mr Howerd's Old Vic creation. Perhaps, too, the associations that his most distinctive intonation evoke made Shakespeare at first sound like a rather uninspired gag writer. But as the play scene followed that of the rehearsal there was no doubt this interesting experiment had succeeded … In addition to his boldness in casting,' Roberts concluded, 'Michael Benthall is to be congratulated for his production as a whole. It secures a very happy balance between the knockabout of the mechanics and the light fantasy of the fairies.'

One comment in the *Daily Telegraph* was even more gratifying for Frankie. 'I feel sure Mr Shakespeare would have approved of Mr Howerd, not only for his acting but for his obedience to his author's injunction: "Let them that play your clowns say no more than is set down for them."' Maybe things changed over the course of the run, however, for Judi Dench herself has said that Frankie was 'hysterically funny, though he just made it up a lot of the time.'

The production was sufficiently high-profile for Galton and Simpson to gently send up Benthall's casting coup in the 1959 *Hancock's Half Hour* episode, *The Knighthood* – when Tony bellows at Richard Wattis' prissy Old Vic flunkey, 'You've had Frankie Howerd here, you can have me!' Publicly, Frankie himself was keen to send up the entire notion of a music hall clown falling for the classics. He dismissed his success with the throwaway gag 'My bottom was the talk of London!' and explained how he initially thought that the Vic 'was the Victoria Palace.'

Privately, however, he was delighted with the adulation. Naturally, he 'got culture' and was tempted to turn away from the comic style that had made him famous, immediately plunging into Molière's *The School for Wives* on television. Indeed, the respected producer Rudolph Cartier, the man behind the BBC's harrowing *Nineteen Eighty-Four* starring Peter Cushing, had asked Frankie to recreate the role of Bottom for the small screen. Annoyingly for Frankie, he was already contracted to a summer season and the proposal came to naught. Earlier, an outside broadcast unit had wanted to film the midsummer forest scenes for television but a mixture of lack of technical facilities and clashing dates conspired against them.

But these television disappointments couldn't undermine the huge success of Frankie's Shakespearean début. Indeed, on 18 March Frankie and the company performed selected scenes for Her Majesty the Queen at an Old Vic gala event. As it turned out, a small screen version would finally be made for ITV some six years later. Bottom was played by Benny Hill.

Frankie's keenness to score in comic plays arose from his feeling that not only music hall but the vogue for revues was on the brink of extinction. Future Carry On screenwriter Dave Freeman recalls that 'I met Frankie on numerous occasions to discuss projects which were aborted for one reason or another. The first of these was around 1958. Peter Saunders was greatly taken with a sketch I had written for Tommy Cooper and asked me if I could devise a revue along the lines of the long-running *La Plume de Ma Tante*. My agent at the time, Beryl Vertue, persuaded me to suggest Frank to star in it. Peter Saunders agreed and I went to see Frank at the flat he had in Holland Park.

'It had an odd, overheated, musty smell to it as if the windows hadn't been opened in the previous hundred years. Frank, who wore a heavy tweed suit summer and winter, obviously felt the cold. His first words were, "I don't want to do a revue, I want to do a musical!" I told him that Peter Saunders wanted to do a revue. Frank said, "Oh, I'm sure you can talk him out of it." While I was trying to talk him out of it Benny Hill was talked into doing *Fine Fettle* in the style of *La Plume de Ma Tante* and I was talked into writing it. Peter Saunders thought I had pinched his idea and didn't talk to me for 30 years.'

Straight after playing Bottom, and while rehearsing in London for the TV production of Molière's *The School for Wives*, Frankie was simultaneously starring in a Northampton revival of the Wallace Geoffrey and Basil Mitchell farce, *The Perfect Woman*, which had starred Sonnie Hale in its West End run ten years previously. The show ran for the prescribed fortnight, starting on 24 March 1958. Frankie's next choice of theatrical enterprise, unfortunately, was rather more high-profile. *Mister Venus* was a new musical presented by opera promoter S A Gorlinsky and penned by revue giant Alan Melville, who had written the *Sweet and Low* trilogy for Hermione Gingold. It concerned a bumbling publican called Alister – played by Frankie – who is visited by an extraterrestrial bent on saving the population of Earth from self-destruction. Shades of Robert Wise's classic film, *The Day the Earth Stood Still…*

Mister Venus

presented by S A Gorlinsky at the Prince of Wales Theatre from 23 October to 8 November 1958
book by Ray Galton and Johnny Speight, music and lyrics by Norman Newell, music by Trevor H Stanford
Cast: Frankie Howerd (Alister), Anton Diffring (Mister Venus), Judy Bruce (Sally), June Grant (Mrs Washington Winthrop III), Alexander Dore (Prendergast), Annette Carell (Sonia), Gavin Gordon (speaker at Marble Arch/Prosecuting Counsel/Fred), Sunny Rogers (Glynnis/actress), C Denier Warren (Plenderleith/Judge), Bill Owen (Mr Brown), Pat Hawkes (Mrs Brown), Raymond Dalziel (Mr Orange), Shirley Gould (Mrs Orange), Keith Galloway (Mr Purple), Nita Howard (Mrs Purple), Paddy McIntyre (Mr Yellow), Leander Fedden (Mrs Yellow), Barry
Irwin (Mr Pink), Valerie Lloyd (Mrs Pink), Brian Scott (Mr Blue), Ruth Denise (Mrs Blue), Natalie Kent (landlady), Vincent Charles (barman), Donald Reid (busker/newsboy), Myra de Groot (married woman), Aidan Turner (married man/BEA official/actor), Bill Clothier (policeman/newsboy), Sonny Clair, John Delaney (speakers at Marble Arch), Wayne Forrest (Boris), Alister Williamson (Ivan), Don Reid (park keeper), Hedley Colson (guardsman/usher), Merv Wilding (TV floor manager), Malcolm Campbell (newsboy), plus John Doye, Kenneth Lacey, Peter Warwick, Laura Hedley, Sonia Peters, Sandra Verne, Frances Youles, Liz Davidson, Maureen Sims, Ann Lewis, Maureen Grant, Jane Hill
Director: Charles Reading; Chief of production: Maurice Fournier; Designer: Henry Graveney; Costumes: Rosemary Carvill, Hilary Virgo; Musical director: Bob Lowe; Musical arrangements: Peter Knight; Choreography: Paddy Stone, Irving Davies

The eponymous alien figure, spouting religious diatribes, was played by the German actor Anton Diffring, descending from the gantry in sparkling jockstrap and angel's wings. 'He looked like a great big fairy queen lost on the way to the Christmas tree,' remarked Frankie roguishly. And poor Anton wasn't the only person crucified with embarrassment. So mortified by the spectacle was Alan Melville that he insisted on his name being removed from the publicity, the regional tour was a disaster and the West End run was the shortest Frankie ever had the misfortune to be involved in.

The piece had apparently been intended for Norman Wisdom. When Frankie was offered the script he decided it wasn't for him and suggested they try his old pal Max Bygraves instead. Gorlinsky was adamant, however. The nominal director was Charles Reading but Frankie recollected that 'The show was distinguished (or extinguished) for an unusual reason: it had no overall director.' As a result, the opening on 1 October at Manchester Opera House was a fiasco. After stints in Liverpool and Cheltenham, the company

With Judy
Bruce in the
disastrous West
End production
Mister Venus.

pleaded for an extension to the tour in order
to delay the London opening.

No extension was given. The show opened
on 23 October 1958 at the Prince of Wales
Theatre, scene of the 758 packed performances
of *Pardon My French*. *Mister Venus* managed
just 20, the curtain falling for the last time on 8
November. Even desperate, last-minute
rewrites by Frankie's trusted band of

scriptwriters – Ray Galton, Alan Simpson and
Johnny Speight – couldn't save it. Galton
recalls that, 'True to form, Frank would ask
everybody and anybody for help. He asked us
to look at this show because there were not
enough jokes in it for him. So we put some
funnies in for Frank. As always, the thing grew
and it got so large that the original writer, Alan
Melville, took his name off it. He thought it

was a load of rubbish and not his play at all. Alan and myself had started work on it and then Alan ducked out and went on holiday, so I worked on it with Johnny Speight.'

Alan Simpson remembers that 'It opened in Manchester and they said, "We can't have all these names on the thing," so I said, "Take mine off. I haven't done much!" So I wasn't on the bill. The book was credited to Ray and Johnny.' Ray Galton continues, 'We opened to pretty indifferent reviews and some of them, like the *Stage*, were terrible. They were all great friends of Alan Melville and we, after all, were mere television writers. We weren't considered of any consequence whatsoever!'

'Not since the fooling of Sid Field has the stage of this country seen such a lovably foolish fellow as Frankie Howerd,' wrote Caryl Brahms in *Plays and Players*, noting, however, that '*Mister Venus* has the kind of plot that would sink a battleship … Reduced to its bones one can see that it could have been funny. It should have been funny. In fact, it was disastrously unfunny … Against the genius of Mr Howerd, the dance routines and a song about 'Love, Love, Love', must be set the most tasteless, outmoded and ill-fitting sets that the West End can have seen for some time.' With personal endorsements like this – and with closure in sight – Frankie opted to send the show up in the style he'd stumbled upon in *Tons of Money*. (Where extra-textual gags were concerned, he observed, 'Anton Diffring's costume was a godsend.') But it was too late, and the damage to Frankie's morale was considerable. He was so ashamed of the piece that he refused to perform extracts from it on TV's *Sunday Night at the London Palladium*.

Frankie spent Christmas in another provincial production of *The Perfect Woman*, this time, at the invitation of entrepreneur Barry O'Brien, at the Grand Theatre Southampton. He then endured a miserable summer season in 1959 alongside Fraser Hayes and Cyril Stapleton and his Show Band at the Futurist Scarborough. A heat-wave dictated poor box-office and Frankie's patter, though resurrected from the 1952 Palladium production of *Dick Whittington*, was

considered too risqué for local audiences.

There followed a disastrous adaptation by Philip Beresford (book) and Arthur Furby (music) of *Alice in Wonderland* produced by former bandleader Maurice Winnick and directed by Stanley Willis-Croft. It opened at the Winter Garden Drury Lane on 26 December and wound up after 50 twice nightly performances on 23 January 1960. Frankie starred as the Mock Turtle, the Mad Hatter and the Caterpillar alongside Richard Goolden, Delene Scott (as Alice), Desmond Walter-Ellis, John English and Frankie's *Out of This World* companion, Binnie Hale. According to Frankie, the show 'proved to be the last production at the Winter Garden before it closed for ever: Frankie Howerd, the man who gave the Winter Garden the deep freeze. It took me only a week into the run to realise that the show was a dead duck. The smaller the audience, the wilder I went – and by the time we'd finished, the Trial Scene at the end would have shamed the Goons. If I say it myself, between us we turned the show into an uproarious success (unless you'd come to see *Alice In Wonderland*), but – as ever – it was too late.' Five years later, incidentally, the Mock Turtle would crop up again, only on record.

The 1960s

1960 was rounded off by Frankie's appearance in front of the Queen Mother at the Palladium's Royal Command Performance together with a pantomime season for Emile Littler at the Streatham Hill Theatre. Frankie, to his surprise, was top-billed as Buttons and his *Cinderella* co-stars included Sonny Dawkes, Garry Webb and Helen Cotterill. But an adoring audience of children and a regal honour from his most famous admirer belied the fact that 1960 had proved the lowest of low points in Frankie's career.

The following year, Frankie eagerly took the opportunity to face a willing gang of supporters when he toured Northern Arabia in a service show for the troops. And the *Evening Standard* Drama Awards were to prove a

Who's your tailor? Anton Diffring and Frankie in the ill-fated *Mister Venus*, Prince of Wales Theatre, 23 October 1958.

'I was a-mazed!' – Frankie takes the Establishment Club by storm in September 1962.

making the film version of *Up Pompeii*, he happily admitted that 'I make suggestions and usually alter lines to make them more comfortable for my style of performance. If I can put it this way, I can cook the meal but others have to provide the ingredients for me.'

In 1961, however, 1970 was a long way off. But even when it seemed the entire show business hierarchy had ganged up against him, the *Standard* were still falling over themselves to get Frankie to deliver after-dinner speeches or hand out awards for performers clearly doing better than he was. Close friend Val Guest, who directed Frankie in two feature films, remembers these personal appearances vividly. 'He was an intelligent comedian. He could talk to anyone about anything. Our mutual friend Kenneth Tynan once told me that "If this man wasn't such a brilliant comedian, he could be an incredible Prime Minister!" – and I believe that! Frankie was the comedian's comedian. There are very few whom the professionals really love – Beatrice Lillie was one, as was Sid Field and Jack Benny. And Frankie Howerd certainly was. Every year the *Evening Standard* Theatre Awards would invite Frankie to appear at the function. It didn't matter what he did, he was always hilarious. An almost assured hoot whether he was up or down. Even when his career was not doing well, Frankie could still deliver the goods.'

By now, represented by Roger Hancock and Beryl Vertue, Frankie was accepting lowly summer season and panto appearances. Facing the spectre of unemployment, Frankie would walk alone round South Kensington, desperate to hit on the winning formula of the past. And a summer season with Tommy Steele at the Windmill Theatre Great Yarmouth brought him to his knees. According to Bruce Forsyth, who was also on show in Great Yarmouth at the time, Steele originally finished the first half of the show with Frankie as top of the bill. As the run went on, however, Steele was given the top spot and Frankie was relegated to the lower position; 'All in the business were heartbroken for him.' Frankie himself maintained in his autobiography that Steele

constant delight for Frankie as a guest speaker. 'We would write material for those, usually the opening lines,' recalls Alan Simpson. 'We did small bits and pieces here and there for a favour. He would go round to Eric Sykes, Johnny Speight, Ray and myself, Barry Cryer, all of us. He wouldn't tell us that he had done the rounds but we would gladly have a look at the material. It was always good fun writing for Frank.'

And Frankie would reward such loyalty with credit where credit was due. Interviewed while ('an absolute charmer: kind, diffident and helpful') was top of the bill from the word go. Either way, though still billed as 'television's favourite comedian', Frankie patently wasn't. His career was on the slippery slope and he was demoralised. And when Frankie was demoralised he just wasn't funny.

An appearance at the 1961 Royal Command Performance did something to revive his self-confidence but mostly the gigs were police benefits and charity shows. He spoke in tribute to Morecambe and Wise at the comic duo's Water Rats Gala celebrating their Personality of the Year Award at the Savoy's Lancaster Room. But Con Mahoney, Tom Sloan and the heads of BBC Radio and Television didn't want him, while Leslie MacDonnell at the Palladium considered him a has-been. It was only corporation producers Pat Hillyard and Jim Davidson and, perhaps most heartening of all, writers like Barry Took, Marty Feldman and Galton and Simpson who would continue to champion the performer they considered the ultimate funny man.

Frankie was still working, but gone were the showy, high-profile pantomimes of his *Variety Bandbox* days. Now he was appearing in *Puss in Boots* at the King's Theatre Southsea for the 1961/62 panto season with Gwen Overton and Joy Marlowe. He was seriously contemplating settling down to run a little country pub and looked upon the show as his swan song. A few days' rehearsal with the London company of *Oliver!* further demoralised him. He had been suggested as Fagin for the show's Broadway transfer, but when the mighty producer David Merrick attended the rehearsals incognito, the idea was vetoed.

The tide was about to change, however, and the beacon of hope came during the Southsea stint early in 1962. At the very moment that he was considering giving up show business before show business gave up him, another invitation came to speak at the *Evening Standard* Awards at the Savoy. In the audience that night were the West End's latest wow, Peter Cook, his fellow *Beyond the Fringe* players and Ned Sherrin, producer of the BBC's satirical revue *That Was The Week That Was*.

It was the beginning of the Frankie renaissance. Frankie was the absolute hit of the night. And the sudden revaluation of Frankie by the young trendies in the audience was running parallel with Beryl Vertue's instinctive pursuit of a suitable cabaret venue for her client. Frankie had never played the sophisicated West End club scene before and felt extremely uncomfortable about the whole idea. After all, here was a lowbrow comedian in his mid-forties trying to compete with the bright young things of Cambridge. Despite Frankie's reservations, Vertue booked him with Max Setty, the owner of the Blue Angel in Berkeley Square. The show was an immediate success and during May 1962 became the hottest ticket in town.

But on 7 June, mid-way through Frankie's Blue Angel run, his mother died. A crushing blow, it was immediately followed by the humiliation of filming *The Cool Mikado* for Michael Winner in July. Impressed by Frankie's *Evening Standard* and Blue Angel triumphs, however, Peter Cook then engaged him for a season at his ultra-fashionable venue, the Establishment Club in Soho's Greek Street. Initially, Frankie felt this was a bridge too far. Having agreed to the engagement he frantically phoned Vertue to instruct her to apologise and get him out of it. Finally, he faced the music and agreed to appear.

Frankie wowed the trendy audience with a bizarre but winning mix of comic dissertation – pondering on why a sausage is funnier than a pork chop – and cosy political satire. The brilliant opening was penned by Galton and Simpson, and played skilfully with the codes and conventions of Frankie's showbiz persona. It was apologetic and chatty, explaining that he was a 'humble music hall comedian' and admitting that the revue was a 'bit different from a Granada tour with Billy Fury.' And Frankie freely faced up to his lean years, claiming to have accepted the engagement because it's the 'nearest thing I get to a West End appearance these days!'

Peter Cook himself, the *Beyond the Fringe*

Frankie admires the shapely Christine Child while Sula Freeman looks on and Kenneth Connor ponders whether he should have made *Carry On Jack* after all. This picture was taken during rehearsals for *A Funny Thing Happened on the Way to the Forum* at the Strand Theatre, 28 August 1963.

crew in general and the Establishment Club ('a snob's *Worker's Playtime*!') were openly mocked too, but it was the political material which really charmed the audiences. The majority of the script was masterminded by Johnny Speight and injected mild references to Harold Macmillan into Frankie's usual absent-minded comic patter. It was an informal, chatty style which addressed the big issues in an unthreatening manner. In 1978, Frankie reflected on his unexpected embrace of the satirical movement. 'I thought then that if I can't beat it, join it. But I joined it in my own way, the Frankie Howerd way. I always try to keep up with the times.'

Interestingly, while all this radical, semi-satirical stuff was going down, Frankie was still happy to embrace his familiar family comedian image. He teamed up with panto débutant Sid James for *Puss in Boots* in the 1962/63 panto season at the New Theatre, Coventry. And his next appearance at the *Evening Standard* Awards was not to dish out an award but to receive one – for 'services to the theatre'. Suddenly, and seemingly overnight, Frankie was back at the very top of the tree. 1963 kicked off when Frankie provided the opening cabaret for a new Manchester nightclub called Mr Smith's, and in August he would star in *Glamorama of '63* at the Jersey Plaza. Then came a show which would revolutionise Frankie's career…

A Funny Thing Happened on the Way to the Forum

book by Burt Shevelove and Larry Gelbart
music and lyrics by Stephen Sondheim
presented by Harold Prince, Tony Walton and Richard Pilbrow at the Strand Theatre London from 3 October 1963
Cast: Frankie Howerd (Prologus, afterwards Pseudolus), 'Monsewer' Eddie Gray (Senex), Kenneth Connor (Hysterium), Jon Pertwee (Lycus), Robertson Hare (Erronius), Leon Greene (Miles Gloriosus), Linda Gray (Domina), John Rye (Hero), Isla Blair (Philia), Ben Aris, George Giles, Malcolm Macdonald (the Proteans), Marion Horton, Vyvyan Dunbar (the Geminae), Sula Freeman (Gymnasia), Norma Dunbar (Tintinabula), Faye Craig (Vibrata), Christine Child (Panacea)
Director: George Abbott; Musical numbers originally staged by Jack Cole, re-staged by George Martin; Settings and costumes: Tony Walton; Lighting: Jean Rosenthal

A Funny Thing Happened on the Way to the Forum had been a huge smash on Broadway, opening at the Anta Theater on 8 May 1962 and eventually clocking up a phenomenal 965 performances. The plum role of Pseudolus had first been offered to Phil Silvers (who would eventually play it in a successful 1971 revival) and was then passed to Milton Berle. But it wound up in the hands of larger-than-life comic powerhouse Zero Mostel, who would recreate his performance for Richard Lester's film version. When it was mooted that the show was to be staged in London's West End, John Gielgud, no less, suggested to the producers, Tony Walton, Richard Pilbrow and Harold Prince, that the perfect Pseudolus would be Frankie Howerd, just as richly steeped in the English music hall tradition as Mostel was in the knockabout smut of vaudeville.

To that end, Frankie visited New York in May 1963 to see the original production and meet the star. The New York-based writers, Burt Shevelove and Larry Gelbart (who had penned the book to accompany the lyrics and music of Stephen Sondheim), had already been

shipped, rather incongruously, to Coventry to watch Frankie in action in *Puss in Boots*. Terrified at the thought of two sophisticated Broadway writers being plunged into the thigh-slapping tradition of regional pantomime, Frankie was amazed when after the performance the pair wholeheartedly endorsed his casting. Indeed, the duo loved the experience of pantomime and noted its similarities to musical comedy. Frankie was in, and with a stunning cast including that quartet of pristine pros Kenneth Connor as nervous slave Hysterium, Jon Pertwee as cunning courtesan dealer Lycus, Robertson Hare as the befuddled Erronius and 'Monsewer' Eddie Gray as the delightfully decrepit Senex, rehearsals began in earnest in August 1963.

Under the direction of George Abbott, the show had a charity preview on 2 October and opened at the Strand Theatre the next day, running until July 1965. Frankie's major film and television glories came immediately off the back of this monumental West End smash. Frankie's role, for those who neither saw the show nor own the essential recording, is, put simply, *Up Pompeii!*'s Lurcio in embryonic form. He is our anachronistic guide through the loves, lives and lusts of Ancient Rome, delighting in the tale of pirates, scantily clad women, star-crossed lovers and every other half-remembered cliché from the amphitheatres. As *Puss in Boots* producer (and the person who had pointed Frankie towards *Forum* in the first place), Pauline Grant, wrote in 1963: 'Howerd lurches through the curtain like some ramshackle Pagliacci, confounded beyond belief to find himself in such a place at

A 12 May 1965 press call as Frankie prepares to hand over his Pseudolus laurels to comedian Dave King.

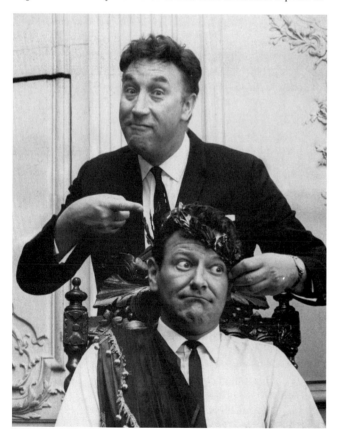

such a time. A glaze of apologetic incredulity besets his introductions.'

The major seed of inspiration for the show came from the writings of Titus Maccius Plautus, a playwright who, as the programme detailed, 'flourished about 200 BC. Twenty-one of his comedies survive and his characters and situations, adapted freely by Shakespeare, Molière and many others, have become the basis for almost all low comedy since.' Frankie first appeared as the Prologus, acting as conspiratorial warm-up man for the performance to follow. He emerged from behind the curtain and delivered a prime piece of front-cloth patter before introducing the evening's entertainment with the rip-roaring, heart-pounding show business anthem that is 'Comedy Tonight'. It's one of the most rousing and emotive starts to any show anywhere and Frankie's tried-and-tested trouper treatment literally bristled with professionalism.

There certainly is something for everyone in *Forum*, and Frankie milked the maximum quota of laughs out of every performance. It quickly became the must-see show in town. Friend and colleague Norman Mitchell recalls vividly the night he was out front. 'Frankie was absolutely marvellous in *Forum*. It was a part he was born to play. I actually went to see the show with my young daughter, Jacqueline. I remember, right near the start of the performance, Robertson 'Bunny' Hare came on stage and said to Frankie, "I have this virgin…" In a clear, loud voice Jacqueline asked me "What's a virgin?" – and without missing a beat Frankie turned to the audience and shouted, "Don't you tell her!" Don't believe anybody who said all his ad-libs were scripted. That one certainly wasn't!'

It is impossible to over-emphasise the importance of *Forum* in Frankie's career. It was quite simply the definitive, archetypal theatre vehicle for his unique, freewheeling talents. During the run, in 1964, the role of Pseudolus won Frankie the Critics' Award for Best Musical Actor and, on a more personal level, Frankie's much-treasured home in Valetta, Malta was called The Forum! After 21 months, Frankie decided, as he put it, 'to quit before I get stale' and on 3 July 1965 the role was taken over by Dave King. Illness caused King to drop out of the production almost immediately, however, and an understudy came in for one week before it was decided to close the show. Sentimental about the piece, Frankie told the management that he would perform the last night, commenting, 'I'll come back and do it free, as a gesture of thanks.' In all, *Forum* had played for a whopping 762 performances. Frankie was seriously considered for the film version but, as already noed, the role eventually went to the Broadway Pseudolus, Zero Mostel.

Immediately after finishing *Forum*, Frankie was turning on the comic charm for free when he entertained British servicemen stationed in Borneo. The 'troupe', this time including Shirley Abicair, singer Mary Murphy and magician Al Koran, travelled to Singapore for two shows and then proceeded to play a series of one-night stands until reaching their final destination of Kuala Lumpur. (One of these shows was filmed for the BBC as *East of Howerd*; see page 170.) Then Frankie signed up for a new revue at the Prince of Wales Theatre.

Way Out in Piccadilly

A musical show by Ray Galton, Alan Simpson and Eric Sykes
presented by Bernard Delfont at the Prince of Wales Theatre from 3 November 1966
The company: Frankie Howerd and Cilla Black with Linda Gray, Glenn Melvyn, Peter Vernon, the Irving Davies Dancers, the Paul Manning Singers, Valerie and Russell Arness, the Charlivels; at the piano: Madame Rogers
Staged by Maurice Fournier; comedy direction by Eric Sykes; musical numbers staged by Irving Davies; décor: Saxon Lucas; costumes: Cynthia Tingay; lighting by Michael Northen; musical director: Derek New

The show was for Bernard Delfont, one of the few major figures in English theatre who had retained his respect for Frankie during the lean years. An all-singing, all-dancing, all-laughing comic classic packed with typically

lowbrow comedy and orchestrated by a hand-picked collection of Frankie's closest allies, the production was scripted by three of the finest comedy writers in the country, Ray Galton, Alan Simpson and Eric Sykes. The latter doubled as the show's comedy director while simultaneously starring opposite Jimmy Edwards in *Big Bad Mouse* at the Shaftesbury. The overall staging was in the hands of Maurice Fournier, sometime ringmaster of *Mister Venus*, and among the treats in store were a *Madam Butterfly* skit called 'Madam Moth' and a 'mellow drama' recycled from an old *Hancock's Half Hour*, 'Jack's Return Home'.

The show was a runaway success, becoming, like *Forum*, the hottest ticket in town. Frankie's Liverpudlian co-star Cilla Black was replaced by Anita Harris on 22 July 1967 and,

A cool and collected Frankie rehearses the Prince of Wales Theatre revue *Way Out in Piccadilly* in 1966.

with nine shows a week, *Way Out in Piccadilly* finally notched up 395 performances (408 including previews). One night, even show business royalty Richard Burton and Elizabeth Taylor were in attendance. La Taylor described Frankie as 'the funniest man in the world', a quote subsequently used to advertise Frankie's late 1980s renaissance. Indeed, Frankie was besotted by the attention, saying, 'What a nice lady! And so intelligent! So perceptive! She won me over in seconds flat.'

Frankie was just as taken with Cilla Black. 'I was worried that as a pop star she might think she knew it all,' he confessed. 'So I was wary of her – and it transpired that she was frightened of me. (Although how anyone could be frightened of sweet, modest, lovable Francis bewilders me.) In the event she was superb to perform with, eager to learn and very hard-working. I soon realised that she was a great pro, and from the sketches we did together I reckoned she had great potential as a comic actress. One asset she had was a mad, piercing giggle. It was quite spontaneous (because the dear girl, in the brilliance of her judgment, seemed to think I was very funny) … and it immediately communicated itself to the audience. No matter how many times we played a sketch, she still thought me a hoot – so she hooted!'

In *Plays and Players*, Hugh Leonard was less enthused by Cilla and also pointed out that 'There is a lot of anonymous scenery and some terrible dancing.' About Frankie, however, he had no qualms. 'Mr Howerd is the funniest thing since Mr Laurel and Mr Hardy,' he maintained, adding that 'There is plenty of Mr Howerd in this show – which, not that it matters, is called *Way Out in Piccadilly* – and, before he has finished, the audience is screaming with laughter and begging for mercy … It establishes him as a great performer; and, in the manner of old bores who drone on about the past magnificence of George Robey, Vesta Tilley and co, anyone who goes to see Mr Howerd will find himself boasting about it 50 years hence. Long before then, let us hope that Harold Wilson, in a sudden burst of sanity, will have the supreme good sense to

nationalise Mr Howerd.'

Towards the close of 1966 Frankie was invited by Bernard Delfont to perform at the Royal Command Performance, while in 1967 the Variety Club of Great Britain named him Show Business Personality of 1966. The year was capped with yet another call to entertain the Royals in the Command Performance. When *Way Out in Piccadilly* finally came to a close, Delfont presented Frankie with a silver cigarette box inscribed 'To Frankie Howerd, who never missed a show'. Towards the end of his days, no one was more surprised than Delfont when Frankie turned up at the Prince of Wales Theatre to help celebrate the launch of the impresario's book, *East End, West End*.

However, the man who seemingly could do no wrong was about to do just that. Even with a theatrical farce especially adapted for him by Ray Galton and Alan Simpson…

The Wind in the Sassafras Trees
by Ray Galton and Alan Simpson
*adapted from **Du vent dans les branches de Sassafras** by René de Obaldia*
presented by the Belgrade Theatre Trust (Coventry) Ltd in association with Arthur Lewis and David Merrick
Belgrade Theatre Coventry from 27 February 1968 for three weeks
Cast: Frankie Howerd (John Emery Rockefeller), Sonia Graham (Caroline Rockefeller), Sarah Badel (Pamela Rockefeller), Glyn Worsnip (Tom Rockefeller), John Franklyn-Robbins (William Butler), Simon Oates (Wayne Nelson), Barbara Windsor (Virginia), John Golightly (Partridge Eye/Lynx Eye)
Director: Warren Jenkins; Designer: Hayden Griffin; Lighting: Barry Griffiths

Rockefeller and the Red Indians
author details as above
presented by David Merrick in Boston and Washington then Ethel Barrymore Theatre, 243 West 47th Street New York City from 24 October 1968
Cast: Joyce Grant (Caroline Rockefeller), Jennie Woodford (Pamela Rockefeller), Norman Allen (Tom Rockefeller), Peter Bayliss (William Butler),

Frankie Howerd (John Emery Rockefeller), John Golightly (Partridge Eye/Lynx Eye), Ann Hamilton (Virginia), Simon Oates (Wayne Nelson) Director: Burt Shevelove; Décor and costumes: Hayden Griffin

The Wind in the Sassafras Trees (*Du vent dans les branches de Sassafras*) was written by René de Obaldia and was basically a Mid-West America piece concerning a Kansas dirt farmer by the name of John Emery Rockefeller. 'Location: John Emery Rockefeller's ranch near that den of iniquity, Pancho City,' explained the programme. 'Time: 1870 … or 1880 … or thereabouts.' Frankie described it as 'a satirical send-up of every cliché of all the Westerns ever screened – and long before *Blazing Saddles* was ever thought of.'

The Rockefeller role had been originated by the distinguished French actor Michel Simon and called upon Frankie to be calmly witty while smoking a clay-pipe and dealing with pesky Injuns. ('Although speaking some very witty lines,' he agonised, 'was it *me*?') Barbara Windsor was in the mix as well, playing a warm-hearted saloon girl. The play was given a three-week try-out at the Belgrade Theatre Coventry starting on Tuesday 27 February 1968 and was a huge success. Then came a big muffed decision. Instead of following the usual practice and touring the show for a while before making a big opening in the West End, it was suggested that the production should immediately go on a tour of the USA.

The big-shot Broadway producer David Merrick had apparently forgotten his rejection of Frankie's Fagin back in 1962. 'Come to America,' he said, 'and I'll make you as legendary as Bob Hope.' Frankie, convinced that the piece was strong enough and, indeed, American enough to work in the States, agreed. He also – amazingly, considering his two-year West End reign in *A Funny Thing* – still nursed the wounds of his earlier West End failure in *Mister Venus*.

So the die was cast. Barbara Windsor dropped out and Frankie's old *Forum* associate, Burt Shevelove, came on board as director. After some rather savage press reactions during the show's two-week run in Boston, there were numerous hasty rewrites and a change of title to the self-explanatory *Rockefeller and the Red Indians*. As Frankie himself put it, 'The management got a touch of the Great Theatrical Panic syndrome … They cut and cut until there was no play left: nothing remained that could be possibly interpreted as politically, racially, sexually, religiously, metaphysically, gastronomically, medically, geographically or veterinarily controversial – or funny! By the time they'd finished, the show had been reduced to an elongated sketch, our opening in New York had been delayed a week – and, as a corollary, our collective nerve was crumbling.'

At the show's second port of call, Washington, it went over rather better; President Johnson's wife and daughter came to see it twice, according to Frankie. But the New York opening at the Ethel Barrymore Theatre followed on 24 October and the nervous Frankie felt 'as though I was giving a private audition to [all-powerful *New York Times* critic] Clive Barnes!' Barnes predictably panned the show (though reserving some kind words for Frankie and the other actors) and David Merrick wasted no time in curtailing the agony. The show closed on the 28th.

Frankie returned home from America with his tail very much between his legs, taking the very last voyage on the Queen Elizabeth. An impromptu Frankie cabaret for fellow travellers was given on the last night, but Frankie felt that 'something of a State occasion' would have been more fitting to mark the ship's passing. 'Instead, we almost seemed to slink shamefaced into Southampton in the foggy gloom of a November midnight. Come to think of it, I felt my own homecoming matched the occasion.'

Alan Simpson reflects on why *The Wind in the Sassafras Trees* – or, rather, *Rockefeller and the Red Indians* – was such a failure in America. The country, he maintains, was simply unfamiliar with Frankie Howerd. 'They just thought he was an actor who couldn't act!' Ray Galton agrees and remembers the

Mark Wynter, Alfie Bass, Dora Bryan and Frankie hand it to the orchestra in the starry London Palladium presentation of *Jack and the Beanstalk*, 15 December 1973.

bewildered reaction. 'The American audience was gob-smacked. They just couldn't understand it. They thought, "What an unfunny man and what a terrible actor." He *was* a terrible actor, there's no doubt about it, but that was half of his charm. In America he appeared without any baggage and they just didn't get it. You have to grow up with him to understand him. He wasn't like Bob Hope. He wasn't a teller of jokes. You had to know the man and his history. Some comedians have nothing but their jokes. With Frank the jokes are not the point. If you are retelling a Frankie Howerd joke you have to impersonate him to make it work.'

Despite facing rejection abroad, Frankie was still one of the biggest names in show business back in England. He gave his umpteenth Royal Command Performance on 17 November 1968 as an unbilled guest artiste under the direction of Robert Nesbitt, filling in for Morecambe and Wise after Eric had

suffered a heart attack. It remains one of the most talked-about and fondly remembered interludes in the show's history. Following a rousing performance by the Supremes which finished with a controversial 'black power' clenched-fist salute, on wandered Frankie, unannounced and unexpected. He paused, waited for the reaction to die down and simply muttered, 'That was a bit political, wasn't it? I thought I was in the wrong place!'

Frankie was deeply moved by the burst of applause that greeted his surprise appearance that night. 'I nearly started in the mood for tears instead of laughter,' he reported. 'I pulled myself together and began by saying how 'Thing' – Delfont – had told me, "We've got a couple of people unable to get here tonight. Very important people." And I said, "Really?" And he said "I'm afraid – well, we want you to take their place." And I said, "*Me*? But I'd feel such a fool sitting in that box all on my own." And so it went on from there.'

The 1970s

Frankie was honoured by the Water Rats in 1969, being named Show Business Personality of the Year. He also won the Radio Industries Award for TV Personality of the Year and landed the Royal Command top spot once more on Monday 10 November. And, as a new decade dawned, the awards kept coming. In 1971, seated at the top table alongside Laurence Olivier, Frankie was presented with the *Evening Standard* Silver Key Award to commemorate (rather inaccurately) his 21 years in show business, while the following year he was named the Variety Club of Great Britain's Show Business Personality of 1971. Also in 1972, he was once again dubbed TV Personality of the Year and, flying high socially, found himself invited to Elizabeth Taylor's 40th birthday party in Budapest. What's more, thanks to his clout from *Way Out in Piccadilly*, he was seated at the top table with such icons as Raquel Welch, Michael Caine and Ringo Starr.

At the end of 1973 it was back to high-profile pantomime, after a gap of over ten years, when Frankie starred as Simple Simon in an 18-week run of *Jack and the Beanstalk* at the London Palladium. The show teamed him with his *St Trinian's* co-star Dora Bryan, plus Alfie Bass, Mark Wynter, *Up Pompeii!* mistress Elizabeth Larner and *Forum* baddie Leon Greene. Unfortunately, a slew of bomb hoaxes (12 in all) was followed by a damaging rail strike and the Three-Day Week, complete with power cuts, all of which made Frankie's Palladium stint a rather frustrating one.

On 2 September 1974, Frankie flew off to Cyprus with singer Lois Lane, the Avons and his stunning *Up Pompeii* co-star Julie Ege. Performing in Tepoi, a sports field in Dekhelia and the Curium amphitheatre, the gang gave six troop shows in just four days. Arranged by Combined Services Entertainment, an organisation Frankie had worked with tirelessly over the years, these performances were followed almost immediately by extensive work in Northern Ireland. At the height of the troubles, Frankie performed in Derry, South Armagh, Crossmaglen, Belfast and even the Maze Prison, where he gave a special benefit concert for the wardens.

Known as 'the tour', these showbiz operations were kept totally secret until after Frankie's return to the mainland. Usually comprising a group of just ten performers, including guest stooges of the calibre of June Whitfield, three musicians, a singer, dancers and a speciality act ('the mighty mannequin' Joan Rhodes), the concerts were organised by the well-respected Major Derek Agutter. Indeed, so well-respected was he that Frankie gave an unrehearsed speech at Agutter's retirement do at the CSE headquarters in Chalfont St Giles. Agutter humbly took the praise and returned the compliment by drawing attention to Frankie's own bravery. What's more, if there was any fee for these troop performances, the money was always given to charity. His Northern Ireland payments, for example, often went to the Royal Artillery Association. In a timely endorsement of both his comic talent and lifetime's dedication to benefit performances, Francis Alick Howard was awarded the OBE in the 1977 Queen's New Year's Honours List. He accepted the honour on 2 March 1977.

Back in 1975, however, Frankie had been briefly crippled by stage fright, frequently forgetting his lines and transposing gags. Trying to locate the source of it, he recalled that, as a boy, 'my obsessiveness to perform had been stronger than my nervous terror of appearing in public – and then it hit me! Now that the obsessiveness had gone, there was nothing to stop the basic fear coming through. It was finally taking over.' He cancelled proposed engagements and even contemplated retirement. But, when reminded of a promise to perform at a children's home, he felt honour-bound to go through with it. 'I braced myself, took a deep breath and walked on,' he remembered. 'Generous applause. I started my patter – and after half a dozen words a little girl in the front row squealed: "You're the man on telly with the funny face! Hello, funny face! … You're going to make me laugh, aren't you?" The audience hooted, so did I – and all my tension suddenly vanished. Just like that! It was extraordinary.'

Frankie may have got over his stage fright, but his interest in 'straight' plays had deserted him since the *Rockefeller and the Red Indians* disaster. According to writer Dave Freeman, 'After Frank's brush with Broadway he took a dislike to the stage. However, in the 1970s I wrote a comedy thriller called *Murder In A Bad Light*. Frank badly wanted to do it, provided that I rewrote it so that he could talk to the audience. I couldn't see any way of doing this. He came to my house for dinner and I accidentally spilt a plate of hot soup over him. Luckily he was wearing his customary thick tweed suit.'

Immediately prior to his OBE award, Frankie had spent the 1976/77 panto season in *Jack and the Beanstalk* at the Theatre Royal Bath, with Nat Jackley and *Up Pompeii!* starlet Georgina Moon. In 1977 he continued to tour the country, from New Brighton or the London Palladium to the King's Theatre Glasgow, with *The Frankie Howerd Show*. The Glasgow dates fell on 18 and 19 May and featured Madame Rogers at the piano plus a bizarre collection of variety turns, including Richard Cromwell, Michael Vine & Karen, and ventriloquist Larry Jones with Thomas the alley cat. And in 1978 Frankie took to the stage of Plymouth's New Palace Theatre to play Buttons in *Cinderella* opposite Julian Orchard, Terry Gardener, John Boulter, Nicholas Smith and Peter Jones. He also chalked up his final Royal Command Performance and entertained the Royals for the very last time at Windsor.

He continued to tour the country and it was at the Grand Theatre Swansea in 1978 that he revealed some plans for the future. 'I might go back to America again to do various things and I might appear in a play after that. I've got two or three plays to look at. I'm hoping to do a modern play at the National Theatre which is currently being written. It is a modern adaptation of an old play and, I hope, a funny one! Then I might go to Australia, New Zealand and Canada because I've been asked to tour there.'

Frankie had just returned from the States, having filmed his Hollywood supporting role in *Sgt. Pepper's Lonely Hearts Club Band*.

In Los Angeles, he had bumped into an old friend from home while attending a performance of Trevor Griffiths' *Comedians* at LA's Forum Theatre. The star of the show, Jim Dale, invited Frankie to take the stage after the performance and lecture the totally bemused American audience on comedy technique and his laughter-packed career. 'Frankie came backstage during the intermission of *Comedians*,' Jim remembers. 'I suggested that I introduce him to the audience at the end of the show. I thought it would be interesting for him to chat to them and he was more than happy about the idea. Ironically the play is all about a load of comics striving to make a living, something Frankie certainly couldn't relate to at that stage of his career.

'I introduced Frankie and, God love him, he went out there cold in front of an audience who really had no idea who he was. It was an amazing experience. He invited questions from the audience and, of course, it's near enough impossible to ask questions of someone when you have no idea who he is or what he does! But Frankie had a charm rare in comedians. He won them over instantly by saying, "I know another question you're simply aching to ask." Then he would proceed to answer the question himself! Man, it took a lot of nerve to do that.'

The 1980s and beyond

In the late 1970s and early 1980s, Frankie's nerve where stage work was concerned began to desert him rapidly. During 1979 he toured New Zealand with his stand-up act, appeared at London's trendy Country Cousin club, performed aboard the QEII and on Sunday 21 October appeared at the Theatre Royal Windsor in a cancer research benefit in memory of Julian Orchard. He then starred in *Robinson Crusoe* at the Birmingham Alexandra with Bernard Bresslaw, Anita Harris, Tommy Trinder and Jack Tripp. Recovering from a broken pelvis early in 1980, he was in residence at the Pavilion Theatre Sandown between 16 June and 19 July for the 'Isle of Wight Holiday Spectacular', accompanied by impressionist Peter Goodwright

Frankie as the drunken gaoler Frosch in the English National Opera production of *Die Fledermaus* at the London Coliseum, 30 December 1981.

plus Emerson & Jayne and their magic flying carpet! And for the 1980/81 panto season he was Buttons in *Cinderella* at Wimbledon. The cast also included Henry McGee as Baron Hardup (complete with the Honey Monster and Uggi: 'friends of the Baron'), Veronica Page in the title role and Terry Gardener and Derek Royle as the Ugly Sisters.

In March 1981, the Variety Club of Great Britain presented Frankie with a Silver Heart to celebrate 35 years in show business. And at the end of that year, Frankie managed to get involved in some highbrow culture again when the English National Opera revived the old Viennese custom of casting a popular comedian as Frosch, the drunken gaoler in *Die Fledermaus*. The production opened at the London Coliseum on 31 December. 'I've attempted to do so many things,' he told the *Daily Mail*'s Lynda Lee Potter. 'This restlessness has always been with me. One is continually testing oneself ... For instance, I don't have to go into this opera, but I've said yes and it was all an accident.

'I was at Covent Garden, seeing *Madam Butterfly*. I was sitting in the stalls in the interval ... and the opera singer Forbes Robinson came up to me ... He said, "When are you going into opera?" And I said, "The only part I could play would be the drunken gaoler in *Die Fledermaus* because there's no singing in it." I meant it as a joke but what I didn't realise was that *Die Fledermaus* was already in their schedule and he thought I was angling for a part. Four days later my agent had a phone call from a man who said, "I hear Mr Howerd wants to be in our opera." ... They made me feel I'd be letting the whole of England down if I said no. I thought, Here we go again...'

As the 1980s went on, however, the big venues tended to elude him, as often as not because of his own self-doubt and nervousness. He turned down a high-profile stint at the London Palladium, preferring to accept a one-night stand in Singapore or a business convention after-dinner speech in Venice or even a quick foreign television advert filmed in the Alps. Anything, in fact, to keep working and earning, while not exposing himself to ridicule or bad reviews from his home audience.

He was still keen to do his bit for the war effort – wherever that war may be – and he was among the first entertainers to volunteer for troop concerts when the Falklands conflict broke out in 1982. In September of that year, the publishers J M Dent invited him to front a collection of one-upmanship anecdotes under the title of *Trumps – and how to come up*. Very similar to the same publishers' collection of Kenneth Williams-collated put-downs, *Acid Drops*, this hilarious anthology was a typical easy read compiled, more or less, by Frankie and illustrated with cartoons from Carry On title-card master, Larry.

From 17 December 1982 until 15 January 1983 Frankie starred as Simple Simon in *Jack and the Beanstalk* at Chichester, enjoying the company of June Whitfield in a memorable duet of 'Spread A Little Happiness'. Easter 1983 was marked by a major knee operation – Frankie reported that his bones were crumbling and that he would have been wheelchair-bound without the surgery – but he returned in style with a three-week run at the Churchill Theatre Bromley from 11 July to 4 August 1984.

This was for *The Fly and the Fox*, adapted by Barry Took from Ben Jonson's lurid 1606 black comedy *Volpone, or the Fox*. Frankie was cast as Mosca, parasitic partner-in-crime to a lustful grandee (Aubrey Woods) who feigns terminal illness to get his claws into a demure merchant's wife, played by Frankie's regular film and TV companion, Madeline Smith. Other familiar faces included Leon Greene and Dilys Watling, with the cast rounded out by Ken Wynne, Brendan Barry, Lionel Hamilton, Bill French and Nick Mercer. The director was Peter Coe, who over 20 years earlier had been behind *Oliver!* and the Broadway transfer which Frankie rehearsed but didn't appear in.

'I can hear faint rumblings as 16th century Ben Jonson turns in his grave,' reported the *Stage*. 'Nowhere does the theatre's publicity indicate that they know which of his plays is the basis for Barry Took's adaptation. Maybe that's as well, since the sharp wit and bite of

Jonson's *Volpone* was entirely missing, although the storyline was not drastically altered. Frankie Howerd is just the cleverly bumbling Frankie we all know and love, getting laughs from asides to the audience, but clogging the pace that Jonson intended.'

Barry Took himself was more brutal. 'To see Frankie Howerd on stage when he was not in tune with his environment, his part or his audience,' he wrote soon after Frankie's death, 'was to witness a man apparently without talent or timing. I know because in 1983 I adapted (at his request) Ben Jonson's *Volpone*, retitled *The Fly and the Fox*, in which, in spite of his enthusiasm during the rewriting – the 'Howerding up' of the Jacobean classic – he was dreadful in the part of Mosca when it finally reached the stage. For one thing his performance lacked energy. If I had known that he was several years older than he admitted I might have understood. How different from his peak, in the 1940s, when he was humour and vigour personified, an electrifying performer.'

On safer ground, for the 1984/85 pantomime season Frankie starred as Wishee Washee in *Aladdin* opposite Trevor Bannister and Anna Dawson at the Congress Theatre Eastbourne. And, finally, it had to happen: in 1986 Frankie starred in the comic revival of all time, recreating the role of Pseudolus in *A Funny Thing Happened on the Way to the Forum*.

A Funny Thing Happened on the Way to the Forum

book by Burt Shevelove and Larry Gelbart
music and lyrics by Stephen Sondheim
presented by Richard Pilbrow, Pamela Hay and Norman Rothstein for Theatre Projects Associates and Spencer Tandy at the Chichester Festival Theatre from 11 August, then Piccadilly Theatre London from 14 November 1986
Cast: Frankie Howerd (Pseudolus), Patrick Cargill (Senex), Ronnie Stevens (Hysterium), Fred Evans (Lycus), Derek Royle (Erronius), Leon Greene (Miles Gloriosus), Betty Benfield (Domina), Graeme Smith (Hero), Lydia Watson (Philia), Richard Drabble, Chris Eyden, Murray Woodfield (the Proteans), Julie and Tracy Collins

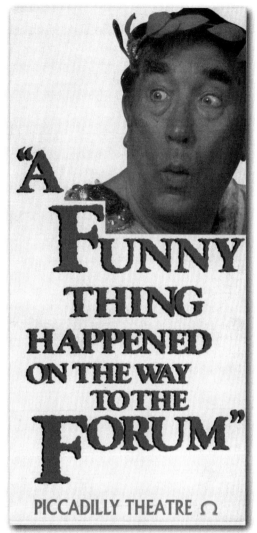

Frankie returned to his greatest stage triumph in 1986, but the revival of *A Funny Thing Happened on the Way to the Forum* failed to recapture former glories.

(the Geminae), Elizabeth Elvin (Gymnasia), Claire Lutter (Tintinabula), Sharon Stephens (Vibrata), Billi Wylde (Panacea)
Director: Larry Gelbart; Musical numbers staged by George Martin; Settings and costumes: Tony Walton; Lighting: Robert Ornbo; Musical director: Godfrey Salmon

The revival kicked off as the centrepiece of the Chichester Festival Theatre's 25th anniversary season on 11 August 1986 and ran until 27 September. On 8 November it opened at the Piccadilly Theatre in London's West End, 'press night' following on the 14th. 'I can think of no comic actor – with the exception of John Cleese – with whom I'd rather spend an evening,' commented the *Times*.

The supporting cast was up to scratch (Patrick Cargill, Ronnie Stevens, Fred Evans, Derek Royle and, returning to his original West End role, Leon Greene) and the show was more or less a carbon copy of the 1963 original, right down to Tony Walton's set and costume designs. But the vim and vigour had faded, and the show closed prematurely on 27 December after only 49 performances, cutting Frankie off from the panto market he might otherwise have enjoyed. Perhaps depressed by this turn of events, Frankie sat out a lot of the musical numbers (literally – making himself comfy on an *Up Pompeii!*-style stone seat while the other oldsters energetically gave their all) and sometimes even wandered off during the finale. He did, however, close the show with a cosy curtain speech ending with a line familiar from the pilot episode and film version of *Up Pompeii*: 'And in the words of

A priceless flyer for a 1987 panto which Frankie never appeared in, his role being taken over by *Star Trek*'s George Takei.

Cleopatra to Mark Antony – if you've enjoyed it, tell your friends.'

Critical responses ranged from 'incredibly limp, tacky and dated' (*Time Out*) to 'It is the most exquisite pleasure to watch Patrick Cargill, Frankie Howerd, Ronnie Stevens and Fred Evans prance around to 'Everybody Ought to Have a Maid', to wallow in the bravura salesmanship on show' (the *Independent*). Michael Coveney in the *Financial Times* observed that Frankie 'looks distinctly fed up, as if resenting the confines of [the] role,' while Mary Harron in the *Observer* looked at it another way: 'Frankie Howerd is low-key, almost bored – as well he might be after playing the role for so long in the sixties – which simply accentuates the elegance and economy of his performance.'

Frankie's sit-down approach to his 1986 Pseudolus was explained the following year when his old leg problems returned, necessitating another major knee operation at the end of November. As a result, he had to bow out of *Aladdin* at Reading's Hexagon Theatre, which was due to start on 14 December with Kathy Staff, Keith Chegwin and *EastEnders*' Shreela Ghosh in the cast. According to Kathy Staff, who was playing the Empress Nora of China opposite Frankie's Genie of the Lamp, 'Frankie was hilarious in rehearsal. My character fancied the Genie and was chasing him round the stage, provoking a string of "Ooh no! Stop it, missus!" exclamations. Luckily for us George Takei, famous as Mr Sulu in *Star Trek*, was in England and, although he had never seen a pantomime in his life, he stepped in to replace Frankie at the eleventh hour. The kids adored him, of course; he used the phrase 'Beam me up, Scottie!' when fleeing from my advances and the song 'Star-Trekking' was also put in to make him feel at home!' From Frankie Howerd to Mr Sulu? The mind boggles.

After a six-month recuperation period, Frankie got back into his stride (in a manner of speaking) in mid-1988 with some London stand-up dates and a one-man show at the

Liverpool Festival of Comedy. And at the end of the year he finally returned to the panto arena, after a four-year absence, as the bemused Baron Hardup in 47 performances of *Cinderella* at Hanley.

However, this proved to be Frankie's final stage performance outside his countless stand-up appearances. With his confidence ebbing away and the young generation of comedians seeming to make veterans of Frankie's era look obsolete, Frankie seriously considered retirement from show business – some 25 years since he had contemplated exactly the same thing at Southsea. Luckily, another turning point was on its way. Having given a notable performance at the Hackney Empire's *Up the Festival* presentation on Sunday 5 March 1989, Frankie was invited to be guest of honour at the Gallery First Nighters' Club annual gathering. This special event was held just over a month later, on 16 April, at the Marriott Hotel in Mayfair. Despite being so nervous that he could hardly get up on his feet to make the speech, a rousing introduction by toastmaster Ivor Spencer and an encouraging word from President Jack Rossiter spurred him on and he literally slayed the audience that day. This success planted the seed that would determine the course of Frankie's final three years.

He accepted a long list of after-dinner gigs and appearances for private business functions. He visited government institutions and lectured on comedy at Cambridge University. However, the major departure was entitled *Frankie Howerd Bursts Into Britain*, a mammoth, back-to-the-fans (old and new) tour which was a sell-out nationwide. It was a one-man show that utilised every ounce of professionalism and gag-telling expertise from 50 years' experience. This 25-date tour ranged from a small club in Wakefield to the Golden Garter in Wythenshawe via the trendy Albany Empire in London's East End and was greeted by an adoring audience of teenagers and 20-somethings. These shows were followed by an awe-inspiring turn at the Hackney Empire's *Holsten Funny Business Show* and more of the same in 1990.

A play-bill for Frankie's sell-out *Tittermost!* shows of 1990.

Quite Frankly Frankie Howerd At His Tittermost!

presented by QPQ Productions Ltd by arrangement with Tessa Le Bars Management at the Lyric Hammersmith and Garrick Theatres, April/May 1990
Frankie Howerd with Madame Rogers at the piano
Producers: Philip Brewin and Tristan Taylor; Lighting: Paul Highfield

This time, however, *Quite Frankly Frankie Howerd At His Tittermost!* was given a run at the Lyric Hammersmith from 2 to 21 April followed by a sell-out three-week stand in May at the Garrick Theatre and a national tour, including the Deptford Albany. 'Frankie Howerd is unique,' said Michael Darvell in *What's On*. 'He is the only funny man who can stand on a stage and talk absolute rubbish for two hours and get away with it … He is certainly a funnier performer than the current breed of so-called alternative comedians.' It was Frankie's final appearance on the West End stage, wallowing in all the usual stuff he had always done on tour but, unlike the seventies, when he did just the second half of the programme… 'Now I do the lot!' In the *Daily Telegraph*, Charles Spencer wrote that 'His look of outrage when the audience responds to an innuendo he pretends he didn't intend is one of the most glorious sights of the British stage today.'

Interviewed in 1978 Frankie revealed that he always wanted to address the young. 'I try to keep young and find out what young people are thinking and doing. I don't mean physically, and I don't dress like a teenager because that would be stupid at my age. But I try to keep mentally young. I also try to change the backgrounds rather than what I do. I don't get stale … Young people today are not used to seeing comedians act on the stage like I used to because they go to discotheques and pop concerts. Obviously, they're the generation who came after the old music halls. But if they see the type of thing I used to do today it's a novelty for them. They're a great audience because they've never seen this type of thing before. It's like these old movies with Fred Astaire and Ginger Rogers they see on television which they think are marvellous because they've never seen people singing and dancing that way. Humphrey Bogart movies have become a cult. It's now become modern again.'

Though he had, amazingly, become the hottest live comedian in the country once more, Frankie was still keen to honour charity appearances and, to this end, made an imposing Richard III for a fund-raising 'Kings of England' historical pageant organised by Gyles Brandreth. He also, rather reluctantly, agreed to speak at University College School,

attended, among others, by Barry Cryer's son. Offered just champers and sandwiches, Frankie muttered, 'What do you want? Twenty minutes?' Cryer recalls with affection that 'He did 70 minutes!'

In December 1990 Frankie was first in the queue to volunteer for troop shows in the Gulf. He was still waiting to hear if his services were required in April 1991. But, instead of bombs and bullets, he faced his final, most adoring crowd of fans ever. 1991 saw yet another major milestone in Frankie's career when the Variety Club of Great Britain presented him with a Silver Heart in acknowledgment of his 45 years in show business. The occasion was celebrated in style and, with yet more regional theatre concerts being booked and Frankie's cult stardom at its peak, his live show was recorded for the one-and-only live video released during his lifetime.

The performance was given on 23 June 1991 at the Birmingham Hippodrome and captured Frankie in all his glory. In particular, Frankie's sheepish reflection on the fact that the fall of the variety circuit coincided with the rise of his career is almost too poignant for words. It's funny and heart-wrenching at the same time. Eager to emphasise that none of the material is highbrow and that the crowd may feel some of the gags are a bit on the corny side, Frankie then plunges into an incredible torrent of every Frankie catchphrase known to man. 'Don't make mock! You're making mock!' he pleads, and from that moment he has the audience in the palm of his hand. He goes through the usual 'phone call from the bloke who hired him' routine and on into the outbreak of war vignette. Resurrected from his Johnny Speight-penned Establishment Club routine, the dramatic recreation of the September 1939 broadcast, perfectly punctuated by humour, is quite breathtaking. Madame Roper emerges and 'Three Little Fishes' is dragged out as well as a brilliant sub-Sinatra deviation, 'Three Wives in the Fountain'.

On the crest of a national wave of Frankie fandom, the old comic warhorse was at a peak of confidence and commercial viability. Fishee Business was his production company, concerning itself with audio tapes and the ever-popular toga wear: 'Frankie Says…' T-shirts. Okay, so it was all very 1980s – the idea and logo had been lifted from Frankie Goes to Hollywood's merchandise – but it was a treat few fans could resist. I mean, it's not often you can buy 'clothing to laugh in!' bearing such legends as 'Get your titters out', 'Nay, nay and thrice nay!', 'Shut yer face!' or the evergreen 'Ooh err, missus!' The really dedicated Frankie Pankie could fork out for a special Yuletide model, featuring a pretty dubious-looking, pink-faced Frankie caricature with a Santa Claus hat plonked on his head. The legend? 'Merry Tittermas!'

Interviewed in *TV Times* in 1969, Frankie had chatted candidly about the thought process behind his stage persona. 'A comedian is someone who ducks when you raise your hand. A comedian dominates you with his weakness. A comedian starts with an instinct … Then you rehearse and practise and eventually get up and do it in front of people and you analyse what they laugh at and don't laugh at. You learn timing and you learn to take in *all* the audience, not just the people at the front. You move on stage so that your face is always on show. I like to wear warm-looking clothes, browns, and have warm-looking scenery. Certain scenes behind you can be so fussy in design that they take attention from your face, and that is really what the audience should be drawn to like a great lit-up moon.'

It was fitting, therefore, that Frankie's final work of any kind, the four *Frankie's On…* programmes recorded for television, were live performances. He always seemed at his most assured and confident with an appreciative audience to work off. In a 1958 interview he confided: 'It's very complicated why people become comedians. Usually they are unhappy and insecure, so they try and laugh at life and be funny … I was a lonely child and was always making up fantasies and used to think that I would be famous and that would make me happy. When I became famous I found I was lonelier than ever.' ●

Frankie holds court at the Lyric Hammersmith, April 1990.

CHAPTER

Nay, Nay and Thrice Again I say...

FRANKIE ON RADIO AND RECORD

'Comedy is like walking through a minefield!' **Frankie Howerd**

A lifetime's familiarity with the comic mannerisms and all-round genius of Frankie Howerd in the autumn of his career makes it well-nigh impossible to imagine the sheer shock value that Frankie embodied in his earliest, freshest, wildest and most challenging days. Think of the establishment-busting, shiny-suited persona of Ben Elton. Mix in the surrealist word pictures of Eric Idle. Add a dash of the rollicking family entertainment typified by Michael Barrymore. And you are approaching something akin to Frankie's effect on the comic landscape of the immediate post-war years.

Nowhere was this comedic bombshell felt more strongly than the British Broadcasting Corporation's Light Programme. In the business called show, real overnight successes are rare indeed but Frankie's rise to the top was truly meteoric. Having only been a professional performer for six weeks, the fresh-faced stand-up comic was selected by the distinguished BBC Radio producer Joy Russell Smith for an audition. She was at that time in charge of the number one showcase for comedy talent returning from the war…

Variety Bandbox

'Is Variety Bandbox just a stepping stone to other heights?'

Gale Pedrick
Radio Times, October 1949

While the Windmill Theatre proved the sorting office for the finest in comic talent fresh from camp shows and troop entertainment, *Variety Bandbox* was the broadcasting favourite that could turn these unknowns into national celebrities. Tony Hancock, Benny Hill, Peter Sellers, Terry Scott, Max Bygraves, Harry Secombe, Bob Monkhouse and Terry-Thomas all appeared but the leading comic light discovered by the programme was none other than Frankie Howerd.

It was on 9 October 1946 that a terrified Frankie journeyed to BBC Broadcasting House – still sand-bagged after the rigours of war – to meet Joy Russell Smith for the very first time. It was a meeting that would make him the most popular and listened-to comedian in the country. Moreover, the call came completely out of the blue. Interviewed in 1949, Frankie revealed that 'When I heard I was to go for a BBC audition I thought someone was pulling my leg!'

Frankie sheds light on another tittersome script.

Frankie performed his usual mixture of shaggy dog stories and comic songs, and the producer was enchanted. In a BBC memo she considered Frankie's comic style 'an entirely new art form.' Frankie's 'very funny, original patter and song' was seen as perfect for *Variety Bandbox*. Joy Russell Smith was joined at the BBC audition by bigwigs Eric Spear and John Hooper, both of whom shared her enthusiasm. Almost immediately Frankie was booked for three appearances on the programme. If the broadcasts went well he would be invited to become one of the show's two resident comedians.

Billed as 'The Borderline Case', Frankie nervously made his broadcasting début on Sunday 1 December 1946 from the Palace Theatre Camberwell. *Radio Times* alerted audiences to the unusual and intriguing quality of the guest performer by explaining that Frankie was 'a comedian who is really different in that he doesn't tell a single gag.' The listings journal went on to heighten the interest by revealing that the show's producer 'wouldn't let us into the secret of Frankie Howerd's humour because it might take some of the surprise from the first show.' This act was clearly going to be something groundbreaking and, of course, Frankie's work in the series crystallised his staccato stage persona and made him a star.

However, Frankie's own reaction to the first broadcast was typically self-critical. Talking in the 1970s, he commented that 'I was on the air for seven minutes and they were seven minutes of sheer torture. I spluttered and stammered, unconsciously pulling faces and running my hands through my hair.' Sadly no audio recording remains of this first broadcast but it proved of immense importance to the development of Frankie's unique comic personality. Naturally, nobody at home could see Frankie's nervous tension; it merely came across as a manic new form of unpolished comic observation. Following his initial appearance Frankie consciously restructured his delivery to match his unfamiliar surroundings. He was a radio natural but only when he worked out how to utilise his

performing skills to the maximum. On stage he had flamboyantly clowned with his expressive face, depending on long pauses and contortions of his features to get laughs: a skill naturally lost on radio. The solution was simple but inspired. He began to clown with his voice. Immediately the timeless Frankie style seemed to fall into place. He would play with language, deliberately mispronouncing words and heightening the accent of familiar phrases to glean the maximum comic effect.

Such was the popularity of Frankie that he was signed up to become the resident comedian and compere for the show. This resulted in over three years' regular employment for the comedian and a fruitful mock-rivalry with smooth-as-silk performer Derek Roy. Speaking in 1978, Frankie explained what the BBC wanted. 'They were looking for a comedian to alternate with the one they had, Derek Roy. So he did one week and I did the other. I think we were the first two to do so over the air … We were the first to do it probably anywhere. The routine became very popular.' The contrast of comic styles was perfect – Frankie seemingly unrehearsed and shambolic, Roy the polished sophisticate. The bitter brickbats and biting banter created a nationwide sensation.

Frankie's style is fascinating at this early stage in his career. It's almost the complete comic persona beloved by each succeeding generation, but there's a freshness and speed which marks it out as arguably his most rewarding and dynamic work of all. Continually dropping in comments about his own machine-gun delivery and screaming 'Quippery!' with an almost childlike glee, Frankie combines the natural comic genius of two of his heroes – the slightly languid campery of Sid Field's 'photographer' sketch and the fast-paced cheekiness of Max Miller. Certainly audiences familiar with his later work will find his delivery much, much faster in the surviving *Variety Bandbox* performances.

Audiences warmed to this new star immediately and within weeks Frankie was rewarded with three solo spots in every show as opposed to the customary one. Naturally, material was being swallowed up at a rate of knots. Gone were the days when a stage comedian could work a single finely tuned routine through every hall in the country for the rest of his life. Frankie needed good, fresh material and urgently. His thoughts flashed to the brilliant comedian he had met during the war years. Although he would find his own comic immortality with an endearing series of BBC situation comedy adventures, Eric Sykes leapt to prominence as Frankie's chief writer. From early 1948 Eric Sykes wrote almost every word Frankie uttered on the show. Instrumental in nurturing the finest post-war comic talent in the country, Eric clicked with Frankie at once and moulded a seemingly endless supply of bizarre and hilarious shaggy dog stories around his personality. Sykes had a wonderful ear for language and, with Frankie Howerd as his interpreter, managed to spin some of the funniest, most imaginative radio interludes ever broadcast.

Sykes' personal favourite involves Frankie's struggle to ship two elephants from Manchester to London and on to Crewe by air. The beauty in these delightful flights of fancy remains Sykes' natural, logical style, even at the tales' absurdist heights. Another celebrated shaggy dog story involved Frankie's reluctance to try a bit of lion-taming at the circus. Elongating the oft-repeated phrase 'The lion moved slowly forward!' relentlessly and hilariously, Frankie closes the piece on a moment of dark humour as he recalls the chap who put his head in Leo the lion's mouth and relates the funeral of the poor blighter. The lion-tamer story is important for containing Sykes' perhaps most lyrical and telling piece of writing. Conjuring up the glitzy, nerve-wracking essence of the big top/big cat experience, Frankie sums up his fear with a single line 'It was so quiet I could hear the lights shining on me!' Sykes the great radio writer creates that scene in the listener's head in an instant.

Although performed at a faster pace, Frankie's personality was already riddled with ultra-familiar catchphrases. Indeed, Sykes and Howerd as a comic partnership created some of his best-loved lines for these legendary broadcasts. Some fell by the wayside in later years – notably 'Ladies and gentle-*men* … I was a-*mazed*!!' and 'The best of luck!' – while 'Dirty old devil', 'What a funny woman!' and 'Not on your Nellie…' were resurrected, reinvented and re-evaluated until the end of his days.

The way these endearing and easily remembered taglines and vocal punctuation marks caught the public imagination was astounding. Moreover, Frankie's 'stream of consciousness' approach, seemingly making up the dialogue as he went along, proved the nemesis of the 'I say, I say, I say' school of music hall jokery. Frankie also had in bucketloads the two essential ingredients of the popular comedian. The audience warmed to him immediately and he radiated an air of down-to-earth ordinariness which made his long-winded comic monologues all the more effective. Frankie proved himself a skilful character comedian as well. A regular comic interlude cast him as 'Francis Howerd – baritone (the lowest of the low)', which allowed him to flex his highbrow muscles and address the audience with a slightly insane, menacing sort of superiority: 'There are those amongst us tonight whom I shall 'do'!'

At the peak of his success with the series Frankie made the brave, but rapidly reconsidered, decision to leave the show. His last regular broadcast came on 20 March 1949 but, despite huge popularity as a stage performer, Frankie was tempted back for a second bite of the *Variety Bandbox* cherry almost immediately. Frankie's return to the show came six months later and almost by default. He was the headlining comedian on the *National Radio Celebrity Gala* which swamped the *Variety Bandbox* spot on Sunday 2 October in two one-hour chunks, from 7.30 pm and 9.00 pm, broadcast from the London Palladium. The benefit was in aid of the British Wireless for the Blind Fund and Frankie joined the likes of Anne Shelton, Max Wall and Jimmy Edwards in the radio festival.

Just two weeks later, on 16 October 1949

Frankie returned in triumph to *Variety Bandbox* itself. Interviewed by Gale Pedrick for *Radio Times*, Frankie was surprisingly candid about his feelings. 'I don't sparkle with wit. I couldn't be an off-stage comic if I tried. I like heavy reading and symphony concerts. It always worries me when people are shocked because I am so serious. I am not the aggressive type some people think. It takes me all my time to cover up an inferiority complex. I cannot help it if I am one of those who never have confidence in the present, but only lots in the future.' Even more interestingly, Frankie addressed his sometimes baffling career moves and, particularly, the reason he dropped out of *Variety Bandbox* at the height of his fame. 'I came off the air because I didn't want people

A vintage Frankie portrait from his *Variety Bandbox* days of 1950.

to get tired of me. Some comedians broadcast too much and go on too long. Even the greatest artists in the world have their own special tricks and surely the secret is trying to keep the act fresh.'

Frankie was also keen to return to one of his earliest passions – writing. He was quite aware of the mockery he might face and certainly wasn't intent on going straight and trying to write something like *Hamlet*. He was aiming for nothing more nor less than 'good light comedies'. *Radio Times* actually gave him the chance to flex his writing muscles when he was invited to pen a short story for the Christmas 1949 issue. Tellingly, it was entitled *The Skeleton in the Armchair* and revealed Frankie's very own skeleton in the cupboard, ticking the comic off for sometimes telling interviewers that he didn't exist!

The delightful tale begins with Frankie facing the fact that his audience probably won't believe his Christmas memories. 'I was at home with my family and I remember suddenly deciding to pop up to my room for a secret toffee.' A quite delightful turn of phrase leads into Frankie's encounter with his disgruntled skeleton in an 'armchair by the fire, warming its hands.' Frankie's 'I was dumbfounded!' links to the skeleton's snappy 'Well, have you lost your tongue?' 'I was about to retort in that automatic way which we comics acquire, "No, but *you* have," when I thought better of it.' The short bit of prose is packed with puns ('I've got a bone to pick with you') but it also reflects the inner thoughts of Frankie himself. In conclusion he writes, 'Of course, as I suggested in the first place you may have reached the conclusion that I concocted this story in order to get my name in the *Radio Times*. Well, if you do think this, all I can say is that if you should go upstairs one night and find your skeleton awaiting you, don't come running to me for sympathy.'

The *Variety Bandbox* format was slightly altered to celebrate Frankie's return. He was once again cast as resident comedian, with Reg 'Confidentially' Dixon in tow, while the sublime patter vignettes were still in the more than capable hands of Eric Sykes. As with the previous 'baritone' business, Frankie was granted another regular interlude of puffed-up pomposity in his role as Professor Howerd. A snotty philosopher and guiding light to the stars, these interludes ushered in the biggest film and television names of the day for a healthy dose of ritual humiliation. In an era of polite refinement and forlock-tugging respect for celebrities, Professor Howerd's bemused, ignorant and dismissive treatment of these huge stars won applause from the regular audiences. Richard Attenborough, Terence Morgan, David Tomlinson and Gilbert Harding were among the legendary names to get the brusque Howerd treatment. Perhaps the most entertaining and inspired episode came when matinée idol Dirk Bogarde required Frankie's help, claiming that, ever since his violent crime in *The Blue Lamp*, he found himself compelled to rob any complete stranger he met in the street.

Despite Frankie's huge radio success having made him famous across the land, there were still some faithful followers tuning in every two weeks who had no idea what Frankie looked like. Interviewed in 1950, Frankie explained that 'The dial and the vocal chords just don't go together. A lot of people, I am told, expect to find that I'm about 50, short and fat and wearing a spiv suit.' After just six months back in the driving seat of *Variety Bandbox* Frankie decided to quit as resident comedian for the second and final time. Such was his sentimental attachment to the programme, however, that when the final edition was broadcast on 28 September 1952 Frankie was the very special guest comedian. It was the perfect close to a programme that shaped Frankie's entire career.

....

Did You Know? Frankie was at his happiest when broadcasting from the intimate Camden Theatre and complained when, owing to better equipment at the Royal Artillery Theatre Woolwich or greater space at the Playhouse, the location was changed. Indirectly this gave rise to his (vastly over-blown) reputation for awkwardness.

....

Guest comedian: Frankie Howerd
1946: 1 December, with Jessie Matthews, Harry Hemsley, Hella Toros and Edward Reach, Stephane Grappelli, Johnnie Riscoe and Violet Terry, Morton Fraser and his Harmonica Rascals. 15 December, with Richard Murdoch and Kenneth Horne, Janet Hamilton-Smith and John Hargreaves, Max and Harry Nesbitt, Ivy Benson, Les Baker, the Regent Singers. 25 December, with Turner Layton, Terry-Thomas, Peter Brough and Archie Andrews, Margaret Eaves, the Doyle Kids, Pat Frost.
Resident comedian: Frankie Howerd
1947: 12 January, with Jack Warner, Maudie Edwards, Mario (Harp) Lorenzi, Ronalde, the Two Rascals, Mario Var. 26 January, with Tessie O'Shea, Ted and Barbara Andrews, Brian Reece, the Beverley Sisters, Len Fillis. 9 February, with 'Hutch', Harry Hudson, Santiago, Lopez and his Rumba Band, Stanley King, Donald Edge, Jimmy Lyons. 9 March, with Mooney and King, Donald Peers, Harry Hudson, Tuppy Oliver, El Mario's All-Girls Latin American Orchestra. 23 March, with Jeanne de Casalis, Harold Warrender, Harry Hudson, Ronalde, Vera Conway, Mervedeff and his Balalaika Orchestra. 4 April, with Max Wall, Beryl Orde, Rudy Starita, Ramon and his Gamba Orchestra, Kevin Eavers. 20 April, with Terry-Thomas, Eric Winstone, Edmundo Ros and his Rumba Band, Paula Grey. 4 May, with Adelaide Hall, Mario (Harp) Lorenzi, Sydney Lipton, Eddie Bankey, the Three Imps, 'Terry'. 18 May, with Anne Shelton, Peter Brough, Santiago, Sacha's Melodists, Hylda Baker, Frank Lane. 1 June, with Terry-Thomas, Peter Cavanagh, Chappie d'Amato, Peggy Brooks, Harry Rabinowitz, Helsa Nevard and Dorice Mann. 15 June, with Vincent Tildsley's Mastersingers, Charlie Chester, Sid Millward and his Nitwits, Betty Powis-Emery, George Crow, Ivy Peace, Geraldo. 29 June, with Terry-Thomas, Johnny Denis and his Novelty Swingtet, Paula Grey, the Five Smith Brothers, Harry Secombe, Sydney Shaw. 13 July, with Ted Ray, Harry Mortimer, Hella Toros and Edward Reach, Bert Waller. 27 July, with Harry Lester and his Hayseeds, Francisco Conde and his Latin American Music, Ian Condie, Flora Ashe, Harry

Secombe, Frankie Higgins. 10 August, with Terry-Thomas, Mario (Harp) Lorenzi, Robin Richmond, Bill Waddington, Sybil Chilchik, Roy Walker. 24 August, with Harry Hemsley, Jack and Daphne Barker, Sidney Burchall, Loren Martin and his Latin American Music, Peter Bernard, Laurie Brewis and Johnny Wood. 7 September, with the Five Smith Brothers, Irving Kaye, Kyra Vayne, Harry Secombe, the El Marios, Stephen Lang. 21 September, with Turner Layton, Mario (Harp) Lorenzi, Macari and his Hot Club de Holland, Percy Edwards, Frankie Higgins, Julie Bretton. 19 October, with Sylvia Cecil, Morton Fraser and his Harmonica Rascals, Harry Secombe, Bill Waddington, Douglas Maynard and Nicky Kidd. 2 November, with Terry-Thomas, Tollefsen and the Radio Revellers, Trevor Watling, Beatrix Clare and Douglas (Cardew) Robinson. 16 November, with Charlie Kunz, Bertha Willmott, Percy Edwards, Stephen Lang, Gordon Jenkins, Felix Mendelssohn and his Hawaiian Serenaders. 14 December, with Tessie O'Shea and Billy Munn. 24 December, Christmas *Variety Bandbox*, with Peter Cavanagh, Davy Kaye and Paula Gray.

1948: 11 January, with Jeanne de Casalis, Ted Ray, Harold Warrender. 25 January, with Davy Kaye. 8 February, with Dick Bentley, Edmundo Ros, Philip Slessor. 22 February, with Percy Edwards, Cardew Robinson, Anona Winn, Rawicz and Landauer. 7 March, with Peggy Cochrane and Douglas Maynard. 21 March, with Vic Oliver, Jack Raymond. 4 April, with Felix Mendelssohn, Billy (Uke) Scott, Michael Howard. 18 April, with Ronald Chesney, Peter Cavanagh, Robert Moreton. 2 May, with Jessie Matthews, the Dagenham Girl Pipers, Ian Melville. 16 May, with Davy Kaye and Harry Mortimer. 30 May, with Adelaide Hall and Billy (Uke) Scott. 13 June, with Avril Angers, Al Shaw, Bob Monkhouse. 27 June, with Max Geldray, Val Merrall, Peggy Brook. 5 September, with Max Bygraves, Bill Kerr. 19 September, with Peter Sellers, Jeanne de Casalis. 3 October, with Davy Kaye, Eric Woodburn. 17 October, with Harry Secombe, April May & June, Bill Williams and the Three Imps. 31 October, with Claude Hulbert, Enid

Trevor. 14 November, with Peter Sellers, Anora Winn, Tony Scott. 28 November, with the Radio Revellers, Max Bygraves, Jackie Allen and Barbara, Doris Gambell, Albert and Les Ward, Beryl Reid. 26 December, with the Ispwich Co-Operative Youth Choir, Charlie Kunz, Suzette Tarri, Peter Cavanagh, Janet Hamilton-Smith and John Hargreaves.

1949: 9 January, with Ronnie Ronalde, Anvil Angers, Tony Hancock. 23 January, with Peggy Cochrane, Jon Pertwee, Janet Brown, Wendford Sandel, Joan Hinde. 6 February, with Anona Winn, Jack Watson, Harry Rabinowitz, Charmian Innes, Lyon and Mason, Joe Crosby, Billy 'Uke' Scott. 20 February, with Flotsam, Bill Kerr, Peggy Desmond, Harry Secombe, 'Terry', Davy Kaye, Johnny Denis and his Ranchmen. 6 March, with Peggy Cochrane, Jack Watson, Tommy Reilly, Beryl Reid, Roy Walker, Alec Pleon, Robin Richmond. 20 March, with Ronnie Ronalde, Joyce Golding, Percy Edwards, Cardew Robinson, the Aspidistras, Allan Clive, the Three Monarchs. 16 October, with Jean Sabion, Peter Brough, Alfred Marks, June Birch, the Maple Leaf Four. 30 October, with Anona Winn, Jack Warner, Tony Fayne and David Evans, Tommy Reilly, Johnny Denis and his Ranchmen and the Cactus Kids. 13 November, with Florence Desmond, Claude Cavalotti, Bill Kerr, Eva Boswell, the Three Monarchs. 27 November, with Charlie Kunz, Janet Brown, George Williams, John Hanson, Jack Freear and his Banjo Kings. 11 December, with Elisabeth Welch, Percy Edwards, Avril Angers, the Burt Twins, Felix Mendelssohn and his Hawaiian Serenaders.

1950: 8 January, with Anne Shelton, George Moon, Ribton and Richards, Miriam Karlin, Robin Richmond. 22 January, with Janet Hamilton-Smith and John Hargreaves, Bill Kerr, Peter Sellers, Barbara Leigh, Jerry Allen. 5 February, with Margaret Eaves, Cyril Fletcher, George Williams, Jacques Lebrecque, Jackie Allen and Barbara. 19 February, with John Hanson and Sylvia Welling, Peter Brough and Archie Andrews, Dick Emery, Ivy Benson, the Three Imps. 5 March, with Elisabeth Welch, Leslie Sarony, Tony Fayne and David Evans, Joan Hinde. 19 March, with Sylvia Marriott and

Douglas Taylor, Janet Brown, Tony Hancock, Tollefsen, the Maple Leaf Four. 2 April, with Barbara Sumner, Harry Hemsley, Avril Angers, Jan Rosel, Frank Baron and his Orchestra. Guest comedian: Frankie Howerd
1952: 28 September, with Stan Stennett, George Williams, Rawicz and Landauer, Billy Ternent
Howerd material written by Frankie Howerd and Eric Sykes. Music from 'the leader of the band!' Billy Ternent and his Orchestra. Broadcast from the Camberwell Palace, the Cambridge Theatre, the Golders Green Hippodrome, the Kilburn Empire, the People's Palace, Queensbury All-Services Club. Introduced by Brian Reece, Philip Slessor and Bruce Wyndham. Producers Joy Russell Smith, Tom Ronald (from 5 September 1948) and Bryan Sears (from 31 October 1948). Sundays, 6.00-7.00 pm, 5.00-6.00 pm (from 2 November 1947), 8.00-9.00 pm (from 5 September 1948), 9.00-10.00 pm (28 September 1952) on the Light Programme

Fine Goings On
Series 1

This first attempt to catapult Frankie Howerd into super-stardom off the back of *Variety Bandbox* proved one of the unhappiest and most puzzling chapters in the comedian's career. Although Frankie's radio work remained prolific afterwards and, indeed, a second series of the programme cropped up seven years later, these 14 programmes first broadcast from 4 January 1951 proved unpopular with listeners.

It's amazing when one casts an eye over the show's winning credentials. The scripts were, in the main, written by Frankie's regular cohort Eric Sykes, while additional material was penned by Sid Colin (who would later script the *Up Pompeii* film). Hattie Jacques, following her sterling character work in the final years of *ITMA*, was recruited as Frankie's comic stooge, while bickering bluster from Bill Fraser (the perfect baddie in the subsequent Up trilogy) and Norman Wisdom (the new wunderkind of British

comedy) made the programme an appetising proposition indeed.

Writing in his autobiography about the horrendous first recording at the BBC's Paris Theatre, Frankie recalled that 'I still needed a large, music hall-type auditorium in which to project myself, even for radio, and I found the Paris claustrophobic and intimidating.' Sykes wisely resurrected Frankie's gloriously familiar *Variety Bandbox* catchphrases – notably 'I was a-*mazed*!' and 'The best of luck!' – while Marjorie Holmes as the prissy Miss Medworthy and hilariously inept romantic duets from Janet Hamilton-Smith and John Hargreaves provided plenty of opportunity for Frankie's acidic, pomposity-pricking comments. But it was all to no avail.

'Maybe the format for the show wasn't right,' Frankie mused. However, this was clearly – to all intents and purposes – *Variety Bandbox* with the resident comedian as complete lynchpin. Whatever the reason, Frankie faced real professional rejection for the first time in his life. His professionalism and perfectionist streak began to glean him a reputation for awkwardness. Not for the last time in his rollercoaster career, Frankie turned to his familiar escape route: long, lonely walks in the country desperately trying to figure out where his career was going.
FRANKIE HOWERD with Hattie Jacques, Bill Fraser, Norman Wisdom, Marjorie Holmes, Janet Hamilton-Smith, John Hargreaves. Written by Eric Sykes and Sid Colin. Music from the BBC Revue Orchestra conducted by Robert Busby. Producer Bryan Sears. Thursdays, 4 January-5 July 1951 on the Light Programme.

Frankie Howerd Goes East

The shock failure of *Fine Goings On* hit Frankie hard. So much so that the perfect solution seemed to be to retreat into himself and return to the type of full-on, audience-led comedy he had excelled at during his time in the army. Thus it was that Frankie, with military cohort and comic genius Eric Sykes in tow, sold the BBC on the idea of an eight-part radio series featuring the stuttering comedian performing for the troops. Produced in partnership with the BBC and the War Office, Frankie advised on a suitable itinerary for the series, taking in such exotic locations as Malta, Egypt and Cyprus. Frankie warmed up for the experience by performing additional concerts for RAF and naval bases although these, never being intended to form part of the series, were not recorded.

The programmes were recorded live and support came from glamorous singer Marcia Owen, serious pianist Eric James and Frankie's 'mascot', the comic pianist Blanchie Moore. And, in a groundbreaking move, amateur servicemen provided the stooge characterisations. Amazingly, Frankie wasn't happy with the end product, considering the Sykes scripts to have been 'written against time and … hardly award-winners'. Several similar transmissions followed, with Frankie's troop concerts in Korea and Hong Kong being broadcast later in 1952, and the BBC couldn't deny the fact that the programmes proved enormously popular with listeners. So much so that Frankie was rewarded with his own, eponymous radio series almost immediately.

FRANKIE HOWERD with Blanchie Moore, Marcia Owen, Eric James. Written by Eric Sykes. Producer Roy Speer.
Show 1: Nicosia, 2 and 3: the Canal Zone, 4: Fayid, 5: Benghazi, 6: Tripoli, 7 and 8: Malta. Wednesdays, 9.30-10.00 pm, 23 April-11 June 1952, on the Light Programme.

Calling All Forces / All-Star Bill

Following the demise of *Variety Bandbox* the format was pretty much resurrected with *Calling All Forces*. Again, the show selected the up-and-coming and fully established cream of music and comedy to entertain the troops. Frankie was a regular. *All-Star Bill* was more of the same and notably teamed Frankie with writers Alan Simpson and Ray Galton for the first time. He introduced three hour-long programmes, with 'interruptions by Graham Stark', on 1 December, 15 December and 22 December 1952.

The Frankie Howerd Show
Series 1

Frankie 'introduces personalities in show business' was how *Radio Times* promoted this celebrated Howerd-headlining, show-stopping, laughter-packed and music-dripping radio series. The format proved an instant success and marked out the comedian's radio style for, on and off, some 20 years.

Joyfully, several features of the glory days of *Variety Bandbox* were embraced, with Eric Sykes still writing material for the broadcasts and the cheeky comic interludes from music master Billy Ternent providing Frankie with the perfect comic sounding board. Old *Variety Bandbox* rival, Derek Roy, guested on one show and long-time host for the series, Brian Reece, was also invited to spar with Frankie on his own ground. Interestingly, the healthy disrespect for the rich and famous of British filmmaking was retained from *Variety Bandbox*'s Professor Howerd interludes. The audiences, again, lapped up the mild-mannered abuse of the country's biggest stars. In the first broadcast, Tony Hancock played the fool and that distinguished thespian Richard Burton was ridiculed without mercy. Other major film star guests included Margaret Rutherford, Dennis Price and Robert Newton, while Julie Andrews, Joan Collins and Katie Boyle made early appearances.

Alan Simpson remembers, 'They were all friends of Frank. He had a photograph of Richard Burton who had just been a big success in *Hamlet*. Most of the guest actors would say, "You're not very good are you?" And, of course, Frank would explode, "How dare you?" He would be outraged at the suggestion that he wasn't a brilliant actor. We wrote a sketch for him and Richard Burton and, naturally, he didn't have Burton on to play the lead. Frank would say, "I'm doing the lead. I want you to play your trumpet!" Frank attracted all the big stars because he was very popular. We had great fun writing the scripts for all these great names. It was a marvellous opportunity and, for us, a wonderful break. Robert Newton was in one. We had him as a schizophrenic madman. He would be terribly

charming and all of a sudden he would go mad. He'd want to kill Frank. The show was a series of sketches with Frank, a Welsh comedienne called Gladys Morgan and Billy Ternent the band leader. They were the three principals and then Frank would introduce the big star and that would be the last sketch. We used to record it at the Royal Artillery Theatre at Woolwich so most of the audience were soldiers and traditionally they were the best audience because they would guffaw at everything!'

Crucially, Frankie was successful in combining the studio-bound comedy style of *Fine Goings On* with his more relaxed and confident performing environment of live, open spaces. Thus, with these comedy revues performed for servicemen, packed with classy

star names and penned by the couple of writers who were to write some of his freshest and funniest material for the next 20 years, the series' success was assured. The Frankie persona was given an extra dimension. *Show 1, with Tony Hancock, Richard Burton, Eve Boswell, Semprini. Show 2, with Max Bygraves, Lee Lawrence, Tito Burns, Margaret Rutherford. Show 3, with Vivian Blaine, Winifred Atwell, Dennis Price, Cicely Courtneidge. Show 4, with Alfred Marks, Vanessa Lee, the Deep River Boys, Claire Bloom. Show 5, with Dorothy Squires, Tibor Kunstler, Gladys Morgan, Anthony Steel. Show 6, with Donald Peers, Eddie Calvert, Kenneth Horne, Margaret Lockwood. Show 7, with the Beverly Sisters, Rawicz and Landauer, Joan Collins, Arthur Askey. Show 8, with Derek Roy,*

An 'over-excited' star struggles to keep awake as Billy Ternent and his Orchestra rehearse for The Frankie Howerd Show at the Camden Theatre, February 1954.

Going through the latest collection of Eric Sykes-scripted quips with the writer himself during February 1954 rehearsals for *The Frankie Howerd Show* at the Camden Theatre.

Julie Andrews, Tommy Reilly, Richard Greene. Show 9, with Val Parnell, Tony Brent, Eve Boswell, Bernard Braden. Show 10, with Shirley Abicair, Ethel Revnell, Josef Locke, Robert Morley. Show 11, with Brian Reece, the Tanner Sisters, Edmund Hockridge, Robert Newton. Show 12, with Bonar Colleano, Bob and Alf Pearson, Maxine Sullivan, Michael Denison and Dulcie Gray. Show 13, with Muriel Smith, Kenny Baker, Billy Butlin, Jimmy James. Show 14, with Harry Dawson, Gladys Morgan, Larry Adler, Catherine Boyle. Show 15, with Marcia Owen, Jimmy Logan, Jack Jackson, Robert Beatty. Show 16, with Josef Locke, Anny Berryer, Diana Dors, Max Wall.

Written by Ray Galton and Alan Simpson with Eric Sykes. Music from Billy Ternent and his Orchestra. Producer Alastair Scott Johnston. Mondays, 23 November 1953-8 March 1954, 9.15-10.00 pm, on the Light Programme.

The Frankie Howerd Show Special

A special edition of Frankie Howerd's comic and musical radio show broadcast from the National Radio Show at Earl's Court with support from Lee Young, Frank Weir, Joy Nichols, Dick Bentley and Billy Ternent and his Orchestra.
Written by Ray Galton and Alan Simpson.

Producer Alastair Scott Johnston. 9.15-10.00 pm, Monday 30 August 1954, on the Light Programme.

The Frankie Howerd Show
Series 2

Having fully found his feet as a star attraction on radio, Frankie was hastily welcomed back for a second series of his own show. Again brought into the mix was that wonderfully eccentric Welsh comedienne, Gladys Morgan, who gelled with Frankie's conspiratorial style of comic observation. Billy Ternent once more joined Morgan as the bane of Frankie's radio life. Indeed the on-air announcement and *Radio Times* listing screamed: '*The Frankie Howerd Show* in which Frankie introduces the vitality of the Tanner Sisters, the versatility of the Hedley Ward Trio, the voice of Lee Young, the nimble fingers of Dolores Ventura, and apologises for Gladys Morgan and Bill Ternent.' Frankie was also 'proud to welcome this week' a starry list of eager guest artistes who continued to impress. The likes of Richard Attenborough, Denholm Elliott, Donald Sinden and Donald Wolfit queued up for comic humiliation. On the scriptwriting front, Galton and Simpson – now also hard at work writing *Hancock's Half Hour* – were joined by another Sykes cohort, a certain Spike Milligan.

With Lee Young, Joan Regan, Gladys Morgan, Billy Ternent, Dolores Ventura (shows 1-4), the Tanner Sisters (shows 4-8), the Hedley Ward Trio (shows 5-8). Guests: Show 1, Terence Morgan. Show 2, Donald Wolfit and Rosalind Iden. Show 3, Jack Hylton. Show 4, Donald Sinden. Show 5, Sheila Sim. Show 6, Anthony Steel. Show 7, Denholm Elliott. Show 8, Richard Attenborough.
Written by Ray Galton and Alan Simpson with Eric Sykes and Spike Milligan. Music Billy Ternent and his Orchestra. Producer Alastair Scott Johnston.
Tuesdays, 9.15-10.00 pm (except show 3, 8.00-8.45 pm and show 7, 9.00-9.45pm), 22 February-12 April 1955, on the Light Programme, with repeats on the following Sundays from 2.15 pm.

The Frankie Howerd Show
Series 3

After a lay-off of just six months, Frankie's radio series stormed back to the airwaves with a further batch of 16 programmes. *Radio Times* heralded the new series by emphasising the differences from the previous two efforts: 'To complete the 'new look' of the programme four new scriptwriters will be engaged in getting Frankie into and out of the kind of situations that his own particular kind of madness seems to thrive upon.' Johnny Speight was the chief writer. His sardonic, mocking observations were ideal for Frankie's indignant and ironic self-importance. A typical example had Frankie explaining the problems he faces in his chosen profession. 'It's not easy to be a comedian. Some do it by wearing funny clothes. Some comedians have a funny face. Me? I have this curse of beauty!' It was Speight building up the assured laughter-line to fever-pitch hysteria.

Other writing contributions for the series came from Dick Barry, John Antrobus and future Dalek creator Terry Nation. Reassuringly, Gladys Morgan and Billy Ternent were still in support and the impressive guest list included Charlie Chester, Gilbert Harding, Stanley Holloway, Gang Show creator Ralph Reader, Max Wall and boxing legend Freddie Mills. The regular supports included Shani Wallis, fresh from the West End hit *Wonderful Town*, Ken Morris (who had impressed as 'Whippit Kwick' in Charlie Chester's *Stand Easy*), and his wife, Joan Savage.

FRANKIE HOWERD introduces 'the glamour of Shani Wallis', 'the vitality of the Tanner Sisters', 'the voice of Lee Young' (except show 1), 'the versatility of Ken Morris and Joan Savage', 'that lovely singing star Joan Regan', and 'apologises for Gladys Morgan and Billy Ternent.'
Announcer Robin Boyle. With: Show 1, John Gregson. Show 2, Terence Morgan. Show 3, David Knight. Show 4, Dennis Price. Show 5, Donald Sinden. Show 6, Hubert Gregg. Show 7, Sam Wanamaker. Show 8, Anthony Steel. Show 9, Gilbert Harding. Show 10, Stanley Holloway. Show 11, A E Matthews. Show 12, Charlie Chester. Show 13, Max Wall. Show 14,

Freddie Mills. Show 15, Ralph Reader. Show 16, Kenneth More.
Written by Johnny Speight, John Antrobus, Terry Nation and Dick Barry. Music Billy Ternent and his Orchestra. Producer Alastair Scott Johnston.
Sundays, 7.30-8.15 pm, 2 October 1955-22 January 1956, on the Light Programme.

Christmas Crackers

Towards the end of the third series of *The Frankie Howerd Show*, Frankie replaced himself with this seasonal offering. 'Frankie Howerd opens a box of *Christmas Crackers* and shares them with Alfred Marks, the BBC Show Band directed by Cyril Stapleton, the Stargazers, Victoria Elliott, Joan Sims, Gladys Morgan and Lee Young.' Ostensibly it was the usual mixture of jokes and songs but, despite the same line-up of writers, wasn't a Christmas special of the regular Howerd show but a special in its own right.
Written by Johnny Speight, John Antrobus, Terry Nation and Dick Barry. Producer Johnnie Stewart.
7.30-8.30 pm, Friday 23 December 1955, on the Light Programme.

Puss in Gumboots

For the pantomime season on BBC Radio, Frankie starred in this deliciously irreverent, all-star Christmas jamboree. Lee Young, Billy Ternent and Madame Blanche Moore provided familiar support, while silky villain Dennis Price oozed charm as the Bad Baron and buxom blonde bombshell Sabrina bounced through the fun as the Good Fairy. Frankie was, quite clearly, flavour of the year at the Beeb. Just 90 minutes after this broadcast had finished he was back, on BBC Television, in the corporation's small screen all-star pantomime!
The Hero FRANKIE HOWERD, The Heroine CAROLE CARR, Rock and Roll, the Broker's Men MONTY STEVENS and LEE YOUNG, The Bad Baron DENNIS PRICE, The Good Fairy SABRINA, Tom the Cat Mr WILLIAM TERNENT, Idle Jack DICKIE VALENTINE, Villagers, town criers etc The George Mitchell Choir.
Music from Madame Rogers and Billy Ternent

and his Orchestra. Script by Johnny Speight and Dick Barry. Producer Dennis Main Wilson.
5.30-6.15 pm, 25 December 1956, on the Light Programme. Repeated from 10.00 am Boxing Day 1956 on the Home Service.

Fine Goings On
Series 2

Returning to his first, ill-fated radio star vehicle seemed a curious idea in 1958, particularly considering that three seasons of *The Frankie Howerd Show* had proved so popular. The reason was clear. This series was a major departure from the usual Frankie format. Tony Hancock had become the nation's favourite funny man by reacting against the pressures of modern living in the brilliantly observed scripts of Galton and Simpson, so this series took the basic, mournful, innuendo-mongering persona of Frankie and cast him in different comic situations each week. In effect, Frankie moved away from the comfort zone of variety towards the more challenging level of character acting.

Playing a character pretty much identified as himself, he was blessed with a sterling support cast including Ronnie Barker, Dora Bryan, Hugh Paddick and (who would argue?) Freddie Mills. The misadventures always rang true and Frankie mugged with gusto. However, as with the first use of this title seven years earlier, the audience didn't seem to go with these programmes. While not a complete failure, Frankie would find himself in radio guest spots and special appearances for the next two years.
With Dora Bryan, Freddie Mills, Lee Young, Vivienne Chatterton, John Ford, Ronnie Barker, Hugh Paddick.
Written by John Junkin and Terry Nation. Producer Bill Worsley.
20 shows: Wednesdays (programmes 1-12, 8.00 pm; programmes 13-20, 7.30 pm) 2 April-13 August 1958, on the Light Programme.

Pantomania

With BBC Television shifting its emphasis to its *Christmas Night With the Stars* format, the old-style *Pantomania* was relegated to

Publicity for
*Fine Goings
On* in April
1958, with
Frankie joined
by boxer
Freddie Mills
and frequent
co-star, Dora
Bryan.

radio and this 1958 seasonal spectacular starred Frankie Howerd alongside such prime comic talent as Stanley Unwin, Thora Hird, Jim Dale and regular Frankie foil, Billy Ternent. The show was recorded in front of a service audience at RAF Halton.

With Stanley Unwin, Thora Hird, the Duke of Bedford, Jim Dale, Joan Regan, Billy Ternent and his Orchestra.

Script by George Wadmore and Johnny Speight. Producer Bill Worsley.

6.00-6.45 pm, Christmas Day 1958, on the Light Programme. Repeated the following Friday from 3 pm.

A 5 May 1956 press call as Blanche Moore, Clarry Ashton, Barbara Leigh, Frankie and Alma Warren prepare to set off to entertain the troops in Cyprus.

Desert Island Discs

A palm tree, a sleepy lagoon and eight gramophone records linked by the tones of Roy Plumley. Frankie Howerd was castaway number 458 on this broadcast from 28 September 1959. In between talking about his life and times, Frankie's selection was:

1: Parry's 'Jerusalem', the Royal Festival Choir, South Australian Symphony.
2: 'Love's Sweet Song' from *The Gypsy Princess* by Kalman.
3: 'Lillibolero' played by the RAF Central Band.
4: 'Waltz Dream' by Strauss.

5: Fats Waller's 'My Very Good Friend the Milkman'.

6: Beniamino Gigli's *Torna a Surriento*.

7. Frankie's own rendition of 'Song and Dance Man'.

8. 'Abide With Me', the Bach Choir.

Frankie's luxury item was a collection of personal photographs while his book was Leo Tolstoy's weighty tome *War and Peace*.

Frankie's Bandbox

In the late 1950s, Light Programme variety show *London Lights* benefited from several Frankie guest spots, performing material written for him by Barry Took and Marty Feldman. By then, however, Frankie was heading into his twilight period and the glory days of *Variety Bandbox* were long gone. Even so, in 1960 it seemed like a good idea to resurrect the title for a new variety show, *Frankie's Bandbox*, in which he was billed as 'the one and only Frankie Howerd'. His old sparring partner, orchestra leader Billy Ternent, was firmly in place to make the whole project feel comfortable and familiar, while Frankie's first feature film leading lady, Petula Clark, was on hand to belt out the songs in programme three. The variety bill was completed by comedy from the married couple, Leslie Randall and Joan Reynolds, and mouth organ exponent Tommy Reilly.

Radio Times explained that this was Frankie Howerd – pure and simple – moving away from experimental comic acting and back to the old variety format. 'In his new series beginning tonight in the Light Programme, Frankie is getting away from the 'story-line' shows which he has recently been doing and concentrating more on his single act with its own fantastic style of humour, expressed in that rich, flexible voice which can convulse some of his fans with the most trivial remark.'

However, this series was anything but old-fashioned. Frankie was keen to point out that 'In this show my humour's going to have a modern slant.' That modern slant was provided by the freshest writers in Frankie's 'joke harem', Barry Took and Marty Feldman. The absolute pleasure of this winning

combination was further enhanced by a sparkling array of guest turns including Alma Cogan, Dick Emery, Peter Jones and Terry Scott.

Show 1, with Max Jaffa, Rosemary Squires, Peter Cavanagh.

Show 2, with Nat Gonella, Margo Henderson, Eve Boswell.

Show 3, with Tommy Reilly, Leslie Randall and Joan Reynolds, Petula Clark.

Show 4, with Kay Cavendish, George Meaton, Edmund Hockridge.

Show 5, with Betty Smith, Ossie Morris, Adele Leigh.

Show 6, with Alma Cogan, Pat Coombs, Kitty Bluett, Stephane Grappelli.

Show 7, with Ian Wallace, Beryl Reid, Joe 'Mr Piano' Henderson.

Show 8, with Andy Cole, Nat Temple, Dora Bryan.

Show 9, with Rosemary Squires, Blanche Moore, Kenny Baker, Tony Fayne.

Show 10, with the George Chisholm Jazzers, June Marlow, Peter Jones.

Show 11, with Max Geldray, Doreen Hume, Terry Scott.

Show 12, with Jack Emblow, Carole Carr, Saveen with Daisy.

Show 13, with Ray Davies, Stephanie Voss, Dick Emery.

Written by Barry Took and Marty Feldman. Music from Billy Ternent and his Orchestra and the BBC Revue Orchestra led by Julien Gaillard. Producer Bill Worsley.

Tuesdays, 8.00-8.30 pm, 5 April-28 June 1960, on the Light Programme.

Music Hall

A popular variety series which recruited the cream of British music hall: for this, week 39 (broadcast 25 July 1960 on the Light Programme), Frankie Howerd was guest comedian.

Leave It To The Boys

In 1956 Frankie was the key comedian on both BBC Radio and Television. By Christmas 1960 he was reduced to a brief, third-billed guest spot on this seasonal radio spectacular fronted

and written by Bob Monkhouse and Denis Goodwin.
With guests: Arthur Askey, Alma Cogan and Frankie Howerd, with 'gate-crashers' Irene Handl and Pat Coombs, and the Avons. Written by Bob Monkhouse and Denis Goodwin. Producer Geoffrey Owen.
9.05-10.00 pm, Christmas Day 1960, on the Light Programme.

Variety Playhouse

Although his film and television careers were becoming distinctly patchy, Frankie still managed to eke out the occasional guest appearance on radio, thanks mainly to the loyalty of his scriptwriting team. Despite the billing, uncredited scribes Bob Monkhouse and Denis Goodwin were hired to write the monologue for Frankie here while Barry Took and Marty Feldman were simultaneously hard at work for the same spot. Cannily, under advisement from his producer, Frankie would take the best elements from both submitted pieces, merge them to perfection and perform a bristling, original, gag-packed and beautifully observed opening for his 1961 New Year broadcast. Kenneth Horne hosted this collection of old gags and old songs with his usual genteel air.

Frankie was given the top-billing guest comedian spot. Speaking to *Radio Times* for a later broadcast promotion, in August 1962, Frankie happily sent up the plight of his writers and, more importantly, his reliance on their services. 'You know my scriptwriters never give me the scripts until it's too late to get a new one! That's how they make sure of the money!' Billed as 'the oldest teenager in the business', Frankie trundled out his familiar patter for an eager audience and in October 1963 he returned as the chief comedy guest in a programme hosted by Vic Oliver.
Kenneth Horne introduces Cicely Courtneidge and Jack Hulbert. Comedy from Leslie Crowther, Ronnie Barker and Frankie Howerd. Written by Carey Edwards, Leslie Crowther and Ronnie Barker. Music Malcolm Lockyer. Producer Alastair Scott Johnston. 7.30-8.30 pm, 7 January 1961.

Frankie Howerd, Cyril Fletcher, Peter Cavanagh, David Kossoff, Carole Carr, Libby Morris. Written by David Cumming and Derek Collyer. Music from the BBC Orchestra conducted by Malcolm Lockyer. Producer Bill Worsley. 7.30-8.30 pm, 25 August 1962.
Vic Oliver introduces Ronnie Barker, Leslie Crowther, Vanda Vale. Storyteller: Donald Wolfit and comedy guest: Frankie Howerd. Written by Carey Edwards and Leslie Crowther. Music from the BBC Orchestra conducted by John Jezard. Producer Alastair Scott Johnston. 7.30-8.30 pm, 14 October 1963, on the Home Service.

Now Listen

With Frankie's entire career suddenly lifted by *That Was The Week That Was* and the satire boom, he was back for this six-part comedy sketch series which, to all intents and purposes, resurrected the successful format of *The Frankie Howerd Show*. Sterling character actors and Frankie's *A Funny Thing Happened on the Way to the Forum* co-stars Robertson Hare and Kenneth Connor gave sublime comic support while guest stars included Arthur Askey, Richard Murdoch and, in his radio début, Harry H Corbett. For Frankie it was back to elongated innuendos and flamboyant character roles. In the first programme alone he played everything from a languid art student to a dithering disc jockey.
With Robertson Hare, Kenneth Connor, Carole Allen. Guests: Harry H Corbett, Andy Stewart, Clive Dunn, Arthur Askey, Richard Murdoch and Kenneth Horne.
Written by Charles Hart and Peter Bishop. Music from the BBC Revue Orchestra conducted by Billy Ternent. Producer Bill Worsley. 8.00 pm, Thursdays, 27 August-8 October 1964, on the Light Programme.

Frankie Howerd!

This was *The Frankie Howerd Show* with sixties attitude and pretty much a semi-sequel to *Now Listen*, retaining the pompous buffoonery of Robertson Hare and adding Wallas Eaton to the mix four years before he played Frankie's boss in the second series of

Frankie and singer Julie Rogers snapped preparing to leave Heathrow on 8 July 1965. Frankie was taking a post-*Forum* break in Beirut, while Julie had a cabaret engagement in Sydney.

Up Pompeii!. The cast also included, to quote Frank Muir, 'God's gift to scriptwriters', June Whitfield.

The format was very familiar, with Frankie's languid pauses, discussions on his medical predicaments and waspishly observant monologues linking cheekily scripted vignettes of everyday problems given the absurd Frankie twist. Thus he would experience hassles everywhere, from a crowded post office queue to an ultra-sophisticated casino. Now, with his nationwide fame at its peak, Frankie could confidently call himself, with tongue planted firmly in cheek, the 'darling of the masses!'

Reflecting his new-found fame as an over-the-garden-wall commentator on political business, Frankie's interlinking patter would include one-sided telephone conversations with the Prime Minister, Harold Wilson. As with his groundbreaking television series scripted by Galton and Simpson, the supporting cast were often dragged away from their sketch characterisations to chat with Frankie as themselves and, even within the most narrative-bound sketch, Frankie could effortlessly break away from the scene and confidentially address his listening audience. In a masterly interlude with Whitfield's frightfully posh Sloane Ranger, Frankie brilliantly pulls himself away from the plot and in hushed tones comments on her Hooray Henry pal (Wallas Eaton) with a wry: 'I see ... Is this Nigel or Penny I wonder?' A sublime vehicle for the all-systems go performer.

With June Whitfield, Wallas Eaton, Robertson Hare.
Written by Charles Hart, Peter Bishop and Bernard Botting.
Announcer Jimmy Kingsbury. Music from the BBC Revue Orchestra conducted by Billy Ternent. Producer Bill Worsley.
Six shows: 8.00 pm, 24 July-28 August 1966, on the Light Programme.

Frankie Howerd

Throughout much of the 1970s, Frankie starred in a string of eponymous Radio 2 variety shows, starting with these programmes broadcast over a seven-week period in June and July 1973. Providing perfect Sunday lunchtime fare from just gone 2 o'clock until 2.30, the shows featured familiar Frankie cohort June Whitfield alongside Ray Fell, Michael Kilgarrif and the Bill McGuffie Quartet. Much the same cast and crew, including writers David McKellar and David Nobbs, joined forces for another series broadcast from late October to early December the following year. June Whitfield and Ray Fell returned to the fold, alongside new comic assistance from Bob Todd, Chris Emmett and Denis McCarthy. The seven editions were broadcast in the same Sunday lunchtime slot.

As usual, the emphasis was on Frankie's culture-vulture self-importance and the shows were prefaced by a corny comic monologue from Frankie, milking his adoring audience and illustrating his comments with sketchy sketches. Interestingly, the writers would frequently pay homage to the past with, on one occasion, an airborne Frankie bore (warbling 'I'm singing in the plane') who is delighted with the in-flight screening of 'one of my old films – Frankie Howerd in *The Runaway Bus...*'

Written by David McKellar and David Nobbs. Music from the Bill McGuffie Quartet. Producer David Hatch.
2.00-2.30 pm Sunday 10 June-22 July 1973 [repeated 8.00 pm the following Mondays], 27 October-8 December 1974 [repeated 7.00 pm the following Saturdays] on Radio 2

The Frankie Howerd Show / The Frankie Howerd Variety Show

The *Frankie Howerd* format was resurrected as *The Frankie Howerd Show* 'with the am-a-a-azing Frankie Howerd' in a series of six shows broadcast from 28 September to 2 November 1975. Again written by Davids McKellar and Nobbs, and enjoying the same Sunday afternoon slot, the shows were repeated from 7.00 pm the following Saturdays and the producer was John Browell. Ray Fell was the only survivor from the *Frankie Howerd* series while excellent new support came from Norma Ronald, Timothy Davies and Barbara Mitchell. And in 1978 Frankie returned to the nation's airwaves for *The Frankie Howerd Variety Show*, his final starring vehicle on radio. Mainly scripted by Laurence Marks and Maurice Gran, the usual smattering of puns, gags and japery was enriched by fledgling work from new kids on the block like Jimmy Mulville, Rory McGrath and Clive Anderson. Griff Rhys-Jones, just months before finding comic fame with *Not the Nine O'Clock News*, sat in the producer seat.

Desert Island Discs

On 23 January 1982 Frankie returned to the popular select-a-tune programme over 20 years since his first appearance. A spiritual consistency remained with the choice for the final disc being the Coventry Cathedral Boys' Choir singing 'Jerusalem'. The other seven were:
1: A poignant recording of the 'Met' music hall audience singing 'Knees Up, Mother Brown'.
2: Chopin's Nocturne in C Minor (opus 48 no 1).
3: Beethoven's Symphony no 9 in D Minor.
4: Nat King Cole singing 'Autumn Leaves'.
5: Puccini's 'Love and Music' from *Tosca*.
6: Sondheim's 'Send in the Clowns'.
7. 'Bruderlein and Schwesterlein' from Frankie's latest stage success, Strauss' *Die Fledermaus*.
His book was Charles Dickens' *David Copperfield* and his emotive personal item was a little cross given to him by his mother. Filmed footage of Frankie requesting this touching item was included in the 1982 *Omnibus* documentary dedicated to the programme.

Carry On Up Yer Cinders

Frankie's fourth, final and 100 per cent unofficial foray into the world of Carry On hit the nation's airwaves at the peak of his latterday renaissance. This was a gloriously awful, tongue-in-cheek Christmas send-up produced by the *Loose Ends* team. Frankie's 1963 telly saviour and 1970s film producer,

Ned Sherrin, was in charge of the fun so it was natural that Frankie, a legend strongly associated with the saucy films, would be dragged into the studio for the re-heated innuendo. Fellow survivor Barbara Windsor was also involved and the likes of future Carry On-er Julian Clary and 'new Sid James' Arthur Smith added to the pleasures. Frankie excelled as one of the ugly sisters, his opposite number being brought to life by none other than Jonathan Ross. An experience, to say the least!

....

Did You Know? In 1989, Harry Enfield wanted to cast Frankie in his affectionate spoof, *Carry On Banging*, as part of his mock-documentary, *Norbert Smith – A Life*. Barbara Windsor, already in the cast, was asked to get Frankie but he was unwell at the time, so his projected role was split between Kenneth Connor and Jack Douglas.

....

Cinderella JULIAN CLARY, Buttons BARBARA WINDSOR, The Ugly Sisters FRANKIE HOWERD and JONATHAN ROSS, Prince Charming ARTHUR SMITH, Fairy Godmother CLAIRE RAYNER, Narrator NED SHERRIN, and RORY BREMNER as Barry Norman, Terry-Thomas and Leslie Phillips.
Script by Arthur Smith.
10.00-11.00 am, Saturday 22 December 1990, Radio 4.

The Nicky Campbell Show

Frankie spent many hours being interviewed about himself on the airwaves, whether in 1970s chats with Jack de Manio or on Pete Murray's *Open House*, through to 1980s chinwags with everybody from John Browell to Gloria Hunniford. However, his final foray into the art of cat's whiskers chatting was probably his most enjoyable. He was a regular studio guest on Nicky Campbell's London Talk Radio show during the early 1990s. 'His Frankiedom', as Campbell fondly referred to him, thoroughly enjoyed the attention, love and dubious Frankie impersonations which greeted his many live phone-in sessions.

★★★★★★★★★★★★★★★★★★★

Frankie gets
with-it and
adopts the
latest craze in
this May 1978
shot publicising
his forthcoming
appearance in
the *Cilla* show.

'Frankie Howerd is the main man.'
Sid Vicious

Frankie Howerd's voice really was his fortune in the early, ultra-successful days of his career. With radio stardom on *Variety Bandbox* it was only natural that he would be dragged into the recording studio and put through his comic paces for vinyl release. Initially these capitalised on his filmic partnership with Margaret Rutherford and his radio reputation with writer Eric Sykes, even trying to reinvent his persona as a credible song and dance man. Never afraid to mock established, notorious chartbusters or even embrace the new musical genres of the early 1990s, Frankie's discography covers charity recordings, gag appearances, stage musicals and major career turning points. This is a complete listing of Frankie's audio recording career released during his lifetime.

Three Little Fishes
The original and definitive 78 rpm recording of Frankie's most celebrated comic song, this energetic, elongated and eloquent bit of aqua-nonsense became a popular request song on the BBC's *Children's Hour*.
Harmony, A1001

Nymphs and Shepherds/All's Going Well (My Lady Montmorency)
This classic venture into the recording studio saw Frankie matched with the ever-helpful presence of glorious acting eccentric Margaret Rutherford. Reflecting their popularity in the feature film *The Runaway Bus*, this celebrated comic excursion remains an oft-resurrected Frankie favourite. The recording features a fairly standard presentation of 'Nymphs and Shepherds' with a rousing chorus acting as a comic background for the flamboyant mugging of Frankie. The record is packed with typical Frankie interjections, from 'Oh naughty Nymph!' to 'Take yer hand off my crook!' Rutherford gets suitably carried away with comments about the joyful chorus and there's plenty of time for Frankie's *Variety Bandbox* favourites like 'Missus!' and 'Nellie!'

The finale is a wonderful sing-a-long chorus of 'Nymphs and Shepherds' with Frankie turning on the strained, high-pitched warbling before moaning 'jealous!' and 'oh...no!' as a climax.

The B-side is an altogether more refreshing bit of scripted comic banter between Frankie and Rutherford. The basic premise is a telephone conversation between Rutherford's snotty Lady Montmorency, calling from her holiday destination and checking on the state of her estate with butler James (Frankie, of course). Lifting the concept completely from a masterly Sandy Powell routine, this bit of vinyl banter with Frankie and Rutherford relies on the frustrated and concerned reaction of Lady Montmorency as Frankie's family retainer desperately tries to relieve her tension before letting out news of another disaster. His continual answer of 'All's going well, my Lady Montmorency' gets more and more high-pitched and whining as the recording goes on. By the end of it, the garden is a mess, the estate is in ruins, fire has destroyed everything and Lord Montmorency has run off with Frankie's wife, while Rutherford's major preoccupation ('What about the pumpkin?') ends with Frankie's 'Delicious!' riposte. It's a bizarre, surreal piece of comedy and the partnership gels perfectly.
MARGARET RUTHERFORD and FRANKIE HOWERD
'Nymphs and Shepherds' written by Purcell with additional bits by Eric Sykes. 'All's Going Well (My Lady Montmorency)' written by Misraki/Parsons.
Philips PB 214

I'm the Man Who's Deputising For the Bull/English As She Is Spoken
Very much basking in Frankie's national superstardom as the host of radio's *Variety Bandbox*, Frankie's regular scriptwriter Eric Sykes penned these two novelty numbers which formed a tasty single vinyl release. Both are nonsensical nonsense but Frankie's freshness and youth shines through. Basically it all plays like one of Sykes' grand flights of fancy with a sliding door accident causing the bull at a bull

fight to disappear. The result is that our hapless narrator Frankie and his pal Charlie are forced into a bull skin to take on the role of chief target for the day. It's frantic, funny and frankly hilarious.

The B-side allows Billy Ternent, *Variety Bandbox* regular and conductor of the orchestra which backs both numbers, to emerge from the shadows and take centre stage with the headline comedian. This is traditional music hall cross-talk and Bud Flanagan and Chesney Allen could very well have claimed responsibility for all the mispronunciation jokes which spatter the rousing chorus of 'English as she is spoken!' *FRANKIE HOWERD accompanied by Billy Ternent and his Orchestra. Written by Eric Sykes.*

It's Alright With Me/Song and Dance Man

This was a fairly straight, fairly nondescript attempt on Frankie's part to do a bit of song and dance man business. 'It's Alright With Me' is performed without a trace of titter-mongering, although obviously flamboyant phrases like 'It's the wrong smile…' and

The definitive recording – Frankie Howerd at the Establishment and at the BBC.

'Charming face!' are slightly camped up for semi-Howerd effect. However, by the close, Frankie gives up the ghost completely and rounds off the proceedings with a full-blooded 'Come and get me!'

'Song and Dance Man' is performed in a more comic style if only for the tongue-in-cheek mockery from Frankie's chorus. Frankie claims he can get ahead like Fred Astaire but by the time he starts banging on about 'Not on your little Nellie I could be the next Gene Kelly,' the lyrics have been adapted for pure Frankie Howerd clout. Both numbers are performed with just the smallest trace of 'Ooh no missus!' style and the comedian seems to relish the chance to wallow in the dated, uncluttered, waspish musical comedy style of Jack Buchanan.

FRANKIE HOWERD with Tony Osborne and his Orchestra. 'It's Alright With Me' written by Cole Porter, 'Song and Dance Man' written by Newell-Stanford. Chappell & Co Ltd 1958, Columbia DB 4230

The Cool Mikado

After another single – 'Abracadabra'/ '(Don't Let the) Kiddy Geddin', Decca F10420 – Frankie was next heard on the totally essential film soundtrack to his lowest cinematic achievement. The great man warbles on four tracks, 'Behold the Lord High Executioner', 'Here's A How-De-Do!', 'The Flowers That Bloom in the Spring' and the 'Finale (For He's Gone and Married Yum-Yum)'.
1963, Parlophone, PMC 1194

Frankie Howerd at the Establishment & at the BBC
'I'm no Lenny Bruce!'　　**Frankie Howerd**

Although this classic 1963 release gives both worthy institutions equal billing, it was the truly scrumptious Establishment Club set which really made this record a winner. As Frankie wrote for the sleeve-note: 'The Establishment is reputed to be the home of satire, famous for its biting, down-to-earth humour. It is not the kind of canteen I usually work in – except as a waiter –

and I was amazed at being asked to lecture there, but one word was uttered which caught my interest – "money". I must admit that as the opening date grew nearer I became more and more nervous. Eventually, the day arrived and I was even more amazed to find how much the audiences seemed to like what I did – in fact, even the proprietors laughed, especially when I asked for more money.'

Recorded on Wednesday 26 September 1962 at the Establishment Club, Greek Street, this is an 'edited highlights' presentation of Frankie's masterly patter routine for Peter Cook's trendy forum. 'Written or stolen by Johnny Speight and myself, with some additional bits by Alan Simpson and Ray Galton', the intellectuals, the Prime Minister, war memoirs and even the famous audience – a raucous Kenneth Williams is continually put down – are mocked with ramshackle delight. There's a real air of confidence in Frankie's delivery, whether it be the tired old jokes or the laid-back satire by the rear entrance. The audience may have a touch of the emperor's new clothes about it – with even the mildest whimsy being greeted with loud laughter, particularly from Williams – but Frankie knows the score and plays the wannabes with gentle disdain. Typically, much of the act is about how Frankie arrived at the place, via an 'audition titter' for Cook, desperation in gearing up 'the old quip factory', a slice of semi-bitter political business and a couple of grey-whiskered gags. For the record, Frankie's ramble about Lenny Bruce and the filth of the American underground rounds off with the 'You can piss off now!' rant being unceremoniously honked out!

The flip side revels in three BBC Radio extracts written by Barry Took and Marty Feldman. Akin to the Speight material, the writers have embraced Frankie's new satire-friendly persona with comments on the Common Market and Britain's place in Europe. Typically, the lecture is designed for a meeting of the Expectant Mothers of Bromley and familiar *Variety Bandbox* catchphrases

('Ladies and Gentle-*men*!'/'I was a-*mazed*!') are peppered amongst the observational humour. The real joy here is Frankie's mockery of the broadcasting medium, turning over two pages, losing the plot, mispronouncing words and, ultimately, cracking up at a gag as if it's the first time he's heard it. It's the ultimate antidote to the adage that great comedians never laugh at their own jokes. The essential Frankie recording. *Establishment Club: Recording engineer Terry Johnson. Editor Arthur Lilley. Producer Hugh Mendl. The Decca Record Company Ltd, 1963, Mono LK 4556*

A Funny Thing Happened on the Way to the Forum

Totally priceless and brilliantly representative recording of Frankie's ultimate West End smash success, this original vinyl record of the Sondheim musical captures the raw, vibrant energy of the stage production to perfection. Restaged for record by George Martin and packed with the original cast members, from the moment the Overture hits home and Frankie belts out the 'Something appealing, something appalling, something for everyone…' opening of 'Comedy Tonight' you know you are in for a winning time. A joyous beginning.

The number, 'Free', a duet with Frankie and his master Hero (John Rye), is kicked off with our slave's pleading for freedom ('Be the first, start a fashion!'), before his daydreaming thoughts of future fun get more and more inviting. Frankie's impassioned 'Can you see me?' literally jumps out of the grooves. 'Pretty Little Picture' is a delightful three-way song with Frankie revealing the plans for his master's escape with his lady love, Philia (Isla Blair). Performed at high speed and with gusto, Frankie's endearing and enduring appeal gives a fairy-tale lightness to the plan. The show stopper, 'Everybody Ought to Have A Maid', really belongs to 'Monsewer' Eddie Gray as Senex, but Frankie's repeated chorus and jaunty style add to the fun. And, following the thrice-muttered line concerning a fancy girl sleeping in, Frankie lets rip with the fruitiest 'Oooh!' of his entire career. 'Bring Me My Bride' is a vehicle for the operatic clout of Leon Greene as the big and burly warrior Miles Gloriosus, with Frankie merely feeding him the big and burly cues.

Act Two features the Frankie vocals sparingly to say the least, with the 'Funeral Sequence and Dance' again casting him as the mock-depressive foil for Greene's heartbroken villain and the 'Comedy Tonight' reprise allowing him a brief wallow in the glorious and happy closure of events. His only other appearance is in a flamboyantly effete, deliciously camp, grotesque reflection of the lover's ballad 'Lovely'. A mightily valuable and instantly re-playable slice of vinyl.

A Harold Prince, Tony Walton and Richard Pilbrow presentation. Recording producer Norman Newell. EMI Records CLP 1685, 1963. CD reissue: 1998

Time For A Laugh

A compilation of 'musical humour' featuring cuts from the likes of Joyce Grenfell, Jon Pertwee and Hermione Gingold. The album also contains 'two great names – Margaret Rutherford and Frankie Howerd – in two of the all-time classics of funny records', namely 'Nymphs and Shepherds' which opens the collection and 'All's Going Well (My Lady Montmorency)' which appears as track two side two.

A Philips Record Wing WL1191, 1964

The Last Word on the Election from Frankie Howerd

A timely single release of Frankie's groundbreaking and all-conquering political deconstruction from the BBC Television satire show of the same name, scripted by Ray Galton, Alan Simpson and Johnny Speight.

Decca 12028, Demo, 1964

The World of British Comedy

Frankie holds his head up high alongside a staggering collection of the finest comedians in British history, from Tony Hancock, Spike Milligan and Benny Hill to Peter Cook and

Marty Feldman. A brief extract from the Took and Feldman-scripted BBC material from Frankie Howerd's *At the Establishment & at the BBC* album was included on this collectable compilation release. Entitled '10 Guinea Cruise', it features Frankie's rant on medical matters, overweight travel agents and the pleasures of Tokyo.

Decca MONO PA39, 1965

Alice in Wonderland

From 1965, a classic all-star recording of Lewis Carroll's immortal surrealist fantasy with a British comedy fan's dream cast. Dirk Bogarde is the languid narrator, Tommy Cooper hams it up as the Mad Hatter, Kenneth Connor twitches through his role as the White Rabbit and the King and Queen of Hearts are played by Arthur Haynes and Peggy Mount. As the Blasé Machin sleeve notes say: 'EMI record producer Norman Newell enlisted a truly galactic selection of comedians. The names speak for themselves but with Frankie Howerd as the Mock Turtle how could he go wrong?'

Indeed, alongside Karen Dotrice's upright Alice and a delightfully Northern Gryphon from Harry H Corbett, Frankie dominates side three of this double album. Entering with a stream of self-pitying 'Oh dear ... dear!' exclamations, this is simply definitive Frankie in a Mock Turtle skin. Best of all, of course, are the songs. 'The Lobster Quadrille' is a solo number detailing the intricate and confused rules of the games the sea creatures play. It's worth checking out if only for Frankie's amazed 'Ooh, naughty octopus – ooh, he is a burden!'

Corbett and Dotrice join in the fun with 'Beautiful Soup', which is blessed with a raucous tuba intro, Frankie's belted-out 'So rich and green, waiting in a hot tureen ... soup of the evening, beautiful soup!' and culminating with an annoyed cry of 'You splashed me!' A peerless, long-forgotten vinyl stint and one of Frankie's most enjoyable performances.

Narrator DIRK BOGARDE, Alice KAREN DOTRICE, White Rabbit KENNETH CONNOR,

Caterpillar IAN WALLACE, Frog Footman JOE
WISE, Fish Footman MIKE HUDSON, Duchess
BERYL REID, Cheshire Cat NICHOLAS EVANS,
March Hare BRUCE FORSYTH, Mad Hatter
TOMMY COOPER, Dormouse FENELLA
FIELDING, Gardener BILLY WALKER, Queen
PEGGY MOUNT, King ARTHUR HAYNES,
Gryphon HARRY H CORBETT, Mock Turtle
FRANKIE HOWERD, Cook DOROTHY
SQUIRES, Knave of Hearts RICHARD FOX
Book adaptation Pauline Grant. Music Philip
Green. Orchestrations and Musical Direction
Brian Fahey with the Lissa Gray Singers. Lyrics
and Production Norman Newell. Music For
Pleasure, MFP 1267/8

Frankie Howerd Tells the Story of Peter and the Wolf

A piece of vinyl which delivers exactly what it
says on the cover. Frankie gives a spirited
reading of the Russian folkloric tale of a small
boy and his animal friends overcoming a
vicious wolf. The classical music score was
provided by the City of London Ensemble,
conducted by Alan Doggett. Andrew Lloyd
Webber and Tim Rice (no less) produced the
disc which was recorded at the Conway Hall,
Red Lion Square, London, in August 1971.
Polydor, Carnival 2928 201

Up Je t'aime/All Through the Night

Probably Frankie's most famous and
celebrated bit of recording heritage. Despite
the fact that, like all the other Frankie
discs, it failed to dent the singles charts on
release in 1971, it has continually been
resurrected on radio ever since. Naturally, its
fame and enduring appeal lies squarely at the
feet of the disc it is spoofing – the October
1969 Number One, 'Je t'aime (moi non plus)',
which added a huge chunk of Gallic raunch to
the British hit parade via the breathy delivery
and relentless organ action of Jane Birkin and
Serge Gainsbourg. With the recurring theme
very much in place, the exotic diatribe
mucked about a bit by the finest writing
team in comedy history (Ray Galton and
Alan Simpson), dream co-star June Whitfield
putting on the romantics and the legend

that was and is Frankie Howerd going
through the sexually disinterested Brit-
in-bed act, how could the record fail?
The fact is that it did fail chartwise, but no
matter – it's still a comedy classic of the
highest order.

Frankie starts the fun snoring away as his
good lady wife gets excited under the sheets.
This less-than-keen sex beast ('Oh give over …
It's not Friday is it?') is more concerned with
getting a good night's sleep in order to have a
fair play on the fairway and beat his pal,
Arthur, at golf. Frankie's extreme Englishness
is typified by his offering to make some cocoa
to calm Whitfield down. Arthur is played to
downbeat comic perfection by writer Alan
Simpson, and Frankie's 'I think I'm going to
beat him tomorrow!' says more about the
patronising stance of the married British
male than a bushel of therapists. With
Whitfield going for the high-pitched singing
bit, Frankie finally has enough and threatens
to get out of bed ('Well, she's such a terrible
singer!'). Sheer comic genius.

The B-side, the much less familiar rendition
of 'All Through the Night', allows the ever-
versatile June Whitfield to change from
French to German for a spot-on Marlene
Dietrich performance. Again, the subject
under the microscope is sex and the British
male's reluctance to go for it. Frankie has
been tossing and turning all through the
night and June is eager to know why.
Unlike the A-side, this is not domestic
sitcom with French undertones, it's merely
two pros camping about in a recording
studio, with the remorseless organ
accompaniment to this less than hymn-like
version of 'All Through the Night' coming to a
grinding halt as Frankie mutters 'I say,
we're finished!'
FRANKIE HOWERD with June Whitfield and
(uncredited) Alan Simpson.
Written by A Simpson, R Galton and S
Gainsbourg (Shapiro Bernstein). 'All Through the
Night' written by J Fishman, A Simpson, R
Galton (Jambo Music).
Produced by Jack Fishman
Pye 7N.45061

Up Pompeii/Salute!

If the television series was a massive hit then the feature film version of Frankie's finest situation comedy forever cemented the comedian in his pole position as Pompeii's most beloved cunning servant. To tie in with the 1971 release of the EMI film, Frankie was dragged into the recording studio to turn out this masterpiece of innuendo-soaked camp. Though a failure in the charts, this remains my all-time favourite Frankie disc.

Though lacking the invention and subtle playing of 'Up Je t'aime', there is something so archetypally British, boisterous and pure Frankie about the cuts here that any self-respecting comedy fan cannot fail to fall under their spell. From those initial magical drum beats at the beginning of the A-side the listener knows a good time awaits: 'I never seem to get it up Pompeii!' Frankie is allowed, nay, encouraged to ham, mug, overplay and generally turn on the flamboyance with every elongated 'Ooooh!' stretched beyond breaking point. A rollicking adventure encompassing orgies, gladiators and delicious over-indulgence in every pleasure known to man, a rasping horn section backs Frankie's gloriously energetic performance and even the most obvious and groan-worthy of rhyming couplets ('There's no decorum in the forum!') have a grandeur and resonance which is above criticism. A jaunty, music hall-flavoured novelty number, this is quite simply a masterpiece of a comedy record. How it failed to reach Number One I shall never know!

The flip side, while lightyears away from the sheer, relentless genius of the Pompeii piece, is nevertheless a worthy companion. This is more of a pop song in construction and tempo. The subject matter isn't much changed from the first song – it's all vestal virgins and drunken behaviour ('pickled as a newtie!'), with a rock beat, winning performance and the unforgettable semi-chorus of 'Bottoms up! Down the cup! Salute!' The three-syllable title – ie, not sa-lute but sa-lu-tay – is presented as the only way to introduce yourself as the heat of the orgy reaches fever-pitch and you find

yourself falling onto a likely candidate for a bit of fun. ('Salute! Salute! Here's a call to us all to do our duty!') Like the TV series and film, the record is, happily, completely obsessed with the pleasures of the flesh. Frankie explains that 'Brother! All roads lead to Rome!' with such delirious passion that you almost grab your passport. A timeless classic of comedy records. *FRANKIE HOWERD 'Up Pompeii' written by Howard-Blaikely, 'Salute!' written by Howard-Blaikely, Sherrin-Brahms. EMI/Carlin Music, Columbia DB 8757*

The BBC Presents Fifty Years of Radio Comedy

A special salute to the best in BBC comedy with extracts from classic programmes (*Hancock's Half Hour*, *The Goon Show*) and classic comedians (Max Miller, Robb Wilton). Track 10 on side one features Frankie Howerd's brilliant lion-tamer piece from *Variety Bandbox*.
Produced by Alastair Scott Johnston and Leslie Perowne. BBC Records REC 138M, 1972

Oh! What a Carry On

Memorable musical recordings from a galaxy of Carry On stars: Bernard Bresslaw, Dora Bryan, Jim Dale, Kenneth Connor, Joan Sims, Kenneth Williams and Barbara Windsor. Frankie Howerd's 1958 single 'It's Alright With Me' appears as track four on the opening side and 'Song and Dance Man' is track four on the other.
Music For Pleasure MFP 1416 EMI, 1972

40 Years of Television: The Comedians Sing

BBC compilation which features Frankie dueting with Margaret Rutherford on the classic 'Nymphs and Shepherds'.
REB 251, 1976

Please Yourselves

'I've paid for these jokes, I might as well use 'em!' **Frankie Howerd**

Classic moments from Frankie's mid-seventies radio shows, recreated for an invited audience at the BBC's Paris Theatre in London. Not simply a compilation from the radio source but specially recorded for vinyl release in 1976, Frankie opens each side with a 'Ladies and gentle-*men*!' ramble and closes them with some tittersome business about the hilarious, non-existent material on the other side. In between there are fair slices of typical Frankie innuendo, half-baked sketches and ritual abuse of the supporting cast. Both Ray Fell and particularly Dilys Laye are reduced to hysterical tatters as Frankie struggles through the script and mercilessly twists the corpsing knife along the way.

As per usual Frankie is obsessed with his health. Laye, quite brilliantly, recognises the Howerd name ('Do you mean that man who is always up something on television?') and is the perfect foil for Frankie's less-than-sophisticated patient. ('I've squashed my sprouts!') The cultural spot, performing 'Old McDonald' with all the relevant animal noises, lowers the tone even further. It's followed by Frankie's recollection of an unsuccessful dirty weekend in Scunthorpe, whereupon side two opens with Frankie defending his corny line in poetry: 'Titter not at my ditty. It's not filth, it's art!' There's also a real sense of Max Miller delivery in a sketch set in a complaints office, packed with schoolboy funnies ('Sex?'/'Ooh, if you don't mind!') and some more Dilys Laye corpsing as she misses her cue. The following sketch, with Frankie resorting to animal impressions to get through to a German waiter, ends with an offer to grunt on German television and the classic throwaway line, 'You wouldn't think we won two wars would you?'

Finally, Frankie tries, unsuccessfully, to become part of the Swinging Sixties generation – about ten years late it has to be said – with a 'She digs me, yeah yeah!' intro and a psychedelic revaluation of his flat. Dilys Laye is unimpressed with his attire ('Is anything worn under the kaftan?'/'No it's all in working order!') and his vegetarianism ('You couldn't say it at rehearsals!'), but it's Frankie's off-trail dialogue which really creates the magic here. A healthy, archetypal slab of 1970s Frankie, he's still obsessed

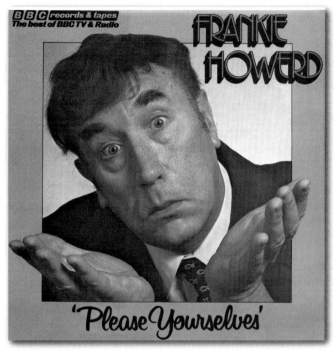

'*Please Yourselves*'

with money (wanting to do the thing on television because he'll get paid more) and obsessed with his youthfulness (the other reason he wants to do television is to show everybody how young he looks). With a stunning support cast and a host of Howerdisms, this is classic stuff.
FRANKIE HOWERD with Ray Fell, Dilys Laye and April Walker.
Written by David Nobbs and David McKellar. Music from Max Harris at the piano. Producer John Browell. BBC Records REH 230

Comedy Special – Highlights from the Top BBC Comedy Shows

A handy 1977 package of extracts from the finest comedy available on BBC Records. Eric and Ernie, the Goons, *The Two Ronnies* and *Round the Horne* are joined by the 'Dirty Weekend' interlude from radio's *The Frankie Howerd Show*, broadcast on 19 October 1975. Produced by John Browell and written by David Nobbs and David McKellar, it is featured as track two on side two.
Compiled by Derek Groom. Pye, BBC Records and Tapes REH 294 (cassette: ZCF 294), 1977

Please Yourselves, recorded at the Paris Studio in London and released in 1976.

Sgt. Pepper's Lonely Hearts Club Band

The obligatory vinyl release for the 1978 Bee Gees/Peter Frampton celebration of the Beatles classic, with celebrity renditions of all the songs. Amazingly, the integrity of John, Paul, George and Ringo remains intact, with their old producer, George Martin, rumbling through the classics for this bumper double-LP collection. Both Frankie's tracks are included, as tracks three and four on side three.

Landing one song from the landmark album, Frankie sings the Beatles on 'When I'm Sixty-Four' (2'38") and the result can be readily imagined. Frankie, clearly having a whale of a time, starts with 'Now ... when I get older...' and puts a very high emphasis on the *many years from now* line. The disc is a duet with Sandy Farina as Strawberry Fields – seriously! – and Frankie happily interjects off-the-cuff interludes and 'scripted' business. He laughs with real evil, almost begs on the 'Will you still feed me?' line, answers Farina's lyrical questions with 'Who indeed?' and lives up to his Mean Mr Mustard image with his tackling of the holiday-home qualification, 'If it's not too dear!' Complete with a climactic 'Ooh!' this is a hidden gem in the recording career of Frankie Howerd.

Frankie's second track follows immediately. 'Mean Mr Mustard' (2'39") is from the *Abbey Road* album and, though it's billed as a solo rendition, Frankie has precious little to do here. Smothered by the mechanical men who share the scene with him in the film, Frankie simply turns on the evil acid for 'Yes, a mean old man!' in response to their artificial chants. Heavy guitar, drum and synthesiser give the track a funky, real-gone seventies feel and there's perverse pleasure to be gleaned from Frankie's vigorous 'Dirty? Old? Yes, dirty old man!'

Musicians: Max Middleton (keyboards & synthesiser), Robert Ahwai (guitars), Wilbur Bascomb (bass guitar), Bernard Purdie (drums and percussion), with George Martin, Peter Frampton and Tower of Power.

Recording engineer Geoff Emerick. Assistant engineers Anthony D'Amico and Nigel Walker.

Producer George Martin. Recorded and mixed at Cherokee Studios, Los Angeles. Polygram, RSO Records

Deus Ex Machina

Not strictly speaking a record, but this early eighties computer game hailed from the time when software was still supplied on cassette tapes. According to *Crash* magazine, the bible for Sinclair Spectrum users in those heady days, the game enabled you to 'control the progress of an accident as it grows, learns and develops into a human being and eventually dies.' A big hit in an era dominated by platform games and sprawling text-only role-playing epics, *Deus Ex Machina* was unique for another reason – once the machine code had been loaded you could flip the cassette over and listen to a synchronised soundtrack while you were playing! Frankie can be heard as a member of the villainous Defect Police, and at one point intones 'War crimes are easy.' The soundtrack also featured Ian Dury as the improbably named rebel Fertiliser. *Crash* concluded that 'it's hard to decide whether this is an extension of the computer video game by music, or an extension of the concept album by the addition of games playing.'

Fertliser IAN DURY, The Machine DONNA BAILEY, Defect Policeman FRANKIE HOWERD, with JON PERTWEE, EDWARD THOMPSON, MEL CROUCHER

Sinclair Spectrum 48k (double cassette), Automata UK

They All Laughed

Double vinyl comedy compilation release from 1987 which includes the Frankie Howerd single 'Up Je t'aime' with June Whitfield and Alan Simpson.

PRT Records PYL 7006

Stars of Variety

A cracking two-record set starring the great and good of music hall and variety. Classic recordings from Flanagan and Allen, Tommy Trinder, George Formby, G H Elliott, Ted Ray and Gracie Fields are joined by both cuts of

Frankie Howerd's 1950s single, 'I'm the Man Who's Deputising For the Bull' (side one track seven) and 'English As She Is Spoken' (side three track five).
Music For Pleasure EMI Records DL 1155, 1989

Three Little Fishes/Primeval Scream (or How to Get Rid of Your Pent-Up Feelings)

Gloriously cheap, tacky and totally indispensable recording of Frankie's most famous and celebrated ditty. A staple part of his stage act since the very beginning, this was a brand new recording to capitalise on Frankie's renewed popularity with the student generation. Never commercially released, this 'audio tape only' collectors' piece was sold in the foyer of theatres where Frankie was performing his *At His Tittermost!* live concerts. Branded 'Frankie Howerd – The Limited Edition Tape', this was an essential souvenir from Frankie's halcyon days. Reassuringly the same as the classic issue, there were slight touches of modernity to the backing with distinct keyboard effects and a more world-weary, experienced tone to Frankie's vocals. He was still happy to send himself up, however, and go through the whole gamut of insane noises and childish bickering.

With a sermon-like organ introduction, Frankie reassures his faithful audience ('No, it is not a hymn – it's Francis!') before embarking on his oft-told tale of the three naughty fishes, Tom, Dick and the pompous Cecil ('dying to get into an aquarium!'), who disobey their mother and swim out of the stream and into the ocean. The primitive, under-funded multi-track recording of three high-pitched Frankies doing the fishy voices is charmingly inept as the great man is reduced to idiotic ramblings and a disgruntled cry of 'This is ridiculous, isn't it?' And so what if the 'You thought the needle was stuckwasstuckwasstuck' bit doesn't really come off on a cassette tape: the sheer exuberance of performance makes this a delight from start to finish.

The supporting track, a brand new number for this release, is another winning slice of

typical Frankie angst. Kicking off with a muttered 'Keep your wits about you and shut your faces!', this is Frankie as a kindly therapist explaining the foolproof way of releasing your tension via ancient bellowing. Basically, 'Your brain's like a kettle' and your mouth 'lets the steam out.' Running through a trilogy of tragic tales, Frankie lets go with a chorus of sorts, a non-connected stream of strained manic screaming of ooohs, ahhhhhs, errrrrrs and the like. As Frankie comments, 'That's what I mean by the primeval scream…' – and it's nothing less than unforgettable, I can tell you.
Written and published by Frankie Howerd/Hatchard/Campbell Connelly. Music written, produced and recorded by Marvin Hanglider. Fishee Business, FISH E 1, 1989

Freudiana

A bizarre musical tribute from Eric Woolfson to Sigmund Freud, originally intended as the eleventh album by the Alan Parsons Project. Recorded in 1989, Frankie joins the likes of Kiki Dee, Leo Sayer, Marti Webb and the Flying Pickets. Frankie's 3'40" track is called 'Sects Therapy', in which an old friend refers him to a Mayfair analyst. 'He asked me if my mother Wore stiletto heels and rubber,' Frankie trills, 'And I realised that this poor soul Was more confused than me … So I wrote to Dr Ruth And she helpfully proposed I should join a nudist colony And throw away my clothes.' Frankie doesn't like the idea, however, and resolves to 'go home to the wife.'
With Marti Webb, Frankie Howerd, Kiki Dee, John Miles, Chris Rainbow, Leo Sayer, Eric Woolfson, Graham Dye, the Flying Pickets, Gary Howard, Eric Stewart
Music and Lyrics Eric Woolfson. Book Eric Woolfson, Brian Brolly, Lida Winiewicz. Conductor Andrew Powell.
EMI 95415

The Spoken Word of Rock 'n' Roll

A laudable and star-packed charity recording in aid of SOS (Stars Organisation for Spastics), recruiting a host of the charity's most famous supporters (Roger Moore,

Michael Caine, Barbara Windsor, Warren Mitchell etc) to do exactly what it says on the tin and speak the words of the greatest favourites in the history of rock 'n' roll. Frankie Howerd OBE was roped into the studio for at least one major number but sharp-eared listeners will catch Howerdisms on several tracks.

Frankie's major contribution comes with the Carl Perkins classic 'Blue Suede Shoes'. Though sharing the limelight with sitcom favourite Gorden Kaye, Frankie leaves his comic mark on the recording, staggering his way through the classic rockabilly lyrics, adding Frankie touches ('Stay off of my shoes … understand?'), elongated catchphrases ('Ooh and ooh again, and thrice ooh!') and brilliantly closing the whole thing with a scream of 'Not the shoes!'

Elsewhere on the recording, several soundbites 'sampled' from Frankie's 'Blue Suede Shoes' vocal crop up. He's audible on the Jerry Lee Lewis classic 'Whole Lotta Shakin' Goin' On', the Queen number 'Crazy Little Thing Called Love', the Manfred Mann song 'Do Wah Diddy Diddy' and, just as you

Frankie stayed hip to the latest trends – in 1991 he appeared on this rap record.

think you've heard Frankie's last bit of business, he storms into the Liverpudlian version of Lulu's 'Shout'. Frankie's brief interludes are a priceless bonus for a fun piece of charity vinyl.

With Michael Aspel, Jean Boht, Janet Brown, June Brown, Frank Bruno, Michael Caine, Tommy Cannon and Bobby Ball, Harry Carpenter, Ronnie Corbett, Leslie Crowther, Barry Cryer, Paul Daniels, Bobby Davro, Judi Dench, Peter Dickson, Ken Dodd, Noel Edmonds, Stephen Fry, Russell Grant, Frankie Howerd, David Jacobs, John Junkin, Gorden Kaye, Ian McCaskill, Vicki Michelle, Warren Mitchell, Bob Monkhouse, Patrick Moore, Roger Moore, Derek Nimmo, Robert Powell, Claire Rayner, Harry Secombe, Dave Lee Travis, Kenneth Waller, Barbara Windsor and Dame Vera Lynn's children of Ingfield Manor School. Telstar STAR 2486, 1990

Oh No Missus/Oh No Missus (Halifax Mix)

If Frankie could resurrect vintage telly situation comedies, wow them at the Oxford Union and star in a pop video, there was surely no limit to his 'hip' potential… Thus ran the reasoning behind this much-mocked (by Frankie himself on several early 1990s chat shows), much-maligned (by Frankie purists who haven't heard it) and much-treasured (by Frankie admirers who have) rap recording. It may be a question of taste, upbringing or musical inspiration but for me this is a priceless bit of vinyl which brilliantly utilises the trendiest sound of the day alongside a hilarious string of Frankie non-sequiturs.

Despite what many people think, this is not simply a torrent of 'Oh no missus!' from the great man. Oh no! For, although 'Oh no … Oh no missus!' is used rather frequently, there are snatches of 'Let me hear more bass' as Frankie gets with the groove, 'Yes, get fresh, get fresh', 'It's wicked, it's wicked!' and several other incongruous, 'happening' observations from the veteran comic genius. The standard mix pays charming tribute to Frankie's on-stage persona with an opening burst of audience applause and Frankie's 'Good evening', while the Halifax Mix, a classic 'beatcom' track, launches straight into the number with joyful abandon, climaxing with Frankie's strained angst of 'That's it, you're away!' Priceless stuff. Very much the zenith of the entire Frankie renaissance, you should fight to get a copy. There's a couple of cracking Frankie cover shots taken by Tristan Taylor to relish as well.

Did You Know? All the sound-bites used for this recording were featured on a track called 'Frankie's Grooving'. Clearly Mike Bennett got cold feet and cut Frankie's contribution down to just the familiar catchphrases. The Grooving track – a 12" version of which was also put together – includes a more narrative-based contribution, featuring Frankie in discussion with a couple of bright young things ('What me? A DJ?') and explaining that he would rather have a cup of tea. The beat is for dancing and Frankie's for prancing as he mutters 'Don't go all limp! … Keep it gyrating!', before facing up to his age, complaining of pulling a muscle and finally revealing, 'I'll have a lie down now … Anyone?' Arguably the coolest, funkiest and most innuendo-packed dance record ever!

POW (Shaun Imrei, Simon Lockwood and Mike Bennett) featuring FRANKIE HOWERD
Producer Shaun Imrei, Executive Producers Mike Bennett and Simon Platz.
Fly Records, Bucks Music, Total Record Co via BMG UK, 12 inch: Flea 6, 1991

Get Your Titters Out/Get Your Titters Out – Part Two (Raise Your Titters)

Frankie was clearly less than happy with his first foray into dance music. The relentless 'Oh no Missus!' certainly wasn't as good as the original Grooving version and this follow-up release tried to make amends. The record happily throws in all the usual audience-pleasers and a load of juicy one-liners ('You must check out his 12" mix!'). The musical content is enhanced by a cheery, all-girl chorus which is full of 'all hang loose … now it's time to get your titters out!' I kid you not – and it's

wonderful! It's even more wonderful when Frankie joins the girls for the final chorus and issues the classic warning, 'The only thing is, once they're out you can't get them back in!' The 'belly laugh' is plugged as 'cooler than Vanilla Ice!' and we're told that 'a titter's better out than in!' The second part, on the other hand, simply lifts Frankie's 'Get your titters out!' business and repeats it ad infinitum. One to empty the dance floor at your kid's party if everything else fails!

Did You Know? With a load of Frankie bits 'n' pieces in the studio, Mike Bennett mixed a few more Frankie-packed discs in London in 1995. Again these utilised familiar one-liners from the great man and resulted in a track called 'Shut Your Face' and another called 'Nay, Nay, Thrice Nay'. The former simply repeats that beloved line relentlessly against a wall of sound which seems to mix the theme from *Mission: Impossible* with extracts from the score for Peter Davison-era *Doctor Who*. Fittingly, Frankie's morphed mutterings take on the sound of a manic Dalek swallowing a wasp and with Hugh Herbert-style 'whoo-whoo!' laughter tacked on for good measure the result is a confused, confusing novelty. The 'Nay, Nay' classic is more of the same, with the phrase repeated over and over, slowed down, accompanied by what sounds like a one-fingered keyboard player, annoying lift muzak and a sense of Orwellian nightmare.

All the Mike Bennett Frankie tracks (complete with remix versions) were gathered together on a compilation compact disc which he produced and issued in 1998. Suitably entitled *Frankie Howerd: The Song and Dance Album* it was released in tandem with Tessa Le Bars (acting as artistic consultant) and Frankie's estate. As a result, the hip hop dance era of Frankie's last recordings was joined by the 'Three Little Fishes' recordings from 1989 and, rather more bizarrely, the two cuts from his 1950s single with Margaret Rutherford and the laid-back 'Song and Dance Man'. ●

CHAPTER

4

Carry on Camping

FRANKIE ON **FILM**

'You can't be funny at 8.30 am!'
Frankie Howerd

Frankie's love of cinema had been a major part of his life from childhood and, in a very spasmodic film career, he proved himself an excellent big screen comedy actor. Over a 25-year period he went from tousle-haired bag of nerves to wild-eyed, Beatle-esque ultra-villain. Finally getting the Hollywood treatment after several profitable British smut-fests in the 1970s, Frankie's long and winding cinematic journey takes in some of the most celebrated high points of his career – and also some of the most brain-numbing low points.

He was always at his best with a live audience and often found it hard to gather enthusiasm for film acting. Speaking in 1978, he claimed that 'Films are even more technical than television. The camera moves there, the cameraman lights the scene, you rehearse, the area is lit again, you work from marks on the floor and you move from one mark to another. They may be chalk marks or bits of wood stuck on the floor and you're told exactly where to go and what to look at in terms of camera technique. So you're much more like a puppet in films. But I enjoy doing films. You do something different every day. Once you've done a scene in a film, you're finished. You can't do it again. Come to think of it, that's a

sad thing about films as well. Once they're done you can't do it again. With a stage show, if it's not right one night I've got a chance to correct it on another night!'

1953
The Runaway Bus

Frankie needed a friendly face and a faithful fan to cajole him into finally making the move into movies and that came in the shape of writer/director Val Guest. From his Palm Springs home Guest remembers that 'Frankie was a wonderful radio comedian and a big star. Both my wife, Yolande Donlan, and myself thought he was a very funny man. I had an idea that I wanted to write a film for him so I went to see him at the Palladium where he was playing and suggested the idea.

'The very thought of making a film horrified him. He explained that people are forced to follow instructions and conform to a set version of their comic personality in a film. He maintained that every 'star comedian' vehicle he had seen had been a complete failure and that was the end of it. He seriously feared that moving away from the medium he knew – radio – would destroy him. His words were "I can say goodbye to my career!" Clearly he was

Frankie as Lurkalot in the 1971 film Up the Chastity Belt.

very reluctant so I put the ball firmly in his court. My final words were "Is there a subject you like?" The rest, as they say, is British comedy history.'

Guest, who had worked with such comic luminaries as the Crazy Gang, Will Hay and Arthur Askey, waited for Frankie's answer and it was pretty vague. 'He said, "No there isn't a subject I really want to do." He then paused and muttered, "But if I were ever to do a film I would like it to be a comedy thriller." He believed that if the comedy failed, the thrills probably wouldn't!' Talking in 1978, Frankie commented that 'I knew the director, Val Guest. He was a friend of mine. I'd seen him direct a film and I wanted to do a comedy thriller. Bob Hope's first real success was in a film called *The Cat and the Canary*. I saw that when I was in the army and thought that if I ever got out I'd make a comedy thriller.'

With this classic, tightly constructed, moodily shot and brilliantly acted piece of spooky, spy-driven, comic capering, Frankie's big screen career was launched in style. Despite that, the film was routinely mocked by Frankie on practically every chat show appearance he made. The film itself, though creaky and old-fashioned in places, remains an endearing and invaluable record of Frankie's early persona. Based completely on his *Variety Bandbox* style, it captures the sparkling, unique and deliberately shambolic delivery of the great comedian during his first and most dazzling flash of stardom.

The pre-credits sequence (detailing a robbery), and the typically British hazard of fog making aeroplane travel an impossibility, sets up the contrived but fittingly farcical narrative. Again, speaking in an unpublished interview from 1978, Frankie remembers that 'In those days we didn't have much money so in order to make the film for £45,000, which was very cheap then, we set the whole thing in a fog so you wouldn't use much scenery. We shot it in five weeks so we worked very fast.' Some ten years later, Frankie maintained that the money-saving fog idea was his, but this doesn't really ring true. Without the plot device of the fog there would be no story in

the first place. And besides, farmhouses, trees and hangars are clearly – well, just about – visible. It obviously wasn't all filmed in an empty shed full of dry ice.

Whatever the truth behind the movie, it was certainly an economic one and also a very successful one. The actual input Frankie had is disputed. Frankie insisted that 'The director wrote the story but I mostly wrote my own part,' while Guest himself recalls that 'I wrote the script for him, using his unique comic style and scripting all his dialogue in that Howerdese that had became such a hallmark of his performances.' However, it is known that Frankie's celebrated telephone rants to his granny were skilfully ad-libbed on the set. They seem Frankie's purest and most relaxed moments in the picture.

The character – that of bemused, startled and just plain terrified relief driver Percy Lamb – is tailor-made for him. Making his confused and staggering first appearance striking a match, moaning 'I don't know!' and burning his fingers, Frankie's perplexed look of anxiety and annoyance hardly changes for the whole 75 minutes. The music underscores his wanderings with a suitable jaunty theme, while Frankie's desperate 'Am I still in England, do you know?' creates a sense of comically dramatic tension. Indeed, as first film appearances go this is a pretty good one. The celebrated Frankie mannerisms are pretty much in place, even at this early stage, and a frantic puffing-out of the cheeks is brilliantly delivered. Treasurable outbursts ('You just stand there and enjoy it, don't strain yourself!') compete with elongated vocal clowning – 'Oooemmm!' – and there's a wonderfully enjoyable bit of banter with Margaret Rutherford's imposing, umbrella-wielding harridan, Miss Beeston. Frankie's muttered 'Silly old bag!' is potent indeed.

Nervous at the prospect of carrying a star vehicle, Frankie was continually looking for approval from his director. Guest remembers that 'Frankie was a very good film actor but he worried about everything. He kept coming up to me, enquiring, "Am I doing it all right Val...?" I would continually reassure him:

Two glorious British eccentrics – Margaret Rutherford helps Frankie make his first splash in movies for *The Runaway Bus* publicity.

"You're fine Frankie… Just pretend you're on stage…" That always seemed to help. The finest comic talents are often nervous about filmmaking. Woody Allen would also need someone to hold his hand during production and Frankie was exactly the same.'

Luckily for Frankie, Guest had assembled a stunning ensemble cast of talented and experienced film actors. Frankie was clearly relieved. 'The great advantage I had,' he said, 'was having Margaret Rutherford. She became a great friend of mine. Petula Clark also appeared. So it had a very good cast.' And the other actors are just as impressive. The stunning blonde bombshell Belinda Lee excels

as the horror-book-obsessed flirt from Basingstoke, diminutive Toke Townley turns on the helpful twittering as he entertains Rutherford with readings from a seed catalogue, the ultra-smooth Terence Alexander dodges in and out in the 'is he or isn't he a crook?' role, while George Coulouris looks alternately bored, menacing and disgusted as only the greatest character players can. Indeed, surrounded by so much talent, Frankie's performance comes across as all the more impressive. To shine at all is a mini-miracle and to shine so brightly in your very first film appearance is extremely rare. And Guest, capitalising on one of the earliest chances to show Frankie in all his visual glory to a mass audience, milks the mobile features and frantic mugging for all their worth.

In particular, the two impromptu, one-way phone conversations with his Granny are the stuff of comedy legend. With the 'poor old soul' mishearing everything; misinformed thoughts concerning a non-existent girlfriend; hilarious interjections to himself ('Bet she's got her shawl in her mouth!'); embittered comments ('It's costing me money!') and long-winded explanations about a cottage pie being in the oven, this is simply Frankie, the ingenious gag-meister, firing on all cylinders. For good measure, there's even a tasty vignette with character star and all-round bumbling figure of officialdom, Reginald Beckwith, as an annoyingly helpful and insistent telephone collection man.

The journey on the ill-fated, fog-bound coach 13 is an eventful one, of course. Frankie is covered with mud, shot at, terrorised by just about everyone and ultimately informed that the stolen loot – a shipment of gold bullion – is stashed in the back of his coach. It all gets very *Lavender Hill Mob*, and it's down to the rubber-faced comic timing of Frankie to keep the comic coach situation funny and fully fuelled. Having hit a fog-shrouded tree and faced the fact that a coach is no place to spend the night, Frankie and the gang decamp to a deserted farmhouse where the plot thickens. Frankie relaxes further in this situation and at one point he almost looks directly into camera as if wanting to drag us, the audience, into the action with him.

The situation gets more and more tense, red herrings are piled onto red herrings, undercover police reveal themselves, the villains are exposed and Frankie can milk his familiar laughter-lines with everything from 'Please yourself!' through a frantic, Rutherford-directed rant of 'Missus! Missus! Loosen anything that's tight!' and on to a half-whispered 'Cow!' There's even a nod to his celebrated stage retorts to his deaf pianist when, suggesting party games as an option to while away some time, he repeats 'Party games!' at the top of his

voice, as if to a bunch of simpletons.

Following another partly ad-libbed bit of banter with his unseen Granny, Frankie ends the film with his thoughts focused firstly on sex and then money. In a winning (and daring) climax to their fraught relationship, the tasty blonde honey Belinda Lee gets a lift back to Basingstoke and offers Frankie the chance to visit her at 25 Nettlebed Road. Dismissive of the offer and thankful to be rid of her, Frankie mutters insincerely 'I will', clocks her stunning figure properly for the first time, repeats with added zest, 'I will!' and cheerfully jots down the address. It's a flawlessly played comic moment and proves without a shadow of a doubt that Frankie was a British film star to be reckoned with.

Sadly, he wasn't to get a big screen assignment to match this one for over a decade. Even his return to the Val Guest fold, with the nautical Hammer flick *Further Up the Creek*, failed to capture the raw, happy-go-lucky, bombastic persona that this film rejoices in. Speaking just a few months before his death, Frankie said that 'Val Guest was the finest film director I ever worked for. He was the only director who really seemed to capture the real me – whatever that is – on camera. In a strange way, my first film was probably my best!' It proved that all those half-hearted japes and moans directed at the film were only in fun and, although I consider his film star period between 1966 and 1973 as the definitive one, there remains an almost Ealing-like charm about *The Runaway Bus*. A perfect one to watch in front of a roaring fire with a piece of toast and a huge mug of tea as the rain pours down, the fog – both outside and on the screen – creeps in and Frankie's fresh-faced powerhouse performance goes through the sainted Bob Hope motions.

....

Did You Know? The film was made under the much spookier title *Scream in the Night*.

....

Percy Lamb FRANKIE HOWERD, Miss Beeston MARGARET RUTHERFORD, Lee Nicholls PETULA CLARK, Ernest Schroeder GEORGE COULOURIS, Henry Waterman TOKE

TOWNLEY, Peter Jones TERENCE ALEXANDER, Janie Grey BELINDA LEE, Inspector Henley JOHN HORSLEY, Duty officer ANTHONY OLIVER, Transport officers STRINGER DAVIS, MICHAEL GWYNNE and RICHARD BEYNON, Telephone man REGINALD BECKWITH, Travel girl MARIANNE STONE, American traveller LIONEL MURTON, Receptionist LISA GASTONI, Security man SAM KYDD, Crooks CYRIL CONWAY and ARTHUR LOVEGROVE, Detective ALISTAIR HUNTER

Music Ronald Binge, Musical Supervisor Philip Martell, Director of Photography Stanley Pavey, Camera Operator Eric Besche, Art Director Wilfred Arnold, Make-up Jill Carpenter, Hairdresser Pauline Trent, Editor Douglas Myers, Sound recordist Cecil Thornton, Assistant Director Tony Kelly, Production Manager George Fowler, Written and Directed by Val Guest
Conquest-Guest Productions
Filmed at Southall Studios

1955
An Alligator Named Daisy

If anything was to convince Frankie that the time was not yet right for film stardom, then this negligible cameo role was it. A frothy and colourful animal picture from the Rank Organisation, the title has come to sum up the corny innocence of mid-1950s British comedy, although the film itself isn't bad at all. Donald Sinden turns on the frightfully English bluster, Margaret Rutherford is quite delicious as the eccentric pet shop keeper who talks to all her stock and there's even a quick glimpse of Diana Dors in the bath. What more does the average red-blooded male moviegoer need?

But for those discerning fans who are only hanging around for an even briefer glimpse of Frankie Howerd, it's a pretty long wait. His sequence comes right at the end, when the wealthy James Robertson Justice is holding a special alligator garden party. (Don't ask.) Frankie is hired as the spluttering master of ceremonies – a role he had performed with aplomb on BBC Radio for nigh on a decade. He starts with the usual 'Ladies and gentle-men' business before making a feeble crack

about all these crocodiles taking part in a rally: 'an old crocs race!' The audience reaction is less than impressive and Frankie mutters 'Oh dear, got a right lot here!' He's then dragged off the stage with a cry of 'Go on, get out of it!' And that, my friends, is that.

Also with JEAN CARSON, STANLEY HOLLOWAY, ROLAND CULVER, AVICE LANDON, STEPHEN BOYD, RICHARD WATTIS, HENRY KENDALL, MICHAEL SHEPLEY, KEN MACKINTOSH and His Band and FRANKIE HOWERD as himself

Screenplay Jack Davies, based on the novel by Charles Trent, Music Stanley Black, Director of Photography Reginald Wyer, Camera Operator David Harcourt, Art Director Michael Stringer, Editor John D Guthridge, Sound Recordists John W Mitchell and Gordon K McCallum, Make-up George Blackler, Costume Supervisor Yvonne Caffin, Assistant Director Pat Marsden, Production Manager Jack Swinburne, Producer Raymond Stross, Director J Lee Thompson
Rank Film Productions
Filmed at Pinewood Studios (VistaVision)

The Ladykillers

A masterpiece of wicked black comedy, this was the last truly classic Ealing comedy. This priceless, brightly coloured gem from director Alexander Mackendrick quite clearly signalled the end of an era. Like a manic Alastair Sim, Alec Guinness leads a gang incorporating both Ealing stalwarts like Cecil Parker and fresh-faced new kids on the block like Peter Sellers. Jack Warner, in between *The Blue Lamp* and *Dixon of Dock Green*, is the archetypal cosy copper, the rousing theme pre-empts flourishes from both *Murder on the Orient Express* and Hammer's *Dracula* and the sinister, smokey railway location is the perfect backdrop for the cloak-and-dagger proceedings.

It's a film of marked contrasts. The subtle, muted villainy of Herbert Lom against the lumbering, gentle-giant approach of Danny Green. The brash American director pinpointing the bizarre eccentricities of a gentle race as only an outsider can. Guinness and Sellers mesh perfectly, while Sellers' fellow young Turks, Kenneth Connor and Frankie

Howerd, leave vintage cinematic marks on this most fascinating of Ealing triumphs. The mixture may not have set the box-office alight at the time but, in retrospect, *The Ladykillers* remains the most daring, challenging and invigorating example of the Ealing output.

Frankie's brief contribution taps into the flamboyant style he had perfected in *Variety Bandbox*. His is a battle of wills and brute strength against Connor's diminutive and belligerent cabbie. All wild hair and goggle-eyes, barrow-boy Frankie is remonstrating with a hungry horse that's taken a fancy to the apples on his barrow. Katie Johnson, the elderly lady whom the ladykillers cannot kill, takes action and the gang, right in the middle of their carefully planned King's Cross getaway, can only look on helplessly as the farcical beating of horse and barrow-boy is played out in the street. Frankie's dialogue is restricted to sharp, one-line abuse. Prodded by Johnson's umbrella he bellows 'Do you

A light for a (future) knight – Frankie obliges Alec Guinness during a break in filming the Ealing classic *The Ladykillers*.

Frankie sets out his stall with director Alexander Mackendrick before shooting his supporting role in *The Ladykillers*.

mind?', while in between calculating the cost of the consumed fruit, he mutters 'Look missus' more times than seems humanly possible – in anybody other than Frankie Howerd, that is.

Dubbed a 'vicious brute' by the avenging old lady, Frankie frantically tries to retain his composure, his business and his apples as he's beaten with the umbrella, annoyed by the cab driver and finally rounded up by the police. The disturbance eventually includes Fred Griffiths' junk man (owner of the horse, Dennis, at the root of the problem) and winds up in Jack Warner's police station, with Frankie ending his moment of Ealing semi-stardom as a defeated wreck with head in hands.

The film happily carries on without him but Frankie himself was mortified by the final product. Speaking about his film career in 1978, he recalled that 'I worked about a week on that. Alexander Mackendrick was a marvellous director but unfortunately something happened to me which happens to a lot of actors. Because the film was too long a lot of my part was cut. Because it had nothing really to do with the film they cut out the middle … It was almost sad to see because it

ruined the sense of the performance.' Indeed, when a stage adaptation, headlining Tim Brooke-Taylor, embarked on a UK tour in 1999, the 'Frankie Howerd' vignette was removed completely. However, *The Ladykillers* was and remains a major part of the Howerd legend. There isn't a great deal to it, but Frankie's manic performance adds an extra dimension to the blackest of black comedies.

Professor Marcus ALEC GUINNESS, Major CECIL PARKER, Louis HERBERT LOM, Harry PETER SELLERS, One-Round DANNY GREEN, Superintendent JACK WARNER, Mrs Wilberforce KATIE JOHNSON, Sergeant PHILIP STAINTON, Barrow boy FRANKIE HOWERD

Story and screenplay William Rose, Music Tristram Cary, Director of Photography Otto Heller, Art Director Jim Morahan, Editor Jack Harris, Assistant Director Tom Pevsner, Production Supervisor Hal Mason, Unit Production Manager David Peers, Associate Producer Seth Holt, Producer Michael Balcon, Director Alexander Mackendrick
Ealing Productions
Filmed at Ealing Studios

Jumping For Joy

In a 1955 *Radio Times* interview, Frankie expressed his desire to make comedy films 'in the Fernandel manner'. The horse-faced Fernandel breezed with bemused innocence through numerous saucy French hits but in *Jumping for Joy*, Frankie's second copper-bottomed big screen star vehicle, he found himself cast in the mould of someone rather closer to home.

With Norman Wisdom triumphing in the 1953 classic *Trouble In Store*, every British comedian worth his salt was groomed as the latest, pathos-driven star turn. Frankie, after a fruitful brush with comic chills in his first film, landed this second star vehicle in the Wisdom mould. Indeed, the following year Wisdom would go through a similar scenario in the horse-racing adventure, *Just My Luck*, ironically with Frankie's first film co-star Margaret Rutherford along for the ride. Here, Frankie is the hapless, sentimental, naïve hero, involved in the corrupt world of greyhound racing.

Made in eight weeks between the second series of *The Howerd Crowd* and Frankie's stage stint in *Charley's Aunt*, the film is awash with little pleasures, from the mouthwatering supporting cast to the vibrant location filming in White City Stadium. Social history and social hysterics merge to form a totally enjoyable, fun-packed film experience and Frankie plays the down-on-his-luck card without a hint of self-mockery. Indeed, he proves that when the opportunity arose he could give a fully rounded characterisation a lease of life without relying on innuendo and flamboyant mugging.

That's not to say there aren't bucketloads of physical and facial clowning in the film; Frankie takes to the slapstick style like a duck to water and matches Wisdom pratfall for pratfall. Indeed, the director, John Paddy Carstairs, and writer, Jack Davies, had been instrumental in the making of Wisdom's classic Pinewood-based flicks and this is the perfect blueprint for 'one that went to another comedian'.

However, it isn't simply a case of moulding Frankie to fit the format of another great performer. The unique vocal elements of Frankie the radio star are included and worked into the sentimental elements of the story. Frankie interjects with 'What a funny

Dog gone? Frankie receives a telling-off when his irate landlady (Beatrice Varley) discovers Lindy Lou the greyhound in *Jumping For Joy*.

Jack Montague (Stanley Holloway) and Willy Joy (Frankie) share a stationary buffet car meal in this scene from the under-rated *Jumping For Joy*.

woman!' twice over, there's plenty of opportunity for over-played 'ooohs!' and 'ahhhs!', his reaction to the death of an unknown tailor is a peerlessly vague 'Oh, shame!' and there's at least one 'Missus! Madam!' interlude as his life is threatened by a poor lady driver (played by the gleefully short-sighted Joan Hickson). Perhaps most tellingly of all, after a dramatic near-death experience, our hapless hero appears unscathed and explains that he wouldn't get killed – 'not on your Nellie!' Frankie's brilliance as a film actor is his ability to embrace the serious elements of his role while contrasting them with vignettes of pure vaudeville.

The Wisdomesque 'she loves me, she loves me not' relationship with the delectable but unattainable Susan Beaumont could have been skin-crawling in the extreme. The fact that it isn't is testament to Frankie's subtlety. Frankie never goes into total sugary overload with her. There's something in their very first scenes that hints at failure – unlike the Wisdom character, where the little man thinks he will never win out in love but as often as not does. Frankie never really thinks he's in with a chance and, in the end, he isn't. Handsome vet, Terence Longdon, has got the hots for the girl; he's also got the looks and the charm. Frankie, Susan and, indeed, the audience clock this from the outset.

Thus, the real sentiment for Frankie to play is focused on the unwanted dog, Lindy Lou. With the most pathetic, helpless eyes of any greyhound caught on film, the dog literally begs for attention. Frankie saves her from the knacker's yard and spends the rest of the movie looking after her and training her for the big comeback race. Akin to Harry H Corbett's plight in *Steptoe and Son Ride Again*, the dog seems a dead loss from the outset but a little love and understanding (plus a special whistle which signals the silly old thing to run) work wonders. Frankie sleeps in a luggage compartment to allow the dog a bed, spends all his dosh on dog food and even risks his own life in a train headed for disaster in order to protect the mutt. The relationship is touching and believable.

A dog-hating boarding house sequence stirs echoes of the Laurel and Hardy short, *Laughing Gravy*, and sets up the fated meeting between depressed Frankie and dapper con man Stanley Holloway. Falling for Holloway's far-fetched tale of a lost fortune, the two team up and create a perfect big screen partnership. As with Margaret Rutherford in *The Runaway Bus*, Frankie has the opportunity to work opposite a delicious pro of the old school and countless classic moments are the result. Holloway's abode, a First Class train carriage, harks back to his appearance in the Ealing classic *The Titfield Thunderbolt* and over a light meal he reveals the fine art of conning the racing world. The scam involves Frankie pretending to be Lord Cranfield and bumbling into an exclusive tailor's shop in order to purloin an Old Etonian tie on the nob's account. Naturally he's taken for the real Lord and gets dragged into a misfitting for the over-sized suit of clothes the old duffer has on order. Typical of these glorious 1950s British movies, the scene delights in three treasured character stars – Richard Wattis, Michael Ward and Reginald Beckwith – before Frankie staggers out and bumps into two more: the real Lord (A E Matthews) and his 'blind old bat' wife (Joan Hickson).

The ultimate sequence, for fans of the best in British comedy, comes when Frankie and Holloway try out their money-making story for the first time. The gullible gambler the two hit upon first is none other than an uncredited Charles Hawtrey. It's a superb little scene featuring three legends sparring for comic attention and creating a minor masterpiece. The rest of the cast is suitably littered with brilliant stereotypes brought into focus by some of the most experienced character players around. Lionel Jeffries turns on the overt, money-mad Jewish style for his devious bookmaker; Alfie Bass becomes ever so 'umble as his distrustful assistant; burly Danny Green, fresh from his mega-success in *The Ladykillers*, does his usual hard-nut thicko routine; Gerald Campion pops up for a cough

Frankie takes Lindy Lou's pulse in *Jumping for Joy*.

and a spit during the closing scenes and Bill Fraser staggers in for a brief drunken turn in the billiards room. Fraser, a big star before the war, was well respected by Frankie and, before he fought back to become a sitcom legend in *The Army Game*, was welcomed into the limelight for an effective cameo here.

The real corruption is perfectly encapsulated by Tony Wright, the ultimate British beefcake, who could play slightly dubious, naïve boxers like no other British actor. Here he's a tough, sharp-suited chap, gleefully stringing Frankie's simpleton along, doping dogs, betting on sure-fire winners and denying all knowledge when the cat's out of the bag. His environment is one of brawls, booze, birds and billiards. And as Frankie wanders into the spider's web – buying some chips for himself and the local kiddies and exclaiming 'Cheeky devils!' when a couple of roughs pinch some and complain about no vinegar – this is clearly troublesville. Naturally, there's a shadowy Mr Big behind all these cheap hoodlums and the final showdown happens at the greyhound stadium. The real corruption is exposed, our hero is awarded the winning cup and all's well that ends well.

A tad old-fashioned – Frankie even resurrects George Formby's cry of 'Turned out nice again!' – there is no denying the real charm at work here. A stunning central performance from Frankie, some delicious moments from Stanley Holloway, a sparkling supporting cast and an unforgettably infectious, post-*Genevieve* harmonica score from Larry Adler, all add up to a joyous British film comedy.

....

Did You Know? Extracts from this vintage Frankie vehicle were featured in the 1977 Herbert Wilcox compilation of British film comedy, *To See Such Fun*. Larry Adler's recording of the film's theme tune was released as sheet music with a mug shot of Frankie and the greyhound on the cover.

....

Willy Joy FRANKIE HOWERD, also starring STANLEY HOLLOWAY as 'Captain' Jack Montague, with Lord Reginald Cranfield A E MATTHEWS, Vincent TONY WRIGHT, Mr Blag

Frankie and Parisian dancer Katherine Kath share a drink during a break in filming *A Touch of the Sun* at Nettlefold Studios, 23 July 1956.

ALFIE BASS, Lady Cranfield JOAN HICKSON, Bert Benton LIONEL JEFFRIES, Susan Storer SUSAN BEAUMONT, John TERENCE LONGDON, Max the commentator COLIN GORDON, Mr Carruthers RICHARD WATTIS, Plug Ugly DANNY GREEN, Mr Smithers REGINALD BECKWITH, with BARBARA ARCHER, WILLIAM KENDALL, EWEN SOLON. Uncredited: Landlady BEATRICE VARLEY, Men CHARLES HAWTREY and IAN WILSON, Mr Pertwee MICHAEL WARD, Drunk BILL FRASER, Farmer GEORGE A COOPER, 'Custard Pie' crowd member GERALD CAMPION
Story and screenplay Jack Davies and Henry E Blyth, Music composed and played by Larry Adler, Musical Supervisor Muir Mathieson, Director of Photography Jack Cox, Camera Operator Jim Bawden, Art Director Michael Stringer, Editor John D Guthridge, Sound Editor James Groom, Special Effects W Warrington, Sound Recordists John Dennis and Gordon K McCallum, Make-up W T Partleton, Costume Designer Joan Ellacott, Assistant Director Robert Asher, Production Controller Arthur Alcott, Production Manager Jack Swinburne, Executive Producer Earl St John, Producer Raymond Stross, Director John Paddy Carstairs
Rank Film Productions
Filmed at Pinewood Studios

1956
A Touch of the Sun

This pleasant little romp was made in July/August 1956. Again, the film was moulded in the saccharine and slapstick image of Norman Wisdom. The whole set-up is similar to Wisdom's 1955 gem, *Man of the Moment*. However, Frankie's film clearly owes a greater debt to an earlier generation, particularly the pre-war antics of George Formby. Indeed, unlike the whimsical Wisdom, there is little sentiment at play here, merely incompetence, one-upmanship and the little man making good against all financial, intellectual and social odds.

At one point in the film, as in *Jumping For Joy*, Frankie even resurrects Formby's celebrated catchphrase, 'Turned out nice

Frankie goes undercover as a waiter in *A Touch of the Sun*.

again!' Moreover, the trio of cigar-puffing, cat-napping, booze-guzzling Northern businessmen (played with delicious relish by Reginald Beckwith, Willoughby Goddard and, would you believe it, Alfie Bass) could have stepped right out of *It's In the Air* or *Get Cracking*.

There's a sense, however, that Frankie is somewhat restricted in his characterisation. Although there's plenty of room for dressing-up, role-play and frantic mugging, there isn't

that spontaneous quality so much in evidence in *The Runaway Bus*. Still, as an example of the early Frankie film catalogue it is a rare and enjoyable treat. In the pre-credits sequence, he stares lovingly into a mirror and prepares himself for the performance of a lifetime – 'Right my lad, you're on…' The acting analogy is quite appropriate, as moments later he has to brave the onslaught of guests in his multi-faceted position as hall porter in an exclusive London hotel.

He bends over backwards to thrill and chill the charming old maids played by Esma Cannon and Lucy Griffiths, he turns on the outlandish Yankee accent for our colonial cousins, goes all Ascot and Wimbledon for the dotty débutante, flirts unashamedly with a lady of a certain age whose sole pride and joy is her dog, gets hilariously aroused by a man-hungry blonde bimbo in shades, spouts nautical terminology to humour an ageing sea dog and even indulges in a bit of Japanese banter for his Oriental vistors. It's all one big performance and, although there's relish in the work, Frankie's mini-creations seem stereotypical rather than believable. The initial stages of the film only warm up, in fact, when he collapses with a deflated 'Ooh, I've had this!'

The hotel sequences are literally jam-packed with rib-tickling attempts to get laughs out of people finishing every sentence addressed to Frankie with a sugar-dripping '…Darling!' – for William Darling is the character's name. Apart from Frankie himself, there is only one fully rounded – also pompous, officious and downright aggressive – performance. Delighting in hard-nosed authority like the ideal baddie in a George Formby flick, the smooth-as-silk Dennis Price, looking at all times as if there's an unpleasant smell under his nose, strolls through the treacle-laden narrative with head held high. Ever-ready with snotty, self-important put-downs and delivering his lines with speed, economy and clipped disinterest, Price provides (as did Rutherford and Holloway before him) the ideal sounding board for Frankie's fledgling film actor. It's a pity that Price isn't used more frequently, for when he's not around Frankie is allowed to get dangerously close to self-indulgence.

Still, there's good support from various veterans of *Jumping For Joy* – notably Richard Wattis as the understanding solicitor and Colin Gordon as a frantic photographer – and there's an underlying sense of self-mockery in Frankie's showmanship. It's all an act, an act he seems to enjoy but an act nevertheless. Behind each cherished re-enactment of a murder mystery for the spinsters or overtly

flirtatious compliment for the floozy, there seems to lurk a darker, more cynical, 'I'm only doing this cos it's my job!' sort of attitude. Indeed, when the charming young lady he admires from afar (Katherine Kath) suggests he needs a good holiday, Frankie bemoans his need for a 'holiday for good!'

As is often the case with these frothy, frolicsome fifties flicks, the opportunity arises almost straight away when the legal bod (Wattis) reveals Frankie's £10,000 inheritance. Suddenly his mind isn't on the job any more. He can now afford to wear smart clothes, smoke a big cigar and walk into the office of his supercilious boss (Price) without a care in the world – or so he thinks.

The classic exchange in Price's office ('I've come to say goodbye!'/'Why?'/'Because I'm going!') leads to Frankie's realisation that he's caught by the well-known chandeliers in the form of a water-tight contract that keeps the ever-popular, indispensable porter very much in his place. Fighting back, Frankie accordingly becomes the ultimate in incompetent hotel workers, with alarm calls to the residents at five in the morning ('Get out of bed, you lazy layabout!'), cheeky comments to the nautical gentleman ('Oh, you saucy old sea dog!') and unsavoury advances towards the American woman, played with gusto by Miriam Karlin ('You're mine!'). Pleading insanity – Frankie explains to a rather worried Price that the voices told him to do it – our hero is finally off the hook, off his contract and on his way to the holiday of a lifetime in the South of France.

The Continental sequences are all fairly standard Brit-on-the-razzle material and play like Eric and Ernie's *That Riviera Touch* a decade early. The typical Cannes sequence is packed with happy holiday-makers, relaxed bikini-wearing and our joyously English Englishman trying to blend in with the locals. He gets buried in the sand, tries chatting up the beach babes and is finally hoodwinked by an erotic nightclub dancer and her champers-guzzling chums. Trying to cheer himself up, he only gets more and more miserable as his farcical attempts at water ski-ing and underwater fishing go totally pear-shaped. It's simply a pretty obvious collection of misadventures orchestrated by the jolly French porter in much the same cheerful manner that Frankie relished his own work. After a winning streak at the casino Frankie gives the lot to a British chappie (Richard Caldicot) and heads back to London. Greeted by pouring rain and seeing that his old hotel is up for sale to the Ministry of Health (depicted by two bowler-hatted blokes suffering from very bad colds – this is satire, folks!), Frankie tries to get the place back on its feet by coaxing a huge wad of cash out of three Northern businessmen.

After a brilliant, self-contained scene in which Frankie pretends to be the nervy photographer's model, it's all systems go with the old hotel gang back in place. Chief among these are the delightfully soft-spoken songstress, Ruby Murray (limited to just a handful of lines and a couple of songs but exuding more charm than the whole of B*witched put together) and gruff old-timer Gordon Harker, who grouches around the place and plays various comic parts to assist in the tricky subterfuge.

The subterfuge gets very tricky indeed – involving the need to impress the trio of brash brass-mongers and convince them that the hotel is full when, in fact, the trio are the only guests. Venturing into Dick Emery territory for the briefest of interludes, Frankie gets to play a flat-topped, bespectacled valet, a hunched, bleary-eyed French waiter and even a dragged-up, refined Duchess who plays up to Beckwith's besotted advances. The entire sequence depends on stretching credibility to breaking point and Frankie's run-ragged cry of 'It's like the Battle of Waterloo!' is one for the 'best of Britcom' compilation. It's like an Ealing comedy played in *Carry On Abroad* mode.

The script is charming, Frankie's performance is delightful and the happy-ever-after ending is endearingly played. As in *Jumping For Joy*, Frankie's little man is given the opportunity to belittle his big-headed former boss. Unlike *Jumping For Joy*, however, Frankie is given the Norman Wisdom reward – in the shape of the girl he loves – and also gets to address the audience. Explaining that the

FRANKIE HOWERD
and introducing
RUBY MURRAY
DENNIS PRICE · DOROTHY BROMLEY
A TOUCH OF THE SUN
with KATHERINE KATH
GORDON HARKER · REGINALD
BECKWITH · PIERRE DUDAN
COLIN GORDON
The New British Laughter Tonic !

Bridal Suite is occupied, he looks at the punters with a wary expression before saying 'And why not? It's all right!' as he reveals the ring on his girlfriend's finger. He plays the romantic finale with just the right touch of camp, Frankie-style bemusement and the fade-out is so quick that nobody can complain about its sentimentality. Probably the least effective and, indeed, least-seen of Frankie's 1950s vehicles, it's still worth catching for the bucketloads of typical Frankie moments and even more so for the less characteristic bits of pathos.

William Darling FRANKIE HOWERD, introducing RUBY MURRAY, with DENNIS PRICE, DOROTHY BROMLEY and KATHERINE KATH, GORDON HARKER, REGINALD BECKWITH, PIERRE DUDAN, COLIN GORDON, RICHARD WATTIS, ALFIE BASS, MIRIAM KARLIN, WILLOUGHBY GODDARD, AÏCHÉ NANA, GEORGE MARGO, ESMA CANNON, LUCY GRIFFITH, NAOMI CHANCE,

IAN WHITTAKER
Story and screenplay Alfred Shaughnessy,
Music composed and directed by Eric Spear,
Director of Photography Arthur Grant, Camera
Operator Harry Gillam, Art Director John Stoll,
Editor Charles Hasse, Assistant Director Frank
Ernst, Production Manager George Pollard,
Production Supervisor Victor Lyndon, Producer
Raymond Stross, Director Gordon Parry
Eros Films
Filmed at Nettlefold Studios

1958

Three Seasons

A 16mm Pathé newsreel short for the British
Travel Association detailing the sights and
sounds in London for the autumn, winter and
spring seasons. The Margot Fonteyn ballet
Burnt Offering and Paul Kletzki conducting
the Royal Philharmonic Orchestra are among
the treats on show. Not forgetting a rare
glimpse of Frankie's legendary Bottom in *A
Midsummer Night's Dream* at the Old Vic.

Further Up the Creek

Low-brow nautical comedy seemed to be all
the rage during the late 1950s. Val Guest had
kick-started the cinematic obsession with his
lukewarm *Carry On Admiral* (no relation to
the subsequent Peter Rogers series) and
resurrected the concept for a cheap and
cheerful – and very, very lucrative – naval
comedy called *Up the Creek*. David Tomlinson
was common to both productions and an on-
the-brink-of-superstardom Peter Sellers
staggered through the latter with merry Irish
charm. Such was the success of *Up the Creek*
that Guest rushed into production with a
sequel, released only a few months after the
first film, at the close of 1958.

However, with Sellers working on *The
Mouse That Roared*, he proved reluctant to
come on board once more. Guest turned
instead to Frankie Howerd. Frankie's big
screen vehicles since Guest's *The Runaway
Bus* had hardly set the world alight but,
backed by the sheer fluster of David
Tomlinson, the stunning glamour of Shirley

Eaton and a healthy roster of seasoned
character actors retained from *Up the Creek*
(David Lodge, Lionel Jeffries, Sam Kydd),
Guest considered him the ideal replacement.

'When Peter Sellers proved unavailable for
the sequel,' Guest recalls, 'Frankie was my very
first choice as replacement. I had to fight for
him, though. The bosses at Hammer weren't
convinced. Still, they hadn't been convinced
about Sellers for the first film, that's why I
brought in David Tomlinson to calm them
down. He was a name they knew and could
bank on. Instead of Sellers as a bumbling
shrewd character, Frankie was ideal for a
bumbling un-shrewd character. Again, David
Tomlinson proved the perfect contrast and
helped appease the Hammer hierarchy.'

As it happens, Frankie does an excellent job
of rekindling Sellers' almost Bilko-style
grandeur. And Guest isn't shy about using
Frankie's familiar radio and television
personality, thus there are plenty of 'Ooh yes!',
'Poor tortured soul!' and 'Slap my Nellie!'
exclamations from the outset. Basically, the
crew of the good ship Aristotle are just as
corrupt and cunning as ever they were under
Sellers. Akin to the narrative strategy of *Carry
On England* some 20 years later, the action
starts with the nervous departure of the
resident authority figure and the rise to
dominance of Frankie's crafty, money-pinching
bosun, providing an illegal betting service for
various personnel and townsfolk while
desperately trying to give the whole
outrageous practice a veneer of respectability.

With the Aristotle sold to some oil-rich
power in the Med, Frankie sees one last
chance for a major scam. Half-price Med
cruise tickets are flogged to the first names
pulled out of a hat, though Frankie makes sure
that Shirley Eaton's sweet-scented letter gets
pulled out first. It is this glorious double-
standard that keeps Frankie's fast-witted
performance afloat; if there are birds or booze
going he will happily look amazed and
outraged at his minions but cheerfully grab the
goods when no one else is looking.

The ship is quickly turned into something
akin to a cruise liner and all is set for the

Bosun Dibble
(Frankie), Jane
(Shirley Eaton)
and Lieutenant-
Commander
Fairweather
(David
Tomlinson)
aboard the
HMS Aristotle
in *Further Up
the Creek*.

ultimate naval rip-off. The only thing Frankie needs for his plan to be secure is a flustered Captain figure. Enter David Tomlinson, who is shocked to recognise personnel from the first film and even more shocked to recognise Frankie from an earlier (sadly unfilmed!) adventure. But at least the crew have regrouped without the nefarious Sellers, so Tomlinson is foolish enough to fall for

Frankie's good intentions and mild-mannered dutifulness.

Throughout Frankie is keen simply to protect his own good name, avoid a court-martial and ultimately lay the blame at the feet of everybody else. With three hour-glass honeys on board there's plenty of opportunity to put on the camp charm, while the ever-moaning Thora Hird only seems to calm down

at the sight of her well-spoken Frankie. His outraged disinterest in her unsubtle advances allows for several priceless Frankie reaction shots. Chuck in Tom Gill's fashion photographer, mincing about the place like Charles Hawtrey on speed, and Esma Cannon putting on the flustered, dotty old lady act and you have a comedy cruise made in heaven.

The plot sort of ambles from outrageous set-piece to outrageous set-piece, all the familiar comic stereotypes are allowed to steal a few scenes and the camera hovers eagerly over Shirley Eaton's scrumptious figure. Naturally, all hell breaks loose when the flirty Eaton lets the cat out of the bag to Tomlinson and the film winds up pre-empting both *Double Bunk* and *Carry On Jack*. Like a nautical Baldrick, Frankie is forever on hand to assist his beleaguered and bemused Captain. His oft-repeated 'Wait a minute, I've got another idea!' sets up a myriad of misadventures before the whole scam is discovered by the naval base, the lads are in deep, deep trouble and the action moves to the mainland.

With a couple of cameos from British comedy stalwarts Eric Pohlmann and Charles Lloyd Pack tossed into the mix, the closing scenes see Tomlinson's foolhardy bumbler hailed as a hero (for flying the flag and causing the Algeroccan rebels to flee), with Frankie restricted to mute agonising as a fly strolls across his nose while he's trying to stand at attention. And, heading back to Blighty, Frankie has cannily filled the vessel with tribesmen and cheerily rolls up his 'Cheap Trips to Britain' banner as the screen fades to black. It's a refreshing, fun-packed and happy-go-lucky little British comedy.

There's not a great deal of taxing action and the plot is the loosest of loose pegs to hang a load of stock characters on, but the acting is exemplary and it's a jolly enough life on the ocean wave. Unfortunately, *Further Up the Creek* didn't perform that well at the box-office. The potential series was dead in the water and Frankie's film star career was awash; he wouldn't headline another film for almost a decade. If Val Guest had had his way, however, it would have been a whole lot

sooner. During production on *Further Up the Creek*, Guest was already hatching the plot for his next film. 'I was planning vague ideas for a third film but Frankie's agent, 'Scruffy' Dale, got far too big for his boots. He demanded millions for another film and what with one thing and another the project was washed up. But Frankie would have definitely been in any further films I made 'up the creek'. He was a successful film comedian and a wonderful man.'

....

Did You Know? The film started shooting on 19 May 1958, less than a fortnight after *Up the Creek*'s West End opening, and was in cinemas by 20 October. 'The trouble was,' Frankie observed, 'that *Further Up the Creek* was made too soon – a matter of months – after the original, and so the public had not had a chance to work up an appetite for it. It followed on far too quickly.' Hammer head James Carreras was blunter still, calling the film 'a disaster'. He needn't have worried, however. *Further Up the Creek* was a rare damp squib in a year that yielded such Hammer mega-smashes as *The Camp on Blood Island*, *Dracula*, *The Revenge of Frankenstein* and *Up the Creek* itself.

As well as making *Further Up the Creek*, Frankie also became the latest recruit to the pages of *Film Fun* in 1958. His cartoon likeness would feature in dozens of comic strips until the paper's demise in 1962. Captured as a fresh-faced, bow-tie wearing, tousle-haired do-gooder, Frankie wandered through the adventures, helping people, foiling crimes and

Our comic strip hero gets the girl in this panel from 'Frankie Howerd Gives a Note-worthy Performance', in the 1959 *Film Fun* annual.

even advising on the dangers of fireworks in the classic 1960 strip 'Light Entertainment'. Indeed, for some of the longer, non-comic strip stories, Frankie himself was credited as writer. But, away from the black-and-white printed page, Frankie's career was less sparkling.

....

Lieutenant-Commander Fairweather DAVID TOMLINSON, Bosun Dibble FRANKIE HOWERD, Jane Cartwright SHIRLEY EATON, Mrs Galloway THORA HIRD, Steady Barker LIONEL JEFFRIES, Perkins LIONEL MURTON, Scouse DAVID LODGE, Cooky JOHN WARREN, Bates SAM KYDD, Webster HARRY LANDIS, Lofty IAN WHITTAKER, Bunts HOWARD WILLIAMS, Chippy PETER COLLINGWOOD, Bennett EDWIN RICHFIELD, Edie Lovelace AMY D'ALBY, Maudie Lovelace ESMA CANNON, Monsieur Phillippe TOM GILL, Kentoni Brothers JACK LE WHITE and MAX DAY, Vicky MARY WILSON, Cleo KATHERINE BYRNE, President ERIC POHLMANN, Porter STANLEY UNWIN, Lieutenant-Commander Blakeney MICHAEL GOODLIFFE, Algeroccan Major WOLFE MORRIS, Despatch Rider JOHN SINGER, Postman LARRY NOBLE, Whacker Payne BALLARD BERKELEY, Chief Wren JUDITH FURSE, Ticket Collector MICHAEL RIPPER, Taxi Driver JOE GIBBON, Dockyard Policeman VICTOR BROOKS, Signalman CAVAN MALONE, Chief Yeoman DESMOND LLEWELYN, Flagship Commander BASIL DIGNAM, Admiral JOHN STUART, Signals JESS CONRAD, First Lieutenant PATRICK HOLT, Algeroccan Officer GEORGE HERBERT, El Diabolo CHARLES LLOYD PACK, British Consul WALTER HUDD, Sea Scout JOHN HALL
Story and Screenplay Val Guest, John Warren and Len Heath, Music composed and conducted by Stanley Black, Director of Photography Gerald Gibbs, Camera Operator Len Harris, Art Director George Provis, Make-up Phil Leakey, Hairdresser Marjorie Whittle, Costume Designer Mollie Arbuthnot, Editor Bill Lenny, Sound Recordist Jock May, Technical Advisor Commander Peter Peake, Assistant Director John Peverall, Production Supervisor Fred Swann, Production Manager Patrick

Marsden, Producer Henry Halsted, Director Val Guest
Byron/Hammer Film Productions
Filmed at Bray Studios (Megascope)

1961
Watch It, Sailor!

With the rip-roaring success of the BBC Radio series *The Navy Lark*, British filmmakers were more obsessed with sailors than ever and the result was a wave of mirthful adventures on the high seas of low humour. Shot in February 1961 and released in August to a wave of public indifference, this feeble effort from Hammer tops and tails the fun with a rousing burst of cod rock 'n' roll sea shanty from the Dallas Boys and defeats its sterling cast with a trite tale of marital confusion and a battleaxe mother-in-law played by Marjorie Rhodes. The film was based on a 1960 stage play by ace farceurs Falkland Cary and Philip King, a sequel to their smash hit *Sailor Beware!*. In the film of *that*, the Marjorie Rhodes role, Ma Hornett, had been memorably played by Peggy Mount.

Though missing Mount, the film is still worth checking out for some delicious character work from flawless players. Irene Handl whines and flutters with ease, officious smoothie Dennis Price breezes his way through the dialogue, while those ultimate British blonde babes, Vera Day and Liz Fraser, also spread a little happiness. But if it's Frankie Howerd you want, prepare for major disappointment. Slap bang in the middle of his career trough, Frankie is caught up in the guest artiste game and has very little to do. Admittedly, his fame grants him top billing in the grab-a-line-and-hope-for-the-best guest crew but that's just the problem. He only has one line and that was probably an ad-lib in a feeble attempt to get more money!

The year before Oliver Reed puffed that cigarette and wowed audiences as a psychotic church organist in Hammer's *Paranoiac*, here we have Frankie Howerd sucking in his cheeks, ripping up his music and generally getting rather frustrated as the church organist at the heart of the 'mistakenly jilted bride' plot. Flamboyantly going for it as the congregation awaits the arrival of our hapless hero (John Meillon), Frankie licks his fingers as an overplayed aid to turning over the pages of his sheet music. He lapses into playing a depressing funeral dirge, waves to the expectant morticians and, embarrassed, quickly reverts to the happier stuff. His single line – wait for it! – comes as he frustratedly wrings his hands, pulls out all the organ stops and then viciously pushes them back in again. One reluctant organ stop provokes an outraged cry of 'Oooh! Get in!' And that's it!

We see him again a bit later, with the women gone and the naval lads panicking in the church during a funeral. Sinister lighting and eerie music give him a touch of the melodramatic Hammer style that audiences knew and loved. He furiously consumes a sandwich and gallops through a nautical number, passes the time as the long wedding wait sets in, yawns, fidgets and finally explodes with silent rage. He's in and out in a cameo that amounts to very little but a warm smile of audience recognition and a wasted

opportunity. But still, it's a Frankie Howerd film credit and in the early 1960s those were as few and far between as, well, funny Hammer films!

Lieutenant-Commander Hardcastle DENNIS PRICE, Daphne LIZ FRASER, Aunt Edie IRENE HANDL, Carnoustie Bligh GRAHAM STARK, Shirley Hornett VERA DAY, Ma Hornett MARJORIE RHODES, Mr Hornett CYRIL SMITH, Albert Tufnell JOHN MEILLON, Church Organist FRANKIE HOWERD, Mrs Lack MIRIAM KARLIN, Vicar ARTHUR HOWARD, Mrs Mottram RENÉE HOUSTON, Solicitor BRIAN REECE, Drunk BOBBY HOWES, Ticket Collector HARRY LOCKE, Ship's Captain WILLIAM MERVYN, Woman with Child MARIANNE STONE, Barmaid DIANE AUBREY, Cab driver JERRY VERNO

Screenplay Falkland Cary and Philip King, Music Douglas Gamley, Title song performed by the Dallas Boys, Musical Supervisor John Hollingsworth, Director of Photography Arthur Grant, Camera Operator Len Harris, Production Designer Bernard Robinson, Art Director Don Mingaye, Make-up Roy Ashton, Supervising Editor James Needs, Editor Alfred Cox, Sound Recordists Jock May and Ken Cameron, Assistant Director John Peverall, Production Manager Clifford Parkes, Associate Producer Anthony Nelson Keys, Executive Producer Michael Carreras, Producer Maurice Cowan, Director Wolf Rilla

Hammer Film Productions

Filmed at Bray Studios

1962
The Fast Lady

Ken Annakin's fantastic semi-trilogy of Leslie Phillips comedies (the others being *Very Important Person* and *Crooks Anonymous*) was completed by this bright and breezy tale of love and vintage cars. James Robertson Justice bellows all over the place, Stanley Baxter wallows in Scottish angst and Julie Christie looks absolutely stunning. Frankie Howerd, again stuck in a tasty one-day cameo, crops up at the very end, when learner-driver Baxter and test examiner Allan Cuthbertson are caught up in a nail-biting car chase through the English countryside. It's a sort of British attempt to usurp the glorious madcap excess of *It's A Mad, Mad, Mad, Mad World* a few months early and at about two and a half hours' less screen time.

Danny Green is part of a bank robbery gang, Fred Emney is hired to simply mutter 'Odd, bloody odd!', Clive Dunn jumps from a burning building, Bernard Cribbins is on a stretcher, Bill Fraser and 'Monsewer' Eddie Gray are playing golf and Frankie Howerd is a maintenance worker who emerges from a man-hole. Lifting the cover to have a quiet fag, Frankie reacts in horror at a fast-approaching car and ducks back down. As he re-emerges, Baxter's car spins into view, he disappears once more and then reappears one final time, disgruntled, dismayed and covered in oil stains. No dialogue, not even a cough and a spit! The film is hardly *Genevieve*, but with jaunty theme music and a spellbinding cast of great comedy character actors in 'blink and you'll miss them' gag appearances, who cares?

Also with KATHLEEN HARRISON, ERIC BARKER, RAYMOND BAXTER, JOHN BOLSTER, GRAHAM HILL, JOHN SURTEES, OLIVER JOHNSTON, DICK EMERY, ESMA CANNON, VICTOR BROOKS, DERYCK GUYLER, TERENCE ALEXANDER, GERALD CAMPION, CAMPBELL SINGER, ANN BEACH, ANNE BLAKE, TERENCE SCULLY, MARK HEATH, TREVOR REID, MARIANNE STONE, EDDIE LESLIE, MICHAEL BALFOUR, HAROLD GOODWIN, HEIDI ERICH, JOHN DUNBAR, MARTIN MILLER, TOKE TOWNLEY, IRENE BARRIE, ANNA OSTLING-THOMAS, MAY LING RAHMAN and FRANKIE HOWERD
Screenplay Jack Davies and Henry Blyth, Music Norrie Paramor, Director of Photography Reg Wyer, Camera Operator Dudley Lovell, Art Director Harry Pottle, Editor Ralph Sheldon, Sound Recordists Peter Davies and John W Mitchell, Second Unit Director Don Sharp, Assistant Director Clive Reed, Production Supervisor Arthur Alcott, Producers Julian Wintle and Leslie Parkyn, Director Ken Annakin
Independent Artists Productions
Filmed at Beaconsfield Studios

The Cool Mikado
'Absolutely incomprehensible gibberish.'
Frankie Howerd

Just before Frankie's career was put back on the straight and narrow by the Establishment Club and *That Was the Week That Was*, he hit professional bottom with this ramshackle reworking of popular light opera. Indeed, the film opens with the typically tongue-in-cheek disclaimer: 'Once upon a time Gilbert and Sullivan wrote the famous comic opera – *The Mikado*. Any resemblance between their creation and this film is completely accidental.' They can say that again.

For Frankie it was a personal humiliation to be involved in the film. In 1978 the comedian recalled it as 'the worst film I've ever done. I'd say it was one of the worst films ever made! It was shot in a month and I was in it for two weeks. I didn't get much money for it, but I needed the money at that time because I wasn't doing very well. It was a good idea, had it been done properly, but the script was appalling.' Indeed, to the end of his days Frankie cited the film as the only thing he was ashamed to have been involved in and, let's face it, he had done some rubbish in his time.

When it was belatedly premiered on home video in 1993 the front cover blurb screamed, 'It's Swinging Sixties time … [a] comical, irreverent romp which encapsulates the true spirit of the 1960s.' The guy that wrote that little lot should get a job as an estate agent. As Frankie put it, 'The film was a disaster, the finished product having all the appearance of being compiled in a wind tunnel.' It also has some of the most mind-numbing dialogue ever written. The dubbing for the principal singers is more obvious than late eighties *Top of the Pops*. The continuity is practically non-existent and most of the direction is so confused that even the camera doesn't know where it should be.

But the most puzzling thing of all is why I have such a soft spot for it. It really is tripe and any number of viewings don't change one's first, jaw-on-the-floor reaction to the never-endingly banal dance routines from

Lionel Blair and his troupe. The grisly romantic leads and the destitute man's Morecambe and Wise turn from Mike and Bernie Winters are absolutely shocking. But it's got something that makes it irresistible. It's not so much a case of 'it's so bad it's good', it's more a case of 'it's so bad it's downright awful'.

Writer/director Michael Winner, the young boy wonder who was about to do his best work (*The Jokers, I'll Never Forget What's 'is name*) before sinking to the repetitive depths of the *Death Wish* films, was hardly the most self-effacing of film directors. Once famously quoted as saying that 'a team effort is when a lot of people do as I say', Winner was not going to take any nonsense from anyone, including his starry cast. As a result, no one seems to be enjoying the experience. Indeed, Frankie vividly remembered that Winner's first words to him on the set were, 'You must understand that I'm a genius!' His garish Gilbert and Sullivan travesty was hardly going to prove this bold claim but Frankie needed the work (and, more importantly, the dosh), so he swallowed his pride and did the film. Ironically, he need not have bothered. The tide was about to turn in his favour and rescue him from a fate worse than death – namely, accepting garbage like this for the rest of his career.

And, in a strange sort of way, I suppose that's why I warm to this film so much. We have a comedian of rare talent, arguably the finest of his generation, reduced to the most grotesque and humiliating of assignments. The performer little knows that he's about to turn the corner but he still gives a professional and, in many ways, very enjoyable performance while singlehandedly combating a tide of the most dreadful one-liners ever compiled. US vaudevillian Stubby Kaye is good value but Frankie's only real support comes from a couple of very minor contributions: a hilarious Tommy Cooper interlude and a refined cameo from *A Touch of the Sun*'s Dennis Price, who, asked if he's attached to the British government, mutters 'Not particularly!'

Although only employed for half of the film's shooting schedule, Frankie appears throughout as the power-mad millionaire, Ko-Ko. The non-existent storyline involves our Yankee hero, Hank (Kevin Scott), fending off a plane-bound bore-a-thon from Stubby Kaye and using the people on the plane as characters in a dreamy musical flashback which comprises the rest of the film. We regularly return to the aeroplane with our handsome hero spinning out the unbelievable story and it's during the initial plane-based sequence that we first spot Frankie. He has no dialogue, just a couple of disgruntled reaction shots and a bit of business when he bangs Kaye on the head with a bunch of flowers, but clearly he is not relaxed with the material. He looks a bit weird as well, with a blonde wig perched on his head like a labrador puppy.

Lew Schwartz, chief among the writers who was commissioned to jolly up the proceedings, had obviously been devouring endless Marx Brothers movies and lifts tons of Groucho Marx-style one-liners. Frankie, acting the big cheese in a nightclub, is distressed to find that the waiter has no wild duck on the menu. Frustrated, he yells, 'Well, bring me a tame one and I'll aggravate it!' Yes, it's that kind of movie, folks.

Nor does Frankie seem at ease when called upon to act the genuine tough guy. Though surrounded by several put-upon heavies (former matinée idol Dermot Walsh among them), he personally threatens death to his intended bride, Yum-Yum (the only blonde Oriental in Japan!), and the fresh-faced American who has won her heart. Frankie is also embarrassing in the sing-song interludes, mugging it up like a Z-grade rep performer but somehow or other getting away with it. He throws in some free-and-easy arm movements, widens his eyes to almost twice their normal size, warbles his overplayed lines to a parrot, strolls over to his co-stars doing an Eyptian walk (post-Wilson, Keppel and Betty but pre-Bangles) and flashes his teeth as if he were trying to impress the judges at Crufts. In other words this is a real pro, knowing he's faced with disaster and grimly making the best of it.

Obviously hired by Winner simply to be Frankie Howerd (albeit in a very un-Frankie

Howerd environment), familiar catchphrases from the past like 'He is a burden!', 'Yesss!', 'What a funny woman!' and 'Silly old fool!' are tossed into the mix but the lines often grate in this bizarre context. Although the musical numbers are enjoyably kitsch in an embarrassing, nerve-shredding sort of way, the great chunks of comedy content are pure Frankie. Dressed to kill – quite literally if his threats are to be believed – Frankie looks natty in suit and tie but the majority of the so-called humour is more schoolboy howler than Palladium prowler. The most telling moment comes when Frankie finds his fame and fortune going unrecognised, whining on about his young love rival obviously not reading the papers or watching the television. This is Frankie, failing comedian, and Ko-Ko, crestfallen anti-hero, bonding as one entity. Ko-Ko finally settles for the leggy blonde bimbo that our American hero has dumped, however, and as a result Frankie ends the movie looking very pleased with his lot indeed.

But it's the comic clash of the titans that the punters really pay their money to see and sadly, when it comes, the Frankie versus Tommy Cooper scene is very short indeed. But there's a distinct sense of perverse pleasure to be gleaned from their single scene together and by this stage everything has gone pear-shaped, in any case. Frankie is nicknamed 'the executioner' merely to allow another 'squaresville' Gilbert and Sullivan classic to get the John Barry treatment and to provide our comic star with an opportunity to do a Sinatra-style gangster number. Hank the Yank looks on in amazement ('Sure is crazy!') and there's another telling moment when, having completed the number, Frankie wheezes 'Thank goodness that's over!'

Stubby Kaye's Judge Mikado comes in to sort things out and the action comes to a head when Frankie kidnaps his love rival (who also happens to be the Mikado's son) and threatens to torture him. All is rapidly resolved when the sexy charms of Hank's ex-girlfriend turn Frankie's head straight away ('Who's that dish?'). During this airport interlude, Frankie,

clearly borrowing a comic lifeline from his pal Tommy Cooper, sports a red fez and, speaking for the entire nation by this stage, caps his evil deeds with the immortal line, 'Isn't this confusing?' With bureaucracy heading into town in the shape of Dennis Price, Frankie can enjoy his romantic pleasures only briefly and, in perhaps the ultimate moment of high camp in his entire career, minces through an unbelievable version of 'The Flowers that Bloom in the Spring'.

Yes, it's an insult to the intelligence of any self-respecting film fan. Yes, it really is the very worst film in Frankie's career. And, yes, it's probably one of the very worst films you're ever likely to come across. But having sat through the thing once more and painstakingly looked at it as part of the overall Frankie canon, I still can't help loving it a little bit. Though it might make you wish that Michael Winner had started making the *Death Wish* films a bit earlier.

....

Did You Know? Filmed in July 1962 and released on 19 May 1963, the film featured the John Barry Seven shortly before Barry composed the scores for *From Russia With Love* and *Zulu*. The single Barry contribution here is 'The Mikado Twist' (aka 'The Tit Willow Twist'), graced with the distinctive guitar sound of Vic Flick and helping to make the soundtrack album a high-priced collector's item.

....

Ko-Ko Flintridge FRANKIE HOWERD, with TOMMY COOPER, DENNIS PRICE, MIKE AND BERNIE WINTERS, LIONEL BLAIR AND HIS DANCERS, JACQUELINE JONES, KEVIN SCOTT, JILL MAI MEREDITH, PETE MURRAY, TSAI CHIN, GLEN MASON, AL MULOCK, DERMOT WALSH, CAROLE SHELLEY, C DENIER WARREN, MURRAY KASH, YVONNE SHIMA, KENJI TAKAKI, FRANK OLEGARIO, THE JOHN BARRY SEVEN and STUBBY KAYE. Uncredited: EDWARD BISHOP, BURT KWOUK, MARIANNE STONE, MICHAEL WINNER.
Screenplay by Michael Winner, based on an adaptation by Maurice Browning of the W S Gilbert and Arthur Sullivan original, with additional material by Lew Schwartz, Philip and

Robert White, Music arranged by Martin Slavin, 'The Mikado Twist' arranged by John Barry, Directors of Photography Martin Curtis and Dennis Ayling, Camera Operator Ronnie Maasz, Production Designer Derek Barrington, Make-up Gerry Fairbanks, Hairdresser Barbara Barnard, Evening dresses Frank Usher, Supervising Editor Fred Burnley, Editor Frank Gilpin, Production Manager Ronnie Bear, Assistant Director Pat Kelly, Producer Harold Baim, Director Michael Winner
Film Productions of Gilbert & Sullivan Operas
Filmed at Shepperton Studios

The Mouse on the Moon

Following the huge international success of the 1959 Peter Sellers vehicle, *The Mouse that Roared*, United Artists were quick to put this rather jolly sequel into production. And with a pre-Beatles Richard Lester at the helm this was clearly a comedy production to be spotted in. In another of Frankie's several 'gag' appearances, here he wanders in for one self-contained scene and disgustedly wanders out again. Hugh Lloyd, dragged in for an equally brief cameo as a construction worker, is slaving away on a blast-proof evacuation centre, when a sheepish-looking Frankie strolls into shot. Clearly in need of a public convenience, he mutters, 'Wait? How long?' When informed it will be three weeks he looks amazed, moans 'Oh dear! I'll have to make other arrangements!' and walks off. He is rewarded with bottom billing (Frankie Howerd … Himself) during the closing credits for his trouble!
The Grand Duchess Gloriana MARGARET RUTHERFORD, Mountjoy RON MOODY, Vincent BERNARD CRIBBINS, Kokintz DAVID KOSSOFF, Spender TERRY-THOMAS, Cynthia JUNE RITCHIE, with JOHN LE MESURIER, JOHN PHILLIPS, ERIC BARKER, RODDY McMILLAN, TOM ALDREDGE, PETER SALLIS, CLIVE DUNN, HUGH LLOYD, GERALD ANDERSEN, ROBIN BAILEY, JAN CONRAD, ARCHIE DUNCAN, GRAHAM STARK, MARIO FABRIZI, JOHN BLUTHAL, RICHARD MARNER, ALLAN CUTHBERTSON, ROBIN BAILEY, GORDON PHILLOTT, GEORGE CHISHOLM, VINCENT

BALL and FRANKIE HOWERD as Himself
Screenplay Michael Pertwee, based on a novel by Leonard Wibberley, Music Ron Grainer, Director of Photography Wilkie Cooper, Camera Operator Kelvin Pike, Production Designer John Howell, Costume Designer Anthony Mendleson, Editor Bill Lenny, Sound recording Dudley Messenger and Bill Daniels, Assistant Director Ross Mackenzie, Production Manager R E Dearing, Producer Walter Shenson, Director Richard Lester
United Artists
Filmed at Pinewood Studios

1965
Missed opportunity # 1 : Help!

Dick Lester, director of *The Mouse on the Moon*, had been put in charge of the big screen version of *A Funny Thing Happened on the Way to the Forum*, in which Zero Mostel was chosen to repeat his Broadway performance. But Lester was keen to re-use Frankie somehow and the opportunity arose when casting his second Beatles vehicle, *Help!*, in 1965. Frankie had first encountered Paul McCartney at the opening of Mr Smith's nightclub in Manchester early in 1963, and later that year the Fab Four had clamoured for

John Lennon tries to out-camp the master and George Harrison enjoys a talent to amuse during Frankie's brief (and ultimately unseen) stint in *Help!* at Twickenham Studios, April 1965.

Frankie flees St Trinian's with fellow train robbers Reg Varney, Desmond Walter-Ellis, Arthur Mullard and Larry Martyn.

this successful comeback, Frankie's career had done a complete u-turn. Now, with his own hugely popular BBC Television series, the time was right, in the minds of Britain's film producers, to give this one-time no-hoper another bite at the big screen cherry. Suitably enough, Frank Launder and Sidney Gilliat, relaunching their St Trinian's franchise in October 1965 after a six-year break, turned to colour, cool Britannia attitude and, of course, the nation's top-rating satirist, Frankie Howerd, as the chief comic.

To be honest, Frankie's top-lining part in this colourful, gymslip-flashing romp isn't particularly rounded or sustained. Dora Bryan and Raymond Huntley have the lion's share of the narrative and Frankie's heavy involvement in the undercranked and farcically constructed train robbery climax reduces his contribution to that of a human cartoon. However, there are at least two or three brilliant, tailor-made sequences for him, while the film as a whole wallows in literally dozens of class acts.

Once considered the weak link in the series – and, indeed, stalling the leggy schoolgirls for a total of 14 years before *The Wildcats of St. Trinian's* limped into cinemas in 1980 – *The Great St. Trinian's Train Robbery* is a strange hybrid. It certainly lacks the charm of the first three black-and-white classics, which were steeped in 1950s warmth and blessed with such cosy, reassuring talent as Alastair Sim and Terry-Thomas. However, the Swinging Sixties infusion works very well indeed. If Dora Bryan's central Headmistress turn is so overplayed it practically jumps off the screen at you, then the cheerfully spiv-like George Cole milks his embryonic Arthur Daley swagger as Flash Harry, for the fourth and final time, to stunning effect.

Basically, the storyline resurrects the glorious girls of the old days courtesy of a Labour-backed grant being given to the dreaded establishment. The corrupt Minister (Huntley) is at the beck and call of la Bryan and a whopping £80,000 is therefore earmarked for the old place, a new establishment is purchased double-quick and the old teaching staff are rounded up. The

tickets to Frankie's Jersey summer show, eventually agreeing to stand throughout the performance because the venue was sold out. So they were more than happy for Frankie to be involved in *Help!*

Filming began on 23 February 1965 in the Bahamas, progressing to Austria and Twickenham Studios and ending with a week of location shooting at the beginning of May. On the afternoon of Thursday 22 April, Frankie turned up at Twickenham to start work with the Fab Four, his scenes being wound up the following day. He was cast as effete drama tutor Sam Ahab, with a then-unknown Wendy Richard playing one of his pupils, 'Lady Macbeth'. Sadly, Frankie's contribution didn't make the final cut. And if you're waiting for the fated footage to turn up as a bonus on any future DVD release, don't hold your breath; the story goes that the scene wasn't merely cut but somehow destroyed altogether.

The Great St. Trinian's Train Robbery

A week may be a very long time in politics but, for a British comedian, three years is almost a lifetime. Indeed, between Frankie's last headlining role in *The Cool Mikado* and group is blessed with the usual mix of battleaxes, drunks and glamour girls, the latter including Doctor Who's former grand-daughter, Carole Ann Ford, as the sexy young French mistress and Carry On stunner Margaret Nolan as the stripteasing art mistress.

Frankie, the good-natured baddie of the piece, is introduced at his place of work. As the prime mover behind the Alphonse of Monte Carlo hair-dressing saloon, he is justly proud of his award-winning Laurence Harvey cut. The gang of crooks narrative allows for the inclusion of several unsubtle and hastily ripped off elements from earlier British classics; indeed, Frankie's under-cover 'clip' joint clearly echoes the Galton and Simpson-scripted Peter Sellers comedy *The Wrong Arm of the Law* as well as the Norman Wisdom vehicle *On the Beat. The Lavender Hill Mob* is also occasionally borrowed from and, most glaringly of all, the entire criminal sub-plot is lifted from the already unoriginal Talbot Rothwell/Sid James caper, *The Big Job*, which was made the same year. Basically, in a thrilling pre-credits sequence, the details of a major bank robbery are revealed and the shadowy gang are spotted hiding the loot in a deserted old manor house. Of course, you've guessed it – it's the very same deserted old manor house that the St Trinian's mob move into.

Six Shepperton schoolgirls threaten to scratch Frankie's paintwork in a 1965 publicity shot for *The Great St. Trinian's Train Robbery.*

The train robbery element was hugely topical at the time and reflects the film's rather ill-advised attempt at being hip and groovy for the mid-sixties audience. Nothing dates quicker than topicality and, indeed, the whole underworld environment is marred by the most outlandish collection of 'up to the minute' gadgetry and crook-friendly devices. Frankie is often reduced to having earnest conversations with a television screen depicting nothing but a single eye and reverberating to the dispassionate tones of Stratford Johns. More toe-curling embarrassment follows: Frankie has to plonk a huge hair-dryer on his head to receive radio instructions and is also required to chat frantically through a shower tap. Chuck in

Falling back on his Rs: Alfred Askett meets Amber Spottiswood (Dora Bryan) in *The Great St. Trinian's Train Robbery.*

lacrosse racquets as aerials and much fiddling with an oversized instant camera which produces black-and-white snapshots of the gang's enemies, and one sees how yesterday's comic twist on the Space Age becomes today's groan-worthy relic of the Stone Age.

No matter, the dialogue, what little Frankie gets of it, is wonderfully droll and dryly delivered by the master comedian. And the gang itself is stuffed with the finest, hand-picked collection of skilled small-part players in the country: the heavily Brylcreemed Reg Varney in the Peter Sellers role, the oafish Arthur Mullard as the Danny Green substitute, the knowing Cyril Chamberlain, the diminutive Larry Martyn and the polished Norman Mitchell. 'For me it was an absolute

joy,' Mitchell remembered. 'It was a wonderful six weeks making that St Trinian's film. Mind you, Frankie was always moaning. He would come up to me at the studio and say, "You worked at Stratford, didn't you, Norman?" "Yes," I would say. "Huh," he would answer. "They wouldn't take me! RADA turned me down as well!" His major desire was to be taken seriously as an actor. Of course, his great skill was as a comedian but I always thought he was a very fine actor in some of his films and, besides, it takes a unique acting skill to deliver stand-up comedy the way Frankie did.

'He threw a party after we filmed the train robbery scenes. We arrived fairly early and Frankie was getting ready to show his guests the Alastair Sim film *Laughter in Paradise*. He asked me, "Do you think they would like this, Norman?" And I said, "Oh, come on, Frankie. People want to come and talk, they don't want to see a film. We've been filming all day as it is." He said, "I'm just worried that if they talk to me for too long they may get bored and go home!" That was the sort of bloke he was. A really charming person. His insecurity was real and very endearing. I shall never forget the time we all had on board that bloody steam engine. We were all cramped together – I'm a fat man as it is and Arthur Mullard was even fatter – and we had some great laughs.'

As well as his merrie band of brothers, Frankie is ably supported by his dubious daughters. With the money hidden in the new St Trinian's property it's essential for an insider or two to case the joint and find the best way to get the loot out. Frankie's two tearaway daughters are the ideal candidates – hand-selected as unlikely public schoolgirls to infiltrate the bowels of St T's. The youngest, Lavinia, is a typical St Trinian's urchin; the elder, Marcia, is typical of St T's sixth form girls – sex-mad. This one's boyfriend is a long-haired 'BBC bottle washer' who grooves with the chick, nods to the transistor radio and gets touchy-feely in the dark. Frankie, outraged at this sexual 'all-in wrestling', delivers his finest line of the movie when the hippie layabout complains that he's misunderstood 'just cos I'm a trend setter!' With perfect timing

John Gregson and Ian Hendry (taking a break from filming TV's *Gideon's Way*) join Frankie between *St. Trinian's* takes at Shepperton.

Frankie mutters, 'You look more like a bleeding Irish Setter to me!' This is class stuff!

The two titans on show here – Frankie and Dora Bryan – only have one scene of any importance together but, thankfully, it's a cracker. Frankie, masquerading as a monied nob (all smart suit and sophistication), drags the two sweeties – complete with brand-new uniforms – to meet the Head. The good manners are soon dropped, of course. Frankie's youngest blurts out the fact that her mum ran off with the milkman and drops big hints about what her older sister's favourite subject is. Frankie steals the scene with a host of dismayed reaction shots but loses the best laugh-line to Bryan – 'It's always good to have your Rs to fall back on, I always say!' But, again, his unscripted facial reaction to the shared innuendo is quite superb.

Sadly, although the film is fun-packed and Frankie enjoys himself hugely, the majority of his screen time is restricted to playful stunts. The celebrated Frankie characteristics – camp bluff and comic bluster – only appear at brief intervals. The gang's initial attempt at retrieving the money ends in disaster when the gang are pelted from above and Frankie himself, emitting a tasty 'Ooh!' as a net envelops him, is hit squarely in the face by a ripe tomato! Hardly Shakespeare, as Frankie was no doubt well aware.

The only remaining means of infiltrating the school is provided by the forthcoming Parents' Day. Putting themselves forward as caterers – and getting the job by undercutting the established firm – Frankie and the gang are on course to regain the loot when the typically inclement British weather dictates that the cringe-making display of Morris Dancing take place indoors. The speeded-up money-grabbing continues apace until a suspicious Morris Dancer peeps through the curtain, is hastily dragged behind it and replaced by a fully costumed Frankie. It's like Dick Van Dyke doing his bit of Old Bamboo in *Chitty Chitty Bang Bang* two years early. The clumsy, ever-smiling, bumbling new recruit staggers onto the stage, mutters 'I'll explain after 32 bars!' and throws himself into the dance.

The money is safely stowed in the van but then all hell breaks loose and both the staff and kids are on the crooks' trail. George Cole's Flash Harry and the sexy 16-year-olds are the hottest in pursuit, with Terry Scott's disinterested policeman and Colin Gordon's deadly earnest insurance man adding comic weight to a Dick Lester-style chase sequence in which trains are boarded, hand-carts pinched, engines mucked about with and the crooks' timetable sent spinning.

In the process, Frankie becomes a mere puppet in the larger universe of the action he is involved in, though he maximises the impact of his close-ups by overplaying with a vengeance. With the gang stuffed into the engine like the complete cast of *A Night at the Opera* and the kids foxing the bumbling adults at every turn, the farcical train business is beautifully brought to life and doesn't outstay its welcome despite the lengthy screen time it takes up. It's all, of course, a homage to the vintage silent days of Buster Keaton's *The General* and the knockabout antics of the Keystone Kops.

That Frankie, very much a dialogue-based talent, can pull off all these sight gags is

testament to his multi-faceted skills. However, he's clearly at his best with the character comedy and comes into his own once more by double-crossing his pals as soon as the opportunity arises. With a cheerful use of his 'And the best of luck!' catchphrase, he rapidly departs stage right as the boys get caught stage left. Frankie dons boot polish and a British Rail uniform to join the bemused Leon Thau in a British Rail walkout. The pair stroll past the police, the gang are less than happy and Frankie tugs a satirical forelock at the coppers with a Pakistani/Welsh cry of 'Knock them about democratically!' It's Frankie's final line and one to be treasured. And, unlike Alec Guinness in *The Lavender Hill Mob*, this ultra-charming crook gets away with the crime if not the money. The girls get that (much to Flash Harry's chagrin), as well as MBEs all round – which, in the film's most subtle and enjoyable gag, is commented on in a newspaper headline reading: 'A diabolical liberty, says Ringo.'

The film can be seen as a cross-over for Frankie, leaving behind his days as a reasonably successful star comedian in the Norman Wisdom tradition and proving him willing and able to muck in with the 'ensemble' school of British comedy. His performance is a well-rounded, understated yet typically flamboyant mix of all his familiar comic tricks with a real character binding them all together. Besides, there's a cheeky in-joke that's worth the price of admission alone. Used in only one scene, Frankie's criminal code-name is – wait for it – Toupée!

THE GANG: Alphonse of Monte Carlo aka Alfred Askett FRANKIE HOWERD, Gilbert REG VARNEY, Leonard Edwards DESMOND WALTER ELLIS, Willy the Jelly-Man NORMAN MITCHELL, Chips LARRY MARTYN, Maxie CYRIL CHAMBERLAIN, Big Jim ARTHUR MULLARD
THE SCHOOL: Amber Spottiswood DORA BRYAN, Mabel Radnage BARBARA COUPER, Veronica Bledlow ELSPETH DUXBURY, Magda O'Riley MAGGIE McGRATH, Susie Naphill MARGARET NOLAN, Drunken Dolly JEAN ST CLAIR, Albertine CAROLE ANN FORD, Flash Harry GEORGE COLE,

Georgina PORTLAND MASON, Marcia Askett
MAUREEN CROMBIF
Uncredited: INGRID BRETT
THE MINISTRY: Sir Horace,
the Minister RAYMOND HUNTLEY,
Bassett RICHARD WATTIS, Butters PETER
GILMORE, Culpepper Brown ERIC BARKER,
Gore-Blackwood GEORGE BENSON, The Lift
Man MICHAEL RIPPER, Truelove GODFREY
WINN, Miss Brenner LISA LEE, Dr Judd
EDWINA COVEN
OTHERS: Policeman TERRY SCOTT, Noakes
COLIN GORDON, Pakistani Porter LEON
THAU, Chairman MEREDITH EDWARDS, Monty
JEREMY CLYDE, Hutch AUBREY MORRIS, Mr
Parker WILLIAM KENDALL
The Voice STRATFORD JOHNS
Screenplay Frank Launder and Ivor Herbert,

inspired by the original drawings of the girls
and staff of St Trinian's by Ronald Searle, Music
composed and conducted by Malcolm Arnold,
'The Beat' by the Brothers Grimm, 'The Tango'
by Philip and Betty Buchel, Director of
Photography Kenneth Hodges, Additional
photography Bert Mason, Camera Operators
Herbert Smith and Dudley Lovell, Art Director
Albert Witherick, Make-up Phil Leakey,
Hairdresser Gladys Leakey, Costume Designer
Honoria Plesh, Editor Geoffrey Foot, Dubbing
Editor James Shields, Sound Recordists Cecil
Mason and Bob Jones, Assistant Directors Peter
Price and Anthony Waye, Production Manager
Eddie Pike, Producer Leslie Gilliat, Directors
Frank Launder and Sidney Gilliat
Braywild Productions
Filmed at Shepperton Studios

Frankie and co-
director Frank
Launder on
location for the
frenetic finale
of The Great St.
Trinian's Train
Robbery.

1967
Carry On Doctor

'If this is the National Health Service, take me back to the leeches!'   ***Francis Bigger***

It was only natural that, after Frankie's success in one celebrated comedy franchise, the longest running and most popular of all British film comedy series would come a-calling. The Carry On series, under the watchful eye of producer Peter Rogers and director Gerald Thomas, had over a ten-year period become one of the most financially successful fixtures of British filmmaking. Although popular in many far-flung parts of the world, their budgets were so economical that the films had already made a healthy profit after only a few days in UK cinemas. The late 1960s and early 1970s saw the series reaching its purplest patch and, although never becoming the major Carry On star that journalists even today label him as, Frankie was very much a part of this pinnacle in popularity.

Indeed, it is amazing that, with just two roles in the film series to his name, Frankie is continually lumped in with the likes of Sid James, Kenneth Williams and Charles Hawtrey as one of the key players in the slap and tickle series. When the Video Collection released the Rank-backed Carry On pictures on videotape in 1987, Howerd's was one of the prominent voices, along with Kenneth Williams and Windsor Davies, impersonated for the trailer. Even after Frankie's death, the back cover blurb of William Hall's biography, *Titter Ye Not*, screamed about the 'inimitable star of the classic Carry On films.'

He was, of course, hardly that and if it hadn't been for the unavailability of Kenneth Williams for *Carry On Up the Jungle*, Frankie's Carry On career would have been restricted to his guest star appearance in *Carry On Doctor*. However, it's fair to say that Frankie, much more than other high-profile guest artistes like Harry H Corbett, Bob Monkhouse or Phil Silvers, made a mark on the Carry On series that remains a unique and endearing one.

He was certainly on the wish-list of producer Peter Rogers. 'I had been an enormous fan of Frankie's for many years,' he says, 'and felt that films were not using him to the full advantage of both his talents as a performer and what he could offer us, his audience. I felt that the Carry Ons suited him perfectly.' The first film Rogers cast him in began life back in 1960, when Rogers registered the 'Doctor' title but decided to leave it untouched while the Doctor series from producer Betty Box (Peter's wife) continued to be popular. And by the time *Carry On Doctor* was seriously reconsidered in early 1967, it was conceived more as a tribute to *Carry On Nurse* than to the Doctor series. The original screenplay was to be filmed as 'Nurse Carries On Again', which was to be retained as one of the film's alternative titles.

In a letter dated 10 August 1967 Rogers wrote, 'Dear Frankie (if I may make so bold), Will you please read the enclosed script with a view to playing the part of Mr Bigger (with an 'I')? I'm sorry to have kept you waiting for so long but you know what typists are with holidays. I am keeping my fingers crossed and hoping. So will you please be prepared to meet and discuss the idea?' Frankie agreed and was rewarded with a healthy pay packet – half as much again as the fee regular leads Sid James and Kenneth Williams could expect. For a five-week period from 18 September until 20 October 1967 he was paid £7,500 with an additional £1,500 for each week over and above that and £300 for each day of any further broken weeks. Of course, with the regimental efficiency of the Carry On production staff, this additional payment was never a realistic prospect. The shooting was effortlessly completed on time and on budget by director Gerald Thomas and Frankie played out his role on stages C and B of Pinewood Studios, plus two days' location filming at Maidenhead Town Hall.

Peter Rogers enjoyed having Frankie in the film. 'The man was so lacking in charm that he almost charmed you – he grew on one like friendly moss!' Having injured himself while toiling in his garden, Rogers was walking with the aid of a stick on Frankie's first day at Pinewood. His first words to the producer

Anita Harris and Frankie relax on the Pinewood set of *Carry On Doctor*.

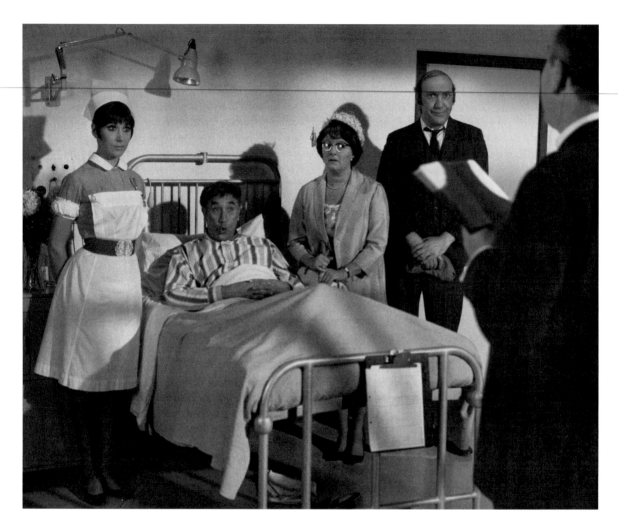

The bedridden Francis Bigger (Frankie) finally commits to the long-suffering Chloe (Joan Sims) in *Carry On Doctor*. Nurse Clark (Anita Harris) and Ken Biddle (Bernard Bresslaw) act as witnesses and the chaplain (Peter Jones) struggles with the vows.

were, 'Hello Peter – what did you do? Trip over your wallet?'

Shrewd as always, Rogers' hunch that Frankie would fit the Carry On style perfectly was dead right. Indeed, Carry On and *A Funny Thing Happened on the Way to the Forum* would be combined for what many consider Frankie's crowning achievement – Talbot Rothwell's *Up Pompeii!*. However, several important figures in Frankie's career considered his involvement in the Carry On films unwise. Eric Sykes dismisses them as too small and formulaic to allow Frankie's comedy to flourish. Sykes insists that 'Frankie was not an actor. He wasn't a Sid James or a Kenneth Williams. He was Frankie Howerd. His talent

was far too vast for those films!' However, generations of Carry On fans tend to disagree. Indeed, Frankie was touched more than most by the eternal Carry On magic. It gave him, if nothing else, regular exposure on television and the cool re-evaluation of the Carry Ons during the late 1980s certainly led to Frankie's renewed appeal to the student audiences who packed out his final live performances.

It comes as quite a surprise, then, to sit down and watch *Carry On Doctor* with your attention focused solely on Frankie's involvement. It's true that he's given a major character, the narrative is often based around his predicament and, indeed, the opening scene allows him a typically flamboyant bit of audience-address, but there are great swathes of the narrative that remove him from the action entirely. Indeed, having started his hospital career as part of the Men's Ward community alongside Bernard Bresslaw, Charles Hawtrey, Sid James and Peter Butterworth, Frankie is hastily removed and relocated in a private room. Thus, if the *Carry On Nurse* angle is to be applied to the entire film – which I think is fully justified – Frankie takes on the grouchy mantle of Wilfrid Hyde-White's troublesome Colonel from the earlier film. Certainly, Frankie's guarded, knowing bark of 'Oh no, you don't! I saw that film!' as sexy nurse Valerie Van Ost gets perilously close with a daffodil remains the most potent, freewheeling and joyous cinematic in-joke in the whole series. The entire film is geared to similar nods and winks and, though a knowledge of the original film is hardly necessary, it certainly enhances the comic set-pieces and characterisations and also the charmingly time-warped screenplay.

Despite his initial reluctance to tackle such a big part in an established film repertory company, Frankie fits the role of Francis Bigger like a glove. Talbot Rothwell, of course, was fully aware of the performer who had been cast as the self-important, charlatan faith healer – even the christian name of the character gives the game away in a 'Sid James playing Sid' sort of way. Though the basic characterisation could have been interchangeable with the acidic camp of Kenneth Williams, Rothwell gave it the distinctive Frankie stamp by incorporating familiar elements from the comedian's public persona.

Thus, during the immortal lecture sequence at the very beginning of the film ('What is mind? No matter … What is matter? Never mind!'), Frankie is given a hard-of-hearing assistant – à la his deaf accompanist on stage – in the shape of mutt-and-jeff spinster, Joan Sims. Not to mention the welcome interjection of that timeless old Frankie catchphrase from *Variety Bandbox* and beyond, 'You will be a-mazed!' And, thanks to Rothwell's brilliantly constructed screenplay, Frankie's continuous

exclamations of pain, suffering and discomfort actually give him an underlying narrative reason for his vocal clowning. Throughout the film, the shifting, wriggling and much-prodded Frankie is able to deliver juicy 'oohs!' with added acting realism, as in the classic ambulance sequence in which a fusillade of Frankie complaints is greeted by sandwich-chomping ambulance man Harry Locke with a nonchalant 'Hurts a bit, does it, sir?'

The memorable X-Ray interlude is another case in point. Frankie maximises the effect of the exploding equipment with not only a ready Rothwell quip – when asked to 'Smile!' he replies, through gritted teeth, 'What with?' – but also a trademark double-take. Almost looking into camera as he reacts to Valerie Van Ost's removal of his bed gown, Frankie the film star is very much to the fore. He is Frankie Howerd being Frankie Howerd in an unfamiliar Frankie Howerd environment. Matters medical had long proved a popular part of Frankie's stage act but to play a part within a tightly structured film narrative while still giving a 'Frankie Howerd' performance was something he had never done before. Where Gerald Thomas succeeded so cleverly was in allowing Frankie basically to do a television spot within a Carry On. As such, Frankie flirts with the rest of the cast on his own terms.

Nobody, before or since, was encouraged to mock the codes and conventions of Carry On. Here, however, the star turn is allowed to react with bemused amazement at all around him – Charles Hawtrey's phantom pregnancy, for instance – and even (shock! horror!) ridicule perhaps the most treasured of all Carry On signifiers by sarcastically imitating the immortal Sid James laugh. With his name listed top and separate from the other headliners during the opening credits, Frankie observes the madness of Carry On's inner world from the sidelines while still coming on as 'substitute' at odd intervals to play along with the rest.

Peter Rogers mantains that he was very careful in his choice of which of the established team members Frankie played opposite. He insisted that the similarly camp Kenneth Williams would cancel out Frankie's contribution and therefore removed scenes which featured the two together. In the scenes that remain, however, the pair interact quite splendidly. The Williams medical examination ('No bleeding, good!') and the knowing Howerd comment ('Just like the service round here!') is one of Rothwell's sweetest sparring dialogues. The majority of Frankie's involvement with Williams revolves around his misunderstanding of Williams' 'a week at the most' comment. It's not, as Frankie thinks, one week to live but merely one week to stay in his hospital bed. Thus, Rothwell can build up the hypochondriac interludes, with Frankie ultimately threatening to do Williams some major surgery-based damage when he finds out the truth.

The climactic operating theatre scene – in which Frankie, Sid and Bernard Bresslaw try to scare a confession out of Williams – is, of course, a darker counterbalance to the laughing gas antics from *Carry On Nurse*. Bleak, dangerous and quite disturbing, it's Frankie's performance that creates the comic tension here. Sid and Bernie seem to be going along with the ruse for a laugh but Frankie is deadly serious about the action. There's real malicious intent in his expression and it's that that creates such a powerful on-screen partnership with Williams – even the familiar Howerdism 'Not on your Nellie!' is tinged with satanic clout.

That same manic determination is also seen, to a lesser extent, opposite that other medical authority figure: Matron Hattie Jacques. Frankie is happiest, however, with characters who bring out his 'innate' superiority. That includes the romantic, hapless hero of Jim Dale, who bumbles into the ward, gets his 'thing' caught, allows Frankie the finest 'I beg your pardon?' of his entire career and proceeds to ram a hypodermic needle into his bruised posterior. And the 'poor old soul' of Joan Sims is the easy target for much of Frankie's suppressed rage and frustration. The initial interest in an unknown lady bearing flowers is dispelled with a disappointed 'Oh

Gawd!' when Sims is ushered in. Frankie's conviction that he's soon to die leads to the painfully hilarious 'hospital bed wedding ceremony' with deaf vicar (Peter Jones) and foot-shuffling witness (Bresslaw). The stuff of Carry On legend, it comes as no surprise when the mousey Sims turns into a vicious, all-hearing nag once the medical treatment is over.

However, perhaps the pick of Frankie's sparring partners is Sid James. There's a real sense of Frankie's intellectual pomposity meshing with Sid's working-class nous like hand in glove. The climactic 'revolt of the slaves' perfectly captures the irresistible comic tension that *Carry On Up the Jungle* would fully exploit. Akin to the community spirit of the Norman Hudis films, class barriers are seen to melt away when British males have a common cause. But it's the initial Frankie/Sid head-to-head that I would vote as the ultimate Carry On moment. Sid's laid-back (literally) bloke about town tries to make Frankie feel comfortable before dropping a truly classic bombshell. Desperately trying to look on the bright side after hearing about the late backache victim who occupied the hospital bed before him, Frankie enthuses about his 'nice warm bed' and Sid counters with 'Should be. They only took him out half an hour ago!'

Frankie's first foray into Carry On comedy is a timelessly brilliant one. For sure, he fits the ensemble playing perfectly, highlights the codes and conventions with ease and, arguably, delivers his finest, most natural slice of screen acting. You know you're watching a master craftsman at work when Frankie grabs hold of the narrative, twists it to his own ends and closes the film with his own, audience-addressing personality to the fore. Saddled with a nagging wife and unhappy prospects, Frankie trips up off-camera and is dragged back into hospital with renewed back pains. His resigned 'I shall be here for months' is squarely aimed at the less-than-concerned Joan Sims and the knowing Jim Dale but the end of the sentence – 'With any luck!' – is sent right down the barrel of the camera lens to the viewer. With a winning wink, Frankie is stretchered away and as the end rolls into view gives a subtle, finger-curling wave.

It's classic, heartwarming stuff; a true pro taking on the most popular comedy collective in the country and, at least for 90 minutes, remoulding it completely to fit his unique skill. A powerhouse comic performance and a true baptism of fire for Frankie's minute but towering contribution to the legend that is Carry On.

Francis Kitchener Bigger FRANKIE HOWERD, Charlie Roper SIDNEY JAMES, Mr Barron CHARLES HAWTREY, Dr Kenneth Tinkle KENNETH WILLIAMS, Dr Jim Kilmore JIM DALE, Nurse Sandra May BARBARA WINDSOR, Chloe Gibson JOAN SIMS, Ken Biddle BERNARD BRESSLAW, Matron HATTIE JACQUES, Nurse Clark ANITA HARRIS, Mr Smith PETER BUTTERWORTH, with JUNE JAGO, DEREK FRANCIS, DANDY NICHOLS, PETER JONES, DERYCK GUYLER, GWENDOLYN WATTS, DILYS LAYE, PETER GILMORE, HARRY LOCKE, MARIANNE STONE, JEAN ST CLAIR, VALERIE VAN OST, JULIAN ORCHARD, BRIAN WILDE, LUCY GRIFFITHS, GERTAN KLAUBER, JULIAN HOLLOWAY, JENNY WHITE, HELEN FORD, GORDON ROLLINGS

Screenplay Talbot Rothwell, Music composed and conducted by Eric Rogers, Title sketches by Larry, Director of Photography Alan Hume, Camera Operator Jim Bawden, Art Director Cedric Dawe, Make-up Geoffrey Rodway, Hairdresser Stella Rivers, Costume Designer Yvonne Caffin, Editor Alfred Roome, Dubbing Editor David Campling, Assistant Director Terry Clegg, Production Manager Jack Swinburne, Producer Peter Rogers, Director Gerald Thomas
Rank Film Productions
Filmed at Pinewood Studios

1969
Carry On Up the Jungle
'*I'm not baring my essentials!*'
Professor Inigo Tinkle

Carry On Doctor enjoyed a hugely successful tradeshow on 12 March 1968 and quickly took the British box-office by storm. Three films later, the team turned its attention to the

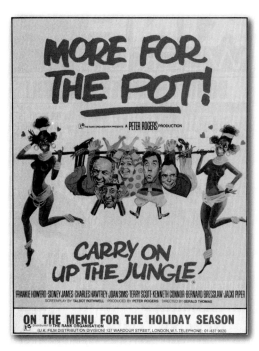

Money-mad trade advertisement for Frankie's second Carry On film.

provisionally titled *Carry On Jungle Boy* in the second half of 1969. Kenneth Williams, however, was proving difficult to obtain for this 19th big screen romp, having found his feet as the bitchy MC of the BBC series *International Cabaret*. He had also been given his own television series, *The Kenneth Williams Show*, and the filming schedule clashed with the dates Peter Rogers had booked at Pinewood. After lowering his sights and attempting to get Williams to play the cameo role that eventually fell to Charles Hawtrey, Rogers reluctantly faced the prospect of the first Carry On since *Cabby* (and, considering that *Cabby* was originally made as *Call Me A Cab*, in effect, the first Carry On ever) without Kenneth Williams.

The second problem facing the Carry On team concerned their first foray into television with the seasonal special, *Carry On Christmas*. Williams felt that the glorious innuendo of Carry On was fair enough for controlled cinema audiences but quite wrong for television, a medium to which audiences of any age could tune in. So there was a flamboyant gap in both the film due to be shot and the forthcoming television special (which, ironically, would be consumed by audiences first). The man to fill both gaps was, of course, Frankie Howerd.

Peter Rogers wrote to Frankie with a view to casting him in the next Carry On film and in a letter dated 21 August 1969 he commented, 'Here I am, cap in hand, tail between legs, eating humble pie, suffering from indigestion.' Much to-ing and fro-ing later, Rogers wrote again on 5 September: 'Rather than go through the rigmarole of pink pages and so on I am sending you Tolly's revisions ... so that you can read them straight away. You will see that he has pasted in type-written slips where necessary ... *It is the only copy.*'

Both Rogers and director Gerald Thomas felt that Frankie would not only require star treatment but also play outside and against the tightly knit squad of regular team actors. Frankie's agent, Beryl Vertue, forwarded a personal, hand-written note from Frankie, dated 30 September, in which the star commented: 'This is to reassure you that *no such thing* will happen. Believe me, I know well your attitudes to work, time schedules and shooting – thus, once I am agreed to be an employee of yours I would naturally expect to abide by all the rules. So now, stop worrying and put a bottle of champagne on ice! Love Frankie Howerd.'

Rogers was quick to respond, sending a telegram on 2 October to Frankie's holiday destination at the Sheraton-Malta Hotel, St. Julians, Malta. 'Message received and understood. Gerald now happy. I look forward to a happy association with you as usual, being one of your fans.' Rogers certainly must have been a fan, for Frankie's payment for the film was in excess of his previous fee for *Carry On Doctor* and in excess of almost anybody in Carry On history. Instead of the usual payment in whole, Frankie was earning £1,500 a week for a guaranteed six-week filming schedule. For each additional week that sum would be repeated with the codicil of £500 per day for any additional broken week of shooting. Again, the film came in on time and so, for 25 working days starting on 15 October, Frankie made a princely nine grand.

In terms of performance and use of the camera, this Frankie Howerd role is clearly far removed from his role in *Carry On Doctor*. There are no knowing looks to the audience, or dreadful puns accompanied by a bemused camera-look. Instead, Frankie is completely restricted to the narrative and interacts only with the characters within the story. Having said that, Frankie is a very strong comic persona and the Carry Ons would not and could not entirely change the actor into a standard Carry On type. His role may have been conceived for Kenneth Williams but – as we have seen from the correspondence above – the scriptwriter Talbot Rothwell was labouring over Frankie rewrites right down to the wire. Judging by the script, the role had been completely reworked and restructured in definitive Howerdese. If anything, the elongated vocal clowning is stepped up a gear from his previous Carry On and there's even time for a disgruntled 'Please yourselves!' Frankie's other beloved phrase – 'Not on your Nellie!' – is also included, twice, but on both occasions it falls, oddly enough, to Sid James rather than Frankie.

Again, it's in his partnership with Sid that Frankie shines brightest. With their characters moulded precisely in the laddish-versus-hifalutin' attitudes that Sid and Kenneth Williams had been perfecting over the past decade, Frankie slips into the age-old battle with consummate ease. From the outset, Sid is the incompetent slouch, chatting up the women, drinking the booze and conning the assembled eccentrics into thinking he's a Great White Hunter. Frankie, on the other hand, is the very embodiment of sophistication, a character whose stint in the jungle must be complemented with the finery of high living and the courtly codes of an exclusive London club. His acidic asides pinpoint Sid as 'vulgar!' from the word go and before long his disapproving comments about the great man being as 'common as muck!' are uttered within ear shot. Frankie's pacifism rests uneasily opposite Sid's gun-toting warrior and it's a real hate-hate, class v class situation throughout – the African Queen against

the Humphrey Bogart-type, if you like.

To put it simply, both are 'fascinated by rare and exotic birds' but not the same ones. Indeed, the loggerheads conflict between them – the cocky wide-boy struggling to bamboozle the learned Professor – sets up the film's comic highlight, the immortal 'mad elephant' exchange. Sid gets the last laugh on this occasion in a screenplay whose cracking gags

are split fairly evenly among the two headlining stars.

Of course, both Joan Sims and Kenneth Connor had worked with Frankie extensively over the years and there's a real sense of professional enjoyment in the ornithological double act he performs with Connor. The two had played *A Funny Thing Happened on the Way to the Forum* countless times; indeed, it

As Professor Inigo Tinkle in *Carry On Up the Jungle.*

Claude Chumley (Kenneth Connor), Lady Bagley (Joan Sims), Upsidasi (Bernard Bresslaw), June (Jacki Piper), Professor Tinkle and Bill Boosey (Sid James) hoist by their own petard in *Carry On Up the Jungle.*

was that show which preoccupied Connor for much of his five-year sabbatical from the Carry On series which he finally broke with this film. Following their bird-related discussion about tits – with Frankie musing that in Africa you only get the 'occasional black one' – Connor is dispatched to use his binoculars while Frankie spies lustfully on Sims in her makeshift shower, finally turning to medical help to stop himself 'getting too excited'. Discovering the perfect cure, he delivers probably the most risqué gag in the series so far: 'Pickett's Muscular Elixir. Eases stiffness – just the thing!' It seems fitting that Frankie, an outsider to the main team, should be allowed to up the innuendo ante.

As with Williams in *Carry On Camping*, Frankie is clearly interested in the opposite sex but feels the whole sordid business is far beneath his social standing. Sims is quite clearly gagging for it, whether it comes from Frankie's naïve boffin or Sid's rough-and-ready man's man. As a result she brushes aside clod-hopping social clangers such as Frankie's observation that she reminds him of something in an English meadow; a babbling brook, he hastens to point out, not a cow. In perhaps the film's pivotal scene – the rogue snake loose in Sims' undergarments routine – it takes a comic master of rare breed to make the simple act of removing his hands from below the table and pouring a drink such a hilarious vignette in a sequence that is already, thanks to Sims' range of discomfited facial expressions, rip-roaringly funny. Indeed, Frankie, as guest artiste, is allowed the climactic tag-line, about something 'rubbing her up the wrong way.'

A quick glimpse of 'milky thigh' and a crafty flick through a naughty French magazine may reveal Frankie's dormant sexual desires but, as with many Carry On characters, the first sign of sexual freedom coming his way for real brings down the emotional shutters automatically. Frightened of the jungle and keen to get a bit from almost anybody, Sims literally throws herself at the repressed bird-watcher – a comically passionate relationship examined even more carefully in a lengthy, tent-bound sequence edited from the final print.

As with the production of *Carry On Doctor*, Sims and Howerd were continually corpsing on the Pinewood set. Joan explains that 'At one stage Frank and I had to sit side by side and chat about the immortal "vind-screen viper" and the fact that the giraffe had such a long neck because its head is so far from its body... all that wonderful silliness from Tolly Rothwell. Well, we just couldn't do it. Gerry Thomas was saying, "Come along dears, come along. We have to get this in the can by the end of the day." But it was just impossible. Frank and I couldn't look at each other without laughing. I did everything in my power to control myself. I was pushing my fingernails into my palms, thinking unpleasant thoughts... all to no avail. Finally we managed to get the scene finished after what seemed like dozens of takes, certainly many more than was usual on the Carry Ons. If you watch the film today you can almost see me lose it. It was just that awful hound-dog expression of Frank's. He was a very funny man. Who wouldn't have cracked?'

Meanwhile, within the plot, the hinted sexual liaison with Sims gets ever closer. Frankie is quick to downplay his eagerness under a guise of sophisicated detachment, gingerly suggesting that any such idea as sharing a tent is 'Unprintable!' And the climactic encounter with the natives presents the superior, upright,

totally British Frankie in full flight of camp fancy. The Nosha tribe sling the Brits into the cooking pot and ultimately become bewitched by Howerd's 'miraculous doings'. For only the second time in the film, Frankie is released into his on-stage persona, actually performing an act for the wide-eyed tribesmen.

The other native population is far more appealing, at least to Connor and Sid, for it comprises the statuesque Valerie Leon and her delicious Lubbie-Dubbies. Faced with the prospect of getting married and attempting to impregnate the entire tribe, Frankie's natural shyness and desire for cleanliness shows through. This is the sort of thing that happens among 'certain classes' and the enforced display of sexual prowess unleashes a torrent of cherishable Howerdisms. To Charles Hawtrey's 'and so on and so on' account of the relentless wedding nights, Frankie, awestruck, mutters, 'Yes, well after two weeks of that it will need sewing on!' The Lubbie-Dubbie venue is home to the mythical (and totally unconvincing) Oozlum Bird, which gets Frankie's pulses racing ('I can clearly see its oozle!'), but the scene is basically just an excuse for the old queens (Hawtrey and Howerd) to taste forbidden fruit and try to out-Sid Sid James.

Frankie himself clearly enjoyed the

Professor Tinkle (Frankie) is molested in *Carry On Up the Jungle*. Boosey (Sid James) finds the natives far from revolting.

experience of returning to the Carry On series. In a letter dated 21 November 1969, he wrote to producer Peter Rogers, 'Dear Peter, I tried to phone you before I left the studio on Thursday afternoon but was unable to contact you so I am writing you this brief note to thank you for a very happy film, in fact, the happiest I have ever done, and to say that if there is anything I can do nearer the release date to help with publicity I shall be happy to do so. I hope the results of the filming will be successful for all concerned and since the last time I worked for you was in October 1967, exactly two years ago, perhaps I may look forward to a similar pleasure in October 1971. All the very best. Yours sincerely, Frankie Howerd. PS For much more money, of course. PPS For very little more. PPPS In fact practically nothing!' The minor pre-filming wrangles had clearly been forgotten, and Rogers replied accordingly on the 27th. 'My dear Frankie, It was very kind of you to write to me telling me how much you enjoyed working on *Jungle*. I must say you're bloody good in the film and I am relieved to feel that I personally may perhaps be back in your favour. Yours sincerely, Peter Rogers.'

Publicity, in the end, tended to focus on the glamour girls, although Frankie was prominently featured in *Woman* magazine of all things. The film enjoyed a successful press show on 6 April 1970 at the Odeon Haymarket; a trade show followed two days later prior to general release and major box-office success. Frankie relished the Carry Ons and, interviewed on the set of the big screen version of *Up Pompeii* in 1970, he said, 'They're such professional people to work with. It's also good to be part of a team, as it reduces the ego. It tends to stop you becoming self-centred when the comedy is shared.'

Ironically, Frankie would never return to the Carry On series. Any chance of his hinted-at reappearance in 1971 – and he would have been ideal for a role in that year's *Carry On Matron* – was out of the question by that stage. His small screen popularity in Rothwell's *Up Pompeii!* had kick-started an entirely new series which kept Frankie fully occupied throughout the early 1970s. For Frankie it really was a case of up, up and away!

Professor Inigo Tinkle FRANKIE HOWERD, Bill Boosey SIDNEY JAMES, Tonka CHARLES HAWTREY, Lady Evelyn Bagley JOAN SIMS, Jungle Boy TERRY SCOTT, Claude Chumley KENNETH CONNOR, Upsidasi BERNARD BRESSLAW, June JACKI PIPER, with VALERIE LEON, REUBEN MARTIN, EDWINA CARROLL, VALERIE MOORE, CATHI MARCH, DANNY DANIELS, YEMI AJIBADE

Screenplay Talbot Rothwell, Music composed and conducted by Eric Rogers, Director of Photography Ernest Steward, Camera Operator James Bawden, Art Director Vetchinsky, Make-up Geoffrey Rodway, Hairdresser Stella Rivers, Costume Designer Courteney Elliott, Editor Alfred Roome, Dubbing Editor Colin Miller, Assistant Director Jack Causey, Sound Recordists R T MacPhee and Ken Barker, Production Manager Jack Swinburne, Producer Peter Rogers, Director Gerald Thomas
Rank Film Productions
Filmed at Pinewood Studios

1970
Up Pompeii

'Honestly! You have to watch every word you say around here!' **Lurcio**

Indeed you do. With a script banged out from the crudest rock around, Sid Colin wrings every last corny old gag and totally unsubtle single entendre from the basic Talbot Rothwell scenario. Nestling somewhere between the flamboyant camp of *Carry On Cleo* and the Latin-bashing satire of *Monty Python's Life of Brian*, Frankie's attack on the laughter and lust of the Roman Empire is a one-track-minded and one-star-moulded comic powerhouse.

Obviously, one comes to the film with half-remembered concepts and half-hearted expectations from Rothwell's BBC sitcom, and naturally the film wallows in the format quite happily. Interviewed on set in November 1970, Frankie commented, 'You have to stick exactly to the script for technical reasons. I don't

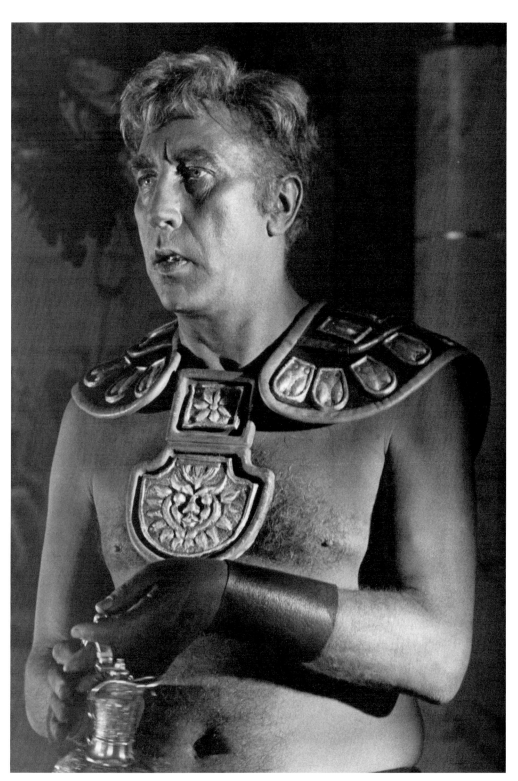

'There's only two things that might give me away!' Frankie as a Nubian eunuch in the big screen version of *Up Pompeii*.

Bare-faced cheek with Frankie and unwrapped friend in *Up Pompeii.*

deviate from the script at all on the film. I still talk into camera and take it into my confidence. But it also calls for a deeper acting performance than on TV.'

It wasn't just Frankie's concentration that had to change, however. There are many more alterations on display, not least in the supporting company. Michael Hordern, a veteran of Dick Lester's film version of *A Funny Thing Happened on the Way to the*

Forum, comes across, surprisingly, as rather uneasy and uncomfortable in his central role as Frankie's boss Ludricus. The delectable Barbara Murray (in her finest film role since Ealing's *Passport to Pimlico* in 1949) smoulders beautifully as Hordern's sex-starved wife, Ammonia. The couple's children – brought to life by Kerry Gardner and Georgina Moon on the box – are played here by a delightfully effete Royce Mills and mouthwateringly wanton Madeline Smith. Smith's interpretation of the role is impressive for a number of reasons, notably because the script calls for her to be a complete little raver as opposed to the naïve figure of the television version.

Caught in the clinches with boxer Billy Walker as Prodigius and Kenny Rodway as the equally contrived Rumpus, Smith's sexual appetite knows no bounds. Indeed, there's more than a glimpse of nudity, certainly fitting for the 'Hey there, orgy girl' setting of the movie but rare for a mainstream British comedy released in 1971. The Carry Ons, for example, would never show as much. As Frankie commented in the film's press release, the girls are 'dressed in little more than innuendos'. Carry On starlet Sally Douglas, as the aptly named Titta, is one of the most outstanding assets in the film, as is another Carry On lovely, Laraine Humphrys, as the wide-eyed innocent, Flavia ('What Flavia? Vanilla!'). There's also a torrent of smut-based misunderstanding between Frankie and Adrienne Posta's nubile Scrubba. And the raucous orgy sequence yields one of Frankie's finest moments, when his comments to camera about the guests' marvellous fancy dress costumes are interrupted by the appearance of a young man and his gorgeous companion, flaunting her extremely naked breasts. 'See what I mean?' Frankie says. 'They're two fellas…'

As in the television series, however, Frankie's Lurcio is a complicated sexual figure. He's desperate for a bit but always counters his lust with a misplaced show of superiority and disinterest. He throws himself into danger to protect his master – blacking up as a Nubian eunuch ('There's only two things that might give me away!') and snogging the delectable Julie Ege with suction skills picked up from playing wind instruments. During this saucy interlude we get a whiff of Frankie the wannabe lover, a whiff counter-balanced by his continual rebutting of Scrubba's all-too-obvious invitations to share a moment of passion. It's this wonderful contrast which makes Frankie's character so lovable and charming. One minute he is the worldly wise bloke who witnesses sexual depravity at its most Roman, the next he's the deeply shocked slave who is affronted when his innocent, throwaway comments are continually misconstrued by Posta's scantily clad bit of stuff.

Even the cameraman shows more interest in Posta, lingering on her breasts as Frankie, aggrieved that the young lady seems to be considered more interesting than the star, pops into view and promises that there will be plenty more of those later in the film. It's all playful and upbeat but against the grain of Pompeii's free-and-easy sexual lifestyle. Indeed, the climactic volcano engulfs everybody but him at the film's close and even swallows up the lovely Scrubba, who was finally beginning to hold some sexual interest for our hapless hero. Frankie's escape proves his innocence and virtue in body at least. To adapt one of the film's corniest gags, Frankie is the classic hero of a British sex comedy – 'always chaste but never caught'!

The basic plot – for what it's worth – revolves around Lance Percival and a missing scroll detailing a list of senators who would willingly kill the Emperor Nero. It's the ultimate comic McGuffin, presenting seemingly endless opportunities for double-cross, triple-cross and false loyalties, as well as presenting Frankie with ample chance to comment on the phallic appearance of both the scroll and his missing cucumber, which Percival ends up with instead. Percival and the monstrous Bill Fraser are larger than life but convincingly ruthless villains and the success of Frankie's throwaway performance relies heavily on the solid believability of the baddies at the centre of the story. The audience and, indeed, Frankie the performer are well aware that it's just a film and there's no *real* danger, but the skill of Frankie's multi-faceted performance needs interludes of genuine panic and danger in order to function. The jokes are corny and dreadful but the actors rightly treat the script like Shakespeare.

References to homosexuality abound and not just in the camp and queeny context of the TV series. Barbara Murray isn't shocked when she thinks her son fancies Frankie; she merely believes that the slave is too old for her little boy. Indeed, Frankie is indignant at her age difference comment more than anything else. His pointed and bitchy cry of 'Saucy cow!' speaks volumes. Ageing queendom is pointed up throughout. Kenneth Cranham's hippie god-worshipper calls Frankie 'Grandad' while Lance Percival, turning on the charm to get back his scroll, is misconstrued as a wanton shirt-lifter. The misunderstanding about what Percival is after – 'It's about this long'/'Flattery will get you nowhere' – remains one of the most impure moments of pure comedy in the film.

What makes *Up Pompeii* the Movie Experience such a joy from start to finish is the fact that Frankie, always the focal point of Rothwell's 30-minute TV scripts, hasn't changed his performance one bit for the film version. (Notwithstanding his comments above about a 'deeper' performance.) He ambles through the action, sending up the entire concept, revealing the film as a film at every juncture and narrating the story like an am-dram production of *A Funny Thing Happened on the Way to the Forum*. He is the master. Frankie's ego is exposed right from the start as his granite-carved name on the opening credits is deemed too small ('Don't be ashamed of it!'). It's almost as if television stardom is being translated into film stardom before our very eyes as Frankie's name suddenly fills the screen and Frankie mutters 'All right, don't go mad!'

Like a tongue-in-cheek version of Alfred Hitchcock's *The Lady Vanishes*, the ominously smoking volcano, the market place and the entire landscape of Pompeii are then painstakingly detailed in an all-too obvious model. Thankfully, this obvious model is quickly revealed as such when Frankie, complete in fetching toga, looms into view from behind the scenery. It's just another movie and Frankie takes great glee in mocking the 'expensive' set with an insincere

'Copulatum expensium, as we Pompeiians say!'

Thus, even before the brilliant close – in which all the dead Pompeiians reappear as contemporary tourists inspecting the petrified remains of themselves – Frankie is seen as immortal and above it all. Halfway through, the larger-than-life Frankie reappears, explaining that an intermission was planned at this point 'but it isn't a terribly long film' and therefore allowing the cast to continue. It's almost Pythonesque in its abuse of the film medium, but tempered with the rougher, more worldly wise stance of a corny old vaudevillian getting away with murder. There's a delicious joy in Frankie's cry to his captors, 'I'm a miserable pleader!', only for the line to be repeated a bit later and counter-balanced with Frankie's dismayed, 'Oh, I've done that gag. You see, I'm so upset I'm forgetting my part!'

Earlier, when the initial search is on for the slave with the scroll, Percival stumbles into the orgy, takes Barbara Murray aside and gives an extremely vague description of the wanted man. Pulling his face every which way to become as unlike the description as possible, Frankie finally gives in, stares into camera and moans, 'If I don't get an Oscar for this lot there's no justice!'

Sadly, the Academy weren't watching, but it takes an astounding character comedian to be able to play a role – admittedly one tailor-made for him – within a story and repeatedly emerge from it while continuing to interact with characters who are totally unaware of the audience involvement angle. Frankie's strengths and weaknesses as an actor are painfully and deliciously on display. Indeed, his pseudo-tortuous interlude in the prison cells – his cry of 'What a terrible place!', his musings about how to escape and his embittered calls to the gaoler – are laughably inept. They are all the more treasurable and enjoyable for that reason. Frankie was a great screen actor so long as he played himself. He could use the camera, script and fellow cast members totally to his advantage – and, as often as not, much to their disadvantage. As long as his cynical swords were sharp and perpetually

A rare shot of Frankie in Lurcio garb and Vincent Price between takes on *The Abominable Dr Phibes*, Elstree Studios, December 1970.

unsheathed there was no one to touch him.

This film is arguably the perfect example. From the moment the stunning title song starts up this is ultimate Frankie movieland: a badly written, cheaply made rag-bag of the corniest gags in the whole wide world, served up perfectly by a shambolic Everyman with a saucy glint in his roving eye. The tacked-on tourist ending may seem a little flat but it's good fun and allows Frankie one final closing monologue in the guise of a tourist guide. Skilfully advertising the movie, suggesting that the audience tonight shouldn't keep it to themselves ('If you've enjoyed it, tell your friends!') and ending with a nod to the nation's desire to see loads of naked flesh via the really rather tame Pompeiian murals, this is a classic transfer from small screen to large.

In it, Frankie – cannily acting as a director of the production company as well as star of the picture – could at last let the full sauciness of Ancient Rome be committed to film. Moreover, it proved that the great British public would happily queue up in the rain and pay hard-earned money to see a variation on something which was, in effect, what they had seen for free in their living rooms. The success of this film and Hammer's *On the Buses* opened the TV spin-off floodgates which didn't close again until 1980. And, for Frankie, it proved the launch pad for his most sustained and popular film work. Forget Luke Skywalker and the *Stars Wars* trilogy. This was to be the Frankie trilogy. Akin to the Carry On series, the notion was to keep the jokes and change the costumes, providing a historical journey for the Lurcio family in the style perfected later by the various *Blackadder* series.

Up Pompeii was a resounding success. Just as well, really, for the second film had already been rushed into production, despite Frankie's comment on the *Pompeii* set that 'We may do another comedy in the Up series but I'll wait and see how this one goes with the public first.' Although the films would come to an end with the First World War instalment in 1972 (making an amazing three films in 18 months), the essence of the family tree idea would limp on into Frankie's final BBC sitcom, *Then Churchill Said To Me*, where the 'Lurcio' figure was let loose on the Second World War.

The film version of *Up Pompeii* was the starting point, but now, historically and hilariously, Frankie would be catapulted into another historical clime. Importantly, this was a historical period with no television format or structure to look to. It was simply *Pompeii* with crusaders. The rest is, quite literally, history.

....

Did You Know? A five-part cartoon serialisation of *Up Pompeii*'s plot was made freely available to local newspapers as a way of promoting the film.

....

Cast in order of disappearance: Lurcio FRANKIE HOWERD, Ludicrus Sextus MICHAEL HORDERN, Ammonia BARBARA MURRAY, Nero PATRICK CARGILL, Bilius LANCE PERCIVAL, Voluptua JULIE EGE, Prosperus Maximus BILL FRASER, Cassandra RITA WEBB, Gorgo BERNARD BRESSLAW, Scrubba ADRIENNE POSTA, Erotica MADELINE SMITH, Nausius ROYCE MILLS, Odius IAN TRIGGER, Villanus AUBREY WOODS, Priest HUGH PADDICK, M.C. ROY HUDD, Flavia LARAINE HUMPHRYS, Fat bather GEORGE WOODBRIDGE, Steam slave DEREK GRIFFITHS, Major Domo BARRIE GOSNEY, Boobia VERONICA CLIFFORD, Biggia GAYE BROWN, First Christian KENNETH CRANHAM, Second Christian ANDY FORRAY, Gaoler RUSSELL HUNTER, Plumpa IRLIN HALL, Procuria LALLY BOWERS, Vinus KEN WYNNE, Satyr MISCHA DE LA MOTTE, Rumpus KENNY RODWAY, Noxius ROBERT TAYMAN, Prodigius BILLY WALKER Uncredited: Titta SALLY DOUGLAS, Sutra LAURA MARSHALL, Belly dancer CORINNE SKINNER, Rant-a-Girls LYNN MARSHALL, PATSY SNELL and ANN COLLINS, Orgy attendee PETER DEAN, Nero's girl CAROL HAWKINS, Orgy girl SAMMI WINMILL, Virginia VALERIE STANTON Screenplay Sid Colin based on an idea by Talbot Rothwell, Music Carl Davis, Title song by Ken Howard and Alan Blaikely, Director of Photography Ian Wilson, Camera Operator Herbert Smith, Art Director Seamus Flannery, Editor Al Gell, Sound Editor Stephen Warwick, Make-up Richard Mills, Hairdresser Eileen Warwick, Costume Designer Penny Lowe, Assistant Director Allan James, Production Supervisor Pat Green, Executive Producer Beryl Vertue, Associate Producer Terry Glinwood, Producer Ned Sherrin, Director Bob Kellett Associated London Films Filmed at Elstree Studios

1971
Up the Chastity Belt

In 1971 Thelma Graves had arguably the easiest job in British cinema. You may never have heard of her but this dedicated soul was lucky enough to be the casting director on this film and its predecessor. As if to stress the fact that Ned Sherrin hoped to catapult his star, Frankie Howerd, into a long-running series to rival the Carry Ons, the cast was awash with supporting actors held over from the Roman caper. And, despite the fact that Frankie's series didn't even get out of school by comparison to the Carry Ons' marathon run, there remains an endearing sense of continuity throughout the Up trilogy.

A glance at even the most minor of supporting parts – whether glam (Sammi Winmill) or authoritative (Barrie Gosney) – will reveal that a sense of acting continuity was at the forefront of the filmmakers' minds. Roy Hudd, who had turned on the cockney charm as the less-than-fair wrestling MC in the first film, returned as the Max Miller-esque locksmith, Nick the Pick. Rita Webb, replacing television's Jeanne Mockford as the ragged

soothsayer last time, kicks up a storm as the grotesque and loud-mouthed Maid Marian, while Hugh Paddick, as a deliciously effete Robin Hood, returns following a brief bit as a High Priest in the *Pompeii* epic. Derek Griffiths, who had contributed a wordless but memorable cameo as the Roman sauna boy, reappears here as the cool hippie dude during the orgy interlude. The well-endowed Veronica Clifford, musclebound Billy Walker and scenery-chewing Bill Fraser are back on board too. Even Lance Percival, clearly unavailable for a leading role but happy to settle for a sitting-down part following a serious car accident immediately after finishing work on *Up Pompeii*, crops up all too briefly as a salacious, seventies-style journalist.

Strangely enough, though, the core members of the family employing our hapless hero are almost entirely recast. Only young Royce Mills – as the effeminate son who is keener on writing ballads than chasing girls – is retained from the previous escapade. (Among other things, Mills happily discusses his love for Max Miller's old bit of stuff, Mary from the dairy, and chucks tact out of the window when he reveals Frankie's age to be over 40!) The young love interest, previously brought to life by the shapely Madeline Smith, called for a new actress here and the successful applicant was none other than *Golden Shot* girl, Anne Aston.

Gretel (Judy Huxtable) and King Richard (Frankie) doing things by the book in *Up the Chastity Belt*.

Frankie surrounded by unpleasant peasants Fred Emney, Dave King and Johnny Vyvyan in *Up the Chastity Belt*.

As she explained at the time, the television hostess seized the opportunity to make her feature film début opposite Frankie Howerd's saucy serf. 'I did meet Frankie before, when he was on *The Golden Shot* singing the theme song of *Up Pompeii* one week. Then I heard him on radio saying that his new film started in April, so I asked my agent to enquire about auditions.' Aston plays her part with the perfect mix of dewy-eyed innocence and blonde-bombshell temptress, finally settling down, sans chastity belt, to a life of pleasure with Frankie himself. Not since *A Touch of the Sun* – discounting the camp booby prize of *The Cool Mikado* – had Frankie actually finished a movie by getting the girl.

Anna Quayle, whose disappointingly sporadic film career included *A Hard Day's Night* and *Chitty Chitty Bang Bang*, replaces Barbara Murray as the curt and overbearing mistress of the family, while Graham Crowden seems to surprise even himself with a brilliantly broad character turn as the bumbling and incompetent Sir Coward de Custard. As with Michael Hordern's 'silly old fool', Crowden is the archetypal ineffectual paterfamilias; indeed, the conception of his daughter 23 years before is cheekily described by Frankie, in one of his bitchiest asides, as 'Custard's last stand!' In the film's pressbook, Crowden maintained that 'I've had a field day in this film, meeting people whose work I've enjoyed so much, such as Roy Hudd and Lance Percival, and opening up a branch of the entertainment world I did not know before. And meeting Frankie again. He is a kind man, highly individual and, like all these big comedians, always vastly entertaining.'

Despite the totally spiffing cast – also including, this time round, such notable guest stars as Fred Emney, Dave King, critic Godfrey Winn and 'the sexiest woman in the world', Eartha Kitt – the desperate, gag-on-gag script tends to drag the majority of the performers through the mire. Unlike the free-and-easy *Up Pompeii*, the format doesn't quite lend itself to the period and Sid Colin – assisted, amazingly, by our finest comedy writers, Ray Galton and Alan Simpson – merely chucks in every historical vignette and half-remembered Olde English custom in the hope that Frankie's sheer comic clout will save the day.

In a quite awe-inspiring central performance, Frankie very nearly does. In fact, let's be honest. Without him this film would be impossible to sit through and very nearly impossible to imagine. It's a tailor-made rag-bag of feeble jokes, semi-saucy situations and delicious overacting, pitched somewhere between *Carry On Henry* and *Monty Python and the Holy Grail* – and also, incidentally, establishing the blueprint for *Blackadder*.

The plot, such as it is, is lifted wholesale from at least two sources. The narrative device of two brothers separated at birth, one becoming regal (Richard the Lionheart here) and the other a serf, comes from Mark Twain's *The Prince and the Pauper*. Obviously, with his film star pulling-power at its peak, Frankie is adept at playing both roles. Lurkalot – a close relation of Lurcio of course – is delivered in typical Frankie style, complete with asides to the camera, smutty observations and bucketloads of Howerdisms. Richard the Lionheart calls for a bit more (though not much) acting skill. A foppish dandy obsessed with sex, he camps about in the background ('I'm so bored … Oh, sod this for a lark, I'm going on a crusade!') and then works his way through the Kama Sutra, first with rubber-limbed Eartha Kitt and latterly with blonde Germanic bit (and Mrs Peter Cook mark two) Judy Huxtable. Moreover, the pre-credits sequence borrows happily from *Tom Jones*. A detailed Bayeaux tapestry-style design is used

to relate the story of the twin births, skilfully heralding the misunderstandings and misrepresentations that aren't resolved within the film's narrative (and, indeed, within Frankie's own mind) until very near the end of the fun.

The story is pretty flimsy – indeed, totally immaterial – for, once again, Ned Sherrin and his team are aware that their film hangs by a single thread, namely, Frankie Howerd. Believe me, some of the 'comic' exchanges are truly awesome in their awfulness. In a 'doth' and 'dost'-peppered duologue with Royce Mills, for example, Frankie earnestly agrees, 'Oh, I dost, I dost … I do all the dusting round here!' If nothing else, however, the film allows Frankie to emulate one of his great comedy heroes, Sid Field, in a role akin to Field's in the historical costume comedy *The Cardboard Cavalier*. It may be a different war, but the essence of poor-boy-making-good and hobnobbing with the nobs is virtually the same.

As with the Pompeiian epic, the film only hits true heights of hilarity when Frankie's cynical commentary on the action is permitted to run riot. When posing for his artistically inclined mistress, a fraught Frankie interrupts a load of wordy exposition with a cry of 'I must speak!' It's not that he has anything particular to say but that, simply, 'Yes, it's my turn!' The film really comes alive at these moments, when Frankie the consummate professional completely sidesteps the job of telling the story in order to comment on the telling of the story itself.

His professional jealousy at the unfair distribution of the film's best moments bubbles up as the villainous antics of Bill Fraser's evil character are listed for us. After much condemnation of the fellow's sexual dalliances and wanton behaviour, Frankie bitterly bemoans the fact that he has 'the best part in the film!' It's *Hellzapoppin*' lunacy with a real slice of British ham chucked on top. Indeed, the fun edges towards Hope/Crosby/Road territory as Frankie heads off to the crusades. During a waterlogged journey across the ocean (or at least the water tank at Elstree), Frankie

Frankie with director Bob Kellett on the Elstree set of *Up the Chastity Belt*.

is joined in the water by a very contemporary-looking (and sounding) bunch of Indians. After a few disbelieving beats, Frankie looks into camera and mutters, 'They're not supposed to be in the film!'

Earlier, when Bill Fraser's gang of baddies is in hot pursuit of the fair Anne Aston, Frankie prepares himself for a corny old visual. Luring the baddies into his den and making ready to trick them with the old locked door/unlocked door ruse, Frankie complains to himself about his own lack of originality. 'Everyone's seen that gag!' he mutters, before hearing an inaudible voice from the crowd. 'You haven't?' he replies. 'Well, I'll carry on then!' 'These old gags are the best!' he concludes. If scarcely that, the reliance on well-worn vaudevillian business and schoolyard smut still serves Frankie very well indeed. Morecambe and Wise made frequent use of the well-scripted, 'off the cuff' put-down aimed at their starry guests, and here Frankie has every right to condemn the brilliantly loud interpretation of Maid Marian from British comedy's favourite harridan, Rita Webb. Reacting with pin-point timing and looking as shocked and outraged as he possibly can, Frankie spits, 'To think we could have got Julie Andrews for the same money...'

En route back to Blighty, the sundered twins finally meet and the scene is set for hilarious confusion and much Shakepeare-style comedy of mistaken identity. Frankie's interaction with the supporting cast is flawless throughout, throwing up some priceless encounters with David Battley's nonsensical 'very vocal local yokel' and Fred Emney's drunken old slob, forever dismissing his claims to be King Richard. Some interludes are unforgettable, notably Frankie's brilliant attempt at playing the court jester ('I have to do everything around here!'), but the Swinging Sixties orgy sequence is a tad overdone and a bit desperate in its attempts to recapture the free-and-easy, sex-on-tap atmos of *Up Pompeii*'s corresponding scene. The girls keep most of their clothes on, Derek Griffiths is a scream and Frankie retains his English eccentricity by ordering 'half a bitter and a scotch egg', but there's a real sense of desperation in the story department.

Moreover, the continual use of Frankie's mystic voices becomes something of an intrusion. Okay, it's an easy plot device to suggest that our hapless hero is made of more regal stuff than his pig-sty upbringing would suggest but the dulcet tones of Lally Bowers – another refugee from *Up Pompeii* – tend to grate after a while. It's repetitive, a bit embarrassing and pretty redundant, although Frankie somehow redeems the entire notion by screaming 'I knew I was a nob!' at one stage.

It's not a classic film by a long chalk, but Frankie continually pulls the plot out of the fire, throws in an off-kilter, out-of-line comment and pumps up the fun as only he can. And the entire film is given a leg-up in the Britcom hierarchy by the camp-as-a-row-of-tents vignette with Hugh Paddick's Robin Hood. Contrary to the opinion that Frankie's unique comic persona would be cancelled out opposite another camp performer, the pair spark off each other perfectly. Royce Mills gets caught up in the limp-wristed fun, a couple of singing sensations (Long John Baldry and Christopher Sandford) mince through their feature film débuts and Frankie takes a real boyish delight in the barrel-scraping puns and semi-bitchy comments.

And the film's absolute highlight comes with Frankie's salacious interest in clapping eyes on Maid Marian and prurient enquiries regarding Robin's sleeping arrangements with her. Of course, once Marian is revealed as Rita Webb, everything falls into place and Frankie can understand Paddick's sexual preference. In a stunning sideways comment to the audience, Frankie reasons, 'That explains a lot of things! I mean, could you?' Delicious stuff.

....

Did You Know? The film was shot at Elstree in double-quick time, from 20 April to 25 May 1971, and was edited down to 90 minutes from what must have been a mind-boggling three-hour original. The American title, dispensing with the Up prefix, was simply *Naughty Knights*. A couple of tie-in items were issued to promote the film. Eartha Kitt's brilliantly sultry song, 'A Knight For My Nights' was released on the CBS label (CBS 7676), while a paperback novelisation of the script ('the incredible and little-known story of Lurkalot the serf and his lady Lobelia') was written by William Rand and published by Sphere Books. A colour shot of Frankie in court jester garb adorned the front cover.

During the daring escape from Judy Huxtable's Germanic husband (played with over-the-top gusto by Iain Cuthbertson), King Frankie, dressed as a nun, muttered the immortal line, 'It must be very hard for you!' The line was clearly too racy, even for this film, and Frankie was forced to dub 'sad' over the offending word. And while we're on the subject of vocals, Lally Bowers was clearly a last-minute substitute for the irritating 'voices' haunting Frankie. The original choice – even up to the printing of the cast list for press publicity – was that immortal 'silly old moo', Dandy Nichols.

....

Lurkalot and King Richard the Lionheart FRANKIE HOWERD, *Sir Coward de Custard* GRAHAM CROWDEN, *Sir Braggart de Bombast* BILL FRASER, *Nick the Pick* ROY HUDD, *Robin Hood* HUGH PADDICK, *Lady Ashfodel* ANNA QUAYLE, *Our Man in the Holy Land* LANCE PERCIVAL, *Archbishop of All England* GODFREY WINN, *Yokel* DAVID BATTLEY, *Knotweed* ROYCE MILLS, *Winnie the Pooh* VERONICA CLIFFORD, *Saladin* DEREK GRIFFITHS, *Gretel* JUDY HUXTABLE, *Master of Ceremonies* FRANK THORNTON, *Chopper the woodman* BILLY WALKER, *Maid Marian* RITA WEBB, *Vegetable stall holder* AUBREY WOODS, *Lobelia* ANNE ASTON, *Little John* JOHN BALDRY, *Locksmith* SAM KYDD, *Sir Grumbel de Grunt* DAVE PROWSE, *Friar Tuck* ALAN REBBECK, *Lucky charm seller* IAN TRIGGER, *Mortimer* FRED EMNEY, *Landlord of the Blue Boar* DAVE KING, *Serving wench* SERRETTA WILSON, *Mistress of the bed chamber* NORA SWINBURNE, *Family at burning* FRED GRIFFITHS, WINNIE HOLMAN and MARTIN WOODHAMS, *Teutonic knight* IAIN CUTHBERTSON, *Peasants* JOHN BARRETT and NICHOLAS BENNETT, *Meat stall holder* BARRIE GOSNEY, *Blacksmith* NORMAN BEATON, *Men-at-arms* JOHN GORMAN and DON HAWKINS, *Horsemen* JONATHAN ELSOM and ROBERT TAYMAN, *Major Domo* MISCHA DE LA MOTTE, *Squill* TOBY LENNON, *Will Scarlett* BERNARD SHARPE, *Man-in-stocks* ALEC PLEON, *Arab* PETER STRAKER, *Vendor* CHRISTOPHER TIMOTHY, *Mutch* CHRISTOPHER SANDFORD, *Chestnut man* JOHNNY VYVYAN, *Lieutenant* IAN WHITE, *First man* KEN WYNNE, *Little man* JIMMY GARDNER, *Belly dancers* NORA WIPP and NIKO LASKI, *Waitress* SAMMI WINMILL, *Battle-axe wife* PARNELL McGARRY, *Young man* JONATHAN DENNIS, *Wife* PATRICIA QUINN, *Troubadour* DAVID KERNAN, *Scheherazade* EARTHA KITT, *The Voice* LALLY BOWERS
Screenplay Sid Colin, Ray Galton & Alan Simpson, *Director of Photography* Ian Wilson, *Art Director* Seamus Flannery, *Make-up* Dickie Mills, *Chief Hairdresser* Ramon Gow, *Costume Designer* Penny Lowe, *Editor* Al Gell, *Sound Mixer* Christopher Moore, *Production Supervisor* Pat Green, *Executive Producer* Beryl Vertue, *Producers* Ned Sherrin and Terry Glinwood, *Director* Bob Kellett
Associated London Films
Filmed at Elstree Studios

Theatrical business re-staged for the movies as Monique (Hermione Baddeley) serenades Lurk (Frankie) in *Up the Front*.

1972
Up the Front

'Funny people, these French!'   **Lurk**

The third and final Up film is a wonderful mix of the best and worst of Frankie's film star vehicles. Clearly this is no *Blackadder Goes Forth*, although the First World War framework initially lends itself very well to Frankie's unique comic persona. In many ways it's not a million miles from the Danny La Rue movie *Our Miss Fred* – which also featured Lance Percival – but while Frankie struggles with a lot of the wartime plot, double-crossing and cross-dressing, there are still some of the most emotive and enjoyable interludes of his entire film canon contained along the way.

Once again, the familiar cast and crew are gathered up by Ned Sherrin to lend immediate familiarity to the frolics. Even supporting faces like Barrie Gosney and Derek Griffiths (quite brilliant as the stunned cockney knife-thrower, with Frankie dragged up as his assistant Isabelle) returned to make it three out of three in the Up trilogy. Lance Percival, thankfully back to full strength and total evil, returns as the second-in-command villain Von Gutz, and Bill Fraser too, returns to complete his Frankie hat-trick with a quite stunning performance as the power-crazed butler-cum-sergeant major, Groping ('That's not only his name, that's his hobby!'). Fraser was delighted to be returning to the Frankie fold, explaining in the press release that 'I like playing villains!'

And this villain is certainly the most enjoyable and well-rounded of his three Up contributions. There's a real sense of mission behind Fraser's eyes, coupled with a genuine loathing for Lurk and his feeble ways. Continually being spied on and walked in on by Frankie's bumbling recruit, Fraser spends most of the film trying to remove articles of clothing from a string of scantily clad glamour girls with his teeth; it's a hard role but somebody had to play it! One such spying routine is my favourite moment in the entire film and one of the great Frankie moments of all time – so obviously hilarious and so spine-tinglingly acted it's above criticism.

The priceless vignette kicks off with a demented Frankie running from the door, staring into the camera lens and pleading, 'I must look for another film!' But it's too late. Fraser has spotted him, he's now in the top-dog position of sergeant major and ready to make Private Lurk's life a misery. With a brilliantly scrambled mouthful of incomprehensible military rant, Fraser slows down for the audible 'I am a sergeant major!' Frankie, still cheeky even in the face of the foe, mutters cheerfully, 'Ahh, sergeant major. I heard that bit!' Fraser turns away slightly, catches the eye of the viewers in his turn and, grinning, comments that, as far as Frankie is concerned, 'the sun shines out me arse!' Frankie's delicious riposte ('It's been a short summer!') is one for the classic archive. It's hardly earth-shattering filmmaking but this is a breathtaking gallop through some pretty dire dialogue by two past masters of the comedic art. Awesome stuff!

The format of the first two films (with Frankie in below-stairs employment and working the action around his servant's duties) is hardly touched on at all. However, the opening of the film remains arguably the most satisfying, despite its reduction of William Mervyn and Linda Gray as Frankie's landed employers, the Twithamptons, to the level of barely glimpsed cyphers. The wet-behind-the-ears son figure is not the Twithamptons' son but a completely separate character, an idiotic Twithampton house guest played in typically 'silly ass' style by Jonathan Cecil. In the token 'daughter' role is the maid character, Fanny. And a collective red-blooded cheer goes up with the return of porcelain beauty Madeline Smith.

Frankie's indulgence in chatting to the

audience, revealing plot and casting details, exposing the film as a film and even revealing historical knowledge well before the time-frame of the story is abundantly catered for and in many ways Frankie seems more relaxed and natural in front of a film camera than ever before. The opening scene is a little address to the viewing public with our smartly clad hero announcing himself as being the latest in a 'long line of Lurks' and admitting that the common thread of the family down the ages has always been cowardice.

Thankfully, our hapless Lurk is no exception. When Madeline Smith's patriotic and raring-to-go maid chats to him about the impending conflict and the need for all able-bodied men to join up, Frankie delivers an impassioned speech in defence of the filthy Bosch, feeling that one should look at the situation from their point of view and basically chickening out as quickly as possible. Extracting a single white feather from her duster, the young lady of his

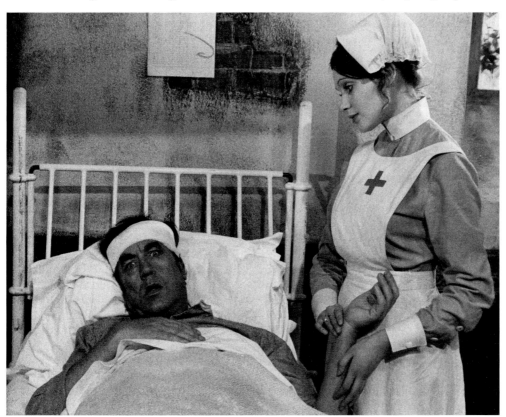

Fanny (Madeline Smith) nurses the stricken Lurk in *Up the Front.*

Drinkies with
Up the Front's
glamour-puss
guest star, Zsa
Zsa Gabor.

dreams storms out. Frankie simply picks up the offending item, opens a drawer stuffed with similar feathers and mutters about storing it 'with the family heirlooms!' It's this sense of continuity and back-tracking which gives the film its heart.

Of course, for the plot to go anywhere our cowardly hero has to be forced into enlisting. The plot device to achieve this is provided by a masterly guest turn from that legendary veteran of film, radio and stage, Stanley Holloway. Having worked as a great comedy team in the Frankie star vehicle *Jumping For Joy* nearly 20 years previously, the on-screen chemistry between the two remains electric. Over 80 when the film was made, Holloway relishes his cameo role and takes on the weird

'voices' part of the *Chastity Belt* scenario by cropping up throughout the French portion of the movie to remind Frankie of his destiny.

Excelling as a permanently drunk hypnotist, Holloway unleashes his buxom assistant (a third well-endowed cameo in the Up trilogy for Veronica Clifford) and Frankie is dragged on stage. The great prestidigitator boasts that his tricks will take the breath away, to which Frankie retorts 'I wish you'd take yours away!' before falling under the master's spell. He enacts a string of heroic Englishmen (Lord Nelson, Sir Francis Drake, etc) much to the amusement of an audience that includes, as well as Fraser and Smith, the future film star, Bob Hoskins. Naturally, Holloway's alcoholic performer collapses before bringing Frankie out of his trance and the appearance of Auntie Cora (a stunning support turn from Dora Bryan) gets Frankie belting out a chorus of 'England, My England' – and signing up to face the enemy.

Bryan was keen to get the chance to work with Frankie again, not just because she enjoyed the comedian's company but because her children would be keen to see her on screen for a change. She explained in the pressbook that 'The children take my shows for granted and don't often watch them, though sometimes I insist! … But they're all dying to see *Up the Front* – no, not because I'm in it, but because of Frankie Howerd!' The film is awash with such class guest stars and another of Frankie's closest showbiz pals is Hermione Baddeley, playing the wide-eyed madame of the local knocking shop. Another Frankie favourite, Zsa Zsa Gabor, is brilliantly exploited as the ultimate sexy spy, Mata Hari, though her much-heralded performance (placed on a par with Frankie's on the poster) is little more than a cough and a spit. Coming towards the end of the picture, when much of the fun has vanished and our hero is reduced to running through plush corridors in a tree disguise ('We've got branches everywhere!'), there's nevertheless a real sense of self-mockery and exotic charm about Gabor's performance.

Throughout, the boundaries between reality and fantasy are totally blurred. Frankie, the great lover, doesn't fall for the obvious charms of the blonde bombshell and instead plays hard to get. Both are fully aware of the espionage games being played; indeed, Frankie looks into camera and points out a glaring chestnut in the script, muttering 'Surely she won't pull that old gag?' But of course she does and thank heavens for it, for her consumption of the truth drug allows Frankie a couple of to-camera comments reflecting his co-star's glamorous and well-publicised love life. When the talk turns to the pleasures of the flesh Frankie comments, 'Course, you've had more practice!' And, when the truth serum really starts to kick in, Frankie eagerly sets the scene for us by muttering,

'This could be very interesting…'

Though the first 30 minutes bang along at a hilarious pace, the subsequent action tends to drag things to a near standstill at times. And, with the secret plans finally being tattooed on his backside, Frankie does his utmost to redeem such a well-worn comic plot, baring the 'cheek' of it with good grace and getting away with it by the skin of his teeth. The deliciously monotone David Battley, complete with dreadful cookhouse habits and an obsession with the local good-time girl, is a godsend for Frankie's comic patter, while Percy Herbert – having enjoyed low comedy with the high-flying Carry On gang in both *Jack* and *Cowboy* – relishes some dreadful one-liners. There are also some last-minute good times to be had with eternal filmic old buffer Robert Coote and frosty-faced authority figure Michael Brennan.

But the most endearing element of Frankie's performance is his ability to drop in knowledge of events yet to come while not interrupting the flow of corny gags and scantily clad can-can dancers. With an earnest desire to complete his mission by 11 November 1918 ('The war ends then, doesn't it?'), Frankie sets things up for the conclusion of battle. In a warm and humane ending, we return to find Frankie cleaning boots in London again. However, the year is now 1939 ('and looking not a day older!'), those spine-tingling military drums start beating, the screen fades to black, a heart-pounding image of Churchill appears and the filmmakers leave their audience on an ultra-high: a reprise of Sid Colin's stirring title song.

It's a fatally flawed movie in many ways, but Frankie's indefatigable style never deserts him. The bad bits are bearable, the average bits absolutely sensational. Thus ended the legacy of Lurk and his bumbling ancestors. The time-frame spanned the Romans to the outbreak of the Second World War and, although the format and characterisation would be re-developed for television, this was very much the end of an era. To indicate this, whereas the first two films had been huge box-office draws, this last effort was noticeably less successful.

....

Did You Know? Some of the nation's foremost comedy writers – including Dick Vosburgh – desperately tried to contribute suggestions and scenes to funny up the First World War but couldn't manage it. None of their material was used. Maurice Sellar – one writer who did work on the film – later took up the story in a way, resurrecting Frankie's blissful fun with the *Up the Front* goat in the shelved Second World War romp, *Then Churchill Said To Me.*

Co-star Zsa Zsa Gabor was so enamoured with Frankie that she had marital designs on him. Frankie skilfully avoided the altar despite the fact that Gabor's mother was heartily behind the idea! Back in the 1950s, incidentally, Frankie had made much of his alleged plans to marry the porcelain Ealing star Joan Greenwood, and claimed to be shattered when she married character actor André Morell in May 1960. For those 'in the know', however, the whole scenario seemed wildly unlikely.

Peter Greenwell, the composer of the film's music, crops up in not one but four Hitchcock-style cameos. He is the piano player at the recruitment hall, a dragged-up accordionist in the brothel, a soldier tinkling the ivories for Dora Bryan's medic performance and a violinist at Mata Hari's ball.

A novelisation of the film, once again written by William Rand and published by Sphere Books, boasted a colour cover featuring Frankie surrounded by the glamorous brothel girls and related 'the amazing adventure of the last of the Lurks in his struggle with the Kaiser – and more pleasant opponents.' Clearly someone somewhere knew that it was definitely the last outing for the rare, ramshackle and totally enchanting Up series.

....

Lurk FRANKIE HOWERD, Mata Hari ZSA ZSA GABOR, Groping BILL FRASER, Von Gutz LANCE PERCIVAL, Fanny MADELINE SMITH, Monique HERMIONE BADDELEY, Vincento STANLEY HOLLOWAY, Lord Twithampton WILLIAM MERVYN, Cora Crumpington DORA BRYAN, Nigel Phipps-Fortescue JONATHAN CECIL, General Burke ROBERT COOTE, Von Kobler PETER BULL, The Music Man PETER GREENWELL,

Donner GERTAN KLAUBER, Blitzen STANLEY LEBOR, Lady Twithampton LINDA GRAY, Mallet NICHOLAS BENNETT, Newsboy MIKE GRADY, Velma VERONICA CLIFFORD, Stage Manager BARRIE GOSNEY, Recruiting sergeant BOB HOSKINS, Muller VERNON DOBTCHEFF, Captain Hamburger INGO MOGENDORF, Lovechild PERCY HERBERT, Midgeley the cook DAVID BATTLEY, Despatch Rider ANDREW BRADFORD, Soldier ANDREW McCULLOCH, Winking soldier ALAN REBBECK, Frou Frou BOZENA, Soldier at Monique's IAN TALBOT, Fat nurse PARNELL McGARRY, Nurse LEENA SKOOG, Buttercup girls TONI PALMER and DELIA SAINSBURY, MPs MICHAEL BRENNAN and HARVEY HALL, Magda, Mata Hari's maid PATRICIA QUINN, Burke's ADC KENNETH FORTESCUE, Diplomat MISCHA DE LA MOTTE, Indian officer MADHAV SHARMA, French officer ROBERT GILLESPIE, El Puncturo DEREK GRIFFITHS, Can-Can dancers LESLEY ANDERSON, JUDY GRIDLEY, MAGGIE VINCENT and WENDY LUKINS, French girl NICOLA ROWLEY, The Waiter PHILIP MILLER, Mademoiselle from Armentières LIZ GOLD Screenplay Sid Colin and Eddie Braben, additional material by Roy Tuvey and Maurice Sellar, Peter Vincent and Bob Hedley, Music composed, arranged and conducted by Peter Greenwell, Title song lyric by Sid Colin, performed by Dora Bryan, Director of Photography Tony Spratling, Production Designer Seamus Flannery, Make-up Richard Mills, Hairdresser Helen Lennox, Costume Supervisor Brenda Dabbs, Miss Gabor's gowns by Zandra Rhodes, Choreography Tommy Shaw, Editor Al Gell, Sound Editor Ian Fuller, Assistant Director Mike Gowans, Producers Ned Sherrin and Terry Glinwood, Director Bob Kellett Associated London Films Filmed at Elstree Studios

The House in Nightmare Park
'The film I enjoyed making the most…'
                                    Frankie Howerd

Having left his mark on the most celebrated and best-loved comedy troupe in the country, and followed that with three starring vehicles built around his most celebrated television persona, Frankie was confident enough to move his big screen career in a different direction. Or, at least, to move it back to where he had started in the first place. Bringing his film star career full circle, Frankie couldn't resist the opportunity to make his very own, copper-bottomed comic-horror flick. It would remain arguably his finest big screen achievement and also, ironically, the best-kept secret in his whole movie career.

The House in Nightmare Park certainly isn't your typical Frankie vehicle and, indeed, the number of full-on Howerdisms can be counted on the fingers of one hand, missus. Still, there's a grandeur in the film's directorial style, an ingrained class about the supporting players and a sense of Frankie's filmic persona finally being toned down to allow the actor simply to act. In his most sustained and satisfying big screen performance, Frankie is cast essentially as an Edwardian version of himself. His Foster Twelvetrees is still very much the self-absorbed orator – a deliciously hammy actor who specialises in tragic readings of Dickens – but one confined within a tightly constructed plot stitched together from *The Old Dark House* (particularly the 1962 Hammer version whose twist this film lifts), *Psycho*, *And Then There Were None* and *The Cat and the Canary*. Indeed, in a characteristically ill-considered judgment, Leslie Halliwell damned the film with faint praise by pointing out that it was 'well enough done though it would have been better with Bob Hope.'

Apart from the fact that both comics hailed – at some time of their lives – from Eltham, Hope and Howerd were alike in that they subordinated themselves to the storyline in their horror-comedies. Whereas Hope is a cowardly, wisecracking radio star, Howerd is a cowardly, pun-dropping stage never-was, but the principle remains the same. Most of Frankie's comic moments stem from his terrified reactions to the weird and less than wonderful things that surround him in the forbidding house of the title. Whether it's a collapsing suit of armour, a collection of Indian snakes or a syringe full of poison, it's the outside danger that brings on the nervous quips, panicked confusion or just plain

terror, elongated with heavy-jowled shock or pitiful whines.

Much of the rest of the humour comes, of course, from the actor's own inflated opinion of himself. He is a shabby tragedian at the best of times, over-egging his Dickens monologues with a deliciously tasty line in curled-lip histrionics. The opening scene sees Twelvetrees' impassioned rendition of *Oliver Twist* set before a meagre audience of raspberry-blowing kids and dozing adults. Still, ever the professional and ever the optimist, Twelvetrees milks the non-existent ovation and 'the greatest master of the spoken word', as his publicity modestly bills him, staggers into the corrupt, contrived and criminally confused plotline within the house in Nightmare Park.

The ill-attended stage performance acts as a pre-credits sequence, establishing Frankie's ham actor persona and the threat from chief ghoul, Ray Milland, before the titles even roll. The action immediately cuts to our hapless, haunted hero emerging from a hansom cab at the house in question. Stacked with every horror cliché known to man, the sequence even picks up the typical 'scared to go any further' cabbie used in everything from Tod Browning's original *Dracula* to the Sid James horror-comedy *What A Carve Up!* In one of the film's few true-blue Howerdisms, the disgruntled star shouts 'I hope your whip shrivels!' after the terrified driver, subsequently embarking on a beautifully

Snakes alive!
Trouble for
Foster
Twelvetrees in
*The House in
Nightmare
Park*.

directed, horror-heavy wander up to the old dark house.

Shadows, thunder, creepy trees, whistling winds, crazy camera angles, sweeping close-ups and discordant piano music are all tossed into the mix to bang home, if proof were needed, the fact that we are in Hammer meets Roger Corman country. (The young Australian director, Peter Sykes, had already directed *Demons of the Mind* for Hammer and would go on to direct their final horror classic, *To the Devil a Daughter*.) The horror techniques are then skilfully defused with arguably the best line in the entire film, as Twelvetrees looks around in amazement and mutters to himself, 'I've played empty houses before but Gawd blimey!' It may well be derived from a Hope line in *The Cat and the Canary* (when twittering Nydia Westman asks 'Don't these big empty houses scare you?' and Hope answers 'Not me, I was in vaudeville'), but it

sets the tone for the whole project.

Twelvetrees is not only an actor who believes himself brilliant, but also a man obsessed with money and convinced of his own youthful good looks. He stocks his room with framed photographs of himself and looks longingly into the mirror with a waspish 'Not bad for 32...' He thrives on applause and is easily duped by a spot of insincere ego-massage. Even the most unwelcoming of welcomes or direst threat to his well-being is ignored if it's accompanied by a compliment. Even money – as in Twelvetrees' initial cry of 'They can stuff their five guineas, I'm off!' – can't reduce him to compliance more quickly than a few well-chosen words of succour. When, in his own words, 'They're dropping like flies!' and he is packed and heading for the main gate, it merely takes a reference to his being the rightful heir to the house to stop him in his tracks and get him back to the murderous madness. Gain and wealth can make a hero of the most cowardly of comedians.

As for his hosts: 'What a funny lot!' he concludes. The funny lot are brought to life by a treasured cross-section of stage and screen stars. Not least, we have self-confessed Frankie fan Ray Milland as the sinister Stewart Henderson, making his first appearance as an agitated pair of gloved hands wringing a white scarf during Twelvetrees' opening performance and skulking off in disgust as Twelvetrees unwittingly intones, 'He had heard enough!' Wielding an axe, ranting with mother-fixated madness and undermining the strangeness of his performance with sweet old-fashioned courtesy, Milland provides a straitlaced, fool-proof foil for Frankie's flamboyantly nerve-wracked central turn.

Of the several scenes shared by the two old pros, perhaps the most rewarding is Henderson's pleading for forgiveness after his mad mother has attacked Twelvetrees. Although Twelvetrees believes it's all *Psycho*-babble and that it was Henderson in drag all along, Henderson ponders calmly on his beautiful childhood, when he would so look forward to his mother's goodnight kiss that he would pinch himself to stay awake, sometimes so hard he would draw blood. It's not manically played, just casually mentioned, and Twelvetrees' mildly concerned 'Oh dear!' is one of the film's absolute highlights.

Hugh Burden, quite brilliant as the bombastic, foul-tempered brother Reggie, wanders through the action continually dubbing everybody and everything 'Swine!' There is clearly no love lost between Twelvetrees and Reggie, the former being a mere 'mummer' and the latter a snobbish boor. The breakfast table sequence is a well-orchestrated farce in which Reggie jockeys for the choicest morsels and Twelvetrees utters a child-like cry of 'Thank you!' as he plucks the mad sister's piece of abandoned fried bread for himself.

Jessica, the mad sister in question, is played with manic detachment by Rosalie Crutchley, governed by her snake gods to such an extent that her tongue darts in and out as she watches them devour a white rabbit. The snake episode follows the sauciest exchange in the film. With the blank-faced Jessica selecting two rabbits for consumption by snake, Twelvetrees gets all luvvie duvvie with the bunnies. With the creatures clutched to Jessica's chest, Twelvetrees is suddenly inspired and mutters, 'What a lovely pair. May I stroke them? The rabbits I mean!' The unimpressed female reaction is awesome, Twelvetrees' frantic embarrassment is tangible and the old pun-master is back to the fore, albeit by proxy. For this is a film of situation over smut, where even Frankie's sexy interrupted dream ('Melanie, you mustn't! It's the knockers, Melanie!') reveals him as a chaste and pure individual.

The last major exhibit on the mad family tree is sweet, innocent and bird-like Kenneth Griffith as the medically inclined Ernest. Akin to the sweet and innocent Saul Femm, as played by Brember Wills in the 1932 version of *The Old Dark House*, Ernest's quiet nature hides a bloodthirsty desire to kill anything and anybody that gets in the way of his inheritance. All sing-song dialogue, gritted-teeth pleasantries and attempted murder, Ernest is the last to arrive and the first to go but he leaves a lasting impression. Perhaps the most intriguing and treasurable sequence sees a

Foster ministers to the swooning Verity (Elizabeth MacLennan) in *The House in Nightmare Park*.

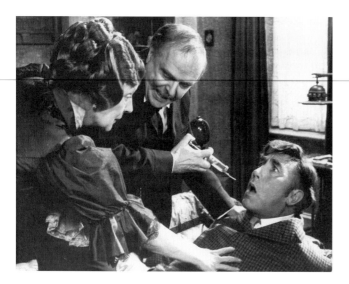

Agnes (Ruth Dunning) and Ernest (Kenneth Griffith) give Foster the needle in *The House in Nightmare Park*.

spooky re-enactment of the family's childhood act as grotesque Pierrots prancing to 'The Dance of the Dolls'. Twelvetrees' simply priceless reaction to this display ('Oh God!') is only topped by his hilarious pay-off line: 'God knows what they do for an encore!'

Thus, this is a very subdued Frankie performance which is dropped into strange territory indeed. The essense of his screen persona is retained but not to the detriment of the plot and atmospheric setting. As such it works brilliantly, complete with lavatorial humour, sexual coyness, self-absorbed self-deception and ingrained cowardliness ('Ooh dear, my stomach went over!'). This is Frankie the actor at full throttle. In one of the film's most hilariously creepy sequences, the head of the supposedly bedridden fourth brother literally drops off in front of our hero and his lady love. The thing is quickly revealed to be a dummy but the camera pans back across the bed to discover Twelvetrees literally fighting for life as he gulps air from a bedside oxygen tank. It is a masterly piece of filmmaking brought bang into focus by Frankie's controlled flamboyance.

Throughout the film, Frankie is clearly enjoying himself hugely. In his scenes with Ray Milland, formerly a card-carrying member of the Hollywood elite, Frankie can be seen almost swelling with pride at being on the

same set as one of the greats. Moreover, he was a lifelong fan of the comedy-thriller genre and this film was the perfect opportunity to really go for the Gothic clowning he loved so much. Six years after making the film, Frankie recalled it with pleasure but remembered the unpleasantness of some of the shooting. 'The only difficult thing about it involved swamps. It was very physically gruelling to make because I was being chased upstairs and downstairs, chased through swamps and generally kicked around. I had to work three days in a pit of live snakes. But it was a good part and good parts don't come around all that often.'

For Frankie at the movies, this would be his very last good part. Perhaps the film moved too far away from what his regular audience expected. Whatever the reason for Frankie's curtailed film career, this final headlining vehicle remains one of his most enjoyable and entertaining. There's something particularly stimulating and timeless about the absurd coda that comes after the sweeping power of the climax. Twelvetrees' loot is buried somewhere in the vast meadow behind the house and it will take a lot of searching to locate it. But his expression is steely and determined, the camera soars up from his toiling figure to the dizzy heights of a helicopter view and the credits roll.

Films first encountered at an impressionable age often fail to hold quite the same magic when re-evaluated later. *The House in Nightmare Park* is a glorious exception. The horror conventions are lovingly embraced rather than mocked and Frankie Howerd is at his best. It needs no greater recommendation than that.

....

Did You Know? Co-scripted by Terry Nation, who had penned material for the third series of radio's *The Frankie Howerd Show*, the screenplay was briefly looked over by Ray Galton and Alan Simpson. However, apart from making the odd suggestion, the writers contributed little to the finished film. The film was made in double-quick time, from 6 November to 16 December 1972, at Pinewood Studios. In America the business may not have been red hot but the two alternative titles were. It was released as both *Crazy House* (which had previously been the title of Ole Olsen and Chic Johnson's madcap follow-up to *Hellzapoppin'*) and, rather brilliantly, *The Night of the Laughing Dead*, in homage to George A Romero's low-budget zombie classic, *Night of the Living Dead*. The promotional tag read: 'Everybody's talking about the MOST CUCKOO COMEDY since *Young Frankenstein*.'

....

Foster FRANKIE HOWERD, Stewart RAY MILLAND, Reggie HUGH BURDEN, Ernest KENNETH GRIFFITH, Patel JOHN BENNETT, Jessica ROSALIE CRUTCHLEY, Agnes RUTH DUNNING, Verity ELIZABETH MacLENNAN, Mother AIMÉE DELAMAIN, Cabbie PETER MUNT
Screenplay Clive Exton and Terry Nation, Music Harry Robinson, Director of Photography Ian Wilson, Camera Operator Neil Binney, Art Director Maurice Carter, Editor Bill Blunden, Dubbing Editor Mike Crouch, Make-up Jill Carpenter, Hairdresser Ramon Gow, Costume Designer Judy Moorcroft, Assistant Director Michael Dryhurst, Production Supervisor Edward Joseph, Executive Producer Beryl Vertue, Producers Clive Exton and Terry Nation, Director Peter Sykes
Associated London Films/Extonation
Filmed at Elstree Studios

1975
Missed opportunity # 2 : The Tempest

The legendary director Michael Powell (*A Matter of Life and Death*, *Black Narcissus*, *The Red Shoes* etc) had long wanted to make a film version of Shakespeare's *The Tempest*. James Mason was just as enthusiastic about playing Prospero and the project finally looked set to get off the ground in 1975. Powell, whose career had been in eclipse for 15 years after the scandal surrounding *Peeping Tom*, had teamed up with Greek producer Frixos Constantine and his partner Costas Carayiannis. The Anglo-Greek co-production was scheduled to start on 5 March in Rhodes

and Athens but then got put back to September. By that stage, Jack Cardiff was pencilled in as cinematographer, André Previn as composer and cartoonist Gerald Scarfe was due to make the monsters.

The actors mentioned in the trade papers included, as well as Mason, Malcolm McDowell, Michael York, Topol, Mia Farrow (Previn's then-wife), Bill Simpson… and our very own Frankie Howerd, presumably to play either the jester Trinculo or the drunken butler Stephano. It didn't happen. Constantine and Carayiannis instead made a Donald Pleasence/Peter Cushing chiller called *The Devil's Men* while Powell was left to await rehabilitation by Martin Scorsese.

1977
Sgt. Pepper's Lonely Hearts Club Band
'They only got me because they couldn't get Ronald Colman!'   **Frankie Howerd**

Or, how the most important and earth-shattering album in recording history became one of the most mocked movies of all time. 'Is it a film? Is it a record album? Is it a poster, or a T-shirt, or a specially embossed frisbee?' asked Janet Maslin in the *New York Times*. '*Sgt. Pepper's Lonely Hearts Club Band* is the ultimate multimedia mishmash, so diversified that it doesn't fully exist in any one medium at all. This isn't a movie, it's a business deal set to music.'

Thankfully, the Fab Four were well out of this one. (Just as Frankie, unwittingly, had been well out of the bona-fide Beatles bonanza, *Help!*, a dozen years earlier.) It was designed instead to make movie stars of the Bee Gees by blessing them with the best back-catalogue in pop history. Still, even the Lennon-McCartney classics couldn't save this and the entire sorry mess sank without trace. Production began in LA on 10 October 1977; it hit US cinemas in July 1978 and crawled shamefaced into the UK the following February.

The response from critic David Castell in *Films Illustrated* was pretty typical. 'The idea of building a film around the Beatles' most famous album is almost as impudent as it is impossible,' he wrote. 'The storyline, such as it is, has to be ineffably silly to incorporate the lyrics of so many disparate songs – the result is rather like a pantomime principal boy torturing the plot out of shape in order to include the latest chart success. The Bee Gees (even augmented by guest artist Peter Frampton) should be heard but not seen: their acting abilities are limited in the extreme. And the scenes involving arch-villain Mr Mustard (Frankie Howerd) carry irrelevant juvenalia [sic] to new heights. If the Beatles themselves couldn't fuse sound with visuals in the filmed television version of *Magical Mystery Tour*, then director Michael Schultz certainly hasn't found the formula. Probably the cartoon fantasy of *Yellow Submarine* was as close as we shall come. This wasteful and expensive ego trip leads only up the long and winding road to self-extinction.'

The film, however, was crucially important for one reason – after some 25 years making movies, Frankie Howerd was finally given the chance to enjoy the Hollywood lifestyle. Talking to Professor Tony Williams in an unpublished interview conducted just before taking the stage at the Grand Theatre Swansea in 1978, Frankie recalled how he landed the role. 'The producer Robert Stigwood is a very good friend of mine. I first met him when he came over from Australia with the Bee Gees. I joined his organisation in London and did a show with the Bee Gees [qv]. When Robert came over last year and met me in his office he mentioned that he had this script of Sergeant Pepper and asked if I'd like to appear in the film. I'm obviously not a pop singer but I thought that it looked interesting and would be a new market for me in reaching youngsters. I play a bumbling comic villain who never has any success, Mean Mr Mustard. I do a couple of numbers but don't talk all that much. It's all mime and knockabout comedy.'

Indeed it is. Frankie is restricted to a few cries of 'I'm a mean old man!' during his title track, performed while a bizarre-looking robot (which does most of the singing) gives our lovable anti-hero a massage. Frankie later relishes the ageing camp of 'When I'm Sixty Four'. He also crops up during the funeral scene alongside comic legend George Burns. 'We mostly discussed British humour,' Frankie observed. 'He was reading a book about Max Bygraves when I was over there so he keeps in touch with British comedy and our show business personalites.' The chorus for the funeral interlude features such names as Carol Channing and Gwen Verdon; 'they even tried to get Bing Crosby but he died a few months before the film began,' Frankie pointed out.

Years later, Frankie's film career was mocked in the *At His Tittermost!* souvenir programme with the crudely drawn Frankie Goes to Hollywood comic strip, but the star thoroughly enjoyed the Sergeant Pepper experience and pondered on the vast differences between making films in the US and in England. 'Coffee was available all the time and they had food such as peanut butter and doughnuts which were never around on British film sets! I worked at the old Culver City Studios where they shot a lot of *Gone With the Wind*. They had built a town called Heartland. I wandered over there and found a jungle pool which is now dilapidated, where Esther Williams used to do her swimming. When I was young, Hollywood was the big thing and I always thought it would be nice to go over and make a film there one day and see the studios. So I was thrilled to do so.'

Thrilling for Frankie perhaps, but with a budget of $6 million the film was a starry folly and a tuneful flop, aptly summarised by the *New York Times*' Janet Maslin. 'When whimsy gets to be this overbearing,' she wrote, 'it simply isn't whimsy any more.'

Billy Shears PETER FRAMPTON, Mark, Dave and Bob Henderson BARRY, ROBIN and MAURICE GIBB, Mean Mr Mustard FRANKIE HOWERD, Dougie Shears PAUL NICHOLAS, B D Brockhurst DONALD PLEASENCE, Strawberry Fields SANDY FARINA, Lucy DIANNE STEINBERG, Dr Maxwell Edison STEVE MARTIN, Future Villain AEROSMITH, Father Sun ALICE COOPER, Benefit performers EARTH, WIND & FIRE, Sgt Pepper BILLY PRESTON, The

Diamonds STARGARD, Mr Kite GEORGE BURNS, The Brute CAREL STRUYCKEN, Saralinda Shears PATTI JEROME, Ernest Shears MAX SHOWALTER, Mr Fields JOHN WHEELER, Mrs Fields JAY W MacINTOSH, Mrs Henderson ELEANOR ZEE, Young Sgt Pepper SCOTT MANNERS, Young Lonely Hearts Club Band STANLEY COLES, STANLEY SHELDON and BOB MAYO, Old Sgt Pepper WOODROW CHAMBLISS, Old Lonely Hearts Club Band HANK WORDEN, MORGAN FARLEY and DELOS V SMITH, Western Union messenger PAT CRANSHAW, Bonnie TERI LYNN WOOD, Tippy TRACY JUSTRICH, The Computerettes ANNA RODZIANKO and ROSE ARAGON Screenplay Henry Edwards, Songs by John Lennon, Paul McCartney and George Harrison, Music arranged and directed by George Martin, Director of Photography Owen Roizman, Production Designer Brian Eatwell, Costume Designer May Routh, Choreography Patricia Birch, Editor Christopher Holmes, Assistant Director L Andrew Stone, Associate Producer Bill Oakes, Executive in charge of production Roger M Rothstein, Executive Producer Dee Anthony, Producer Robert Stigwood, Director Michael Schultz Robert Stigwood Organisation/Geria Film ●

Frankie goes to Hollywood: flying the flag in Tinseltown while filming *Sgt. Pepper's Lonely Hearts Club Band.*

Tantrums and Togas

FRANKIE ON **TELEVISION**

*'I work all the time but it's not for the cash …
I love working!'*
                                                    Frankie Howerd

Having leapt to fame via radio and stage, it was only natural that Frankie would be seized by the British Broadcasting Corporation and propelled into the new-fangled medium of television. Well before the benchmark telly event – the broadcast of the Coronation of Queen Elizabeth II in 1953 – Frankie landed his first high-profile assignment on the box. And for the next 40 years he would rarely be off it.

The Howerd Crowd
Series 1

With his radio popularity renewed by *Frankie Howerd Goes East*, the natural progression to TV came with these three, hour-long, monthly comedy spectaculars which relied on Frankie's relaxed, conversational style with a live audience. Well aware of the confusions and complications that were plaguing television at the time, Frankie insisted on bringing in his very own cameraman who had strict instructions to focus on and follow the star, no matter what the rest of the action was. Frankie's transition to television was made easier thanks to the fact that Bill Lyon-Shaw, who had cast the comedian in his first major theatrical

break, *For the Fun of It*, was producing the series.

Broadcast live from the People's Palace, the programmes welcomed variety guests such as the Beverly Sisters and were peppered with studio-bound live skits, notably a messy cookery class vignette with far too many cooks (including Frankie and Bill Fraser), ensuring that the kitchen ended up like a war zone. Frankie remembered 'some madness involving the making of Tittlepong Tarts and Bees' Knees Puddings in which (needless to say) everything went wrong.' Feeling hampered technically, Frankie was uncomfortable with the final result ('of course, my nerves were shockingly emphasised by the TV cameras'), but the viewers and BBC bosses were more than pleased. Importantly, as with other pioneering small screen comedians like Arthur Askey, Benny Hill and Terry-Thomas, Frankie's initial bash at television fame depended on acute and biting parodies of television itself. The medium provided the material for much of the humour and, as such, the shows had a primitive but telling sophistication.

FRANKIE HOWERD with the Beverly Sisters and Ernest Maxin
Written by Eric Sykes, Choreographer Ernest

A publicity shot from the 1981 series *Frankie Howerd Strikes Again.*

Maxin, Producer Bill Lyon-Shaw
Three programmes: 8.45-9.45 pm, Saturdays,
12 January-8 March 1952, in black and white
on the BBC

Frankie Howerd's Korean Party

Having created a hugely popular radio show
out of troop concerts (*Frankie Howerd
Goes East*), Frankie continued on this
morale-boosting roll by performing for
British servicemen in Korea in 1952.
Entertaining home audiences for the festive
season, Frankie gave the classic material
another airing for British-based servicemen
at the Nuffield Centre. This was recorded
and broadcast as an hour-long Frankie
special on the BBC with support from Eve
Boswell.
*Written by Eric Sykes, Producer Kenneth
Carter*
*8.15-9.15 pm, Tuesday 9 December 1952, in
black and white on the BBC*

Frankie creates
culinary chaos
while Bill Fraser
apes popular
TV chef Philip
Harben in *The
Howerd Crowd*
(1952).

Television's Second Christmas Party

A special Christmas Day broadcast which pre-
empted the more familiar *Christmas Night
With the Stars* tradition. An ensemble piece
featuring the best-loved names in television,
Frankie was signed up as guest comedian and,
apparently, stole the show from the likes of
Norman Wisdom, Arthur Askey, Tommy
Cooper, Ethel Revnell, Betty Driver and John
Slater. The performer was less than happy with
his performance, feeling that the time-slot
given (about halfway through the broadcast)
was wrong for him. He felt he should be nearer
the top of the bill. However, these were the sort
of end-of-term jamboree programmes where
billing didn't really matter. To be included at
all was the measure of your popularity and
Frankie's performance clearly marked him out
as one of the key funnymen in the country.
Produced by Bryan Sears and Bill Lyon-Shaw
*7.30-9.15 pm Thursday 25 December 1952 in
black and white on the BBC*

Nuts In May

In between radio and television series, Frankie's resident scriptwriting genius, Eric Sykes, wrote this special 'spring frolic' which the *Daily Express* dubbed 'a triumph'. A comedy revue with music, Frankie held court, delivered his monologues, performed skits and introduced his guests – grumpy broadcaster Gilbert Harding and singing personality Carole Carr.
Producer Kenneth Carter
8.45-9.25 pm, Wednesday 13 May 1953, in black and white on the BBC

The Frankie Howerd Show

A one-off special television experience with Frankie Howerd and guest Joan Turner live from the 1953 Radio Show at Earl's Court, London. Scripted by the ever-dependable Eric Sykes and his Goon pal, Spike Milligan.
Producer Kenneth Carter
9.05-9.50 pm, Thursday 10 September 1953, in black and white on the BBC

What's My Line?

Uncertain about the direction his television career was taking, in February 1953 Frankie had accepted a guest star spot on this popular 'what-does-this-bloke-do-for-a-living?' telly parlour game. In a letter guaranteed to appease Frankie, the producer T Leslie Jackson wrote: 'We have never had a better celebrity (and that includes Bob Hope) … On behalf of seven million viewers, many thanks.'

Having been such a smash hit, Frankie was invited back in March 1954 as a replacement for professional grouch Gilbert Harding, joining the standard team of Isobel Barnett, Barbara Kelly, David Nixon and host Eamonn Andrews. But it was hardly the success that people expected. Frankie himself was ultra-critical, explaining that 'I was absolutely appalling in the show … I sat there, lunatic with fear, frozen like a rabbit caught in the headlights of a car … Barbara Kelly sat next to me, and felt so sorry for me that she passed me bits of paper on which she'd scribbled questions for me to ask. I was so paralysed I couldn't even read them! I was a spectacular

Marianne McCourt packs a punch with a game Frankie in the 1953 show *Nuts in May.*

flop, so much so that the telephone lines to the BBC were jammed with complaints. The press was scathing – and rightly so.'

Later, when Noël Coward organised the Palladium-based 'Night of a Thousand Stars' benefit for the Actors' Orphanage, Frankie teamed up with old cohort Margaret Rutherford. 'We did a sketch as two women aboard a cross-Channel steamer, and Margaret had something to say about getting away from all the things that were wrong with England. To which I replied: "Yes, including *What's My Line?*" – and it brought the house down.'

Tons of Money

Frankie starred in this breakneck, madcap and door-slammingly hilarious adaptation of the classic Aldwych farce by Will Evans and Valentine, concerning a poverty-stricken married couple (Frankie and Eleanor Summerfield), whose life together is packed with bills and writs. However, when they unexpectedly inherit a fortune and continue to

Tea for two ... Frankie shares a farcical moment with Eleanor Summerfield in rehearsal for the 1954 comedy *Tons of Money*.

dodge debts their troubles really begin. Commenting on the television version in a February 1955 issue of *Radio Times*, Frankie wryly remarked, 'That show had a mixed press but viewers seemed to like it and I'm going to do a similar show for television later this year.' That didn't happen, but in 1956 he did take part in a stage revival of *Tons of Money*. In the meantime, Frankie was immensely proud of the TV version, claiming that 'It was an experiment on my part and the first public demonstration of stirrings of restlessness: the feeling that had slowly grown over the months that I needed to diversify my talents.'

Aubrey Henry Maitland Allington FRANKIE HOWERD, Louise Allington ELEANOR SUMMERFIELD, Sprules, a butler JACK MELFORD, Simpson, a parlourmaid ROSEMARY DAVIES, Miss Benita Mullett JOAN YOUNG, Giles, a gardener's boy LEE YOUNG, James Chesterman, solicitor GEORGE BENSON, Jean Everard BARBARA SHOTTER, Henery BILL FRASER, George Maitland ROLAND GREEN Designer Frederick Knapman, Producer Graeme Muir
9.15-10.45 pm 26 December 1954, in black and white on the BBC

The Howerd Crowd
Series 2

After a break of three years, Frankie returned to the series which had launched his small screen career. The deliciously intricate and well-tailored scripts were still penned by Eric Sykes. An elongated bit of business which saw Frankie lecturing on the pleasures of lovemaking by using a lifesize rag doll to illustrate his instructions was deemed degrading and disgusting by several viewers!
Producer Ernest Maxin
Two programmes: 9.30-10.30 pm, Saturdays, 11 June and 27 August 1955, in black and white on the BBC

Frankie Howerd

'Now – listen – Now – Ah! Frankie Howerd invites you to join him at 7.50' enticed the *Radio Times* blurb for the first of these Frankie specials with music, laughs and guest stars. The first broadcast rejoiced in familiar supports from his radio success, *The Frankie Howerd Show*, including Lee Young and Shani Wallis, while the second featured Joan Sims from the 1955 Light Programme *Christmas Crackers*.
Written by Johnny Speight and Dick Barry, Orchestra directed by Malcolm Lockyer, Designer Norman James, Producer George Inns Show 1: 7.50-8.20 pm, Thursday 11 October 1956; Show 2: 9.45-10.15 pm, Monday 3 December 1956, in black and white on the BBC

Pantomania or Dick Whittington

1956 had been a vintage year for Frankie – in June, he had made his first appearance on *Sunday Night at the London Palladium* and at Christmas he starred in the Beeb's traditional Yuletide extravaganza. As *Radio Times* stated, despite its fairly standard title this was no ordinary pantomime. Chock-full of the best-loved BBC personalities and presenters (including telly chef Philip Harben as the back end of the panto cow!), the comedy quota was set to overload with a sparkling script from Eric Sykes and appearances from Hattie Jacques and Spike Milligan. Frankie starred in the principal comedian role, Idle Jack, wallowing in Sykes' surreal imagination and jolly twisting of pantomime convention. It was a double-header for Frankie, also appearing in the BBC Radio pantomime, *Puss in Gumboots*, the same day. On stage that year, he gave pantomime a miss to star in the farce *Tons of Money*.

Dick Whittington JEAN KENT, Alice Fitzwarren SYLVIA PETERS, Alderman Fitzwarren BILLY COTTON, Idle Jack FRANKIE HOWERD, Good Fairy HATTIE JACQUES, King Rat SAM KYDD, with David Attenborough, Roger Avon, Fred Emney, Edward Evans, Bill Greenslade, Peter Haigh, John Hall, Philip Harben, the Max Jaffa Trio, Jacqueline MacKenzie, Mary Malcolm, Spike Milligan, Freddie Mills, Robert Raglan, Nancy Roberts, Bruce Seton, Eric Sykes, Jimmy Wheeler and the Mitchell Singers.

Orchestra conducted by George Clouston, Music arranged by Alan Bristow, Choreography Leslie Roberts, Writer/comedy director Eric Sykes, Producer John Street

7.45-8.45 pm, 25 December 1956, in black and white on the BBC

The Howerd Crowd

Not a further batch of specials for the BBC but Frankie's first major appearance for the other side, this commercial showcase ironically resurrected the title for Frankie's television début on the BBC. It also, wisely, welcomed another winning script of sketches, skits and stand-up from Eric Sykes. Frankie's next non-BBC appearance would follow rapidly, in an ATV *Saturday Spectacular* broadcast on 11 May 1957.

Executive Producer Val Parnell, Directed and produced by Brian Tesler

An ATV production. 9.00-9.45 pm, Saturday 23 February 1957, in black and white on ITV

Val Parnell's Sunday Night at the London Palladium

Perhaps the most cherished and influential television variety programme of them all, the show enjoyed a string of totally professional hosts from Bruce Forsyth to Jim Dale over its long and hugely successful run. During one stint in the compere position, distinguished actor Robert Morley introduced the great and good of British light entertainment. In this particular edition Morley introduced arguably the greatest, Frankie Howerd, as top-lining guest comedian, alongside fellow guest artistes the Beverly Sisters, Edmund Hockridge, Los Brasilieros and the Tiller Girls.

Dance Director George Carden, Executive Producer Val Parnell, Produced and directed by Brian Tesler

An ATV Production. 8.00-9.00 pm, Sunday 16 March 1958, in black and white on ITV

Play of the Week: The School for Wives

This Associated-Rediffusion offering was Frankie's first major misreading of what his adoring public would and would not tolerate from him. Fresh from his Old Vic triumph as Bottom, Frankie played Arnolphe, a scheming old man who wants a wife tailored to his exact specifications in Miles Malleson's adaptation of Molière's 1662 satire *L'école des femmes*. A real shock to the system for many of his most loyal fans.

Associated-Rediffusion's head of drama, Norman Marshall, had seen Frankie interviewed in the *On Stage* programme and

Camping about with the George Carden Dancers during rehearsals for ATV's *Saturday Spectacular*, May 1957.

Not the ideal career move: Frankie tackles Molière in the April 1958 *Play of the Week: The School For Wives*, seen here in rehearsal with Kenneth Griffith and Joan Newall.

was inspired to ask him to make his ITV drama début. As Kendall Macdonald put it in the *Evening News*, 'His appearance in Molière would seem to indicate that the acting bug has bitten Frankie hard. He says, however: "It's the same picture in a different frame. It's a question of… well, I think I'm slightly graduating. I'm giving things a little more depth instead of just telling jokes. I plan to continue along these lines. I've got a film to do next and then a musical play, but it's still light…" Producer Cyril Butcher told me: "We've made this an absolute romp in the scenes which can be rompish. There are a lot of moral issues and we don't fool about with those, but otherwise it is a rip-roaring romp."'

But, as Frankie put it later, 'The Old Vic is the Old Vic – when you go there you've a pretty shrewd idea of what you're going to get. But for a large proportion of the TV audience, the name Molière meant nothing, the title

didn't matter – what they expected was the familiar Frankie Howerd … The sound of switched-off sets was like a thunderclap across the land.' With the upcoming film (*Further Up the Creek*) proving a damp squib, and the musical play (*Mister Venus*) an out-and-out disaster, Frankie vowed never to stray too far from his popular comic persona again.

Arnolphe (a rich man) FRANKIE HOWERD, Chrysalde (his friend) LESLIE FRENCH, Alain (a countryman) KENNETH GRIFFITH, Georgette (a countrywoman) JOAN NEWALL, Agnes ZENA WALKER, Horace (Oronte's son) CHARLES LAURENCE, Enrique (who has been in America) JOHN BAILEY, Oronte (a friend of Arnolphe) FREDERICK FARLEY

Adaptation Miles Malleson, Settings Reece Pemberton, Director Cyril Butcher

An Associated-Rediffusion Production. 8.30-10.00 pm Wednesday 23 April 1958 in black and white on ITV

The Frankie Howerd Show

Having pinched the title of his first BBC vehicle *The Howerd Crowd*, the ITV network again lifted the self-explanatory name from Frankie's 1953 BBC television special. This was the usual mixture of funny sketches, Frankie's long-winded introductions and tasty guest stars. However, this very special hour-long revue boasted some extra-tasty guest stars in the unmistakeable shape of eccentric character legend and Frankie's *The Runaway Bus* co-star Margaret Rutherford and blonde bombshell Sabrina. Michael Denison and Joyce Shock also appeared.
Executive Producer Bernard Delfont, Producer Kenneth Carter
An ATV Presentation 8.30-9.30 pm Sunday 17 August 1958, in black and white on ITV

Frankie Howerd In...

With Frankie's latest West End appearance an embarrassing flop, Kenneth Adam, controller of programmes for the BBC, penned an internal memo which read: 'The disappearance of *Mister Venus* presumably leaves Frankie Howerd without work. I have considerable interest in this comedian. Do not let us be slow in seeing if we can make use of him.' This was the result. Before *Comedy Playhouse* and *The Galton & Simpson Comedy*, the BBC, now clearly desperate to find the perfect television vehicle for Frankie Howerd, commissioned a couple of self-contained situation comedy playlets for him. Reflecting diverse episodes in the manic life of Frankie Howerd – 'the laughing stock of television,' as *Radio Times*' publicity dubbed him – these two programmes would prove instrumental in lifting his television reputation onto a higher plane, though not immediately.

1: Pity Poor Francis

Less a situation comedy and more a cosy evening in with one of life's failures, with Frankie reflecting on life, his 'laughing stock' reputation and the world in general.
Written by Johnny Speight, Designer Richard Henry, Producer Eric Miller
7.30-8.00 pm, Tuesday 16 December 1958, in black and white on the BBC

2: Shakespeare Without Tears

This, the most popular of the two programmes, proved the ideal vehicle for Frankie's pompous self-importance, wild flights of fancy and endearing eagerness to succeed. Often referred to at the BBC as 'the Old Vic comedy', it was a frantic, pathos-edged farce about a stagestruck shop assistant who dreams of appearing in the plays of William Shakespeare. The aspiring employee with his head in the theatrical clouds is sacked from his mundane job and eagerly grabs employment as a dresser to the star of the Old Vic. Owing to numerous farcical situations Frankie finds himself having to impersonate the star on stage and ultimately saves the day, and the good name of the distinguished thespian, by confessing to the performer's 'dalliance' with a persistent female fan to the woman's outraged husband. The BBC's Light Entertainment department considered the programme a major triumph and the wheels were set in motion for a Frankie series scripted by the two writers.

....

Did You Know? Co-writer Phil Sharp wasn't credited for his written contribution thanks to binding contractual obligations from his previous work on American television sitcom classics *The Phil Silvers Show* and *I Love Lucy*.

....

Written by Reuben Ship and Phil Sharp, Producer Eric Miller
8.40-9.20 pm, Wednesday 28 January 1959 in black and white on the BBC

Frankly Howerd

This series, which sprang directly from *Frankie Howerd In ... Shakespeare Without Tears*, seemed doomed from the outset. Frankie was unhappy with the quality of the scripts and the inability of the writers – the Canadian Ship and the American Sharp – to fully grasp his comic persona. Indeed, to Frankie's astonishment, one had never written for him before and the other didn't even know who he was. However, having impressed the BBC powers-that-be and been commissioned for a series of six half hours, the writers were pretty

With screen girlfriend Gladys (Helen Jessop) in the opening episode of the ill-fated BBC series *Frankly Howerd*.

helpful performer, aiding new writers and 'making a script more Howerdish.' However, at the BBC's insistence, Frankie was forbidden to advise his writers, who were working to establish Frankie as the next major sitcom star. Indeed, Eric Maschwitz, Head of Light Entertainment for BBC Television, had a clear plan. In February 1959 he had written to Frankie's agent with the opinion that *Frankly Howerd* 'should follow Tony Hancock in a series of six or seven half-hour programmes in early April when we can make the series one of our Big Guns for Spring.'

Unfortunately, with Frankie on tenterhooks and the scripts failing to complement his acting strengths, the series was considered a disaster. In a BBC memo from Eric Maschwitz, dated 25 May 1959, Frankie was dismissed as a 'neurotic performer' who is 'unable to make up his mind whether he wants to be a slapstick comedian or a comic actor.' Moreover, although the writers are carefully left blameless, Frank Muir and Denis Norden are cited as writers who, had they 'been available for script supervision', could have improved the situation. Maschwitz's comments were blunt and hurtful, explaining that 'the poor quality of the present Frankie Howerd series is causing me a great deal of concern.'

In later years, Frankie was keen to explain that the finished scripts were 'excellent' but 'just not me'. One of the scripting problems, akin to the first few seasons of *Hancock's Half Hour* on radio, was the insistence on giving the star a girlfriend (played here by Helen Jessop). Hancock's comedy was at its finest in defeat and Frankie's persona was equally mournful. Relationship comedy was not his style; it had to be either complete rejection or, as with his finest situation comedy *Up Pompeii!*, complete, tongue-in-cheek crumpet overload. Whatever the ins and outs of the problematic series, the show's failure to attract good audience figures signalled the end of the comedian's initial golden era. Three years of brief guest appearances and blackballed non-employment were to follow.

much protected by the men in grey suits. Even when discussing the Old Vic comedy Tom Sloan, the Assistant Head of Light Entertainment Television, had informed Frankie and his agent that not one word of the finished script was to be changed. He was eager to point out that this was a comedy drama and not a collection of stand-up routines.

Frankie's 'difficult' reputation was beginning to haunt him and, with his popularity visibly slipping, the performer became paranoid. As a result his performance was affected. Frankie was adamant that his so-called difficult reputation was nonsense. Writing in his autobiography, he comments that his advice to scriptwriters to include the seemingly 'unscripted' oohs and ahhs made him the ultimate professional. Whereas the reams of comedy banter seemed to be ad-lib, in reality every word was scripted and rehearsed.

In public, of course, Frankie was all for the show. He told Rowan Ayers in an April 1959 issue of *Radio Times* that 'Television seems to be a medium in which familiarity no longer breeds contempt. The public, in fact, may not know what it likes, but it certainly likes what it knows. That's why I'm glad this is to be a regular series.' Frankie considered himself a

With SIDNEY VIVIAN as Fred Thompson and HELEN JESSOP as Gladys Thompson, and SAM

KYDD (shows 1 and 2), JOHN BAKER (show 1), BRUNO BARNABE (show 2), ROGER AVON (show 2), TOTTI TRUMAN TAYLOR (show 3), DENYS GRAHAM (show 3) and BERNARD HUNTER (show 3)
Written by Reuben Ship and Phil Sharp, Designers Norman James (shows 1, 2, 5 and 6) and Alan Anson (shows 3 and 4), Music Bruce Campbell, Producer Harry Carlisle 7.30-8.00 pm, Fridays, 1 May-5 June 1959, in black and white on the BBC

Mother Goose

By the end of 1959, after a gruelling summer season in Scarborough and while embroiled in the disastrous West End *Alice in Wonderland*, Frankie could refer to this BBC Boxing Day frolic as 'the teeniest glimmer of hope' in a rapidly declining career. The show was recorded in front of an invited audience of 1,500 people and was Frankie's first stab at playing Dame. According to producer Richard Afton, 'Frankie is at his funniest, and it's a real panto as the kiddies know it – and by kiddies I mean anyone from two to a hundred-and-two.' He also pointed out that 'Harry Granley, whose knees are bent throughout the performance, is perfect as the goose.'
Mother Goose FRANKIE HOWERD, the Goose HARRY GRANLEY, Johnny JOE CHURCH, Colin ANNE DALY, Jill WENDY COOK, the Mayor EDDIE LESLIE, the Fairy RHODA ROGERS, the Demon LESLIE ADAMS, King Goose AUSTEN GAFFNEY, King Frog MYRTA ESTEVES, Water Lily GILLIAN BLAIR, the Broker's Men TRIO SPARKES
Plus the Dagenham Girl Pipers, 12 Peggy O'Farrell Juveniles and the Television Toppers
Written by Bertram Montague, Dance Director Jack Billings, Orchestra conducted by Woolf Phillips, Producer Richard Afton 7.40-9.10, Saturday 26 December 1959 in black and white on the BBC

Ladies and Gentle-*men*

1960 wasn't a good year. Among other humiliations, Frankie did a stint on *Juke Box Jury* ('Pop was a subject about which I knew absolutely nothing,' he lamented later) and

was involved in an ill-fated TV version of radio's *Twenty Questions*. The producer was Maurice (*Alice in Wonderland*) Warwick, the chairman was Stuart McPherson and Frankie's fellow panelists were Stephen Potter, Isobel Barnett and Muriel Young. And on 5 March he had swallowed his pride and struggled through a bottom-of-the-bill slot on *Sunday Night at the London Palladium*. *Ladies and Gentle-men* was a happier experience. That superior character actor Richard Wattis introduced this one-off television special of comic monologues and hilarious sketches. Rather warily described as '45 minutes of unpredictable entertainment', the show had another tantalising guest star in smooth-as-silk Dennis Price. Here he proved the ideal, high-profile authority figure to thwart Frankie's airy flights of fancy.
Written by Johnny Speight, Ray Galton & Alan Simpson and Barry Took, Producer Richard Afton 8.50-9.35 pm, Saturday 24 September 1960, in black and white on the BBC

★★★★★★

Frankie's annus horribilis of 1961 is well documented. After over-running on ITV's live *Sunday Night at the London Palladium* show he was almost ousted from television completely. He made a single guest appearance on the Peter Haigh cartoon game show *Laughline*. The following day Tom Sloan sent Frankie a memo regretfully informing him that Kenneth Adam, controller of programmes, had axed the show.

The following year featured a guest star turn in an untransmitted 30-minute pilot for a comedy detective series called *The Secret Keepers*. Alma Cogan, Harold Lang and PeggyAnn Clifford were the stars; Shirley Bassey, Jess Conrad and Cardew Robinson were the other guest stars; writer/ producer/ director was Kenneth Hume.

1962 was also to include Frankie's now legendary stint at the Establishment Club and several noteworthy, career-turning spots on television variety programmes. He was once again hired by Bill Cotton and enjoyed a celebrated guest spot on the Alma Cogan variety show *Startime*. It was his semi-triumphant return to the small screen but it was satire which would really drag him back to the top of the tree in 1963.

★★★★★★

Comedy Playhouse: Have You Read This Notice?

Following the parting of the ways between Galton & Simpson and Tony Hancock after the single series of *Hancock* for the BBC, the writers found a new lease of life for the old Hancock versus Sid James banter in *Steptoe and Son*. However, so prolific was the duo and so much in demand by the BBC that they were invited to write for any comedian they wanted. Having worked with the comedian on radio and, most recently, on the television special *Ladies and Gentle-men*, both asked immediately to write for Frankie Howerd. They were categorically told to 'Forget him, he's finished!' Regardless, they penned a second season of *Comedy Playhouse*. Seven potential pilots were written (the previous batch had spawned *Steptoe and Son*), including the Leslie Phillips and Bernard Cribbins mind-game, *Impasse*, Alfred Marks as *The Handyman* and this vehicle for their favoured comedy star, Frankie Howerd.

Ironically, the Hancock connection was reinforced with the casting of Tony's old radio pal, Bill Kerr. Frankie starred as the mild-mannered Norman Fox, returning from his holiday in Switzerland and plagued by his conscience as he desperately tries to get a Swiss watch past customs. Ray Galton remembers that Frankie was hardly flavour of the month at the BBC. 'They weren't keen on us writing for Frank at all. Tom Sloan said that Frank's last show was terrible and his PA, Queenie, brought in all these audience appreciation figures for Frankie's latest shows and they were all disastrous. He said, "There you are, I'm right." He offered us the *Comedy Playhouse* deal which was fantastic and far too good to turn down, but he did say, "If you want to put Frankie Howerd in one that's fine." And we did! It didn't resurrect his career but I like to think it helped.'

Norman Fox FRANKIE HOWERD, 1st Customs Officer BILL KERR, Aeroplane Passenger EDWIN APPS
Written by Ray Galton & Alan Simpson, Producer Graeme Muir
8.20-8.45 pm, Friday 29 March 1963, in black and white on the BBC

That Was The Week That Was

Despite the BBC's reluctance to employ Frankie, Galton & Simpson's faith in him was almost immediately borne out when the great comedian was discovered by the satire generation. Having been spotted regaling his audience at the fashionable Establishment Club in London's Soho, Frankie had been signed by Ned Sherrin for a brief deconstruction of the Budget for this, the Beeb's ultimate comic exposure of politics and pomposity. Sherrin reasoned that 'If he can do an hour at the Establishment he could certainly do 15 minutes on national television.'

With Reginald Maudling's Budget still fresh in the audience's mind (it had been announced just three days earlier), Frankie's gentle conversational delivery and the hidden timebombs in Johnny Speight's explosive observations created a relaxed, biting satire which played like over-the-garden-wall tittle-tattle. The result was electric. In the era of Frostie and Cookie, any joke aimed at political bigwigs and the ultimate target, Prime Minister Harold Macmillan, couldn't possibly fail. The satire boom wasn't to last and, indeed, 1963 can be cited as the movement's last golden year, but Frankie and Speight's peerless scripts caught the zeitgeist while retaining Frankie's uniquely uncertain style. It was homely satire in which the Prime Minister's wife was reduced to 'Dot', just another meddling woman controlling the country from the top.

Frankie was slightly uneasy before the show began but an over-running schedule relaxed him and allowed him a dig at the show straight away ('I've been waiting!'). At ease with his material and growing in confidence by the minute, he throws in unscripted asides, sends up the contemporary big boys of television (describing David Frost as the one who wears his hair backwards and commenting on the 'cruel glasses' of Robin Day), mocks the song sung by Millicent Martin ('the one you can't hear the words of!') and grabs the chance to change from stand-up to sit-down comedian. ('I should be dynamic, the money they're paying me!') This is Frankie on bristling, world-beating form.

Sherrin believes that the piece succeeded because it was 'reducing international politics to kitchen conversation.' Indeed, Frankie's cosy barbs aimed at political incompetence were never blatantly cynical but their controversial message was delivered even more powerfully because of, not in spite of, the gentle, chatty approach. The *TW3* appearance was a national sensation and, after three lonely years in the wilderness, Frankie found himself the hottest comedy star in the country. Indeed, just three weeks later he made a triumphant starring appearance on *Sunday Night at the London Palladium* with sparkling material penned by Sid Green and Dick Hills.

With David Frost, Roy Kinnear, David Kernan, Lance Percival, Willie Rushton, Millicent Martin and Bernard Levin with guest comedian FRANKIE HOWERD Producer Ned Sherrin 10.35-11.25 pm, Saturday 6 April 1963, in black and white on the BBC

A Last Word on the Election

With Frankie having become the darling of the Oxbridge set and the acceptable face of political satire on British television, the BBC happily commissioned this Ned Sherrin special for him. With a roll-call of some of the finest writers working in television (from Galton & Simpson to Dennis Potter, no less) and with Frankie at the peak of his performing confidence, this timely (the General Election had taken place the previous Friday) look at government and the future under Labour's Harold Wilson was a ratings winner and a comic masterpiece. Frankie was simply firing on all cylinders and doing his, by now, familiar stand-up routine, with the coveted, late-night slot allowing him to be sweetly cynical in his own inimitable fashion.

Written by Frankie Howerd, Ray Galton & Alan Simpson, Frank Muir, Denis Norden, David Nathan and Dennis Potter, Directed and produced by Ned Sherrin 11.15-11.40 pm Sunday 18 October 1964, in black and white on BBC1

Frankie Howerd

With Tony Hancock having exited stage left and their thirst for pathos-driven sitcom quenched by Wilfrid Brambell and Harry H Corbett, writing legends Ray Galton & Alan Simpson finally got their wish to write 'a series of unlikely situations' for Frankie. Alan Simpson maintains that it's 'the best thing we did for him. A sort of situation comedy Frank would introduce himself!' With a downtrodden and woebegone comic persona similar to Hancock's, Frankie relished these beautifully constructed scripts. Naturally, blessed with the same scriptwriters and producer, these programmes were very much akin to the Hancock style and, indeed, Frankie's nervousness around the opposite sex and reluctance to reveal his real age are running themes throughout.

Like Hancock, Frankie was often depicted as a failed actor. Whereas Tony had Sid James as a dodgy, unhelpful agent, Frankie had the blunt Warren Mitchell. The likes of Beryl Reid and June Whitfield would crop up too and the emphasis was very much on Frankie the comic loser in the glorious Hancock tradition. However, the brilliance was in the subtle differences. Importantly, whereas Hancock yearned for reality and believability in his comedy, Frankie was happy to reveal the entire programme as simply that: a programme. Pioneering the behind-the-scenes exposures of Marty Feldman and the Monty Python boys, Frankie would often break into scenes of the supporting actors sitting around chatting, drinking tea and relaxing between takes.

The star was introduced in the same fashion each week. Frankie would stride out onto the studio floor, make himself comfy on a stool and simply chat to the audience. As often as not it would be a mild rant about the government or his penny-pinching BBC bosses, the disinterest of his producer and the prison-like regime of the corporation: 'The better behaved you are the quicker you get out!' Gradually a thematic thread would emerge from his observational humour and a self-contained, reflective, elongated sketch, with every sitcom convention firmly in place, would illustrate the problematic topic. The writers even sent up their own work by characterising Frankie as 'a sort of cross between Bertie Wooster and Albert Steptoe'. It proved the perfect vehicle for Frankie's comic style and, even taking into account the ultra-successful *Up Pompeii!*, many consider these shows his funniest, best-performed and most representative television work of all.

Series 1

The first batch of six Frankie stand-up sitcoms cast our hapless hero in various silly situations and farcical frolics. The first show saw him visit the BBC staff doctor, played by Hancock's 'legalised vampire' Patrick Cargill. The second programme was a masterclass in how to survive the bleak periods of resting between theatrical engagements, while the third featured Frankie getting away from his hassles on a continental trip. It was more holidaying in the fourth show with Frankie on a winter cruise, show five had our bumbling star panic over a threatening letter and the final half-hour took a wry look-back at the show's final rehearsal.

....

Did You Know? How times change. *Radio Times* eagerly made Frankie their cover star for the issue of 5-11 December 1964, detailing the opening episode of the first series. And on Christmas Day 1964, during the run of this groundbreaking series, Frankie cropped up to introduce a broadcast inviting the seasonal audience to meet unfortunate kids in hospital.

....

With: Show 1, Patrick Cargill and Audrey Nicholson. Show 2, Norman Bird, Arthur Mullard, Anthony Sagar, Ken Roberts, Rita Webb, Margaret Flint, Lala Lloyd, Louis Mansi, Trevor Barrie and Walter Swash. Show 3, Colin Gordon, Anthony Sharp, Len Lowe, Alec Bregonzi, Don Smoothy and Stella Kemball.

Show 4, Alfie Bass, Derek Francis, Frank Thornton, Delphi Lawrence, Bill Shine, Dennis Chinnery, Bill Maxim, Barney Gilbraith and Frank Littlewood. Show 5, William Kendall and Terence Edmund. Show 6, Glenn Melvyn, Hugh Paddick, Arthur Mullard, Yootha Joyce, Julian Orchard, Felix Bowness, Barbara Archer, David Grahame and Marian Collins
Written by Ray Galton & Alan Simpson, Music Peter Knight, Designer John Hurst, Producer Duncan Wood
8.00-8.25 pm Fridays, 11 December 1964-15 January 1965, in black and white on BBC1

East of Howerd

In a return to the ethos of Frankie's popular radio series *Frankie Howerd Goes East*, this one-off special, recorded for the BBC by Mithras Films, captured the great comedian doing his stuff in Malaysia. Again, the format was simple but perfectly suited to Frankie's down-to-earth comic persona. He rounded up a gang of entertainers and brought a bit of home comfort and jollification to the British servicemen stationed in the humid back-of-beyond. The film crew not only recorded the concert but also captured some priceless back-stage antics with Frankie and the cast. The programme also included touching interview soundbites from the troops themselves, missing home and loved ones and reacting to the conflict around them. The result is not only a very funny, very poignant piece of television but a valuable social document to boot.

Looking relaxed and confident in an open-neck shirt and shambling around a bare, makeshift stage, Frankie is in his element. Basically, it's the same routine, with the same jokes and the same sending-up of authority, that would be his staple comic diet until his very last television series, *Frankie's On…* Indeed, it's almost criminal how similar the material is (in fact sometimes it's exactly the same), but only Frankie could trundle out the most ancient, moth-balled groaner and present it as new. Some of these gags were doing the rounds years and years before the great man's birth, but who cares? Certainly not the British servicemen in the audience for this show.

His prime target for authority-baiting and disrespectful condemnation is, of course, the Colonel, and even the merest insult aimed at this lofty individual is greeted with rousing cheers and uncontrolled laughter. Frankie is clearly having a whale of a time as he spins through his oft-repeated paces. The brilliance of Frankie was that his basic routine could be amended and adapted at will. Here he sends up the pompous, public school education of the officer class, abbreviating Twickenham to Twickers and Edinburgh to Edders. This presentation remains one of Frankie's finest television ventures, and although uncredited to any writer, was skilfully gleaned from his wealth of Sykes, Galton, Simpson and Speight material. A comic performance for the classic time capsule.

FRANKIE HOWERD with Shirley Abicair and Al Koran

Director John Irvin, Producer Joe McGrath

A Mithras Film Production. 8.45-9.35 pm, Saturday 1 January 1966, in black and white on BBC2

Frankie Howerd
Series 2

A second helping of the irresistible mix of Frankie and writers Galton & Simpson, this proved just as brilliant as the first series in 1964/5. Frankie would link a couple of sitcom-style sketches with his familiar monologues and observations, spar with some of the character actors left over from *Hancock's Half Hour* and continually break away from the narrative to share a cheeky thought with the audience. The series featured Frankie in another collection of misadventures, ranging from a trip to see his member of parliament at the House of Commons, a failed attempt to break into films, another failed attempt to become part of the Swinging Sixties and a

High society with Beryl Reid in the second series of Galton and Simpson's *Frankie Howerd*, February 1966.

classic encounter with Peter Butterworth who takes Frankie's parting 'If you're ever in London look me up!' invitation all too seriously.

However, perhaps the classic example from this series and one which, thankfully, survives in the archives, centres on the general theme of loneliness and Frankie's disastrous attempts to find the ideal life partner through a lonely hearts agency. John Le Mesurier is typically languid and dry as Janice Goodbody ('Ltd!'/'Well, I should think you must be!'), the girls on offer are shocking ('A Bunny Girl … judging by the ears!') and Le Mesurier's wife (the busty Sheree Winton) offers no comfort at all. In the end Frankie is lured to an art gallery to meet the deliciously insane June Whitfield, playing the manic, desperate-to-wed Beryl Cuttlebunt. ('I thought, I'm not surprised with a name like that!') In a breathtakingly hilarious vignette June begs for passionate lovemaking in the Tate ('Old Harry would turn in his grave!') and insists on being bitten: 'Bite you? I can't dear, I'm a vegetarian!' A superbly structured comic tour de force.

With: Show 1, Arthur Mullard, Anthony Sagar, Julian Orchard, Dennis Ramsden, Ken Wynne, Tim Buckland and William Raymor. Show 2, Warren Mitchell, Beryl Reid, Arthur Mullard, Rita Webb, Valerie Bell, Felix Bowness, Henry Longhurst, Sheree Winton, James McManus, Emmett Hennessey and Keith Ashley. Show 3, John Le Mesurier, June Whitfield, Edwin Brown, Sheree Winton and Peggy Ann Clifford. Show 4, Nora Nicholson, Garry Marsh, Coral Atkins, Evelyn Lund, Harry Brunsing, Eddie Malin, Anita Moore, Ronald Alexander, George Myddleton and Peter Perry. Show 5, Peter Butterworth, Gretchen Franklin, Gerald Rowland, Alan Baulch, Bill Maxim, Marie Makino, George Hirste and Anthony Buckingham. Show 6, Hugh Paddick, Sheila Steafel, Arthur Mullard, Dennis Ramsden, Michael Robbins, Ian Trigger, Joan Ingram, Peter Diamond and Tim Buckland. Written by Ray Galton & Alan Simpson, Incidental music by Peter Knight, Designer Chris Pemsel, Producer Duncan Wood 9.30-10.00 pm Tuesdays, 22 February-29 March 1966, in black and white on BBC1

The Blackpool Show

With Tony Hancock facing his darkest hour, he was less than equal to compering this variety series broadcast from the ABC Theatre in Blackpool. Indeed, he missed two shows entirely. The fourth instalment saw guest star Frankie Howerd climb aboard. The package also included the Kaye Sisters and Terry Hall with Lenny the Lion – boy, they don't make shows like that any more. Hancock suggested that Frankie perform a tried-and-tested old music hall piece with him. Interestingly, Frankie (the star comic here) was to stooge for Hancock.

Frankie wasn't convinced that the material was good enough – or that the working relationship would gel. He told the producer Mark Stuart, 'What Tony's got in mind just won't work. It was written for somebody else, and for me to play it (apart from it being dreadfully old-fashioned) would be bad for us both. Also, it's so long I wouldn't be able to do the patter act you also want.' It was eventually decided that Frankie should do his own act as usual and then trade a few gags with Hancock in the finale. What Frankie didn't know was that Hancock was on the slippery slope which would lead to his demise in Australia less than two years later. Speaking fondly of his colleague, Frankie noted that 'Shortly after his death I was interviewed on television and asked "Have you ever contemplated suicide?" I was so furious at this patent exploitation of [Tony's] going that I looked the gentleman straight in the eye and replied coldly: "Suicide, no. Murder, yes!"'

With JOHN JUNKIN, PETER GORDENO AND THE DANCERS, BOB SHARPLES and the ABC Television Showband
Written by John Muir and Eric Green, Produced and directed by Mark Stuart
An ABC production. Recorded from 8.30 pm on Sunday 10 July 1966 and broadcast the same night from 10.05-11.05 pm

The Bruce Forsyth Show

That rubber-limbed, huge-chinned, totally professional and evergreen all-round entertainer Bruce Forsyth enjoyed his eponymous variety series on ITV from 1959. In this edition from August 1966, Bruce was joined by a very high-profile comic guest, a certain Frankie Howerd, and it was a partnership that proved particularly popular. So popular indeed, that the duo were reunited almost immediately for a seasonal special at the end of the year.

The Canterville Ghost

A lavish TV musical for the American market, with book by Burt Shevelove (of *A Funny Thing Happened on the Way to the Forum* fame) and tunes from *Fiddler on the Roof* duo Sheldon Harnick (lyrics) and Jerry Bock (music). First aired on ABC's 'Stage 67' strand on Wednesday 2 November 1966, Frankie's co-stars ranged from screen legend Douglas Fairbanks Jr and stage legend Michael Redgrave to Herman's Hermits frontman, Peter Noone. Others in the cast were David Charkham, Mark Coleano, Natalie Schafer and Tippy Walker. *Variety*, however, was not impressed. 'Burt Shevelove's musicalised adaptation of Oscar Wilde's *The Canterville Ghost* was a spiritless, soggy effort with few redeeming qualities … What it added up to was a waste of a considerable amount of good talent … It's another miss for Stage 67.' The soundtrack is preserved on *Four Television Musicals* (Blue Pear 1019).

Frankie and Bruce's Christmas Show

A rollicking and laughter-packed variety revue of the kind that television simply doesn't make anymore. The talent packed into this feature-length Yuletide treat was quite astounding and at the head of the table 'your agreeably disagreeable hosts', the mournful Frankie Howerd and the spritely Bruce Forsyth, presented 'a 90-minute holiday spectacular' to celebrate the 'season of goodwill to all men except each other!' In effect, it was a belated resurrection of the Howerd versus Derek Roy feud of *Variety Bandbox* and the banter, bickering and biting comedy proved an irresistible combination.
FRANKIE HOWERD and BRUCE FORSYTH with Cilla Black, Tommy Cooper, Tom Jones, the

Kaye Sisters, Aleta Morrison, the Malcolm Goddard Dancers and Bob Sharples Written by Sid Green and Dick Hills, Music from the ABC Television Showband, Musical associate Colin Keyes, Choreography Malcolm Goddard, Designer Neville Green, Executive Producer Philip Jones, Director Peter Frazer-Jones, Producer Peter Dulay
An ABC Production. 9.40-11.10 pm, Saturday 24 December 1966, in black and white on ITV

60s Commercials

Frankie was the perfect person to sell you things and, in a unique and groundbreaking move, began his pitch by taking a negative attitude. The best of these commercials appeared on British television in 1967 when he was hired by Lyons Maid Ice Cream and supplied with a script by future Carry On writer Dave Freeman. Surrounded by pots of the stuff and bemoaning his assignment ('I never touch the stuff'), Frankie figuratively grabs the money and forces some of the muck down his throat. Of course, impressed by the array of flavours and won over by the delectable taste, he endorses it fully and mutters, 'Very good … I might have to buy one myself!'

Those Two Fellers

As two of the country's most prolific and endearing comedy writers, Sid Green and Dick Hills became celebrities themselves. Writing for Dave King and Morecambe and Wise, the duo would often crop up as supporting players in sketches (notably the Eric and Ern gem, 'Boom-Oo-Yatta-Ta-Ta' from *Two Of A Kind*) and were frequently referred to as 'those two fellers'. Having scored with their own sketch series, *That Show*, in 1964, Green and Hills were back with this six-part comedy programme. Frankie Howerd, a comedian they had often written for on radio and had just worked with on *Frankie and Bruce's Christmas Show*, agreed to be the star guest on the first episode. Frankie was a frequent and welcome guest on other variety television shows. Just over two months after his work with Sid and Dick, Frankie cropped up as the top-billed guest comic on the ITV spectacular *The Blackpool Show* on 23 July 1967.

SID GREEN, DICK HILLS, DIANE RACHELLE with guest comedian FRANKIE HOWERD
Written by Sid Green and Dick Hills, Director Keith Beckett
An ABC Production. 9.10-9.40 pm Friday 5 May 1967, in black and white on ITV

Frankie and Bruce's Christmas Show

Another tinsel-stuffed Christmas special from that dynamite duo Frankie and Brucie, with music, dance, comedy and lighthearted insults. The one and only Tommy Cooper was the guest comic: now that's what you call a Christmas cracker!

Written by Sid Green and Dick Hills Produced and directed by Peter Frazer-Jones
An ABC Production. 9.35-11.05 pm Saturday 23 December 1967, in black and white on ITV

Hattie Jacques flirts with western hero Frankie in the May 1968 special *Howerd's Hour*.

Howerd's Hour

Frankie's first solo small screen special in over two years – since *East of Howerd* for the BBC – this marked a nostalgic return to the scriptwriting brilliance of Eric Sykes and provided plenty of sketch-based opportunities to mug away opposite one of his favourite leading ladies, Hattie Jacques. That bombastic character star from *The Power Game*, Patrick Wymark, also joined in the fun as Frankie reminisced on the amazing exploits of his gallant and foolhardy explorer grandfather. Pop sensations Sandie Shaw and Scott Walker added further lustre.

Producer Keith Beckett
An ABC Production. 8.25-9.25 pm, Sunday 12 May 1968, in black and white on ITV

Frankie Howerd Meets the Bee Gees

Nowadays if a programme is postponed we get repeats of documentaries relating the fascinating story of coffee-making in Java but in the glorious days of 1968, when *An Evening With Jack Benny* was cancelled the unsuspecting viewing public was treated to this unheralded and unscheduled gem: a musical comedy evening with the Antipodean songsters belting out the hits, Francis belting out the witty, whimsical monologues and the original big-toothed quintet even joining the great comedian in three scripted sketches from the masterly Ray Galton & Alan Simpson.

FRANKIE HOWERD and THE BEE GEES (Barry Gibb, Robin Gibb, Maurice Gibb, Colin Peterson and Vince Melouney) with Arthur Mullard, Valentine Dyall, June Whitfield, Julie Driscoll and Brian Auger and the Trinity
Written by Ray Galton & Alan Simpson, Produced and directed by John Robins
A Thames Production. 8.55-10.00 pm, Tuesday 20 August 1968, in black and white on ITV

The Frankie Howerd Show

Following his successful appearance on the Green and Hills show *Those Two Fellers*, Frankie was rewarded with this single variety special, which gathered together a host of celebrities for songs and sketches. Frankie played a faithful family retainer in a skit on pomposity, position and public image opposite the beautiful Diane Cilento and reinterpreted Shakespeare's *Othello* with himself as the Moor and Cilla Black as his Liverpudlian Desdemona. Frankie also presented his unique take on ITV's beloved *News at Ten* opposite that 'master' of current affairs Joe Brown and even indulged in a friendly warm-up routine with English sports legends Bobby Moore and Lew Hoad.

With Cilla Black, Joe Brown, Diane Cilento, Bobby Moore, Lew Hoad, Ken Parry, Nosher Powell, the New Faces and Eric Delaney
Written by Sid Green and Dick Hills, Orchestra conducted by Ronnie Aldrich, Designer Brian Eatwell, Producer Peter Frazer-Jones
9.10-10.00 pm, Wednesday 25 September 1968, in black and white on ITV

The London Palladium Show

This was to all intents and purposes a retread of the classic *Sunday Night at the London Palladium*. Indeed, in the *TV Times* blurb it was even identified as such. As Frankie Howerd, who was guest compere on this edition, commented, 'My personal view is that people prefer variety at the weekends … the time they relax with their families. They feel the need to be escapist which is why *Sunday Night at the London Palladium* is ideal.' Just three months later, Frankie was the guest comedian, alongside that gap-toothed master of smooth talk Terry-Thomas, on the Easter family spectacular, *Variety Parade*, broadcast on ITV on 30 April 1969.

FRANKIE HOWERD with Vince Hill, Fred Roby, Peter Nero, the Palladium Dancers, Jack Parnell's Orchestra under the direction of Peter Knight
Frankie's material written by Sid Green and Dick Hills, Choreography Malcolm Goddard, Designer Michael Bailey, Producer Albert Locke
An ATV production. 7.25-8.25 pm, Sunday 26 January 1969 ITV

David Frost presents … Frankie Howerd

This colourful showcase for Frankie represented another brush with the Beatles.

Made for US TV by the former *That Was the Week That Was* frontman David Frost, the show was recorded on Sunday 16 June 1968 at the Intertel studios at Stonebridge House in Wembley. Frankie's musical guests were none other than Paul McCartney and Apple protégée Mary Hopkin but the eventual broadcast, on Sunday 23 February 1969, didn't succeed in cracking the American market for Frankie.

Frankie Howerd at the Poco a Poco

As *TV Times* screamed: 'Following the tremendous success of Frank Sinatra at the Sands Hotel Las Vegas, Sammy Davis at the Coconut Grove Los Angeles and Tony Bennett at the Hollywood Bowl, Thames Television proudly presents Frankie Howerd at the Poco a Poco, Stockport.' Frankie was on blistering form with the same old banter for this specially presented live concert from the Cheshire venue. Frankie's guest star from his May 1968 special, Patrick Wymark, returned to the fold to give an aggrieved Frankie an acting masterclass, ex-Shadow Hank Marvin joined Frankie for a song or two, while the script was from frequent Frankie collaborators Sid Green and Dick Hills. Ted Brennan, the Mike Sammes Singers, Doreen Chung and the ever-faithful Sunny Rogers were in support. Interviewed by *TV Times*, Frankie reflected that 'I don't know what I'm going to do tonight!' Of course, every last ooh and ahh had been carefully rehearsed.

Produced and directed by William G Stewart
A Thames Production. 8.00-9.00 pm
Wednesday 7 May 1969, in black and white on ITV

The Frankie Howerd Show

Sid Green and Dick Hills returned to pen this six-part variety series for Frankie, in which the resident glamour and music were provided by Pan's People and Jack Parnell's Orchestra respectively. It was the familiar and all-conquering mixture of downtrodden monologues, skits, songs and star names billed in *TV Times* as 'Lanky Frankie and his guests in a tornado of fun and music.' Rehearsals took place at the folk club, Cecil Sharp House in London.

Show 1: Salena Jones, the Tremeloes, Jack Haig, Peggy Mount. Show 2: Danny La Rue, Dilys Watling, the New Seekers. Show 3: Wendy Craig, Janie Marden, the Moody Blues. Show 4: Warren Mitchell, Ronnie Carroll, the Virgil Brothers. Show 5: Edmund Hockridge, the Jonson Sisters. Show 6: Patrick Cargill, Janie Marden.

Written by Sid Green and Dick Hills, Choreography Flick Colby, Designers Richard Lake (shows 1-3) and Ray White (shows 4-6). Producer Sid Green, Director Milo Lewis

An ATV Production. 6.15-7.00 pm, Saturdays, 9 August-13 September 1969, in black and white on ITV

★★★★★★

Up Pompeii!

Despite Frankie's many years at the top, it wasn't until this rich, raucous, raunchy, randy and relentlessly risqué slab of comic brilliance came along that he finally found his popular niche on television. For the rest of his life he would be, somewhat misleadingly, linked with Ancient Rome in the hearts and minds of the general public. All the more amazing to think, then, that only a handful of episodes were filmed and, indeed, the entire run of just two series were both originally broadcast in just one year – 1970.

The connection between Frankie and lowbrow hi-jinks in historical costume was first made when he landed the fruitful and fruity role of Pseudolus in the West End production of Stephen Sondheim's *A Funny Thing Happened on the Way to the Forum* in 1963. In tandem with his television comeback in *That Was The Week That Was*, Frankie was suddenly big, big news. Legend has it that Light Entertainment big shots (and, till then, anti-Frankies) Michael Mills and Tom Sloan were on holiday in Pompeii. As the pair strolled around the ruins, Mills reputedly muttered: 'It's amazing! I expect to see Frankie Howerd come loping round the corner!'

Thus was the seed planted. It was decided

that a television situation comedy, with copious amounts of innuendo based around the vaudevillian success of the *Forum* show, should be commissioned. For the star, there was no-one else but Frankie Howerd. And for the sauce-dripping script the only writer up to the job was Talbot Rothwell. Having already written for the likes of Arthur Askey, Terry-Thomas and the Crazy Gang, Rothwell was at the time most celebrated for his bludgeoningly hilarious Carry On screenplays. His thirteenth contribution to the series, *Carry On Up the Jungle*, was just about to go into production with none other than Frankie Howerd heading the cast. Rothwell was sent a copy of the 2000-year-old writings of Plautus and was basically told, 'Rewrite this for Frankie Howerd!'

The result was accurately described in *Radio Times* as 'a sort of Carry On Up the Forum'. However, it was much, much more than that. With Rothwell's keen knowledge of and passion for history, particularly ancient civilisations as plundered in 1964 for his masterwork *Carry On Cleo*, the scripts for Frankie's sitcom were invested with a love and understanding of the period. It may have been a two-set, economically produced comedy show held together by Frankie's powerhouse performance, but the writing was sublime.

The initial 35-minute script written by Rothwell was met with approval by everybody at the BBC. Frankie's friend Barry Took was then in the enviable position of adviser to the BBC comedy department. As a freelance, Took's opinions often helped make or break a programme and in his short tenure he successfully brought together the Oxford and Cambridge elements to make *Monty Python's Flying Circus* and green-lighted Rothwell's classic comedy for Frankie Howerd. Took recalls that, unusually for a first script, 'I laughed out loud!' – as did Frankie himself, who considered it packed with 'splendidly broad and corny gags, both visual and spoken.'

Indeed, while the general consensus was that the jokes were a tad on the naughty side, it was decided that Frankie's charm and easygoing manner would defuse a lot of the shock value. Intriguingly, Frankie himself was uncertain about doing the series. 'I said to the BBC, "Can we get away with it? Is it going too far for the small screen? For people's drawing rooms?" "Don't worry about that," said 'Thing' at the BBC. "Will you do a series?" "Don't worry" meant that since the series had been designed for me, *I'd* carry the can: not 'Thing' … I may have had my cheeky moments but was this going to be too rich for the viewers' blood?' According to Frankie, the solution was to film and broadcast a pilot show (using the first of Rothwell's scripts) and judge the audience reaction accordingly.

Pilot

'Can you see the plot thickening now? Can you? Notice we're using cornflour…'
Frankie Howerd

Recorded on 4 July 1969, the *Up Pompeii!* prototype was filmed in colour and subsequently repeated in all its glory; the initial broadcast, however, was in black and white owing to the fact that BBC1 was still transmitting only in monochrome. The series proper was to make a virtue of its ramshackleness, but this pilot is something else. It sometimes seems as if cameras had been unexpectedly present at an early dress rehearsal. And Frankie himself is visibly feeling his way. But the studio audience's response is warm and encouraging and he battles on.

'Greetings, noble plebeians, crafty artisans and arty courtesans,' he beams, proceeding to give the viewers an inspired geographical tip. 'Imagine Italy is the shape of a woman's leg. Well, Pompeii is situated not quite high enough to be interesting.' We're then introduced to all the regulars, though the soothsayer (later to be called Senna and played by Jeanne Mockford) is for the time being a scrawny creature called Cassandra, played by Ruth Harrison. Young Erotica isn't the naïve character of the later series, more the bit of hot stuff featured in the film version (in a complicated bit of Rothwell wordplay, Frankie describes her as 'one of the original libertine-agers'), while Frankie is saddled with

a tightly curled and unflattering wig, abandoned later on in favour of his own trademark rug.

There are two ill-fitting filmed interludes, one in which Ammonia, breasts bobbing in 20 gallons of asses' milk, loses her soap (a routine repeated in the film) and another in which Frankie goes up onto the balcony with seafaring Phrygian slave trader Captain Bilius ('I thought I saw some Phrygian in the rigging'). But there are plenty of tasty in-jokes – introduced to a shapely slavegirl called Cilla, Frankie clucks 'Such a pretty nose!' – and an absolutely hysterical Frankie-tying-himself-up-in-knots introduction for Ammonia. 'She's my mistress,' Frankie tells us. 'Well, I say mistress… I don't mean… I mean, I serve her. Well, no, I don't mean I serve – I mean, if she fancies a bit – I mean, if… I have to give her what she wants. If she – if she…' He finally admits defeat and segues straight into 'The Prologue!'

Frankie's scheme to raise the 500 drachmas needed to buy his freedom winds up at the Ludi Puerorum Club (Playboy Club, geddit?), where John Junkin's Jewish MC sizes up the extremely scantily clad merchandise, all of it imported from swinging Britannicus. The

Nausius pulls the chain and feels the flush of success: with Kerry Gardner in rehearsal for the pilot episode of *Up Pompeii!* (1969).

presentation may be a bit ropey, but the basic format is present and correct. The popular reaction was tremendous and plans for a series were put into motion immediately.

Lurcio FRANKIE HOWERD Ludicrus Sextus MAX ADRIAN Ammonia ELIZABETH LARNER Odius JOHN JUNKIN Captain Bilius AUBREY WOODS Nausius KERRY GARDNER Cilla JULIA GOODMAN Erotica GEORGINA MOON Cassandra RUTH HARRISON Senator RICHARD McNEFF Plautus WALTER HORSBRUGH Agrippa DANNY DANIELS Slavegirls BARBARA LINDLEY, VALERIE STANTON and MARIE

Written by Talbot Rothwell, Music Alan Braden, Lighting William W Poole, Sound John Holmes, Camera Max Samett, Editor Bob Rymer, Wardrobe Reginald Samuel, Make-up Cynthia Goodwin, Designer Sally Hulke, Producer Michael Mills

9.10-9.45 pm Wednesday 17 September 1969 in black and white (later repeated in colour) on BBC1

★★★★★★

Carry On Christmas

For their first venture into television, the core Carry On team were joined by the explosive talents of Frankie Howerd, catching him between starring in the *Up Pompeii!* pilot and the broadcast of the first series. Here, Carry On's most prolific and inspired scriptwriter, Talbot Rothwell, ripped open and rearranged the Charles Dickens classic *A Christmas Carol* and injected elements of pantomime, Hammer Horror and an end-of-the-pier romp.

The show's producer, Peter Eton, writing to film series producer Peter Rogers on 20 August 1969, reported that 'When the cast first heard they were doing *A Christmas Carol* there were near riots, as they felt it was outmoded rubbish.' However, Sid James made a deliciously nasty Scrooge brilliantly supported by the likes of Bernard Bresslaw, Peter Butterworth, Charles Hawtrey and Hattie Jacques. But it was Frankie who removed himself from the narrative and addressed the viewers.

First cropping up in the second of Sid's trio of ghostly visitations, Frankie emerges from the fireplace in full Santa Claus outfit and

mournfully mutters 'Ah … Greetings' to the assembled yobbos. As the dreadful poet Robert Browning, Frankie is in character, sort of, but nobody seems to mind him sending up the entire production, ad-libbing furiously and ignoring co-star Hattie Jacques for an age. Most of his comic interjections, of course, were scripted, the best being the post-watershed warning to watching families: 'I should get the kids to bed, it's hotting up now!' But there's at least one genuine off-the-cuff moment as he urges the camera to look at his distressed, languid girlfriend. A split-second image of Hattie instantly cuts back to a bemused Frankie. His blustering delivery shows it's a geniune ad-lib as he mutters, 'That was a quick look, wasn't it? What, are you saving film?' There's another priceless moment when Frankie loses it completely during a romantic interlude and chuckles 'I'm laughing and I'm in it!'

The original script was quite different to the final version. Indeed, the entire speech to the studio audience was absent and, instead of a chimney entrance, Frankie's Browning appeared in a hot air balloon. In a letter dated 10 November 1969, Peter Rogers was less than happy with this particular part of the programme, commenting that 'The Browning sequence appears to have lost something. Has it been cut down at all?' The final version, however, remains one of Frankie's finest television performances.

And that's not all. Frankie returns in drag for the third part of the show, making an ultra-camp appearance as a Mae West-style Fairy Godmother. Dripping with sequins and topped with a flamboyant blonde wig, there are plenty of shared 'old queen' references with Charles Hawtrey's Aladdin before the miserable old miser Sid James turns up, has a bash at Barbara Windsor and attracts the unwanted advances of Frankie's sex-mad maneater. What's more, the whole section is done in punful rhyme. 'An ambitious project as far as television is concerned,' said Thames head Philip Jones to Carry On director Gerald Thomas in a letter dated 1 January 1970. And it proved to be the biggest ratings winner of the 1969 Christmas season.

....
Did You Know? A letter from Peter Eton Productions Ltd details the rehearsal schedule for the show, beginning on Monday 1 December 1969 at Teddington Yacht Club and moving to rehearsal room 3A two days later. Staying there until Friday 12 December, the cast then moved into Studio 1 for pre-taping, with a camera rehearsal on Saturday and further rehearsal on Sunday until 8.00 pm, when the entire programme was recorded in one block before a studio audience. Editing began the following day and a final cut was completed on 19 December, just five days before broadcast. Frankie promoted the show at the ITV Christmas schedule press conference held at the Mayfair Hotel, London.
....

SID JAMES, TERRY SCOTT, CHARLES HAWTREY, HATTIE JACQUES, BARBARA WINDSOR, BERNARD BRESSLAW, PETER BUTTERWORTH and Guest Star FRANKIE HOWERD as Robert Browning and Cinderella's Fairy Godmother
Written by Talbot Rothwell, Choir routine staged by Ralph Tobert, Comedy consultant Gerald Thomas, Designer Roger Allan, Director Ronnie Baxter, Produced by Peter Eton by arrangement with Peter Rogers, creator and producer of the Carry On series
A Thames Production. 9.15-10.15 pm Wednesday 24 December 1969, in colour on ITV

★★★★★★

Up Pompeii!
Series 1
'What do you expect? Wit?'
Frankie Howerd

72 BC: and the BBC were set for their corniest, rudest and most belly-achingly hilarious comedy ever. From the moment you hear that rousing, jaunty, totally representative theme music, the comic soul knows it's set for good-time overload and, of all the classic sitcoms, this has a real freshness and vitality largely because it is so far removed from anything resembling social comment, domestic humour or, indeed, situation. It's simply a rollercoaster of awful puns, face-pulling, bird-watching and script bypassing.

Frankie was still slightly uneasy about the whole thing – 'After all, it was full of busty girls and mildly saucy dialogue and innuendo, and sexy (if comic) situations' – but the viewing figures and public opinion were such that his misgivings were soon quashed. He was distressed when that doyenne of informed criticism and champion of national taste, Mary Whitehouse, dismissed the show as 'sordid, cheap, and a disgrace for a man of Howerd's undoubted talent'. But, as the Goodies realised, an attack or two from that bespectacled lady was coveted by and helpful to most comedy shows. It certainly didn't affect the popularity of Frankie's Pompeiian sitcom. He happily accepted that Rothwell's urn-scraping double-entendres were 'cheeky, cheerful, seaside-postcard bawdiness designed for a relaxed belly-laugh' and seized the script by the scruff of the neck and went for it.

There has never been anything like it from the BBC – before or since. For one thing, and uniquely in the annals of television situation comedy, the plotline was almost totally irrelevant. The point was to get Frankie in a comic situation whereby he could address the audience, step outside and beyond the mock-historical narrative and become contemporary in an ancient environment. 'Think of the phone calls we'll be getting in!'

It was, to all intents and purposes, a very amateurish am-dram set-up with the egotistical acting giant (Frankie) reduced to the slave role when he would much rather have played the master or a God. Frankie would even address the scriptwriter, with either disgust or complaint, and on occasion would fill in with a co-star's line to keep the action going. He would also keep his audience on their toes if the plot was slowing down by chucking in a corker like 'Don't doze off now...!' Thus, with the style set, Rothwell could wind up his innuendos and let them go. Although the writer's love of history shines through, the actual historical essence of the show was, thankfully, played down, the show resolving itself into a traditional three-set sitcom: the forecourt, the house interior and the market place.

Flamboyant, scene-stealing performances from supporting turns like Jeanne Mockford's soothsayer or one-off guest players, notably Barbara Windsor, would be met by Frankie with ill-concealed mock-jealousy. The most camp and melodramatic of Frankie's co-stars was that glorious old queen, Max Adrian, as Frankie's master, the wheezing and befuddled Ludicrus Sextus. Often forgetting his lines, frequently cracking up in response to that master corpser Frankie and staggering around the place as if he had just wandered in from the National Theatre and become hopelessly lost, Adrian was the perfect sounding board for the broadest of broad comedy, a solid-gold gift to Frankie's quick wit and ready tongue.

Elizabeth Larner, playing the Senator's lubricious wife, Ammonia, had been a distinguished opera singer before taking up acting. Her busty screen presence, man-hungry energy and booming voice proved to be a winning combination throughout the series, while Georgina Moon (later to appear in *The Benny Hill Show* and *Carry On Behind*) provided unchallenging and demure glamour as the daughter of the household, Erotica. The maximum camp element was injected by the limp-wristed, sweetly naïve, lovestruck Kerry Gardner as her brother, Nausius. His uncompleted and dubious odes of blind devotion were one of the most popular and eagerly anticipated parts of the show. Every week he would pen some new love ode, leaving the final line unwritten ('I couldn't think of a rhyme…') and Frankie would milk the audience reaction with an eye-rolling 'You're the only one who couldn't, I can tell you that!' or some such variation.

And that remains the sheer bliss of the programme. It is simply an excuse for Frankie to run the gamut of corny gags, eye up seductive vestal virgins, try and protect his master and household from outside influences and struggle to deliver his forever-interrupted prologues. Nothing really taxing happens, the audience are assured that Frankie will top and tail the show with a prologue-attempt and everything will work out in typically farcical fashion.

....

Did You Know? The enormous success of *Up Pompeii!* followed Frankie throughout the world and throughout his life. He was rather disconcerted when, during a tour of Australia, journalists insisted that he don a white sheet and surround himself with scantily clad ladies for his photo shoots.

When the BBC finally released two volumes of *Up Pompeii!* on video in 1991, the archive nature of the shows was justified by this tongue-in-cheek disclaimer: 'WARNING – You may feel some of these pictures are showing their age. But remember, they are 2000 years old.'

They also superimposed episode titles not present on the original transmissions or even in *Radio Times*, getting one of them (*Jamus Bondus*) wrong. Stranger still, the season one selections had 'and Sid Colin' added below Talbot Rothwell's writer credit, a refinement not featured on the original broadcasts until season two.

....

Lurcio FRANKIE HOWERD, Ludicrus Sextus MAX ADRIAN, Ammonia ELIZABETH LARNER, Nausius KERRY GARDNER, Senna JEANNE MOCKFORD, Erotica GEORGINA MOON (not in episodes 'The Senator and the Asp' and 'Spartacus'), Plautus WILLIAM RUSHTON, plus SUI LIN, BARBARA LINDLEY, ANITA RICHARDSON, JOANNA ROSS, VALERIE STANTON and JEANETTE WILD
Written by Talbot Rothwell, Music Alan Braden, Lighting William W Poole, Sound John Holmes and Michael McCarthy, Costumes Penny Lowe, Make-up Sylvia James and Penny Needham, Designers Kenneth Sharp and Sally Hulke, Produced and directed by David Croft
Seven episodes: 9.10-9.40 pm, Mondays, 30 March-11 May 1970, in colour on BBC1

Vestal Virgins
'Only two? This is virgin on the ridiculous!'   **Frankie Howerd**

The first episode is also, by the shortest of heads, the best in the entire Pompeiian canon: a bristling pace, packed with stunning girls, Frankie's relentless undermining of the situation, Max Adrian's most out-of-breath performance ever and some gloriously laid-back bingo-calling from guest star Hugh Paddick. Basically, there is a big public holiday in Pompeii: the 2,462nd Miss Vestal Virgin competition, 'commonly known as VV Day!' The master of ceremonies is unavailable and Lurcio has to front the virgin celebrations. The search for suitable virgins is what fuels the comedy. The baddies – played with Italianate flamboyance by Leon Thau and high-pitched camp by Geoffrey Hughes – are on course to sabotage the contest. Ludicrus, you see, is campaigning against the pleasure houses which provide the guys' income. The two demure virgins are duly replaced by two busty vixens. The Gods will be furious and Ludicrus will be shamed.

The contest sequence is a gem. Frankie happily sets up the ancient-beyond-words 'What's a Grecian urn?' gag, bounds onto the stage as cheerful host for the event and stumbles through his off-stage discussion with the stunning Tittia, played with boundless energy by Penny Brahms. The 'Two Ts but they're not pronounced'/'Ooh, I wouldn't say that!' banter goes perfectly, but the remainder of the dialogue ties up Frankie's tongue. He laughingly mumbles, 'I'll say that bit again', pleads to the audience ('It's a lot to learn, all this, you know!') and finally suggests to his co-star that her assets are putting him off. You can always tell when Frankie's ad-lib crack-ups are scripted or not. He's so brilliant at the scripted ones. When it's for real, he smiles, gets shy and comes completely, but subtly, out of character. This, probably my favourite Frankie telly moment of all, is one of the genuine ones and it's a heartwarming, hilarious display of a man struggling to cope with the giggles, a confusing script and a fear of public exposure. Magic television!

Back to the plot, and having scoured the neighbourhood and even asked for a volunteer from the audience, Frankie drags up Nausius. He bluffs his way through and ends up in the Temple of Vesta with his master, the daughter of the house, a load of virgins and the gorgeous Trisha Noble as a glamour-puss with a secret. An absolute joy from beginning to end, this is the pinnacle of Frankie's toga-wearing career and a masterclass for any writer or performer who wants to get away with the corniest material and still create an unsurpassable slice of classic comedy.
Noxius LEON THAU, Pitius GEOFFREY HUGHES, Priest HUGH PADDICK, Tittia PENNY BRAHMS, Virginia JANET MAHONEY. Guest: TRISHA NOBLE as High Priestess of the Virgins

The Ides of March
'Do not adjust your set. There is a fault in the script.'   **Frankie Howerd**

A classic episode that runs out of steam (and over time) at the end but still has more than its share of blissful bits. Frankie's prologue theme is Leda and the swan, but he's soon interrupted by the arrival of three hissing conspirators ('Psst!'/'I am not!') who are plotting the assassination of Caesar with Ludicrus. And, of course, it falls to Frankie 'to plunge a dagger into Caesar's foul black heart'. The situation, right down to the 'foul black heart' bit, would reappear in the film version. Here, though, it comes with the added bonus of Frankie himself doubling as Caesar. 'It's me again,' he confides. 'I'm playing two parts, you see. What? Laurence Oliver [sic]? Are you kidding? I should get an Oscar for this.'

Ammonia comes to warn Caesar of the plot against him and they're soon horizontal on Caesar's chaise longue. The steamy exchange that follows is another for the classic comedy time-capsule. 'Oh, your lips are like ripe cherries,' Frankie pants. 'Your throat is like a swan's. Your shoulders are like the Venus de Milo. Your bosoms are like the round hills of Rome…' 'What of my eyes?' 'I'm not going that way, I'm sorry. Oh, be mine, be mine!' 'Oh, do you really think we ought to?' 'Well… May

Up Pompeii! –
Lurcio keeps a
breast of the
matter with
Valerie Leon in
*The Senator
and the Asp.*

as well. It's bitter out.' Cue well-deserved cheers from the studio audience.

Frankie's shuttling between Caesar and Lurcio becomes increasingly frantic, culminating in a dressing-room screen toppling over to reveal our hero (in string vest and jazzy boxer shorts) struggling with his dresser, a little bald bloke in a blue blazer who gets bustled off screen by the embarrassed Frankie. ('What do you think this is, an audition?') Caesar finally tells his general, Ponderus, to 'Bring the slave Lurcio to me here now and let us confront each other face to face,' whereupon Frankie, in another classic moment, turns to camera and says, 'Oh Gawd, what have I said?'

There's loads more to enjoy, including some tasty one-liners ('Oh Ponderus, in the words of the Persian carpet salesman, you may beat it'), a delicious 'miserable pleader' moment from Frankie done at the top of his voice ('Nobody goes to sleep when I'm on, I tell you') and, finally, one of the rudest visual gags in the whole series, when Ammonia, shot from the waist up, is seen bouncing up and down and squealing 'Oh Caesar, this is a lovely game.' The camera rapidly pans down to reveal that it's nothing more than... a game of piggy-back. *Ponderus JEREMY YOUNG, Soppia WENDY RICHARD, Mucas ROBERT GILLESPIE, Hidius NICHOLAS SMITH, Caushus MICHAEL KNOWLES, Centurion COLIN BEAN*

The Senator and the Asp
'Something tells me I've got everything asp about face!' **Frankie Howerd**

How true. Like *Spartacus* and, in season two, *The Peace Treaty*, this episode doesn't seem to have been reshown in the UK (much less released to video) for some 30 years. The reason could be as simple as this: all three episodes are pretty much below par. In *The Senator and the Asp*, Frankie's still saddled with the silly Romanesque wig he wore back in the pilot episode, suggesting that this show was the first of season one to be shot but was shrewdly shown third so as not to put anyone off.

Even so, there's some cherishable stuff at the outset. Frankie hoves into view bearing a covered chamber pot ('I have to empty this ten, 15, 20 times a day: believe me, it's all go, go, go'), but it turns out to be full of *pips*. Romulus and Remus provide the theme for Frankie's prologue (with a guest appearance from Pegasus), during which he informs us that puberty is 'a small town north of Rome, the place where they fought the Pubic Wars.' He's soon oiling Ammonia's back and helping her out of her clothes behind a screen. 'The things a slave has to do,' he sighs. 'Who would want my job?' And as the camera moves enthusiastically in: 'Get back, dirty beasts. Control yourselves. What do you think this is, *The Wednesday Play*?'

It's during Ammonia's toilette that we get an inkling of the plot. Senator Lecherus Maximus of Thrace is keen to rekindle his romance with Ammonia but she wants no part of him. Ludicrus, meanwhile, receives a message from Caesar himself ('Yours truly, Julie'), telling him to expect a visit from Senator Stovus Primus. Naturally, the latter turns up first – 'You with the big quiff' is his opening shot at Frankie – and is mistaken for Lecherus. Frankie locks him in with Ammonia's deadly asp and has a tedious battle with the creature when it keeps popping back through the keyhole. When the real Lecherus turns up (played by Frankie's future *Whoops Baghdad* co-star, Derek Francis), he thinks the surprisingly welcoming Ludicrus is suggesting a bit of group sex, while Ludicrus himself – or rather, poor confused Max Adrian – trots out his trademark 'tut tut tut' babble and even has difficulty pronouncing his own name. The whole thing peters out, like Stovus Primus, in record time.

Things are perked up a bit by Nausius' latest lady love Daili, played by the spectacular Valerie Leon from *Carry On Up the Jungle*. 'The girl with the big prospects,' as Frankie calls her, makes a meal of her cockney accent but has the distinction of being the only subject of a Nausius ode who's actually present when Frankie reads it out. *Senator Lecherus DEREK FRANCIS, Stovus Primus NORMAN MITCHELL, Daili VALERIE LEON, Scrophulus JAMES OTTAWAY*

Pax Britannicus

Ladies and gentle-*men*, Frankie settles down onto his comfy seat and starts with his usual disjointed and rapidly interrupted prologue. This time it concerns those fabulous mythical creatures, the sirens. Half-woman, half-fish and always going off, Frankie's magical tales of fishy tails are destroyed when his master and mistress embark on another crockery-smashing argument. Senna then weighs in with dire warnings about gods, monsters and escaping 'their bloody fangs', and Frankie can't resist a hasty look at the audience as he mutters, 'No bloody fangs to you, love!'

The marital upheaval in the Sextus family is paralleled by the bloody threat of international warfare. Soon enough, we're off to ancient Britain, soldiering duties and more than a dash of camp command. Lurcio's army number (IV or Ivy) inspires any number of relentlessly milked gags and, with his master and now general in the field arriving ('Here's Charlton Heston!'), Frankie finds himself with the unenviable task of trying to keep Ludicrus from realising the true identity of his bit of hot stuff – it's Ammonia. Meanwhile, the Britons (including one very camp follower played by Robin Hunter) attack via their Trojan cow – inspired by the Trojan horse and prefiguring *Monty Python and the Holy Grail*'s rabbit. ('I thought it was something or udder!') Escaping an off-screen beheading, finding his long-lost love and ultimately getting back home with a blonde bit of stuff encased in the cow, Frankie gets off scot-free and smiling. Salute!
Sgt Jankus WALLAS EATON, Britons ROBIN HUNTER and PETER NEEDHAM, Camp followers FIONA KENDALL and ANDI ROSS, Soldiers STEPHEN CHURCHETT, DAVID HILTON, NIGEL PEGRAM, MICHAEL SHARVELL-MARTIN and VIC TAYLOR

The Thespians

This is a tragic tale of acting tragic and tragic acting. Frankie, in whimsical mood, begins his short-lived prologue about the Gorgons and legendary jockey 'Gorgon Richards'. Basically, he gets the special effects chaps at the BBC running scared by giving a huge build-up to the extraordinary actress who is due to play the part. With snakes in her hair and the whiff of greasepaint in her nostrils she is, throughout the show, waiting in the wings to come on – and although 'It's wicked to mock the afflicted', Frankie and the audience have a darn good try.

The plot – such as it is – disrupts the prologue in characteristic fashion and Frankie finds himself up to his neck in actors from the Olympia Theatre Company. Hernia, one of the leading starlets of the troupe, has captured Nausius' heart and, of course, there's a poem on the way. The final word of the penultimate line ('crystals') sets us up for the inevitable 'bristols' pay-off and Frankie's controlled reaction to the concluding line ('truly wondrous pair of…') is sublime. He simply pauses, looks into the audience and mutters 'Hello…' Sheer genius.

It turns out that Frankie's aged master once had a fling with the battleaxe actress in charge of the wandering players. Frankie himself has acting aspirations and the lady thespian has a drunken, no-good acting husband who staggers around like Charles Hawtrey on New Year's Eve. To cut a long, farcical, brilliantly performed story short, Frankie finds himself rehearsing a scene with Nausius' lady love and finally donning the acting garb to play the part of the inebriated star. Seized by mistake and beaten up, Frankie moans, 'I don't get a penny extra!'

There are countless delights along the way, notably Frankie's split-second timing as he dons the incorrect emotion masks for the serious-and-happy piece, plus Bill Maynard, in a stunning cameo as the theatre manager, turning on the bespectacled, gruff, no-nonsense, working men's club attitude. And in one of the great series moments, Max Adrian explains the situation, milking the scene with extended bursts of rasping laughter and allowing Frankie the 'spontaneous' comment, 'I wish to God he was sitting in the audience!'
Hermione OLWEN GRIFFITHS, Percentus BILL MAYNARD, Hernia AUDREY NICHOLSON, Cuspidor DOUGLAS RIDLEY

Spartacus

*'We spent four hours rehearsing this;
you'd never think so, would you?*

Frankie Howerd

You certainly wouldn't. Another show denied
to UK audiences for some 30 years, with Willie
Rushton's heavenly Plautus delivering gags
even more ineffective than usual and a
climactic gaol sequence which, though partly
recycled in the film version, is a complete
and utter mess – hence the Frankie line
quoted above.

Things kick off with Frankie bedevilled by a
fearsome dog; its offstage barking is clearly
human and at the end it turns out to be a tiny
little terrier. In the meantime, though, it takes
a bite out of Frankie's behind, revealing
another pair of irridescent pants, and puts him
off his stroke during the prologue, which this
time focuses on Icarus. Stumbling over his
words, Frankie breaks up and winningly
mutters, 'Oh Gawd help us, the pills are
wearing off already…' Thanks to Senna, he
hears about the slave uprising led by Spartacus
and soon meets the man himself hiding under
Ammonia's couch. Frankie's reluctance to join
the cause leads to a classic bit of Bob Hope-
style crosstalk. 'What are you, man or mouse?'
growls Spartacus. 'Pass the cheese please,'
replies Frankie.

Nausius is more public-spirited and is
addressing a bunch of girl bondservants
gathered in the street. Decked out in flowers,
he tells them that 'All you need is love, love,
love' and reprises an old Carry On gag when
he presents Frankie with a daffodil. ('You
dare!' Frankie tells the audience.) When the
meeting breaks up at the approach of the
'fuzz', Frankie carries the can for Nausius and
is put in gaol by a grim centurion, who at one
point, contrary to the usual *Pompeii* practice,
has to feed Frankie with his lines. 'All right,'
Frankie replies, 'but you try to get another part
in this show…' Ironically, Wallas Eaton, who
had already appeared in *Pax Britannicus*,
would take centre stage in the next series as
the new-look Ludicrus Sextus.

'Talking of titters,' Frankie mutters in jug, 'I

must bust out of here.' Though the priceless
Larry Martyn plays the giggling gaoler, the
impetus flags completely at this point. 'Here
look, look: real tears,' Frankie says as he starts
emoting. 'Ooh, no glycerine rubbish – real
tears. Mind you, it's not difficult for an actor
like me to cry, you know. I just have to think of
the money they're paying me for this show and
I'm in floods.' Soon the cell is packed to the
rafters with Ludicrus, Ammonia, Nausius and a
mob of glamorous bondservants led by the
shapely Iris. ('What pretty bumpers!') Finally,
Spartacus' all-too-temporary triumph sees a
reprise of the 'lost soap at bathtime' routine
from the pilot show – only this time it's
Frankie afloat and Ammonia attending to him
– while poor Ludicrus mopes about with a
broom and is contemptuously dubbed
'Cinders'. Not quite a classic, then.

*Spartacus SHAUN CURRY, Centurion Captain
WALLAS EATON, Centurion Private VIC
TAYLOR, Gaoler LARRY MARTYN, Iris ANITA
RICHARDSON*

The Love Potion

With probably the most star-studded cast ever
assembled for the series, this one starts off
with Frankie dutifully hanging out the washing
and appearing from behind a pair of knickers:
'Honestly, I do feel smalls!' Rome is all sex,
sex and more sex, and while Frankie is a mere
slave he still has his eye on a bit of 'covet' of
his own. Every member of the household is
paying Frankie off (ten drachmas apiece) so
the house will be clear for their sexual
dalliances, but our hapless, hopeless pal doesn't
get the hint and eagerly awaits the arrival of
the blonde bombshell next door, making off to
the apothecary for a love philtre.

Frankie's battle with the overacting-and-
proud-of-it John Cater as the medical man, Dr
Castor Oilus, is a classic interlude. Cater's
ramshackle delivery and scruffy appearance
steal the scene, so much so that Frankie,
exiting disgruntled as the old man wheezes
with laughter, comments: 'That's right – enjoy
your last appearance on this show!' However,
the masterstroke comes with the earnest
doctor's determination to prove that his love

potion works. With a dead straight expression he mumbles, 'Would you like to see my testimonials?' And without a beat, Frankie resurrects the essence of wartime entertainment with a knowing, 'No, thank you very much – I've got no time for old concert party gags!' It's a breathtaking moment.

Back at the senator's pad, all's looking good for a Frankie fun-fest. Dressed up in his master's gear and eagerly awaiting his bit of crackling, Frankie pours the entire potion into the wine and prepares himself. The scantily clad Trisha Noble (returning for a second time this series for maximum audience titillation) is all long blonde hair and come-hither looks. She pouts and purrs her way through the attempted seduction, revealing that she only came round to ask Lurcio to remove his washing line from her property. Naturally, everybody returns home in sequence, the wrong people drink the potion at the wrong time and the house erupts into a sex-mad kiss-chase. Frankie, alas, ends up with the unwanted advances of a boastful gladiator.

Chuck in a gaggle of future sitcom favourites (*Open All Hours*' Lynda Baron, *Are You Being Served?*'s Mollie Sugden and *Just Good Friends*' John Ringham), a remorselessly farcical plot and Frankie's mounting frustration, and you finish up with a classic episode. In the end, with the scene approaching madness ('It's worse than swinging Londinium!'), Frankie finds himself being chased by a lovestruck, wine-soaked Senna the Soothsayer... Pity poor Francis!

....

Did You Know? Talbot Rothwell happily included a gag ('What ails you? ... He's full of ale!') that had just been cut from the final print of *Carry On Up the Jungle*. The actor who originally delivered the line in the film and saw it hit the cutting-room floor? Why, Frankie Howerd of course!

....

Ambrosia LYNDA BARON, *Prodigius* DAVID KERNAN, *Bumshus* JOHN RINGHAM, *Lusha* TRISHA NOBLE, *Dr Castor Oilus the apothecary* JOHN CATER, *Flavia* MOLLIE SUGDEN, *Lusha's maid* QUEENIE WATTS, *Castor's assistant* ANITA RICHARDSON

Royal Television Gala Performance

Less than a fortnight after the first season of *Up Pompeii!* had come to an end, Frankie and the other regulars joined the cast of *Dad's Army* (plus Morecambe and Wise, Dave Allen, Basil Brush and Derek Fowlds) in this right royal BBC bash broadcast on 24 May 1970.

Up Pompeii!
Series 2

Such was the instant popularity of *Up Pompeii!* that the BBC rushed a second batch of episodes into production, the cameras rolling on 6 September 1970. However, despite the fact that only four months had elapsed since the end of the initial series, this further instalment of six episodes was markedly different.

Firstly, Talbot Rothwell – still up to his innuendo-tinted eyeballs with various Carry On film scripts – couldn't manage the new series on his own. He turned to his old cohort and co-writer, Sid Colin (whom he had worked with on *Ray's A Laugh*, *Educating Archie* and *Carry On Spying*), to write the show with him. The production was now in the hands of Sydney Lotterby (before working on such shows as *Porridge* and *Last of the Summer Wine*) who took over from David Croft, himself tied up with the fourth series of his scriptwriting baby, *Dad's Army*. Furthermore, Frankie's right-hand man and wheezing comic sounding board, Max Adrian as Ludicrus, was gone. Adrian, who died two years later, was replaced by the younger character actor, Wallas Eaton. Indeed, Eaton had appeared in cameo roles in two episodes of the first season, as well as having been a regular part of the rep company for Frankie's 1966 radio series *Frankie Howerd!*

With Eaton playing old rather than actually living it, some of the bumbling pleasure of Adrian's masterly and charmingly ghoulish Ludicrus was lost, but Eaton's almost Moore Marriott-style character proved equally adept at bamboozling Frankie's hapless slave and creating heights of sex-mad mayhem. Although there's no great fanfare to alert the audience to the cast-change, there is a brief mention.

Typically, it's underplayed and thrown away but in *The Legacy*, Frankie quickly explains that 'You may notice a little change in him; he's had a face-lift. I think the lift broke down. Never mind!'

The rest of the supporting cast remained the same, although Senna acquired white hair and a corpse-like pallor while the Olympian comic interludes from satirist Willie Rushton were dropped altogether. His self-contained observations as Plautus always seemed a bit forced and tended to jar with Frankie's freewheeling style. In retrospect, Rushton's contribution seems more Python than Carry On, if you will, and clearly it didn't fit the format. In series two, there are a couple of 'godly' encounters with the camp messenger Hermes, played by Bunny May, but these are interactive with Frankie's mocking persona and, like the odes and soothsaying, are simply a comic cypher to signpost the laughs. Still, despite some discreet alterations behind the cameras and some major adjustments in front of it, Frankie and the show seemed reassuringly unaffected.

Lurcio FRANKIE HOWERD, Ludicrus Sextus WALLAS EATON, Ammonia ELIZABETH LARNER, Nausius KERRY GARDNER, Erotica GEORGINA MOON (not in episode 'Jamus Bondus'), Senna JEANNE MOCKFORD, Hermes the messenger BUNNY MAY (in episodes 'The Legacy' and 'Exodus') plus PENNY BEECHING, LUCIENNE CAMILLE, MONIKA DIETRICH, JACKIE LEAPMAN, ANITA RICHARDSON and HEATHER WRIGHT
Written by Talbot Rothwell and Sid Colin, Music Alan Braden, Costumes Ann Halle, Make-up Lyn de Winne, Videotape Editor Michael Adley, Lighting Derek Slee, Sound Mike McCarthy, Designers Gerry Scott and Michael Young, Produced and directed by Sydney Lotterby
Six episodes: 9.20-9.50 pm, Mondays, 14 September-26 October 1970, in colour on BBC1

Sunday 6 September 1970: while filming The Legacy at BBC Television Centre, Frankie relaxes with 'the new line-up of Roman dollies' – Jackie Leapman, Penny Beeching, Heather Wright, Lucienne Camille, Monika Dietrich and Anita Richardson.

The Legacy

'Can you get Filfia for me?'
'In this show! We're lucky to get away
with this, aren't we?'
Kerry Gardner and Frankie Howerd

A tired old plot – weren't they all? – is given a new lease of life with Frankie's flamboyantly mocking performance and the knowing, wonderfully disjointed script. Like a poor, mistreated Cinderella, Frankie is lumbered with all the work but the usual prologue (this week about the goddess Vesta) and the Senna interlude set him off on a tangent. A peerlessly executed moment of high camp with sing-song banter from Bunny May as the blue-rinsed messenger Hermes ('This is turning into a musical!') sees the show collapsing into blissful chaos. So much so that both television terminology and the fickleness of the viewing audience are addressed when Frankie insists the camera follow him in case the viewers get restless and turn over to the other channel. Indeed, at the climax, the stage scenery is revealed as the camera passes through a wall to follow Frankie's exit accompanied by a cheeky 'Isn't that clever?'

The basic thread of story revolves around a wealthy relative of Ludricus dying and leaving the family a load of money. But Filthy Lucre will only bequeath the dosh if the family has a son and heir to continue the Lucre name. The master and mistress are, naturally, dumbstruck and the call goes out for some artificial aid to help their sex life. Frankie gets the job and is packed off to the local madwoman for some rejuvenating liquid. Pat Coombs, in wild fright wig and screaming with insane laughter ('I wish to God she was sitting in the audience, I'll tell you that!'), turns in a delicious cameo. Getting all the best lines, cackling continually ('Well, she's enjoying the show if nobody else is!') and forever stirring her cauldron, she mutters 'We shall meet again!' and Frankie comes right back with 'Not on this show we won't!' A sparkling vignette.

The potion works but the master takes both doses and reverts to childhood, while the daughter of the family seems to have a guilty secret which might just save the day. Frankie, believing she's pregnant and too ashamed to tell her father, interjects a number of elongated 'oooohs' and finally works out a plan. However, it's a broken chariot and not out-of-wedlock pregancy that's been worrying the poor child, the master sees his chance to claim the inheritance dashed and the family end up debating about rechristening the son: 'Lucre – that's a filthy name!'/'We've done that gag!'/'Nausius!'/'That's a sickening name!'/'We haven't done *that* gag!' But, with the prologue unfinished and a few drops of the naughty juice remaining, Frankie offers his sexual services to the studio audience, is mobbed and makes a rush round the back of the flimsy Pompeiian scenery!

Tarta the sorceress PAT COOMBS, Gladiator WILLIAM CORDEROY, Filfia ANITA RICHARDSON

Roman Holiday

'Don't overact, we've got the message!'
Frankie Howerd

Probably the pick of series two, this is a brilliantly scripted, perfectly acted bit of Roman farce with a rip-roaring guest star turn from Kenneth J Warren, some fetching, dewy-eyed innocence from Grazina Frame and a bucket-load of corn from a firing-on-all-cylinders Frankie.

Frankie is concerned by the possible effects of stage fright on his trusty steed ('Stand there and do nothing,' he tells the donkey, 'and I do mean nothing!'), while Senna's piercing cry of 'Speak to me, oh ball!' brings forth the hilarious aside, 'I've heard of talking balls…' The prediction, however, is no laughing matter. Two fair maidens, in flight from the slave trade, are set to complicate Lurcio's simple life. Enter the big, beefy, burly and bellowing Kenneth J Warren, hot on the trail of the two terrified young ladies. Frankie, referred to as the man 'with the big thing dangling' and milking remorselessly the 'Ooh, so it's scum to this' gag, is on a promise if he helps the girls. With the girls concealed in an empty fruit sack, Warren has a quick feel of the merchandise and thinks they feel like melons. 'I hope he's right!' mutters Frankie.

As it turns out, the girls are not equally blessed ('One all peas, the other all pod'), but Frankie's got offers from them both. A bath with plenty of loofah action is hinted at and it's all systems go for a night of aquatic passion. Even the cameraman is denied access to the scene ('Where do you think you're going?'), but the promise is short-lived. Concern about public taste ('You should have seen some of the letters we got in after the last series!') and the climactic arrival of Frankie's sex-mad master put paid to his best-laid plans; Ludicrus selects the fruitier of the two girls and Frankie glumly concludes that 'I'm in for a flat evening!'

With the slave traders dispatched at last, Frankie mourns his loss ('Pity pity, bang bang!') and we are given a choice of viewing: Frankie and his 'flat' mate or Ludicrus and the bustier babe. Before long, Senna storms in with her oft-repeated 'The time has come, the end is here!' bit, Frankie interjects a final 'Please would you shut your gobs?' and breaks down into giggles as the show comes to an end. There is a sense of sheer, undiluted pleasure about this episode; it's one of the plums in Frankie's entire television output.

Felonius KENNETH J WARREN, Letitia GRAZINA FRAME, Twiggia PENELOPE CHARTERIS

Jamus Bondus

A wonderfully constructed, beautifully overplayed exposé of espionage and intrigue in Ancient Rome. George Baker, guest-starring as the woman-satisfying, smooth-as-silk OOVII (007, get it?), is the perfect contrast with Frankie's wannabe, languid man of mystery. The spying plot, never anything more than the briefest of brief narrative bridges to hang a load of old gags on, revolves round the missing plans for a deadly weapon, a catapult that can hurl coconuts 25 feet.

Everybody is after it, from Frankie's aged master to the busty Pussus Galoria ('cheeky cat!'), played with refined elegance by Patricia Haines.

The scriptwriters throw in every corny cliché and knowing gag, allowing their star to send up the entire story, mock the performances, deconstruct the setting and generally reveal everything as just a silly entertainment from the BBC Television comedy department. Frankie starts the fun down on his luck, as usual, having to shift an armless, busty statue and stagger through a few tantalising moments of the prologue. There's a masterly put-down on Senna's 'Whoa! Whoa!' entrance: 'Sounds like the milkman calling his horse!'/'Nay, nay!'/'I think it *is* his horse!'

But it's Frankie's comic asides and bemused reactions that create the true gold-dust here, and with the arrival of Larry Martyn the episode is effortlessly lifted into the classic bracket: 'What a funny man! … What do you mean – this show needs one?' A totally stereotypical cypher of a character, spouting nonsense espionage passwords, his dramatic death, stabbed in the back and going out with a relentless string of 'oohs!', 'ahhs!' and 'owws!', is a shameless resurrection of Victor Maddern's departure from *Carry On Spying* but here, with no narrative ties at all, Martyn can milk the scene remorselessly, refuse to die and keep on ahhing into infinity. Frankie's comment is typical: 'You can't die here, this is the living room!'

He tries to impress upon his enchanted audience that 'You wouldn't get this from Harold Pinter!' and happily reverts to narrative mode when the body vanishes and he desperately tries to explain the situation to his mistress. The problem is finally sorted out, the deadly coconut hurler is safe and Larry Martyn returns, still caught in his death pangs. 'I'm going … I'm going!' he moans, to which Frankie finally yells, 'I'm coming with you!' A classic example of the ancient art of situation comedy at its best.

Jamus Bondus GEORGE BAKER, Pussus Galoria PATRICIA HAINES, Spurios from MIV LARRY MARTYN

The Peace Treaty

'Ooh no, I'm not able-bodied, sir. I have this funny tremor running down my back; it's called fear.'

Frankie Howerd

Pan forms the prologue to this, another 'lost' (and limp) episode. Ludicrus appears in single file and full body armour ('Sinister dexter, sinister dexter'), only to find his troop has disappeared. 'When you sinistered, they must have dextered,' Frankie suggests. 'There he goes: Hercules unchained,' he adds as Ludicrus sinister-dexters off. Apparently, Pompeii is all set to go to war with the Barbarians (cue any number of tired rugby gags), but Frankie has no intention of joining up, even for the fearsome Captain Bumshus (played by future *Whoops Baghdad* regular, Alan Curtis). 'They get me down, these army types,' he explains. 'They're so arrogant, aren't they? Honestly, I've never seen anyone with arrows so gant.'

Bumshus is in charge of the aptly named ENSA cohort (East Naples Suicide Army), and to avoid conscription Frankie takes up Nausius' suggestion that the women of Pompeii should try the old Lysistrata dodge: ie, withdraw their sexual favours until the men call the war off. Frankie gets a resounding 'Yes' from the female members of the audience when he asks if they'd be willing to go along with the plan, and pretty soon is dragged up as the rabble-rousing Titticata. 'Ban the Bang Bang' read the placards in the market place, and Frankie's oratory goes down a storm, despite Ludicrus' attempts to reason with 'her'. 'Madam, I appeal to you,' Ludicrus pleads. 'You don't, you know,' Frankie snaps back.

To foil Titticata's schemes, Bumshus attempts to seduce her and Frankie's frontal bolsters subside at his every move; 'It's like cohabiting with an octopus,' Frankie complains. The scene is an exact trial run for the final *Whoops Baghdad* episode, *Saved From the Harem*, and Frankie finally refuses the offer of a large drink with the classic line, 'If I drink this lot I shall be up and down all night.' Peace is eventually restored, and a

battalion of female warriors, led by the breastplated Ammonia, are going on manoeuvres as Senna, also in full battledress, starts to make eyes at our horrified hero.
Alan Curtis CAPTAIN BUMSHUS, David Anderson LIEUTENANT PRESHUS

Nymphia

Of all the *Pompeii* episodes this one contains the only guest star turn that almost (almost!) overshadows Frankie himself. Barbara Windsor, the bubbly blonde toast of the Carry On series and the ideal choice to overact, over-expose and overflow in this Rothwell television masterpiece, bursts into the action with full-on cockney charm.

That cheeky 'little plighter' Nausius has another crush, this time on a sweet, demure, refined young lady by the name of Nymphia, and has composed the expected, un-rhyming ode to the latest flavour of the month. Frankie's called upon to give a bit of sex education chat but he, the audience and everybody else in the show realises that he's wasting his time. For the sweet, demure and refined young lady is none other than the cockney sparrow herself, Barbara Windsor, man-hungry, falling out of her costume and bounding on with a raucous 'Evenin' all!' Frankie, looking into camera with delicious indignation, mutters 'Common as muck' before further sordid revelations about Barbara's sexual prowess emerge and he re-evaluates his initial opinion: 'Muck itself!'

Basically, Nausius' obsession with busty Babs could cause the family problems and Frankie is assigned the difficult job of showing the young lad what the girl is really like. This involves donning a crazy disguise as Frankie masquerades as a powerful Caliph. (He does this simply by adding a beard: 'Who did you expect? Omar Sharif?') Rothwell, never one to let a successful gag go unrepeated, resurrects *Carry On ... Up the Khyber*'s immortal 'Up yours' banter, lays on the totally unsubtle comments with a trowel ('I like to get my dipper out occasionally!') and winds up his star with hurtful digs at his 'ancient' appearance. Frankie, borrowing a trick or two from

Morecambe and Wise, bemoans the casting ('To think we turned down Vanessa Redgrave for this part!'), while the entire script seems to be geared towards Barbara's long-anticipated striptease routine.

Frankie, having cracked up Barbara with a twist-the-knife corpsing interlude, sets up the major attraction in classic style: 'For the first time on your screens … that well known pair, left and right!' However, before the clothes start dropping off, Barbara's dear daddy rescues her from a fate worse than death. Frankie gets beaten up but at least the 'saucy cow' is well out of the way. A classic locking-of-horns routine, with Frankie winning by a short head!

Nymphia BARBARA WINDSOR, Ambi Dextrus MICHAEL BRENNAN, Jeremy the Nubian ROY STEWART

Exodus

'A moving story' in more ways than one. Ammonia is barely involved – she's off to scout out the Rome apartments – and the rest of the family spend most of the time looking at Lurcio's 'tired old camel face' and crying. For with money in short supply – Ludicrus having lost his seat in the Senate and an expensive house move on the cards – Frankie's up for sale at the slave market. Frankie starts the fun by shoving up a Pro Venditio sign, or For Sale notice for those of you who don't know Latin. The man-hungry 1940s star Jean Kent is prowling round the place, initially putting Frankie's back up by condemning his pathetic prologues and finally putting him on his back in a manic seduction attempt.

Frankie launches into the remnants of the prologue and enjoys a bit of sooth-saying nonsense with Jeanne Mockford. Her innocent request to 'Let me feel your bumps!' gets the desired reaction and Frankie chuckles 'Isn't she naughty?' before going for the kill and explaining he wouldn't dare feel hers, 'even if you had any!' Frankie is subsequently knocked down and knocked off at the slave market and his life is made even more uncomfortable by his new-found friend, Verminus, played with ragged brilliance by Larry Martyn in his

second characterisation in the series. His pathetic 'You think I'm mad!' comment is poignantly touching and brilliantly sets up Frankie's hilariously brutal riposte, '*Think*? My dear little chappie, I'm bloody sure of it!'

Jean Kent's rich widow, having exhausted poor old Larry Martyn, has her sexual sights set on Lurcio and despite his protests ('I'm sorry, I don't do auditions!') he's whipped away for a pre-auction trial run. Frankie tries to appeal to her maternal instincts, unflatteringly likening her to his mother, and finally claims to be quite satisfied: 'I only had it half an hour ago!' (The 'it', of course, is a drop of ass's milk.) His previous owners are listening outside the door, however, and a plan is hatched to buy the old slave back. The auction is a farce as sex-beast and ancient old master fight it out, the keen-as-mustard Kent is tricked into bidding for the slave seller instead while Frankie – having taken over the auction – knocks himself down to 100 drachmas and gratefully falls back into the hands of his old master.

Aphrodite JEAN KENT, Nefarius PAUL WHITSUN-JONES, Verminus LARRY MARTYN

★★★★★★

Cucumber Castle

A bizarre, surreal and totally bewitching comical/musical trip through mediaeval fantasy, devised by, showcasing and promoting the talents of the Bee Gees. The then-Mrs Gibb, Lulu, is also on hand to add to the pop star clout of the piece, Vincent Price pops up, too, but the major attraction is in the almighty seasonal line-up of top comedy stars. Spike Milligan and old Bee Gees cohort Frankie Howerd were the laughter-making top-liners.

THE BEE GEES (Barry Gibb, Maurice Gibb and Robin Gibb) with Eleanor Bron, Pat Coombs, Julian Orchard, Frankie Howerd, Spike Milligan, Vincent Price, Lulu and Blind Faith Written by Barry and Maurice Gibb, Executive Producer Robert Stigwood, Producer Mike Mansfield, Director Hugh Gladwish 1.30-2.25 pm Saturday 26 December 1970, in colour on BBC2

Frankie Howerd:
The Laughing Stock of Television

In 1971, Frankie not only promoted the *Up Pompeii* movie theme on ITV's *The Golden Shot* but also made a stunning return to the hour-long variety-cum-sketch show format he excelled in, recruiting five of the finest comedy writers in the country to pen a trio of self-contained skits. Here he wallows in television parody and sweetest innuendo. The pieces are: 'Dr. Inlay's Bookcase', a beautiful mockery of the BBC medical drama *Dr Finlay's Casebook*, written with typical bite by Marty Feldman and Barry Took; 'The Photographer', packed with character, observation and knowing pathos by Ray Galton & Alan Simpson; and finally 'Horatio and Nelson', with Frankie hamming it up as Lord Nelson. A favourite co-star, Hattie Jacques, goes over-the-top as a larger than life Lady Hamilton in this classic bit of semi-Carry On business from Talbot Rothwell.

With Hattie Jacques, Peter Copley, Patricia Hayes and Pearl Hackney, Carmel McSharry, Arthur English, Michael Hawkins, George Tovey, John Bindon, George Roderick, Jenny Lee-Wright, Lesley Goldie and Richard McNeff Written by Marty Feldman, Barry Took, Ray Galton & Alan Simpson and Talbot Rothwell, Musical Director Albert Elms, Designer Neville Green, Directed and produced by John Robins A Thames Production. 8.00-9.00 pm Wednesday 14 April 1971, in colour on ITV

Parkinson

Frankie's first encounter with legendary king of chat Michael Parkinson was in Granada's *Cinema* series, in an instalment devoted to Frankie and transmitted on 6 May 1971. Directed by Michael Becker, this programme was adapted for use as a cinema short and led to Frankie's début appearance on Parkinson's self-named BBC show in its very first season. The programme was broadcast exactly 25 years to the day since Frankie made his maiden broadcast on BBC Radio and, as Frankie explained in the interview, 'I'm still doing the same jokes!'

However, typically of Parkinson, a more serious side of Frankie is revealed. With the relatively recent suicide of Tony Hancock in

A match made in heaven with John Bindon, Lesley Goldie and Arthur English in 'The Photographer', an April 1971 moment from *Frankie Howerd: The Laughing Stock of Television.*

1968, Parkinson addresses the bleakness of the laughter-maker and although Frankie makes a joke out of it (he's 'contemplated murder!'), there is a brief moment of unease, reflection and openness which is a Frankie rarity in interviews. Frankie discusses the pitfalls of his trade, whether it be mistiming gags, not being very good at delivery, feeling a 'bloody fool' and forgetting the tagline. Still, he ultimately proves his split-second brilliance with the tired old gag about the old bloke who marries a young girl, takes medical advice, gets a lodger and makes them both pregnant! *Carry On Matron* please copy – and it did! Finally, with a plug for the *Up Pompeii* film and Frankie's sincere defence of 'honest vulgarity', the interrogation was over.

Frankie demanded a scripted interview from Parkinson and wanted to rehearse the responses before going on. In fact, his opening gamut is a check of the notes to make sure they are the 'same questions that I've got the answers for!' Frankie's fellow guests on this show were singer Marian Montgomery and distinguished actor Sir Ralph Richardson.

....

Did You Know? Frankie's first appearance on *Parkinson* was one of literally dozens of small screen talks. He made appearances on both *Russell Harty Plus* and its late-1970s successor, *The Russell Harty Show*; a transcript of the former interview was published in a book based around the series in 1974. And in 1978, he was interviewed by Brian Johnston about the great old comedians, Jimmy James and Sid Field ('the best').

....

Frankie Howerd's Hour

Another hour-long sketch-based special scripted for Frankie by loyal scribes Ray Galton & Alan Simpson. Frankie's special guest was Jean Kent, who had also been in *Pantomania* and the last episode of *Up Pompeii!*, and his other co-stars were Angela Baddeley, Allan Cuthbertson, Paul Haley, Michael Savage, Michael Standing, Raymond Farrell and Nicholas Bennett. In a revealing *TV Times* interview accompanying the

Brits in the bedroom: reunited with Sheila Hancock 15 years after the Bromley *Tons of Money* for *Frankie Howerd's Hour* in September 1971.

programme, Frankie admitted that 'I've never been fully satisfied with my work. And I hope I never will be. If you give me satisfaction, then I'll have nothing to aim for … It's almost depressing when I think of the number of British comedians better than me.'
Directed and produced by Peter Frazer-Jones A Thames Production. 8.00-9.00 pm, Wednesday 1 September 1971, in colour on ITV

Frankie Howerd's Hour: The Frankie Howerd Show

A second batch of skits and sketches from Ray Galton & Alan Simpson featuring Frankie's return to his wartime experiences. Here the skits include our hapless hero journeying back to 1944 and meeting Adolf Hitler, with co-stars Sheila Hancock, Allan Cuthbertson, Tim Barratt and ex-boxer Billy Walker. 'The first show was a great success with viewers,' enthused Thames TV's publicists, 'and was number one in the London ratings and number two on the network.'
Directed and produced by Peter Frazer-Jones A Thames Production. 8.00-9.00 pm, Wednesday 29 September 1971, in colour on ITV

★★★★★★

Whoops Baghdad

'New costumes but the same old jokes!'
Frankie Howerd

It's a tough job but somebody's got to do it … Frankie in Whoops Baghdad *heaven with Judi Stevenson, Anika Pavel, Cherri Gilham and Christine Donna during the August 1972 recording of the series.*

Up Pompeii! had proved to be one of the BBC's biggest situation comedy successes. As with other greats like *Dad's Army* and *Fawlty Towers*, the ratings seemed to get bigger and bigger with each new repeat season. *Pompeii* re-runs had been greeted with great popularity in 1971. The BBC thought it would make sense to make further programmes. But Frankie was reluctant on several counts. Firstly, although only 14 half-hour programmes had been made, Frankie had been very vocal about the way the scripts had started to become repetitive towards the end of series two. He couldn't see how the show could remain fresh and funny if they continued. The one person who could have helped make the corny old chestnuts and

dubious innuendos seem totally new was chief scriptwriter and series creator Talbot Rothwell. Sadly, Rothwell was tied up with his film work on the Carry On series and couldn't oblige the BBC with further shows.

The solution was simple. Rothwell's co-writer for the second series of *Pompeii* had been Sid Colin. Colin, who had also written the *Up Pompeii* film, was commissioned to resurrect the old format of the *Pompeii* television shows and merely change the historical context. The trick – similar to the films *Up the Chastity Belt* and *Up the Front* – was merely to drop the familiar Frankie persona into a fresh environment. In this series of six programmes, Frankie was cast as Ali Oopla, a disgruntled bondservant to the frustrated and flustered Wazir of Baghdad. Everything in the garden was rosy and nothing had really changed since the *Pompeii* shows.

Filming started in August 1972 (for Frankie, mid-way between the films *Up the Front* and *The House in Nightmare Park*), and transmission began the following January.

The Wazir was played with wheezing buffoonery by Carry On veteran Derek Francis in a tubbier variation on the aged Max Adrian and Wallas Eaton. Francis was perfectly suited to Frankie's off-the-wall, off-the cuff and off-the-point mutterings. Scripted comments about the cheapness of the show ('Don't clap, he'll want money!') and the innocence of his co-star ('I told him this is an audition!') effortlessly give Frankie the upper hand. Most enjoyable of all, however, are the ego-deflating moments as Frankie's hard-done-by slave goes off on a dramatic rant only to have his fellow actor disappear stage right. In one memorable encounter Frankie fumes 'I'm used to audiences walking out on me but not the cast!'

Wisely, popular *Pompeii* guest artiste, Larry Martyn, was employed almost throughout the *Baghdad* series as Derti Dhoti the beggar. Basically, this was a carbon copy replacement for Jeanne Mockford's wailing soothsayer, with Martyn's smelly, wild-haired whinger hamming up his performance and stealing scenes with uncontrolled laughter. Usually greeted with an unsubtle reference to his pervading odour (from 'the desert pong!' to 'aroma wasn't built in a day!'), Martyn laps up the insults with relish. The series is almost stolen, too, by that splendid pantomime baddie, Alan Curtis, who – in various villainous guises – appeared in all six episodes. Treating subtlety as a dirty word, yelling at the top of his voice, cracking his whip and twirling his moustache, Curtis provides the perfect contrast to Frankie's self-mocking, show-mocking attitude.

The element of camp, so popular with Nausius and the others in *Pompeii*, was selectively resurrected via spasmodic cameo roles for Norman Chappell's eunuch and Lee Young's genie of the bottle, while the bountiful glamour was embraced just as fully as before. With countless harem girls and belly dancers decorating the place, most of the female action was left in the capable hands of Hilary

Pritchard and Anna Brett as the Wazir's daughters. The delicious Pritchard is a constant delight as the innocent Saccharine ('Isn't she sweet?'), granting Frankie a new and oft-repeated catchphrase, 'She's soooo naïve!' Anna Brett, on the other hand – as the well-endowed and certainly well-named Boobiana – is the sex-mad glamour girl of the two, nicknamed June 'cos she's busting out all over!' Playful attention was continually drawn to her skimpy costumes, stunning figure and frightfully upper-class performance.

But the chief delight of these programmes is Frankie himself. Each show starts with a story prefaced with the generic phrase 'It came to pass…' It was the running gag equivalent of Lurcio's prologues and if the 'Salaam!' greeting didn't quite catch on as 'Salute!' had done, then Frankie was still more than eager to expose the shortcomings of the programme. Ultra-critical of the scripts, he would yell off-camera, 'I told you that gag wouldn't go!', or admit that the plot situation was critical because the script hadn't got a laugh yet. As was Frankie's wont, he would also plead for more tittering for particular gags and re-deliver dialogue that seemed unsatisfactory the first time round: 'I'll do that again, that wasn't very good!' Perhaps the finest example occurs in the opening episode as the Wazir spies a beautiful girl and asks, 'Who's that lady?' To which Frankie responds (wait for it), 'This is no lady, this is your wife!' Milking the laughter he shouts, 'You never thought you'd hear that old gag again, did you?' – before turning to the folks back stage with a cutting 'Neither did I!'

It's all in fun on the screen but Frankie was indeed unhappy with the way the scripts turned out. The mixture of sexy girls, dubious gags and silly character names may have been the order of the day but with Colin only working on some of the shows (the majority of gags being farmed out to a horde of other writers), the carefully structured smut of Rothwell was often sadly lacking. Having said that, as a Frankie vehicle this is an excellent programme and if some of the characters don't quite gel and some of the gags are more genuinely groan-worthy than endearingly barrel-scraping then so be it. It's more than worth it for the spine-tingling theme music from Ted Astley, the joyous shared pleasure of the cast, the relentless mugging from one and all and Frankie trying to keep a straight face as he murmurs, 'May your bullocks never be tightly tethered!'

....

Did You Know? When this classic show finally resurfaced courtesy of UK Gold, the playfulness of the original programme was retained with one enforced advert break. Frankie, in the middle of some long-and-winding dramatic rant, is interrupted by the title card and screams out 'I haven't finished yet!' The action cuts back to Frankie who does his last bit of dialogue and thanks the audience, whereupon the folks at UK Gold finally cut back to the ad break. Fab!

UK Gold also presented different titles (possibly originated by BBC Enterprises) for most episodes. The titles given below are the scripted titles, though they did not appear on screen or even in *Radio Times*. UK Gold left the first title intact, but subsequently came up with *Royal Command* instead of *Festival of Magic*, *Dear Dowry* for *Genie of the Bottle*, *Cattle Market* for *A Cargo of Crumpet*, *Tamberlane the Terrible* for *Ali and the Thieves* and *Come to No Harem* instead of *Saved from the Harem*.

....

Ali Oopla FRANKIE HOWERD,
Wazir DEREK FRANCIS, Saccharine HILARY
PRITCHARD, Boobiana ANNA BRETT (not in
episode 2), various villains ALAN CURTIS (not in
episode 3), Derti Dhoti the Beggar LARRY
MARTYN (not in episode 4), Imshi NORMAN
CHAPPELL (episodes 1, 4)
Costumes Sally Nieper, Make-up Penny Norton,
Lighting Bill Millar, Sound Jack Sudic, Sound
mixer Tony Rowe (episode 5), Music Ted Astley,
Designers Rosamund Inglis (episodes 2, 3, 5),
Tony Snoaden (episodes 1, 6) and Gerry Scott
(episode 4)
From an idea by Dennis Heymer
Produced and directed by John Howard Davies
Six episodes: Thursdays, mostly 10.10-10.45
pm 25 January-1 March 1973, in colour
on BBC1

The Wazir Takes a Wife

We meet our hapless hero stuffing… cushions. The oft-repeated but never quite as catchy introduction of 'Greetings … Salaam!' welcomes the audience into Pompeii Mark II. Treasurably, Hilary Pritchard as the painfully naïve Saccharine delights in revealing the identity of her secret admirer and his pleasure in picking bluebells. Frankie, of course, is concerned for her virtue and goes off on an intriguing and confusing rant ('What am I talking about?'). Thankfully Hilary knows ('She must have read the script!') but her line is drowned out by laughter and Frankie, keen to keep the story clear, mutters, 'They didn't hear that, dear!' Pritchard, having repeated her line through suppressed giggles, rushes off and leaves Frankie to milk the scene alone.

Alan Curtis, the bellowing, black-hearted villain, brings a touch of pantomime pleasure to the show; on one of his appearances Frankie comments, 'Here he is again … Henry Irving!' Curtis also brings in the minor detail of a plot device: the newly attained and quickly lost concubine who finds her way into Frankie's care and ultimately escapes a life of sexual slavery thanks to Curtis' dark secret. For it is Curtis who is the mystery bluebell-picker. Naturally, all the plot and intrigue is as nothing to Frankie's amazed reactions, double entendres and deliciously limp-wristed banter with Norman Chappell's distressed eunuch.

Besides, Frankie has to search for a woman for his master and faces an overacting masterclass from Josephine Tewson as the manic marriage broker, a supporting turn in the grand tradition of Pat Coombs and John Cater in *Pompeii* (ie, a wonderfully controlled performance which nevertheless goes over the top and out the other side). In the end, the chosen girl finds her freedom, the Wazir's potential wife is dismissed as a bad influence on his public image and Frankie almost gets to tell his shaggy camel story before the credits roll.
Fatima JOSEPHINE TEWSON, Captain of the
Guard ALAN CURTIS, Shanana VALERIE
STANTON, Ahmed NEVILLE SIMONS
Written by Sid Colin with David McKellar and
David Nobbs

Festival of Magic

'Don't forget, it's free tickets – don't expect Harold Pinter!'   **Frankie Howerd**

A 'first of the phew!' beggar flogs Frankie a ticket to the ultimate entertainment in town – the Royal Command. The bill is impressive indeed, with everybody from Bendi Afendi to Mustaphaslash (which gets probably the biggest single laugh in Frankie's sitcom career), but it's the celebrated Wizard Prang who is the real attraction. Bill Fraser plays him with just the right amount of flamboyant evil, but it's Alan Curtis who is, as usual, the real villain of the piece. Frankie, of course, finds time to reminisce about his performing credentials: his mother ran theatrical digs and was the first person to say 'Hello sailor!' to Sinbad.

But it's hastily back to the plot and the appearance of both Wizard and Wizard impersonator. Both have identical assistants (Ronnie Brody), one enhanced with a convincing Arabian accent and the other a real frog-and-toad cockney. Curtis, yelling about his nasty plans to find fame and power via the magic powder, keeps up the deception by drawing attention to the 'remarkable' similarity between his boy and the wizard's. Naturally Frankie, trapped inside a magic box, dispels the myth completely by shouting '*Remarkable?* It's the same bloody man! He plays a tree later on!'

Even by this, only the second show, the scripts are starting to repeat themselves and Alan Curtis' glorious overplaying is remorselessly mocked. ('To think we turned down Roger Moore for this!') And with almost the entire cast being climactically turned into frogs (with the giant Derek Francis frog getting huge applause), even Frankie starts getting bored with the fun. At one point – in jest, presumably – he turns to the audience and moans, 'I've lost interest in the show!' Meanwhile, the stolen magic dust has done its worst, Frankie is disguised as the wizard (having blagged his way past a stuttering guard and a deaf guard five years before Terry Gilliam and Eric Idle had a bash at

the same routine in *Monty Python's Life of Brian*) and he's in danger of facing Bill Fraser's vengeance. Thankfully, with a bit of jiggery pokery, 'a frog warning' and some dodgy BBC special effects, everybody turns out happy.

Wizard Prang BILL FRASER, Fake wizard ALAN CURTIS, Mustapha Shufti RONNIE BRODY, Short guard MARK NICHOLLS, Tall guard LEE YOUNG, Belly dancer MAHED KHAIRY, Juggler DANNY GRAY Written by Peter Vincent and Bob Hedley

Frankie and frog in the *Festival of Magic* episode of *Whoops Baghdad*, broadcast on 1 February 1973.

As camp as a row of tents: Frankie with longtime friend Lee Young in the *Genie of the Bottle* episode of *Whoops Baghdad*, broadcast on 8 February 1973.

('I don't remember rehearsing this bit!') and ultimately the lost plot turns farcical with the appearance of a wizened little old man, played to perfection by Jackie Wright – immortalised as the bald man whose bonce was regularly slapped by Benny Hill.

Money is tight, the diminutive old Sultan is demanding huge dowries for the daughters and Frankie is threatened with redundancy. Life as a galley slave ('I'm no good with oars!') looks set to be his lot until his destiny is altered with the appearance of a very friendly genie. Played by Frankie's old *Pardon My French* and radio chum Lee Young as an out-of-control Charles Hawtrey clone, the character – dripping with pink drapery and unsubtle innuendos – launches into a camp, limp-wristed torrent of flamboyant magic and high-pitched ramblings. Frankie, clearly relishing this ultra-camp interlude, follows suit. It's perhaps the most satisfying and hilarious set-piece in the entire series.

Genie LEE YOUNG, Major Domo GERTAN KLAUBER, Messenger LOUIS MANSI, Cassim JOHN LEVENE, Sultan JACK WRIGHT, Wine merchant ERIC KENT
Written by Sid Colin with Roy Tuvey and Maurice Sellar

A Cargo of Crumpet

'We'll see you again next week, so don't forget: under the palm tree, it's a date!'
Frankie Howerd

Genie of the Bottle

Our beloved bondservant encounters the smelly old beggar flogging perfume ('camel number 5') and delights in unleashing the most tired and obvious joke in the Baghdad book: 'He wazir, now he's over there!' Sex rears its beautiful head with the reappearance of the twin attractions of the lovely Boobiana. The over-zealous camera operator is quick to focus on the girl's assets, much to Frankie's outrage: 'I'm the star of this show, not those!' Mind you, 'those' do play an important part in the feeble narrative – namely the need to marry off the Wazir's two daughters to a wealthy and powerful Sultan. The plot thickens, Frankie loses the plot

Uniquely, in this episode Frankie actually gets to the end of his opening diatribe about the Caliph and his cousin. But it's the return of Norman Chappell that creates the real comic magic. Frankie's genuine delight at the way the script is going is priceless ('I'm laughing at me own jokes!') and their giggling duologue leads brilliantly into the inevitable arrival of the Wazir and his two daughters. Boobiana is banging on about women's rights and has plastered the place with women's lib slogans. Some classic business with a bemused Derek Francis concerning the purchase of a woman for the Caliph precedes the slave market scene, in which busty liberator Boobiana sells herself off for the cause.

Of course, Frankie's 300 dinas ('Can I borrow your dinas card?') goes into buying her back. The ample Janet Webb – as Gigantima – is sold to a scenery-chewing Alan Curtis, playing a bellowing Arab this time round, and Frankie must return home empty-handed. Dejected, he nips off to the El Wimpy bar where he is joined by the ranting Curtis, desperate to buy his large female something to adorn her hair. He's after a bejewelled tiara and, as Frankie observes, these are very popular: 'There's a tiara-boom today!'

Curtis laughs long as Frankie's plan of attack is hatched. Webb, like a poor man's Hattie Jacques, continually (and scriptedly) bangs into the set furnishings: 'Mind the props, dear, there's a good woman!' A quintet of harem girls is given to Derek Francis as a reward. Luckily his daughters are outraged so Frankie is quickly given custody of them instead. However, his lustful anticipation is short-lived as a bombastic Curtis returns, whips them away and makes off for the desert via the Street of a Thousand Armpits ('Just follow your nose!'). Salaam!

Akbar the Vile ALAN CURTIS, Gigantima JANET WEBB, Auctioneer ROBERT BRIDGES, Little old man JACK WRIGHT, Beggar DOUGLAS EMERY, Chinaman JOHN A TINN
Written by Roy Tuvey and Maurice Sellar

Ali and the Thieves
'Satire this week – not just old jokes!'
Frankie Howerd

A truly outstanding episode thanks to a tasty, unexpected guest actor and some brilliantly over-the-top ranting from Alan Curtis. Frankie, of course, delivers his usual sublime bit of opening business, finally breaking down into non-comic strike action after an insulting rumble from the audience. Sitting down on the job and refusing to go on, the voice of God – or at least the Director General – bellows out 'You won't get your money!' and without a

pause Frankie resumes his story-telling immediately.

The ragbag of vintage gags is happily wheeled out again – his shopping list includes a sheep's head 'to see us through the week' – and that 'dreary old fruit' Derek Francis bumbles in for some more dithering Wazir business. Larry Martyn's dirty old beggar comes on bearing worrying news that Avabanana, the leader of the band, is in town and on the prowl. Indeed, it's Alan Curtis in yet another variation on his bellowing villain, admitting that 'I prowl everywhere!' and ultimately kidnapping the poor Wazir. Frankie knows that if the Wazir dies, then his servant's contract insists on death by wild tiger ('the tiger clause!'). Frankie, in disguise again (this time in a variation on his Wizard Prang get-up from episode two), journeys to rescue his boss with the naïve daughter and the dirty beggar in tow.

Acting as a wise soothsayer, Frankie gets an audience with Avabanana's boss, Tamberlane the Terrible, and it's a treasurable meeting between a great comedian (Frankie) and a great actor (Patrick Troughton). Troughton is in scene-stealing, scenery-chewing mode, delivering his comic lines with just as much intensity as his serious threats. Frankie finally sends Troughton and his guards into a deep sleep and gets the biggest laugh of the show with his disgruntled plea of 'Oh astral plane, oh astral plane, try not to balls it up again!' Luckily, Frankie's fake soothsayer turns out to be genuinely gifted and gets his reward – wealth, women and the return of the Wazir. But all he ends up with is an old hag cast off by Troughton, who has kept the Titian-haired beauty Tangerine for himself. With a flat and feebly greeted reprise of the sheep's head gag, Frankie's out of there!

Tamberlane the Terrible PATRICK TROUGHTON, Avabanana ALAN CURTIS, Chief guard ROBERT BRIDGES, Tangerine JANE MURDOCH, Short tribesman JACK WRIGHT, Tall tribesman JOHN G HUGHMAN, Crone WINIFRED SABINE
Written by Sid Colin and David McKellar with Roy Tuvey and Maurice Sellar

Saved from the Harem

The final show in the series, though an excellent example of style over content and containing a stunning central turn from Frankie, clearly illustrates that the basic format was very tired indeed. In fact, the entire thing is an almost exact remake of the *Up Pompeii!* episodes, *Vestal Virgins* and *The Peace Treaty*. It's still hilarious but clearly the series had little imagination left of its own.

Frankie's opening monologue ('Now I must ask you to shut your gobs') gives way to the basic narrative, concerning the pure and innocent Saccharine's status as the only virgin in the area, ripe for plucking by the all-powerful Caliph. When selecting new female companions for the leader, the rule is simple – 'If they've had it, they've had it!' – and the busty Boobiana ('Don't point, dear, it's rude!') is more than keen to get the job of Caliph-comforter, though she hardly stands up to the purity test. No, it's Saccharine who is the chosen one. She's met a charming young man, however, who has 'plighted his troth'. Within the confines of the script Frankie reflects on the precise meaning of the phrase and someone from the audience shouts, 'Get married!' Laughing and amazed, Frankie checks that this contribution did indeed come from the crowd and goes into a genuinely off-the-cuff attack: 'You keep your mouth shut, if you don't mind! Don't interfere with us artists! Taking our living away... Bloody amateurs, they get everywhere!' A magical moment of television at its very best.

Equally enjoyable, although far from spontaneous, is the expected acting battle with Alan Curtis. The bellowing warrior makes a meal of his simple dialogue, as usual, and Frankie is finally not going to stand for it. He demands a script and insists on being shown where the flamboyant dialogue is written down. Unable to oblige, Curtis kidnaps Pritchard, a very camp harem hairdresser turns up and is turned out, Frankie disguises himself and infiltrates the harem as 'Ali the Barber'. Insisting that the camera shouldn't focus on all the scantily attired dolly birds, he is soon attacked by the sex-starved dollies and meets a seductive June Whitfield ('I am Charisma, the titular head of the harem'), all beads, twirled tassles and seduction tactics.

The keys, dropped down her cleavage and retrieved with gentlemanly elegance by our hero, enable Frankie to get into the boudoir, comfort the naïve daughter and quickly take her place ('It's such a drag!') before Bill Fraser turns up. Fraser, having brilliantly played the Wizard Prang earlier in the series, returns as the equally flamboyant, bombastic and underwritten Caliph character, desperately trying to have his wicked way with the new 'girl', finally looking upon the uncovered features and fleeing in horror. Finally, free but still in his feminine attire, Frankie is clocked by Milton Reid's randy Sinbad the sailor and chased into oblivion. And poor old Ali Oopla was never seen again.

Caliph BILL FRASER, Charisma JUNE WHITFIELD, Captain of the Guard ALAN CURTIS, Sinbad MILTON REID, Hairdresser GEORGE BALLANTINE, First lady CHERRI GILHAM Written by Sid Colin with David McKellar and David Nobbs

★★★★★★

Frankie Howerd in Ulster

During the run of *Whoops Baghdad*, Frankie made three consecutive appearances on his friend Cilla Black's BBC showcase *Cilla*, on 10, 17 and 24 February 1973. This special recording of Frankie's Ulster concert performance at a military base followed a fortnight after *Whoops Baghdad* finished its run, on 14 March. The stand-up patter is supplemented by a memorable court martial sketch that recruits old mates like June Whitfield and *Up Pompeii!* co-star Elizabeth Larner as back-up. The monologue material is deliciously inspired and would be oft-repeated. The plummy officer muttering 'Ha'ard! ... Are you Ha'ard?' and then observing that 'I'll be in the club' sets up Frankie's pomposity-pricking riposte, 'Working men's, social or pudding?' The line would stay in his repertoire until the end.

With June Whitfield, Wendy Richard, Allan Cuthbertson, Paul Haley, Elizabeth Larner, Andee Silver, the Tremeloes, Pan's People

Written by Ray Galton & Alan Simpson, Chris Allen, Johnny Speight, Talbot Rothwell, Roy Tuvey and Maurice Sellar, Produced and directed by Terry Hughes 9.25-10.10 pm, Wednesday 14 March 1973, in colour on BBC1

Show of the Week: An Evening With Francis Howerd

Following superstardom as a sitcom favourite and a successful return to 'live' television performance with the Ulster programme, Frankie starred in these three brilliantly constructed variety shows. Mixing parody, sketches and comic monologues, Frankie bombarded the audience with wit and whimsy, while beloved co-star June Whitfield was on hand for every edition.

FRANKIE HOWERD and JUNE WHITFIELD, with: Show 1, Norman Bird, Wolfe Morris, Pamela Cundell, Raymond Mason, Tricia Newby, Jacqueline Stanbury and Ken Alexis. Show 2, Robert Keegan, Patricia Haines, Alan Curtis, Betty Duncan and Keith James. Show 3, John Arnatt, Norman Bird, Alan Curtis, Allan Cuthbertson, Kerry Gardner, Keith James, Robert Lankesheer, Geoffrey Lumsden and Bernard Severn
Written by Eric Merriman, Ray Galton & Alan Simpson with Peter Robinson (Shows 1 and 2), Chris Allen (Show 1), Roy Tuvey and Maurice Sellar, Tony Hare, David McKellar, David Nobbs (Show 2), Mike Craig, Lawrie Kinsley, Ron McDonnell, Dave Freeman (Show 3)
Produced and directed by John Ammonds 9.25-10.10 pm Mondays, 30 April-14 May 1973, in colour on BBC2

Comedy Playhouse: Howerd's History Of England

A return to the ludicrous, innuendo-based historical costume comedy that had made Frankie a television star. This 30-minute slab of hilarious English history was originally intended as a pilot for another situation comedy. Sadly, the series was not forthcoming.
FRANKIE HOWERD, PATRICK NEWELL, PATRICK HOLT, JOHN CAZABON Written by

Barry Took and Michael Mills, Produced and directed by Michael Mills 8.30-9.00 pm, Tuesday 30 April 1974, in colour on BBC1

Francis Howerd in Concert

Another hour-long slice of stand-up and corny sketch comedy. The comic pedigree was high indeed, with a notable guest star on leave from *Dad's Army*, John Le Mesurier, plus all-round entertainer Kenny Lynch and Norwegian bombshell Julie Ege. Two of Frankie's finest and most frequent writers, Johnny Speight and Barry Cryer, wrote the script.
Music arranged and conducted by Ken Jones, Choreography Roy Gunson, Producer Duncan Wood, Director Vernon Lawrence A Yorkshire Television production. 8.00-9.00 pm Wednesday 18 September 1974, in colour on ITV

A dapper chappie hosts Francis Howerd In Concert, September 1974.

Back to Lurcio
basics in the
first *Further Up
Pompeii!*,
broadcast
Easter Monday
1975.

Further Up Pompeii!

Frankie's mid-1970s turns included *Petula Sings Christmas*, a seasonal special for singing star Petula Clark's popular series *The Sound of Petula*. Frankie, who had made his feature film début opposite Clark in *The Runaway Bus,* was the show's special guest star on its BBC1 transmission on 21 December 1974. The following year, Frankie contributed to the BBC's *2nd House* documentary, *The Sound of Laughter*, accompanied by Arthur Askey, Richard Murdoch, Hattie Jacques, Deryck Guyler,

Maurice Denham, Galton & Simpson, Sam Costa, Tim Brooke-Taylor, John Junkin and Barry Cryer. Presented by Melvyn Bragg and directed by Ben Rea, the show was broadcast on 3 May 1975.

A few weeks earlier, and exactly five years after the BBC had launched Frankie as a television star who looked great in a toga, the original writer and the original producer of *Up Pompeii!* returned to the ancient setting and ancient jokes for a one-off Easter Monday revival. Frankie, of course, was back at his peak as the confiding, conniving, cunning and thoroughly hilarious slave Lurcio, while Talbot Rothwell managed to throw in the odd mid-1970s gag, as when Frankie urges smut-hungry viewers to go to the Rialto to see *Last Tangent in Pythagoras*.

Nothing seems to have changed in Frankie's performance although he is working opposite the third and final Ludicrus (Mark Dignam) and Jennifer Lonsdale replaces an unavailable Georgina Moon as the sexy but innocent daughter, Erotica. *Forum* chum Leon Greene turns up as Erotica's beau Prodigius, whose sister Scrubba is played by future theatre and TV star Lindsay Duncan. Thankfully, enough old favourites – Elizabeth Larner, Kerry Gardner and Jeanne Mockford – were recalled, but there were never any plans to resurrect the series. To all intents and purposes this was designed as the last hurrah for Lurcio. However, he was to return over 15 years later, when ITV thought they were being original by making a one-off special entitled *Further Up Pompeii* (dropping the exclamation mark).

Lurcio FRANKIE HOWERD, Ludicrus MARK DIGNAM, Ammonia ELIZABETH LARNER, Nausius KERRY GARDNER, Pollux JOHN CATER, Senna JEANNE MOCKFORD, Prodigius LEON GREENE, Hernia OLWEN GRIFFITHS, Erotica JENNIFER LONSDALE, Claudius CYRIL APPLETON, Scrubba LINDSAY DUNCAN
Written by Talbot Rothwell, Producer David Croft
9.10-9.55 pm, Monday 31 March 1975, in colour on BBC1

Frankie and Bruce

The irresistible combination of light entertainment legends Frankie Howerd and Bruce Forsyth had proved an instant hit in the 1960s and after almost eight years the pair were reunited for this autumn season opener. The mixture of music and laughs scripted by Sid Green, Dick Hills and Barry Cryer was as powerful as before.

Produced and directed by David Bell
A Thames production. 8.00-9.00 pm Wednesday 3 September 1975, in colour on ITV

Frankie Howerd's Tittertime

An hour of titters, tall tales and talent scout baiting with Frankie and a dream team of writers running the gamut through stand-up, sketches and skits. Ray Galton & Alan Simpson's beloved, bum-flashing vicar creation was resurrected from the 1971 *Frankie Howerd's Hour* shows.

With Hughie Green, Caterina Valente, the Anderson Sisters, Norman Chappell, Derek Seaton, Raymond Farrell, Michael Bangerter, Willi Bowman, Gideon Kolb, Peter Kodak and David Valentine
Written by Barry Cryer, Ray Galton & Alan Simpson, Produced and directed by Peter Frazer-Jones
A Thames production. 8.00-9.00pm, 1 October 1975, in colour on ITV

Adolf antics as General Von Vintel in the 'Night of the Generals' sketch from *Frankie Howerd's Tittertime*, October 1975.

A Touch of the Casanovas

Frankie himself came up with the idea of transplanting the Lurcio concept to 18th century Venice. The faithful Sid Colin was on board as co-writer, while familiar Frankie co-stars like Madeline Smith, Leon Greene, John Cater and Patricia Haines abounded. So the format was hardly changed. Escaping the Doge's wrath, Casanova flees to Padua and swops identities with his loyal bondservant, Francesco. Result: farcical misunderstandings all round. The idea was frankly lifted from the 1953 Bob Hope vehicle *Casanova's Big Night*, while also paving the way for *Blackadder the Third*. The New Year's Eve pilot seemed to have hit all the right notes, audience appreciation was high and a series was announced for 1976. Sadly, it fizzled out before production began.

Francesco FRANKIE HOWERD, Casanova STUART DAMON, Isabella MARGUERITE HARDIMAN, Captain of the Guard LEON GREENE, Bartoldi JOHN CATER, Clementina PATSY ROWLANDS, Teresa MADELINE SMITH, Count Pelligrini ROGER BRIERLY, Countess Pelligrini PATRICIA HAINES, Count Malatesta CYRIL APPLETON, Doge's guardsmen GREGORY POWELL, BILLY HORRIGAN, TERRY MAIDMENT

Written by Sid Colin and Hugh Stuckey, Designer John Wood, Fight arranger Arthur Howell, Producer/Director Michael Mills A Thames production. 10.15-11.00 pm Wednesday 31 December 1975, in colour on ITV

Up the Convicts

With sitcom work thin on the ground in England, Frankie went to Canada in autumn 1975 to star in a 13-part series made exclusively for CBC Toronto, predictably entitled *The Frankie Howerd Show*. And with the classic *Up Pompeii!* proving a popular import for the expat-packed Australian community, he then agreed to make a series Down Under. The result was *Up the Convicts*, with all the usual talking to the audience, mildly blue gags and cheerful self-mockery. Frankie starred as Jeremiah Shirk, a smart ex-convict situated in Sydney Cove during the early 1800s. BBC colleague, Wallas Eaton, lent familiar support, while the bumbling

authority figures, Sir Montague and Lady Fitzgibbon, were played by Australian actors Frank Thring and Carol Raye. Frankie's friend Lee Young, Crystal Redenks and Anne-Louise Lambert (fresh from *Picnic at Hanging Rock*) filled out the supporting cast. The scripts were written by Hugh Stuckey who, having co-penned the *Casanova* romp, went on to write for *The Howerd Confessions*. Originally planned to be a series of six episodes, the shows were instead edited into two marathon chunks – a two-hour special broadcast on 7 Network on 18 June 1976 and a one-hour special aired on 19 July.

The Howerd Confessions

A series of six half-hour Frankie sitcom rants with a different subject each episode but all based around a common theme. An interesting concept – a sort of freewheeling, unstructured way of presenting Frankie in a myriad of different time-zones and institutions – the basic hook was Frankie revealing all about a given aspect of his life. The situations ranged from a criminal Frankie being dragged to court to inside information about Emmanuelle's business in the attic and, most intriguing of all, Frankie's secret wartime work with the French Resistance. This particular episode, perhaps the most adventurous of the series, saw Frankie tackle Adolf Hitler and pay delightful homage to the script's feel of *Let George Do It* with a toothy George Formby impersonation. Interviewed in *TV Times* Frankie commented that '*The Howerd Confessions* are just a series of script situations. They are not my memoirs or in any way autobiographical. Quite a few folk seem to have taken them seriously! I mean, I've actually been asked to bring my banjo-thing to parties. Cheek! The only thing I play with any confidence is the gramophone.'

The peerless Joan Sims played supporting roles in three of the programmes, ranging from a sexually forward and shockingly blunt dinner guest to a stern, hard-faced and hard-nosed hospital matron. In the medical skit, Sims brilliantly undermines Frankie's entire career, complaining that she has seen his shows and dismissing his innuendo as 'self-indulgence!' The glamour girls were top drawer as well, with the delectable Madeline Smith almost popping out of her nurse's uniform ('Oh look! Pinky and Perky!') and really creating a sense of 'Carry On Frankie'. Even better is the stunning Caroline Munro, who had already scored as a Hammer babe and would go on to 007 immortality followed by further Frankie work on *3-2-1*. Her appearance in episode two as a lusty French Resistance girl is remarkable. Seducing Frankie's green-as-grass British soldier and rolling about in the hay with bags of pent-up passion, this is a classic slice of British comedy. Indeed, Frankie seems never to have enjoyed a female's advances quite as much.

'It was a fantastic show to do but I almost talked myself out of the job,' Caroline remembers. 'I really didn't think I was right for the part and I hadn't done any comedy to speak of. But Michael Mills insisted and simply told me to "Play it straight," which I did. Frankie was great to work with. He made the whole thing so easy. We hardly had a chance to rehearse and it was recorded in front of a live audience so, being used to film, I was a little nervous to say the least. But Frankie dragged me through in one take. I think by that stage he had a say in the female co-stars he worked with so I was very proud. And there was a real chemistry between us. I really liked him.'

FRANKIE HOWERD *as himself with: Show 1, Nellie JOAN SIMS, Dr Morgan CHARLES MORGAN, Security guard KEN KITSON, Matron VIRGINIA BALFOUR, Mrs Palethorpe ELSPETH MacNAUGHTON; Show 2, Captain Latour CAROLINE MUNRO, Pierre ALEX SCOTT, Lieutenant Gruber HANS MEYER, Sergeant CYRIL APPLETON; Show 3, Matron JOAN SIMS, Nurse MADELINE SMITH, Dr Smelley NICHOLAS McARDLE, Agent TOMMY GODFREY, Mr Cockspur GEORGE MOON, Miss Pettigrew DOROTHY FRERE, Old man JACK LE WHITE, Probationer BEVERLEY KAY JENNINGS; Show 4, Mrs Beachum JOAN SIMS, Sergeant JOHN JUNKIN, Magistrate RUTH KETTLEWELL, Suspect RONNIE BRODY, WPC Taylor ISABELLA RYE, Prosecutor ROLAND MacLEOD, Girl KATE BROWN; Show 5, Chalky White ALFIE BASS, Eve LINDA THORSON, Sergeant Hardman ALAN CURTIS, PC Simpkins*

BUNNY REID; Show 6, Mrs Parsley MARGARET COURTENAY, Mr Parsley GEOFFREY CHATER, Deirdre APRIL OLRICH, Ludovic ROGER BRIERLEY, Lola SARAH DOUGLAS, Emmanuelle MIREILLE ALLONVILLE, Melissa MARGARET DALTON
Written by Dick Hills (episode 1), Hugh Stuckey and Peter Robinson (episodes 2, 4 and 5) and Dave Freeman (episodes 3 and 6)
Music Peter Knight, Designers Peter Elliott and Robin Clarke, Produced and directed by Michael Mills
A Thames production. 9.30-10.00 pm, Thursdays 2 September-7 October 1976, in colour on ITV

Drop 'em ... Dr Logan (Charles Morgan) dishes out some bad news to Frankie in *The Howerd Confessions*, September 1976.

This Is Your Life

Despite still combining regular headlining sitcom roles and stand-up showcases, Frankie was more than happy to inject a few guest titters into almost any assignment that came his way. During the run of *The Howerd Confessions* he returned from a brief holiday in Malta to feature in the 21st anniversary celebrations of ITV, hamming it up opposite Eamonn Andrews on a special edition of *This Is Your Life*. A two-hour salute to the best in the ITV archive and the best of ITV stars, it was broadcast live from the New London Theatre Drury Lane from 8.00 pm on Wednesday 22 September 1976. Andy Allan produced and Philip Casson directed. A month or so later – in the middle of celebrating his 40 years in show business – Frankie himself was honoured with the easy grin of Eamonn Andrews and the most famous red book in the history of broadcasting. Regular co-stars, friends and future *Sgt. Pepper* stars, the BeeGees, joined June Whitfield and Cilla Black among the special guests. It was a Thames production broadcast on 27 October 1976 on ITV.

★★★★★★

Frankie's late-1970s TV assignments were as varied as ever. *Those TV Times* was a cheap and cheerful trawl through the best and worst moments of television history and the likes of Tim Brooke-Taylor, Kenneth Williams and Frankie made up the dial-a-celeb game show panel. An ITV time-filler, Frankie appeared on the show broadcast on 31 August 1977. He was also frequently seen rubbing shoulders with his pal Cilla Black on the ITV version of her eponymous variety show, *Cilla*. Frankie interacted, insulted and informed the show twice, on 24 May 1978 and 8 August 1979.

Frankie also proved an invaluable guest star on the special festive edition of Bob Monkhouse's ITV panel game, *Christmas Celebrity Squares*. The show was broadcast on 23 December 1978. A few days later, on the 26th, Frankie was back in the Denis Norden

nostalgia fest *Looks Familiar*, a show he'd return to on 20 March 1980 and 20 June 1986. And on 18 January 1979, he was the star attraction in the popular Edwardian music hall showcase, *The Good Old Days*.

★★★★★★

Just So Stories

Frankie was the cosy narrator of a dozen Rudyard Kipling fables for Thames TV across a six-week period in spring 1979. The ten-minute programmes, which went out at midday every Tuesday, were *The Elephant's Child* (3 April), *The Cat that Walked by Himself* (10 April), *How the First Letter was Written* (17 April), *The Beginning of the Armadillos* (24 April), *The Crab that Played With the Sea* (1 May) and *The Butterfly that Stamped* (8 May).

The Plank

Having started life as an episode of *Sykes*, Eric's legendary battle to locate a missing plank of wood became a film featuring a dream cast of comedy heroes like Jim Dale, Bill Oddie and Tommy Cooper. This sparkling television remake managed to gather an equally impressive cast including such masters of the art as Charles Hawtrey, Harry H Corbett and, of course, Frankie Howerd. All the star guests play very much second fiddle to Sykes himself, naturally, but Frankie leaves a charming mark on the fun as a flamboyantly decked-out man with a cine-camera.

Cropping up about 13 minutes into the fun, he is earnestly filming the stunning blonde Carrol Baker as she drapes herself over a park bench. An interruption from dogged plank-pursuers Sykes and Arthur Lowe sees Frankie ranting in gobbledegook bad language and indignantly rubbing his banged posterior. Five minutes later we meet him again in more cheerful mood. He has positioned his model on a horse trough and desperately orders her to 'Smile!' Lowe, complete with plank, obliges, knocking the dolly into the water to the amazement of Charlie Drake and the distress of Frankie himself. It's hardly the most earth-shattering telly credit of his career but to be included in this sort of cast at all was testimony to Frankie's top-table status.

ERIC SYKES and ARTHUR LOWE with CARROL BAKER, LIONEL BLAIR, HENRY COOPER, HARRY H CORBETT, BERNARD CRIBBINS, ROBERT DORNING, DIANA DORS, CHARLIE DRAKE, JIMMY EDWARDS, LIZA GODDARD, DERYCK GUYLER, CHARLES HAWTREY, FRANKIE HOWERD, JAMES HUNT, WILFRID HYDE-WHITE, JOANNA LUMLEY, KENNY LYNCH, BRIAN MURPHY, KATE O'MARA, ANN SIDNEY, REG VARNEY, FRANK WINDSOR
Written and directed by Eric Sykes, Music Alan Braden, Camera Operator Tom Ingle, Editor John Plummer, Dubbing Mixer Gordon Temple, Costumes Janet Bevan, Make-up Gillian Wakeford, Location Manager Brian Heard, Stage Manager Auriol Lee, Designer David Richens, Producer Dennis Kirkland
A Thames production. 8.00-8.30 pm Monday 17 December 1979, in colour on ITV

Comedy Tonight

Frankie's TV appearances in 1980 ranged from judging a 'Glamorous Grandmothers' contest on the magazine programme *Nationwide* on 18 March, joining Kenny Everett and presenter Mavis Nicholson on *Afternoon Plus* ten days later, and indulging in the *Easter Star Games* broadcast on 4 April. The same week, *Comedy Tonight* had Frank Muir hosting an exhaustive tribute to the finest comedy sketches of the previous 50 years. The galaxy of stars included Richard Briers, Ian Carmichael, Harry H Corbett, Sheila Hancock, Patricia Hayes, Arthur Lowe, Ian Ogilvy, Lance Percival, Beryl Reid and Dennis Waterman, with Frankie on hand to recreate Tony Hancock's immortal 'Budgerigar' sketch.
Written by H F Ellis, Reginald Purdell, Ray Galton & Alan Simpson, Douglas Furber, John Mortimer, Cole Porter and Michael Brown
Produced and directed by Michael Mills
A Thames production. 8.00-9.00 pm Wednesday 2 April 1980, in colour on ITV

Chaos Supercedes ENSA

A fascinating two-part investigation into the history, heritage and horrors of the 'Every Night Something Awful' performers who struggled through war-torn terrain to bring a bit of ramshackle entertainment to servicemen during the war. Many of the finest comedy talents of the post-war era tittered for the cause and some of the best, including Kenneth Williams, Spike Milligan, Tommy Trinder and our own Frankie Howerd, contributed interview material to this ITV documentary broadcast in two parts on 29 June and 27 August 1980. The shows were hosted, produced and directed by Patrick Garland. Later in the year, on 2 October, Frankie was funny for nothing on a spectacular ITV marathon charity telethon.

Parkinson

After an intermediate appearance on 16 April 1979, Frankie's final stint with the doyen of chat show hosts came on 3 December 1980, when his fellow guests were Trevor Nunn and Bryan Forbes. Typically, Frankie immediately begins interrogating the interrogator ('How are you?') before getting started proper. Parkinson skilfully extracts Frankie's memories of RADA failure before challenging him to go through his dramatic expressions, whereupon Frankie drags on a shy blonde teenager to be his 'co-star'. Instantly changing from 'humility' to 'passionate', it's a one-man, camp masterclass in overacting, topped off with Frankie dragging in the host for some embarrassed play-acting. A joyous trawl through Frankie's public persona with an intriguing, extremely brief glimpse into the private domain. Besides, there's a totally fresh and never-repeated Frankie catchphrase to cherish – 'I'm just a tiny tot!'

....

Did You Know? When Parkinson returned as the conquering hero of chat in the 1990s, his vintage interviews were resurrected in handily edited 'best of' chunks, including a 1995 presentation called *The Parkinson Interviews: Tommy Cooper and Frankie Howerd.*

....

Mystic madness with Henry McGee in the philosophy episode of *Frankie Howerd Strikes Again,* September 1981.

Frankie Howerd Reveals All

'I'm only acting, love – I'm too convincing … I should take this up!'
                          Frankie Howerd

Another glorious one-off comic investigation, this time into the British class system. From the opening 'Ladies and gentle-*men*!' to Frankie's climactic eruption through the Yorkshire Television logo, this is a brilliant variety special in which Frankie launches into a high-minded dissertation on the class system. Frankie's inspired pieces to camera and amazement at YTV's cheap scenery act as brilliant bridges between the guest star turns. His only pre-filmed work involves a handful of historical vignettes, playing a Civil War turncoat, the bowls-obsessed Sir Francis Drake Howerd and the deeply confused Bonnie Prince Charlie Howerd. Deluxe support comes from a Benny Hill second banana, a ghost of Motley Hall and a Carry On legend, all of whom appear in Francis-free, pre-filmed interludes and studio pieces, while the rousing finale ('the classy bit') sees 'Howerd Sing Coward'. With a hammed-up, sometimes

poignant, sometimes painful rendition of 'I'll See You Again', Frankie peppers Noël's lyrics with corny observations before the cast interrupt with 'The Party's Over' and Frankie trips the light fantastic with Henry McGee.
With HENRY McGEE, SHEILA STEAFEL, KENNETH CONNOR, CHRIS EMMETT, BRIAN OSBORNE, THE BARRON KNIGHTS
Written by John Bartlett and Mike Goddard, Additional material by Laurie Rowley, Musical director and original music Laurie Holloway, Senior Cameraman Chris Clayton, VT Editor Bill Duff, Make-up Di Lofthouse, Lighting Director Brian Hilton, Designers Howard Dawson and Desmond Crowe, Produced and directed by Alan Tarrant A Yorkshire Television production. 8.00-9.00 pm Wednesday 10 December 1980, in colour on ITV

Frankie Howerd Strikes Again

'I hope you don't regret that applause!'
                          Frankie Howerd

Following the success of the *Reveals All* special, Alan Tarrant recruited much of the same talent for this stunning six-pack of

Frankie frolics for Yorkshire TV. Built up as an antidote to the lacklustre television programmes audiences were used to, this was 'the thinking man's show' designed to get you 'stimulated and aroused' with a weighty topic tackled each week via stand-up monologue and sketches.

Each edition would start with Frankie reading a letter from Ethel Clutterbuck of Harrogate; Frankie would then chat on the given subject (psychology, the occult, the media etc) for about five minutes prior to a self-contained and often underwritten sketch featuring authority figure Henry McGee. After the much-mocked commercial break, that legendary singer-songwriter Neil Innes would then be insulted and asked to perform a number suitable to the subject under discussion. A second sketch would follow and the programme would wrap up with Frankie taking questions from the audience in the regular slot, Francis' Fretters Forum. This slot started out with actors coming on and asking Frankie for advice but was eventually substituted with the cheaper procedure of Frankie reading 'audience questions' from cards.

Frankie was on bristling form throughout and even the most hackneyed gags came up fresh and sparkling. He could get a huge laugh just by tripping over some line or other and muttering, 'I must rehearse this more!' Old catchphrases ('Well, please yourselves!' and 'What a funny woman!') were joined with experimental new ones ('a quick peep!'), while shortcomings in the dodgy sets were pinpointed ('I wobbled that then!') and old glories resurrected – one week Frankie journeyed back to the ancient world in his time-machine to chat things over with Norman Chappell's Socrates. The rudiments of philosophy were effortlessy distilled: 'Why are we here? Well, I'll tell you. I'm here for the money and you're here 'cos you got free tickets!'

Finally, as if to cock a snook at Frankie's infamous and much-exaggerated reputation for over-running, these recorded programmes would close with Frankie getting excited about the 'book of the week', which always mixed the subject of the show with 'the erotic', leaving Frankie to cry 'I haven't finished!' as the credits rolled. Patchy is hardly the word but this was Frankie's final headlining stand-up vehicle until he returned for the last hurrah of *Frankie's On…*

With HENRY McGEE, LINDA CUNNINGHAM, NEIL INNES and David Brierly, Annie Rice, Muriel Rogers, Ray Ternet, Jacqui Ross, Ronnie Brody, Hilda Fenemore, Bartlett Mullins, Lesley E Bennett, Colin Meredith, Wendy King, Carl Gresham, Norman Chappell, Claire Davenport, Jeanne Mockford
Written by John Bartlett with Mike Goddard, Barry Cryer and Spike Mullins, Sound Mike Naylor, VT Editors Lance Tattersall and Bill Duff, Make-up Pam Fox, Lighting Terry Mounsey, Peter Hardman and Brian Hilton, Designer Andrew Sanderson, Executive Producer Alan Tarrant

With Henry McGee in the final instalment of *Frankie Howerd Strikes Again*, October 1981.

What's a Grecian urn? Frankie with Madeline Smith, Chris Emmet and members of the Brian Rogers Connection in the December 1983 3-2-1 epic 'It's All Greek To Me'.

A Yorkshire Television Production. 9.30-10.00 pm, Tuesdays 1 September-6 October 1981, in colour on ITV

Does the Team Think?

A television treatment for Jimmy Edwards' brainchild which allowed members of the great British public to fire questions at a distinguished comic panel and await the (hopefully) hilarious answers. The peerless Tim Brooke-Taylor gritted his teeth and battened down the hatches as the chairman of the fun while series inventor Edwards was joined by Beryl Reid, Willie Rushton and Frankie Howerd on the panel. The television critics greeted the antics with typically smug comments like 'Does the Team Think? Of itself, highly!'

Programme associate Eric Merriman, Designer Tony Borer, Producer Robert Reed
Nine editions: 7.00-7.30 pm Thursdays 14 January-11 March 1982, in colour on ITV

3-2-1

Ted Rogers, Dusty Bin, scantily clad hostesses, incomprehensible riddles and super guest stars were just some of the reasons why the nation tuned into ITV every Saturday night for Yorkshire Television's quiz-based feast of kitsch, corn and confusion (based, oddly, on a Spanish original called *Uno Dos Tres*). Frankie made his first of three appearances on the programme in a camp, comic and cod-Sherlock Holmes edition screened on Saturday 6 March 1982. Next, he appeared in a frolicsome Foreign Legion skit, transmitted on 9 May 1983, alongside Christopher Beeny, Chris Emmett, Dilys Watling, Felix Bowness and Caroline Munro. And Frankie's final appearance came in the 'It's All Greek to Me' instalment, broadcast on 17 December of the same year.

....

Did You Know? Frankie was keen to present his own game show. He was aggrieved when, in 1978, Larry Grayson – a comedian he often cited as stealing his act – was awarded the plum BBC job of hosting *The Generation Game*. It was a job he would have killed for. However, his desperation to work didn't cloud his judgment. In 1990, Pinewood producer Kevin Francis was hard at work fashioning a television quiz show tailor-made for Frankie. However, after an initial burst of interest and enthusiasm, Frankie concluded that the vehicle wasn't right for him and withdrew completely.

....

★★★★★★

Then Churchill Said To Me

'You think yourself lucky – there's only half an hour of this; it could be worse!'
Frankie Howerd

The legendary lost Frankie sitcom, this *Up Pompeii!* meets World War II series was originally filmed in late 1981 for scheduled broadcast in early 1982. However, the series was pulled before screening in light of Britain's involvement in the Falklands conflict. More recently, it has been suggested that the corporation considered the final results less

than satisfactory and used the contemporary events as an excuse to shelve the series indefinitely. Whatever the reason, this final attempt to resurrect the spirit of Frankie's historical toga-thon in another historical context remained unseen during Frankie's lifetime.

While hardly *Blackadder Goes Forth*, there is still much to enjoy. In terms of British comedy it comes somewhere between the final Rowan Atkinson series and *Carry On England*. Indeed, in the black-and-white credit sequence presenting a mini-tour of Winston Churchill's wartime bunker, the highly unsubtle 'WC' gag is recycled direct from the khaki Carry On. The format was pure *Up Pompeii!* and although the scripts were hardly in the same league – Maurice Sellar and Lou Jones had been additional writers for the far funnier *Whoops Baghdad* shows – Frankie easily overcame all the problems. He delivers the most mind-numbingly awful gags in comedy history with boisterous enthusiasm.

The script may never set its sights higher than the lowest common demoninator but there's something reassuringly cosy and hilarious about the establishing sequence, in which the Anne Shelton vocals seem just as potent as Bud Flanagan's *Dad's Army* theme but without the gift of total familiarity. Panning across the cluttered Churchill office, settling on the back of a huge office chair with the V-sign digits of its famous occupant protruding, the comedy juices start flowing in classic style as the chair swivels round to reveal Frankie in all his khaki glory.

Basically, Frankie is the work-shy, cheeky and cowardly Private Percy Potts, continually trying to make a quick buck out of Winston souvenirs and forever facing the vengeful might of the military. In terms of *Up Pompeii!*, the Ludricus figure is brought wonderfully to life by *Doctor Who*'s very own Brigadier, Nicholas Courtney. Demoted to play Colonel Robin Withering (so-named so the writers can throw in constant Robin and 'batman' cracks), he struggles to avoid conflict and chases energetically after his posh secretary, given just the right amount of cynical, self-important venom by Joanna Dunham.

The major bugbear in Frankie's army career, however, is the Scottish sergeant major played with fiery, Bill Fraser-esque aplomb by Shaun Curry. Carry On veteran PeggyAnn Clifford is underused as the friendly tea-lady and, ditto, Linda Cunningham, fresh from Frankie's recent work for Yorkshire TV. James Chase is quite outstanding as the over-sexed, old-before-his-time batman who wheezes, moans and suffers for his country with deliciously fretful dialogue and hard-done-by mannerisms, while gormless Michael Attwell as Norman ('Four more brain cells, he'll make a good idiot!') allows Frankie some classic moments of mockery.

Frankie eagerly embraces all the old catchphrases, skilfully injecting everything from 'It's wicked to mock the afflicted!' to 'Please yourselves!', but the script lets him down on many occasions. 'What do you mean it's old?' Frankie pleads. 'It's a good 'un!' This falls a tad flat because all too often it simply isn't. The major flaw in the fun is the writers' coy avoidance of 'deconstruction'. Unlike Frankie's other historicals, there is never a sense that this is merely Frankie acting at the BBC; the historical situation is played for real. Lines like 'You've paid your licence' are few and far between, while the script – which, at its worst, is very bad indeed – is never openly mocked, with no opportunities for Frankie to point the finger at the faceless scriptwriters responsible for the corny one-liners. Frankie manages to come out of the fun smelling of roses but the show's cancellation was hardly the most auspicious end to Frankie's BBC career.

....

Did You Know? The series was first broadcast in 1993 on that saviour of classic British television, UK Gold. A couple of BBC video releases of the entire series appeared in the same year. However, it wasn't until 8 April 2000 that the show made its terrestrial début. Uncelebrated and unheralded, the scheduling for the show was all over the place; amazingly, the sixth and final episode didn't get an airing until 10 September. Co-writer Lou Jones had been employed as editing supervisor on the programmes for the 1993 broadcast and, as a result, not only do some of the lines disappear completely but the editing remains confused, sloppy and grating. The original planned running time of 30 minutes was trimmed so that each show weighed in at just 25 minutes. Although PeggyAnn Clifford and James Chase were originally featured in all six programmes and are credited accordingly, several of the shows drop their contributions completely.

....

Private Percy Potts/General Fearless Freddy Hollocks FRANKIE HOWERD, Colonel Robin Withering NICHOLAS COURTNEY, Petty Officer Joan Bottomly JOANNA DUNHAM, Sergeant-Major McRuckus SHAUN CURRY, Batman MacKensey JAMES CHASE, Sally Perks LINDA CUNNINGHAM, Private Norman Pain MICHAEL ATTWELL, Tea-lady PEGGYANN CLIFFORD
Written by Maurice Sellar and Lou Jones, Signature tune composed by Ronnie Hazlehurst, Sung by Anne Shelton, Costumes Robin Stubbs, Make-up Shirley Channing Williams, Production team Gavin Clark, Jan Hallett and Alison Roddy, Lighting Peter Smee, Sound Malcolm Johnson, Senior Cameraman Peter Ware, Designer Vic Meredith with Barrie Dobbins (episode 1) and Les McCallum (episode 6), Producer Roger Race, Director Martin Shardlow

Operation Panic

Plundering *The Prisoner of Zenda* for the opening episode's narrative hook, the distinguished Freddy Hollocks looks exactly like Frankie with glasses on. Frankie's belligerent and sex-mad boss is preparing for a bit of hanky-panky with his snotty WREN secretary. But his leave application inadvertently ends up in an 'out' tray for volunteers for a suicidal mission to Antwerp. Frankie must retrieve the Colonel's application or face going on the deadly mission himself. Hence, it's rather handy that Frankie is the dead spit for the General! With the General in the shower Frankie can easily whip his uniform, whip the application and save the day. The Colonel, however, catches Frankie in the General's room, slips on the soap, exposes the Howerd rear and breaks his own leg. So, although the Colonel is saved from the mission, he can't go on his dirty weekend because his leg is in plaster!

Frankie is in sparkling form throughout, but the script does him no real favours. Indeed, the show's funniest moment comes when Frankie and Courtney struggle to keep straight faces as the batman's shammy leather starts smouldering (the Churchill cigar butt has set it alight). Courtney's suppressed grin as he bravely tries to keep his cool in the face of Frankie's mugged reaction is one for the 'best of' archive.

....

Did You Know? General Horrocks was the name of an actual officer whom Frankie served under during his time stationed in France. The General was continually banging on about 'no fraternisation' with the locals.

....

ROGER AVON, BRIAN HAINES, FRANK GATLIFF

A Mole In the Hole

There's a spy in the bunker (or, as Frankie puts it, 'Someone down here is leaking') so everything is covered in a special powder which leaves an indelible green mark. The finger of suspicion points at Frankie when his hand turns green and our hapless hero is thrown into a cell. He makes room for a familiar comic rant – 'I'm too young to die, aren't I? Well, don't take a vote on it!' – before his bewildered boss is caught green-handed and tossed in the cell as well. Obviously that devious Welsh boffin Dai Jenkins is at the bottom of it all (as Frankie observes, 'That's all you can expect from a Welshman – a leak!'), and a search of the bunker exposes the gun-toting Nazi-supporter. Frankie is in the firing line with Taffy pointing the gun at the star's nether regions and bellowing 'I'll blow his brains out!' before Frankie moves the weapon to the appropriate place! Frankie then cries 'Heil Hitler!', the Welshman's gun arm flies to a Nazi salute and the villain is overpowered.

It's all exciting stuff but George Formby and Will Hay had done it all before and much,

much more powerfully in the 1940s. Still, Frankie's round-up is a joy, pointing out that the baddie has been sentenced to watch never-ending ENSA shows with people like Harry Secombe, Spike Milligan, Max Bygraves, Kenneth Williams and Frankie Howerd: 'They're so old-fashioned – except one!'
TALFRYN THOMAS, MARTIN WIMBUSH, RUSSELL WOOTTON

Nanny By Searchlight

Resurrecting memories of *Up the Front*, Frankie is lumbered with the regimental mascot, a nanny goat, and finds that the Colonel's missing bearskin hat is being used as the batman's tea cosy. It's hardly stimulating stuff but it gets better as Frankie chews the fat about sex and moth-balls with his knackered cohort before the corniest, most groan-worthy goat gag – 'Why don't you get him a pen?'/'Cos he can't write!' – reveals what an absolute genius Frankie was at getting away with absolute murder! The dreadful goat-based punning finally gets a bit out of hand when Frankie chances his arm with 'Stop acting the goat ... Who do you think you are, Billy the Kid?'

But the barrel-scraping script is instantly redeemed when the old *Up Pompeii!* style is revived, with the dim-witted Norman mumbling about buying the animal a pen and Frankie screaming 'We've done that gag ... I wish you'd watch the show!' The blonde bombshell Perks (played with effortless charm by Linda Cunningham) comments that the goat reminds her of film star Monty Woolley, the nanny goat chomps through a few important letters and sets up the final narrative mix-up involving General De Gaulle and a Nazi prisoner. Frankie is allowed some gloriously over-played 'oohs' as he listens to the intercom chat between the Colonel and his stuck-up bit of skirt, after which a cliché-ridden, underwritten, fog-strewn duel sequence pads out the episode. Although there are a few titters along the way – notably Frankie's shocked reaction to 'I would like to examine your weapon!' – this one drags along.
JOHN CHALLIS, MICHAEL COCHRANE

Those Who Loot We Shoot

Perhaps the funniest Churchill-based opening precedes the appearance of the dreaded McRuckus. Frankie's observation that 'I bend over backwards – but that's another story!' is classic and he reacts with trademark unease to the bellowed request, 'Show me you're a man!' Colonel Withering orders Frankie to fetch him an Encyclopedia of Battles, there's a rare return to *Pompeii* vein with Frankie's 'Enjoy your farewell appearance' to the gormless Norman, and a delicious three-tier 'Oh Joan!'/'Oh Robin!'/'Oh blimey!' moment.

The narrative – for what it's worth – sees Frankie bring the Colonel the wrong book (as well as a truly awful joke about being 'left on the shelf'). Moreover, the Colonel's naughty weekend is jeopardised yet again, this time due to a bang on the head and a regression to childhood. Frankie's Private P Potts is, meanwhile, salvaging stuff from the Colonel's house and gets arrested as a looter. Of course, with the Colonel's memory gone, Frankie's in deep trouble. Blessed with a glorious, stammering cameo from Gordon Peters ('They'll sh-sh-sh-shoot you!'), Frankie milks the imprisonment storyline, calls for a Hattie Jacques sub, takes a leaf out of Toad of Toad Hall's book, dons the drag and gets past the camp prison guard with a hasty 'Hello sailor! … Thank God he never looks at a woman!'
NEVILLE BARBER, DAVID CLEEVE, BERYL COOKE, CHARLES PEMBERTON, GORDON PETERS, JOYCE WINDSOR

Blow Out

The bunker is struck with a jamming device and the lads are on the case. The rather unconvincing explanation is that a poltergeist has taken up residence and Frankie gets cracking on a booby trap to catch it. The Colonel, of course, is less than impressed and sums up the whole episode with 'I've never heard so much rubbish in my life!' Frankie is quick to answer, 'Lots more to come yet, sir!' Unfortunately there is.

This is the series' ultimate sub-*Dad's Army* scenario, resurrecting one of the classic Croft and Perry routines – the unexploded bomb – and remorselessly trying to squeeze every drop of laughter from the situation. Frankie, gamely overacting with a vengeance, just about saves the day but the supporting turns are lacklustre and the script is simply not firing on all cylinders. An inspection of the attic – with Frankie's fear of mice coming into play – pads the plot out a bit. However, the obvious patter concerning a flying mouse ('It's a bat, man!') raises a smile and the sudden air-raid triggers the narrative into overdrive as the hapless Frankie and his bellowing boss find themselves trapped under an unexploded bomb. (Asked to describe the thing Frankie memorably mutters, 'Bloody big!') The bomb is finally revealed to be a dud, Frankie looks with almost shamefaced apology into camera and the show grinds to a halt.
CYRIL APPLETON, ALAN HOCKEY

The Goose Has Landed

Rumours abound that Nazi intelligence is intending to infiltrate the bunker and kill Churchill. Thus the PM is whisked off to safety and Frankie is given the unenviable task of wheeling round Mr Churchill's lifesize, wheelchair-bound dummy. The totally unconvincing decoy (on loan from the Marquis of Bath's Churchill collection at Longleat) is used by our hapless hero to con people out of money for petrol coupons. Naturally the humour is fairly workmanlike and the script doesn't really aim its sights any higher than the obvious, as when Frankie comments to his boss that 'We'll have a dummy run!'

The real spy – Pamela Salem as blonde temptress Baroness Hannah Von Thrump – attempts a seduction of Frankie, his drink is drugged and pretty soon he's leglessly babbling about the confused plot. It's all very reminiscent of *Up the Front*, with Frankie going into overacting overdrive and the dastardly plot being fooled by a combination of good luck and British bulldog spirit. Finally, as the series winds down and Frankie addresses the nation, he sums up the entire ill-fated exercise in one phrase: 'Never has so much been done to so many by so few …

Thankfully so far I've got away with it!' The *Life* magazine-style closing credits and Shelton's patriotic song are then rolled out for the final time.
PAMELA SALEM, LES DOVE, DICK HAYDON

★★★★★

The Gilbert and Sullivan Collection

It had been nearly 20 years since Frankie had suffered the indignity of hipped-up Gilbert and Sullivan in Michael Winner's messy *The Cool Mikado* so it must have felt sweetly ironic when Frankie accepted the chance to star in two more faithful productions of the great duo's comic operas. Presented by George Walker and produced for the American market, screen legend Douglas Fairbanks Jr was dragged in to introduce each production while Frankie and the cast cavorted at Shepperton Studios.

In 1981 Frankie was cast as the Judge in the one-act piece, *Trial By Jury*, originally conceived as a frothy curtain-raiser but quickly becoming one of the team's earliest and most celebrated successes. A brilliant satire on the legal system, it is unique in the annals of Gilbert and Sullivan for being the only opera they wrote completely devoid of dialogue – until Frankie Howerd got his hands on it, of course. This television presentation utilised Sullivan's 'Di Ballo' as an overture to introduce the principals in a mimed opening. Frankie is seen waking up, refusing tea and struggling into a corset in a brilliantly evocative comic mime. The highlight comes when a discarded wig lands on the head of his maid, Frankie looks aghast at the sight, stares into the mirror and mutters to his audience 'What a funny woman!' This is pure Frankie indulgence and quite breathtaking.

His musical performance is wonderfully fraught and energetic, working his audience – the jury – with ease, taking the applause for his musical history of how he became a judge with glee, playfully banging a counsel on the head with his brief and frantically flirting with the attractive plaintiff, Angelina (played with manipulative charm by Kate Flowers). Looking petulant at every revelation, boozing before he faces the court, consulting saucy literature and winking at the camera at every opportunity, this is Gilbert and Sullivan according to Frankie Howerd and a masterclass in how to adapt a classic to your own style. He even injects a haughty 'I haven't finished yet!' as his line is interrupted.

The supporting cast includes the earnest Ryland Davies as Edwin the defendant and Benny Hill's faithful cohort Anna Dawson as his new lady love Miss Ann Other. The production was staged by Wendy Toye, directed by Derek Bailey and produced by Judith De Paul, but it's Frankie's riveting and rousing performance as the Judge – 'and a good judge too!' – that brings fresh life to this musical classic.

Frankie also appeared for the Brent Walker organisation as Sir Joseph Porter, ruler of the Queen's Navy, in their production of *HMS Pinafore*, staged this time by Michael Geliot and directed by Rodney Greenberg. Here, Frankie was partnered by Peter Marshall, long-serving MC of *Hollywood Squares*. This one was also made available on record (Pioneer Artists PA 84-067), and both shows were released on video in 1982. They later surfaced on BBC TV, under the collective title *The Compleat Gilbert & Sullivan*, on 30 August 1983 (*HMS Pinafore*) and 3 June 1984 (*Trial By Jury*).

Trial By Jury: *The Learned Judge FRANKIE HOWERD, The Plaintiff KATE FLOWERS, The Defendant RYLAND DAVIES, Counsel for the Plaintiff TOM McDONNELL, Usher ROGER BRYSON, Foreman of the Jury BRIAN DONLAN, First Bridesmaid ELSIE McDOUGALL, Miss Ann Other ANNA DAWSON*
HMS Pinafore: *Sir Joseph Porter FRANKIE HOWERD, Captain Corcoran PETER MARSHALL, Ralph Rackstraw MICHAEL BULMAN, Dick Deadeye ALAN WATT, Bill Bobstay GORDON SANDISON, Josephine MERYL DROWER, Little Buttercup DELLA JONES, Hebe ANNE MASON*
Ambrosian Opera Chorus, London Symphony Orchestra (conducted by Alexander Faris)

The Other Side Of Me

As part of ITV's commitment to religious broadcasting, popular entertainers were quizzed on their beliefs. Here the sincere spiritual side of Frankie's clerical aspirations and days as a Sunday School teacher were discussed while he was filmed delighting an audience of pupils. A TVS production, Frankie's episode was broadcast on 27 August 1982.

★★★★★★

Also in 1982, Frankie hosted an edition of the dreaded *Summertime Special*, was interviewed by Russell Harty again and contributed to a BBC *Arena* documentary devoted to the radio favourite *Desert Island Discs*. Originally broadcast on 23 February 1982, the programme, partially revamped, was repeated on 27 January 1992.

In 1983, Frankie turned up on *The Noel Edmonds Late Late Breakfast Show* and, early in the life of TV-AM's morning news and reviews show, *Good Morning Britain*, found himself a regular gig as a gag-cracking, on-the-spot roving reporter in September and October 1983. He would also be dragged into the studio to interact with the station's greatest spin-off character, Roland Rat, when the self-promoting rodent superstar was given his own show, *Roland's Yuletide Binge*, on 25 December 1985.

The remainder of Frankie's mid-1980s TV output was patchy, starting with a turn as Plautus – the original source of reference for *Forum* and *Up Pompeii!* and much else – in the *Makers of Magic* segment of Ronald Harwood's BBC documentary series *All the World's a Stage*, broadcast on 29 January 1984. More conventional gigs later that year included *Who Dares Wins* on 23 June and *Entertainment Express* on 29 August. Frankie also put in a hilarious appearance on the weekend children's favourite, *Saturday Superstore*, on 19 October 1985.

Also in 1985, Frankie was roped in to put his name and caricature features to the exclusive Marks and Spencer book, *Howerd's Howlers*. Published by Octopus Books for St Michael, the flimsy paperback was a 'hilarious collection of anecdotes gathered together with the assistance of Frankie Howerd.' His involvement didn't extend much beyond an introduction and an 'Ooh don't laugh … it really happened!' tag-line on the front cover, but there were reminiscences on making the record 'Up Je t'aime' and enough dodgy Howerd cartoons by Mick Davis to keep the most discerning fan happy.

★★★★★★

The Gong Show

Having set out their stall as purveyors of cult viewing with one eye on the past and another on the future, Channel 4 secured the rights to the wacky American talent show and gave it a homely British sheen. Frankie was drafted in to keep control of the judges (Barbara Windsor, Barry Cryer and Mike Newman) while such manic acts as three little maids from St Trinian's, a German tit willow and a Snow White who sang a duet with herself tried in vain to impress. Devised by Chuck Barris and Chris Beard, this pilot for the home audience was broadcast on 9 December 1985. It didn't gel but remains an interesting failure.

Saturday Live

When the so-called 'alternative comedy' invasion was at its height, this groundbreaking showcase for the best in contemporary stand-up comedy proved the perfect launch pad for Ben Elton and featured vintage work from Harry Enfield, Stephen Fry, Rik Mayall and many others. Amazingly – some 25 years after Peter Cook, the Establishment and *That Was The Week That Was* had relaunched Frankie as a cutting-edge comedian – he was invited (fast approaching 70) to do his stuff on this, the ultimate platform for hip new comedy. Peter Cook himself and fellow veteran Spike Milligan were also featured. Frankie grabbed the challenge with both hands and delivered his usual shambolic but painstakingly polished routine with razor-sharp perception and self-mockery. The kids loved it!

A London Weekend Television production. 25 January-29 March 1986/7 February-11 April 1987, in colour on ITV

The Bob Monkhouse Show

An invaluable record of the great and good of comedy, presented by the ever-great and good Bob Monkhouse in a series of in-depth interviews and stand-up routines. The host's healthy obsession with vintage comedy was reflected in the delicious animated credits which utilised the Marx Brothers, W C Fields, Laurel and Hardy and the like. The guest list included, as well as Frankie, veterans Peter Cook, Les Dawson, Tommy Cooper, Bob Hope and Joan Rivers, while providing a useful platform for fresh young talent. On Frankie's edition, the fresh young talent came in the form of Sandra Bernhard.
Director David Taylor, Producer John Fisher
9.30-10.10 pm Monday 10 February 1986 in
colour on BBC2

The Blunders

A long-running Filmfair cartoon series (30 episodes were produced in 1985 and ran over a six-week period from 22 April to 4 June 1986) concerning the accident-prone Blunder family and their wacky pets, Trouble the dog, Zebra the cat and Patch the canary. Frankie provided the irresistibly lugubrious narration and the stories veered from standard domestic sitcom (rivalry with the neighbouring Puddlebum family) to bizarre flights of fancy (the family bumping into a prehistoric monster in *An Idle Idol*). A weekly repeat season ran into 1987.
1: At the Circus Tuesday 22 April; 2: Looking After Doris Wednesday 23 April; 3: Central Heating Thursday 24 April; 4: Dog Bath Friday 25 April; 5: House of Horror Monday 28 April; 6: Dogs Don't Migrate Tuesday 29 April; 7: Ye Blunder and Ye Dragon Wednesday 30 April; 8: UFO Spotting Thursday 1 May; 9: The Trouble with Trouble Friday 2 May; 10: At the Manor Tuesday 6 May; 11: A Blunder on the Run Wednesday 7 May; 12: Lucky Thursday 8 May; 13: Bean Blunder Friday 9 May; 14: The Invisible Blunder Monday 12 May; 15: Life On Spudnook Tuesday 13 May; 16: School Report Wednesday 14 May; 17: Bobby and the Prunestones Thursday 15 May; 18: An Aunt In Time Friday 16 May; 19: An Idle Idol Monday 19 May; 20: Stage Struck Tuesday 20 May;
21: Dog Diet Wednesday 21 May; 22: The Burglar Thursday 22 May; 23: Never Kiss A Frog Friday 23 May; 24: Double Act Tuesday 27 May: 25: The Blunder Family Tree Wednesday 28 May: 26: The Genie Thursday 29 May; 27: The Bugs Meringue Gang Friday 30 May: 28: Ma Goes Ape Monday 2 June; 29: The Invasion of the Burger-Snatchers Tuesday 3 June; 30: A Blunder on the Landscape Wednesday 4 June 1986
Written and directed by Ian Sachs, Executive Producer Graham Clutterbuck
A Central Production

Superfrank!

The boy was back in town and the home for radical television, Channel 4, caught on to the growing Frankie cult a couple of years early to present this bristling live performance recorded at the Playhouse Theatre, Weston-super-Mare.
Written by Vince Powell, Miles Tredinnick and Andrew Nickolds, Producers Cecil Korer and Derek Clark
An HTV production. 10.00-11.00pm Monday 12 January 1987, in colour on Channel 4

All Change
Series 1

Although to all intents and purposes this was a children's comedy drama, it remains the very last scripted situation comedy series Frankie appeared in. Very much a token star name to hook the narrative on, Frankie headlined as the rich and gloriously unpredictable Uncle Bob. (Yorkshire TV's publicity described him as 'filthy rich eccentric millionaire biscuit baron and barmy birdwatcher Uncle Bob.') Apparently dead and buried, and communicating with his dreadfully rude and greedy relations via television screens, videotape and sheer good luck, the basic story found little room for the great man. Instead, he contented himself with brief appearances, chucking in treasured one-liners, looking with disgruntled amazement into camera and generally resurrecting every code and convention from his 30-odd years' experience in television. The story revolved

Frankie as a barmy birdwatcher in his final situation comedy *All Change*, broadcast in November 1989.

around the frightfully posh London family and the gritty working-class Oldfield family, swopping lifestyles in order to secure the massive million pound legacy of the 'late' Frankie. Wonderfully buoyant stuff for the younger generation of all ages!

Uncle Bob FRANKIE HOWERD, Henry Herewith ROGER MILNER, Fabia London MAGGIE STEED, Julian London WILLIAM McGILLIVRAY, Charles London DAVID QUILTER, Polly London LISA BUTLER, Brian Oldfield TONY HAYGARTH, Maggie Oldfield PAM FERRIS, Vicky Oldfield DONNA DURKIN, Nathan Oldfield ROBERT ELLIS, Hornbeam ANDREW NORMINGTON Written by John Stevenson (6 episodes), Tony McHale (3 episodes), Morwenna Banks and Chris England (1 episode), Chris England (1 episode), Chris England and Paul Simpkin (1 episode), Producers Peter Tabern and Greg Brenman, Director Graham Dixon

A Childsplay Production for Yorkshire Television. Six episodes: 4.40-5.10 pm Wednesdays 15 November-20 December 1989, in colour on ITV

★★★★★★

Frankie's other appearances in the late 1980s included a charity bash at the invitation of Lenny Henry and Griff Rhys Jones. Bob Geldof and *Live Aid* having provided the music industry's answer to Third World famine, the comedy fraternity – with Lenny and Griff – presented a recurring fund-raising telethon which became the mammoth *Comic Relief* movement. Practically every comic in the country, from Ben Elton to the Goodies, was roped into the charity rabble-rousing and Frankie Howerd was no exception. Lumbered with an early spot but gleefully giving his all, Frankie took part in a mock-newsreading item with master of the craft, Michael Buerk. The show took place on Friday 5 February 1988 on BBC1.

Also in 1988, Frankie turned up at a televised Variety Club lunch, as well as endorsing the moderately successful board game, Orgy. On 27 July 1989, some of his ITV back-catalogue resurfaced in the archive special *The Birthday Show: 21 Years of Variety from Thames Television*, while in November he announced the winner of the Best Situation Comedy category at the Jonathan Ross-hosted British Comedy Awards. The winner? The historical masterpiece, *Blackadder Goes Forth*.

1990 was the real year of the Frankie renaissance. He was the darling of the student generation, Oxford was about to embrace him to its cultural bosom, the BBC were finally releasing a couple of *Up Pompeii!* videos, the other side were seriously considering resurrecting the series and his one-man show was about to launch him into, arguably, his most critically acclaimed period of live performance. As a result, he was a frequent and welcome guest on just about every television chat show worth its salt, and a few that weren't.

Clive Anderson, irreverent host of Channel 4's *Clive Anderson Talks Back*, had been part of that merry band who had been taken under Frankie's comic wing, scripting material for him alongside other 'urchins' like Jimmy Mulville and Rory McGrath. Entering the Anderson chat forum with a healthy 'Shut yer face!', Frankie is on sparkling form throughout, commenting on Anderson's 'clammy' hands and hastily explaining the pulled faces and clowning-with-vocals technique that had shaped his comic art for some 45 years. Frankie's contribution is almost entirely taken up with an impromptu reading of a new Clive Anderson monologue, crammed with loads of oohs, ahhs and no missus moments; Frankie tongue-in-cheekily comments, 'It must have taken you hours to write this!' Clive's other guests were Jonathan King, Chris Langham, Ann Webb and Steve Punt as the bell boy; a Hat Trick production,

the show aired on Channel 4 in March 1990.

In the absence of Michael Parkinson, Terry Wogan had provided the best line in mainstream chat for much of the 1980s and early 1990s. As always, Frankie Howerd proved the perfect guest and during his 1990 plug-a-thon, Tel welcomed the comic great with open arms. Frankie was happy to chat about his early army days, 'Three Little Fishes' and the poverty-row budget of *The Runaway Bus*. During one of Terry's holiday breaks, that legendary all-rounder Bruce Forsyth stepped into the chair and insisted on booking Frankie as his first guest. A regular cohort on television, Frankie bounced into the old routine immediately and the result was one of the most relaxed interviews he ever gave. The classic climax, a duet of 'Spread A Little Happiness', was an endearing success, comically enhanced by Frankie's sincerity in praising the 'lovely voice' of his co-star and then, without missing a beat, looking straight into camera and muttering 'Shocking, wasn't it?'

Doing the chat show rounds, Frankie cropped up twice in April 1991. ITV's *Aspel & Co* provided a classic interrogation with Frankie happily plugging his *Blue Suede Shoes* contribution to *The Spoken Word of Rock 'n' Roll* and the impending ('escaping next week') appearance of the *Up Pompeii!* videos. Hopes of making 'some new ones' were revealed, as was his volunteering for Gulf War troop shows (yet to be met with a response) and memories of performing similar shows with Julie Ege. Michael Aspel enquires about the dodgy legs of the great Howerd, the stunning legs of fellow guest Natasha Richardson catch Frankie's eye ('You're just young enough to be my wife, you know!') and the now-legendary interaction with David Attenborough creates television magic.

The finest Frankie Howerd interview in the world, however, was broadcast on Channel 4 on Good Friday. That ultimate follower of the Frankie cult, Jonathan Ross, introduced his one-and-only guest for the evening with an enthralled and excited build-up. As 'Sir Francis of Howerd' wandered onto the stage it was almost as if the comic saviour had arrived.

Frankie was special guest on *Tonight With Jonathan Ross*, recorded on 29 March 1991 and broadcast on Good Friday.

There is a debate as to whether any more Carry On films will be made (and would Frankie be involved if there were?), a salute to the importance of scriptwriters, a chance to ponder on the legion of Frankie impersonators (of which Jonathan confesses himself a member) and even an opportunity to create an impromptu and endearing new catchphrase: 'little puppy!' Frankie's cheerful and charming 'I'm everybody's little puppy!' walks the fine line between corn and magic that only he could manage. A televisual chat treat, with more of the same being dished out on 23 October when Frankie guested on ITV's *Des O'Connor Tonight*.

★★★★★★

Arena: Oooh Er, Missus!
The Frankie Howerd Story or Please Yourselves

At the peak of the Frankie Howerd renaissance that bastion of cultural analysis, *Arena*, put the legendary comedian under the spotlight in a documentary sporting no fewer than three titles. At its centre is a surprisingly candid and almost totally humourless interview with Frankie himself, continually putting himself down and pondering on his mysterious success with the youth audience. With the shield of laughter removed and the emphasis very much on what makes the great man tick this is at times an awkward experience but a rewarding one nevertheless.

The most poignant moments top and tail the

documentary with a lonely and isolated Frankie, clad in heavy overcoat, scarf and hat, strolling through the countryside rehearsing his stage material. He is seen in a field full of cows, sitting on a fast-being-consumed bale of hay. Later he stands in a picturesque country church dishing out his finely tuned live performance and he cuts a quiet, introspective figure as he stares forlornly into nothingness on a beach. The use of Frankie's own recorded past accompanies these intimate, thought-provoking moments – from his classic recording of 'Nymphs and Shepherds' with Margaret Rutherford to the 'voices' interlude from *Up the Chastity Belt*.

Frankie also recorded a linking narration which, rather more jokily than the interview footage, tells the story of his birth in York, his family, the move to Eltham and his early acting ambitions. There's fascinating footage of Frankie's return to the Bob Hope Theatre, formerly the Eltham Parish Hall where his ambition first bore fruit during local talent contests. He is shown being chauffeur-driven from his London home to the Garrick Theatre in the West End for his sell-out season of *Quite Frankly Frankie Howerd*, there are copious extracts from the show itself and several embarrassing Frankie impersonations from his young crop of admirers. Most powerful of all, an ultra-nervous and softly spoken Frankie is followed through the backstage area, up the steps, into the darkness and onto the stage to a rousing response. It's a spine-tingling piece of television and, perhaps more than anything else, fully captures the stomach-churning experience of facing an audience on your own.

Earlier in the programme Frankie mocks his biggest filmic flop, *The Cool Mikado,* and tries to re-enact the Bette Davis/Paul Henreid cigarette-lighting moment from *Now Voyager* with June Whitfield. The actual history of his career is rather uneven and rushed between all these personal and potent riches. Much is made of his early days and early success on *Variety Bandbox*, while rather too much time is spent on his downward spiral and the depressing downers of his career. Suitably there is a huge chunk of *That Was The Week*

That Was, his major career turnaround, but the last ten minutes gallops through the many highpoints of his career.

As such, masterpieces like *Up Pompeii!, Carry On Doctor, A Funny Thing Happened on the Way to the Forum* and *The Ladykillers* are barely mentioned. Indeed, Frankie isn't even featured in the clip chosen from the Ealing film which rather defeats its purpose. But as a brief and informative trip through the majestic highs and lows of an unforgettable comic career this is very hard to beat. The interview footage is bristling with emotion, the *Comic Roots*-style return to important places in Frankie's life is priceless and the sheer, bewildered delight in his twilight years reappraisal brings a real lump to the throat. A masterpiece.

....

Did You Know? The complete and unabridged Frankie Howerd interview recorded for this documentary was broadcast as *Frankly Frankie* on UK Arena in 1999. This invaluable material included everything, from impatient comments and reel changes to moments of enjoyably languid dismissal.

....

FRANKIE HOWERD with Max Bygraves, Vera Roper, Johnny Speight, Eric Sykes, June Whitfield and Michael Winner
Film cameramen Chris Seager, Colin Case, Richard Adam, Mike Dauncey and Andrew Spellar, VT Editor Chris Kane, Film Editor Colin Knijff, Series Editors Anthony Wall and Nigel Finch, Director Helen Gallacher. 9.30-10.30 pm Friday 1 June 1990, in colour on BBC1

Frankie Howerd on Campus
'I'm not what you'd call an intellectual ... oh no!' **Frankie Howerd**

The crowning glory of Frankie's new-found cult status with the nineties student generation, this classic live recording was the result of a request from Melanie Johnson, 'bossy boots' president of the Oxford Student Union, for Frankie Howerd to address the university. In many ways it's a touching tribute to some of the finest comedy writers ever to work for Frankie. The material is a refreshing round-up of some of his funniest routines of the previous 30 years and the audience are like putty in his hands. The style is as reassuringly familiar and shambolic as ever, but every ooh, ahh and shut yer face is beautifully delivered for maximum clout. The basic stand-up monologue format is firmly in place. He embraces the new breed of alternative comedian (fearing that some people are expecting Ben Elton) and happily plays down his expectations of the venue (thinking the Oxford Union was a pub!).

Typically, Frankie gets everyone's attention by revealing the subject of tonight's lecture as perversions, but the ensuing comedy is anything but perverted as the grand old master milks his audience with every trick in the book. Tellingly, the mask of comedy is dropped on occasions. The hilarious tales of bed-wetting and childhood may be tailor-made for Frankie's self-deprecation but there's a sense of darkness behind them. More importantly, Frankie literally lectures the young audience, advises them to 'be happy while you can', celebrates them as 'the future' and jokes that they shouldn't 'end up like me ... don't end up a shambles like me!' – one of the most poignant moments of Frankie's career.

However, for a cracking close, Frankie reflects on his lost career in the church and delivers a closing sermon vignette in the person of a face-pulling, vocally eccentric country vicar of Much-Rutting-in-the-Wold. With outrageous lip-pursing, eyeglass-adjusting and dismayed comments ('Obscene letters have been thrust through my letter box ... indeed, other things!'), this is a stunningly well-observed comic creation from writers Ray Galton & Alan Simpson. The infamous bare bum exit is a legendary close to a legendary live performance. With a cheery 'Up the Students!' farewell, Frankie leaves to roaring applause. 'Well, please yourselves!'
Written by Barry Cryer, Dennis Berson, Steve Knight, Spike Mullins, Mike Whitehill, Peter Vincent and Ray Galton & Alan Simpson, Script associate Ian Davidson, Title music David Mitcham, Senior Cameraman Lisle Middleditch,

Stage Manager David Matthews, Production Manager Peter Hall, Designer Robert Day, Director Ian Hamilton, Producer Paul Lewis A London Weekend Television production. 10.10-11.10 pm, Saturday 24 November 1990, in colour on ITV

All Change
Series 2

A final burst of Frankie's brilliant children's situation comedy, this series explains that last time Frankie was only *pretending* to be dead. The series again revolves around bizarre tasks, family feuds and the ever-greedy pursuit of financial gain. Peggy Mount was recruited as Frankie's bombastic sister while the rest of the cast – with the exception of Bobby Knutt replacing Tony Haygarth – remained the same. Once again Frankie was restricted to very minor appearances and every opportunity to reprise familiar catchphrases was grabbed wholeheartedly. Thus, with an older, more experienced Frankie in the autumn of his telly days, his young audience could savour every 'Not on your Nellie!', 'How dare you? How very, very dare you?' and 'Oh, please yourselves!' The basic plot concerns the chase for a million quid stuffed in a china pig and the frantic attempt to capture Uncle Bob and stick him in the Home For Distressed Gentlefolk. But the chief joy is Frankie's delicious facial reactions to camera, off-the-wall video diaries and the supremely surreal vision of this national treasure being driven around in the back of a lorry.
Uncle Bob FRANKIE HOWERD, Aunt Fanny PEGGY MOUNT, Henry Herewith ROGER MILNER, Fabia London MAGGIE STEED, Julian London WILLIAM McGILLIVRAY, Charles London DAVID QUILTER, Polly London LISA BUTLER, Brian Oldfield BOBBY KNUTT, Maggie Oldfield PAM FERRIS, Vicky Oldfield DONNA DURKIN, Nathan Oldfield ROBERT ELLIS, Hornbeam ANDREW NORMINGTON, Driver PAUL BARBER
Production Manager Barney Reisz, Art Director Sonja Klaus, Costumes Alan Lightfoot, Make-up Claire Faithfull, Camera Paul Barton, Sound John H Marchbank, Music Colin Gibson and

Kenny Craddock, Production Designer Lizzy Ashard, Editor Chris Wright, Executive Producers Chris Jelley and Peter Tabern, Producer Greg Brenman, Director Garth Tucker A Childsplay Production for Yorkshire Television. Six episodes: mostly 4.30-5.00 pm Tuesdays 5 February-12 March 1991, in colour on ITV

Sinful!

Liverpudlian beat combo, The Farm, had already chalked up a number of hit singles when their 1990 album *Spartacus* produced a single release for the song, *Sinful!* The group were Frankie fans and aware that the master was preparing to re-launch himself as Lurcio, the *Up Pompeii!* slave. Thus, Frankie was invited to do a bit of Roman face-pulling for the song's promotional video. His last appearance on 'film', this was very much made for the MTV generation and played on Britain's Saturday morning pop-filled kids' shows during April 1991.

The Craig Ferguson Story

A unique and fascinating attempt on Ferguson's part to combine a standard live recording of his stand-up act at the Glasgow Pavilion with situation comedy interludes featuring the cream of classic British comedy. Frankie's brief but memorable appearances cast the ultra-hip veteran as the God of Comedy. Ferguson occasionally trips off into dreamy dream sequences to consult Frankie regarding all manner of comic ideas. A delightfully effete and ineffectual heavenly body, Frankie dishes out useless advice and irrelevant observations and proves an unhelpful albeit heartwarmingly welcome addition to the show.
CRAIG FERGUSON, with Fergus Ferguson PETER COOK, Mrs Ferguson JUNE WHITFIELD, God of Comedy FRANKIE HOWERD, Stage doorman GERALD HARPER, Beezie JESS ANGUS, Agnes NAN FORSYTHE
Written by Craig Ferguson, Jane Prowse, Paul Whitehouse and Charlie Higson, Additional material by Jon Canter, Executive Producer Charles Brand, Producer Sarah Williams, Director Jane Prowse

A Tiger Television production. 11.50-12.50 pm Thursday 12 September 1991, in colour on Channel 4

Further Up Pompeii

Although this wasn't presenting Frankie in a toga 'for the first time in 20 years', as the publicity blurb would have had us believe, and the title, too, was rather unoriginal – the BBC had quashed both claims with their 1975 effort *Further Up Pompeii!* – this was, indeed, a contemporary attempt to revive the old Lurcio character in the light of Frankie's popularity with the university generation. For us, Frankie was born to wander through ancient Rome and the bosses at LWT were eager to capitalise on this. The theme music may have gone – it seems to have been cheaper to adapt genuine classical music rather than the familiar jaunty tune of old – and the outstandingly polished scenery almost distracts from the glorious corniness of the script, but everything else in the garden is as rosy as ever.

Frankie admirers are split on the success of this final foray into Lurcio territory. Clearly, at 74 years of age and carrying a bit of weight, Frankie had to adopt a longer, leg-covering garment. But the sparkle in the eye, the delivery of the corny lines and the sharpened skill at putting down his fellow actors is as potent as ever. The opening monologue is one for the classic compilation video, with a disgruntled Frankie complaining about a damned goat 'nibbling at my courgettes' before turning to the expectant audience and launching into the public address-cum-prologue as if he'd never been away. Frankie collaborates in the corporate dismissal of the BBC's mid-1970s effort with comments like 'Long time no see ... XX years at least!', but he's as mock-vain as ever ('They tell me I haven't changed a bit!') and immediately sets the show in the context of a mere television programme by interjecting the best line of the piece: 'It is not now BC, it is not now BBC!'

For those concerned with the almost non-existent plot, Frankie is now a 'mature' chap with a trio of his own slaves. He's still in trouble, of course, for the villains of the piece

Frankie went
*Further Up
Pompeii* for the
last time in
London
Weekend
Television's
1991 revival.

and, best of all, the stunning and ideally pitched naïve and busty beauty of Elizabeth Anson. ('She's young and innocent … just like me!') The hard-nosed figure of police authority (Ben Aris), the double-dealing, double-crossing crook (John Bardon) and the flamboyantly caddish youngster (Russell Gold) add to the background delights, and there's even a suitably pox-ridden and atmosphere-fogging beggar from the wizened Roy Evans.

As for the script, new writers Paul Minett and Brian Leveson, paying tribute to Rothwell and Colin, throw in every *Pompeii* trick in the book. The character names are rich in obvious hilarity (the plague-ridden Typhus; the high-pitched Ambiguus; Umbilicus: 'that name strikes a cord!') and the deliciously old-fashioned, politically incorrect innuendo flows like fine wine. Unbeatable elements from old scripts are shamelessly resurrected ('Hey there, orgy girl' for example) and poor acting is condemned as of old. As Roy Evans wanders off with a cheery 'See ya later!', Frankie can't help but mutter, 'Not in this show he won't!' A frantic and dramatic speech, delivered with real incoherent rage by Frankie, comically culminates with 'If that doesn't get a BAFTA nothing will!'

The show's finest encounter is pure Rothwell-for-the-Nineties. Barry James, going wonderfully over the top as the limping, stuttering Claudius ('We've only got 15 minutes!'), is perfectly suited to the near-the-knuckle nature of the piece. Frankie is obviously delighted with their scene ('What a shocking actor!') and milks the dubious innuendos for all they're worth. Absolutely classic stuff. Resurrecting Frankie's most celebrated comic creation just in the nick of time, *Further Up Pompeii* is the perfect example of how to retread an old hit. There could be no better exit for a sitcom favourite.

....

Did You Know? Although some critics consider that Frankie is slow and cumbersome in performance, there is an occasional need for real audience reaction to the script. It was at Frankie's insistence that no studio audience be allowed into the recording. It was only after

have discovered that the will of his late master, Ludricus, was forged, and the clause allowing Frankie his freedom was a falsity written by Frankie himself. Naturally, as a result, Frankie becomes the general dogsbody and put-upon whipping boy of the family, toiling in the fashionable Bacchus Wine Bar, getting involved in the fixed gladiatorial games and generally trying to avoid being caught for breaking the law by the local bobbie. There's gambling, corruption, dodgy wine, stolen money, lost virtue and fruity comments throughout.

The supporting cast, in the main, are perfectly suited to the overblown style of the piece and all the clichéd comic types of the original programmes are gleefully resurrected. There's Frankie's three slaves – the grotesque battleaxe (Joanna Dickens), the plump, plumless and effeminate eunuch (Peter Geeves) several technicians, laughing during rehearsals, had heightened Frankie's comic touch that he quickly changed his mind. Sadly, by that stage it was too late and the show was recorded at the London Studios without an audience; a laugh-track was added later to give the impression of the old raucous days at Shepherd's Bush. No series was commissioned. It was always intended as a one-off and, as it turned out, no series could have resulted in any case. Frankie died less than six months after the show's transmission.

....

Lurcio FRANKIE HOWERD, Colossa JOANNA DICKENS, Petunia ELIZABETH ANSON, Villainus Brutus JOHN BARDON, Noxius RUSSELL GOLD, Ambiguus PETER GEEVES, Typhus ROY EVANS, Gluteus Maximus TIM KILLICK, Umbilicus GARY RICE, Claudius BARRY JAMES, with BEN ARIS
Written by Paul Minett and Brian Leveson, Created by Talbot Rothwell et Sid Colin [sic], Senior Cameraman Alan Fawcus, VT Editor Graham Sisson, Costumes Sue Formston, Make-up Louise Furness, Production Manager Peter Hall, Lighting Director Colin Innes-Hopkins, Designers John Demetri and Mike Oxley, Executive Producer Robin Carr, Producer Paul Lewis, Director Ian Hamilton
A London Weekend Television production. 7.55-8.40 pm Saturday 14 December 1991, in colour on ITV

90s Commercials

Frankie's final commercial, directed by Frankie fan Mel Smith and aiming to sell Panama Cigars, became a classic of the form. Packed with the nation's favourite funny men – from Peter Cook to Ronnie Corbett – it famously ended with Bruce Forsyth accepting and relishing the cigar after everybody else has turned it down. The tag-line ('Comedians hate them') resulted in Bruce's legendary 'I'm an all-round entertainer!' plea, which caught on big time. Frankie, caught off guard in the street, is simply part of the negative comic narrative, looking deep into camera and moaning, 'Oh no, missus, no!' Mel Smith subsequently agreed to make a series of

adverts for Boddington's Bitter, all starring Frankie. Wearing a Bitter Ye Not T-shirt, Frankie went through various pub-based vignettes muttering 'It's bitter out' and enjoying the bitter in. Sadly this mini-collection was never screened owing to Frankie's death. A one-off Frankie appearance to promote R White's Lemonade, with our hero creeping downstairs in his pyjamas to grab a crafty mouthful, failed to hit the screens for the same reason.

Frankie's On...

The last stand and final hurrah, this was Frankie's return to his roots – variety performance – in the wake of his new-found status as everybody's favourite funny OAP. Akin to the motormouth Ben Elton series for BBC, *The Man From Auntie*, *Frankie's On...* delivered his well-honed live act in tasty chunks for the home audience. Despite brilliantly structured routines from the writing duo behind the latest *Pompeii* escapade, plus young, up-and-coming scriptwriter Mark Bussell, Frankie was happy to rely on familiar old favourites. Indeed, he even told the classic, well-worn gag about the unfortunate old woman who couldn't part her legs, visits the doctor and is told that she has two legs down one knicker. Now that particular Frankie gem dated back to the *Variety Bandbox* days of 1947 but the 1992 audience howled with laughter as if it was freshly minted.

Basically the format was well-timed, polished and totally scripted. Frankie would introduce himself to an audience of professionals (varying each week), a few unsubtle cracks would be aimed at the television bosses and/or television audiences at home, while the chief aim for the comic barbs was authority in all its ghastly shapes and sizes. After a peerlessly delivered monologue concerning the head of whichever establishment he was in, Frankie would eagerly promote audience participation as the name of the game. This would prompt scripted and often unscripted questions from the floor which Frankie would use as a springboard for his latest comic observation or acidic put-down. Finally, hands would be shaken, the audience would break into applause and Frankie would leave his fans with the treasured victory salute and a suitably tailored 'Up the miners!' or 'Up the Navy!' farewell.

Complete with a jolly animated title sequence, these shows are totally priceless records of Frankie's final professional engagements. Only four of the six planned programmes were filmed. Frankie's final trip to hospital interrupted recording and the last two programmes, although scripted and scheduled, were never performed. The completed shows were broadcast some two months after Frankie's death as a tribute to a beloved comic performer. To be honest, in them Frankie cuts an unlikely and ungainly figure. His suit is even more dreadful and ill-fitting than usual. And he is carrying an awful lot of weight. However, there is an energy and fire in the comic belly which is quite amazing in the circumstances. He is as playful and mentally agile as ever he was. Quite simply, these shows are the final legacy of a national institution.

....

Did You Know? In 1971, Frankie scriptwriter, biographer and close friend, Barry Took, suggested resurrecting the *East of Howerd* format for London Weekend Television. The idea was to film Frankie entertaining audiences in such locations as Gibraltar, Cyprus, Hong Kong, Malta, Gan (in the Indian Ocean) and a base in Germany. The *Frankie's On...* series, some 20 years later, was the nearest ITV got to the notion.

....

Written by Mark Bussell, Paul Minett and Brian Leveson, plus Ian Davidson (Board), Steve Knight and Mike Whitehall (Board and Call), Dennis Berson (Coals and Call), Marc Blake (Coals), Hugh Stuckey (Call)
Theme music Jonathan Cohen, Designer Dave Allen, Associate Producer Mark Bussell, Executive Producer Paula Burdon, Producer Trevor McCallum, Director Dennis Liddington
A Central Television production. 10.00-10.30 pm, Sundays 21 June-12 July 1992, in colour on ITV

Frankie's On... Board!

Frankie doing his stuff from the Ark Royal aircraft carrier at Gibraltar, this first edition kicks off with the expected play-acting telephone conversation with the boss man employer ('Are you Haaard?'), some telling telly send-up ('Have we started? What camera are we on?') and some biting political satire ('Slash half the Navy and sell them the idea it's an achievement!'). The naval main man is condemned as a 'cheeky bugger', there's yet another on-the-spot catchphrase ('pixie face!') and the audience put-downs are extremely choice ('We don't want a mini-series!') in this brilliant and timeless performance. It's as if the decades fall away and we're back in *East of Howerd* terrain.

Frankie's On... the Coals!

Entertaining a group of Nottinghamshire miners at the Cotgrave Miners' Welfare, Frankie reveals details of his new job with the Chippendales... in an advisory capacity. There's chat about honeymoon couples and some risqué banter about 'Blow on me! Give me a blow!' – thanks to the very hot television lights, of course. The authority-baiting is aimed at the chairman of British Coal, the 'very badly managed industry' comment hits the satire button and a tasty, innuendo-tinged instruction to 'Get back to your shaft!' hits all the right comic ones.

Frankie's On... Fire!

Some blazing gags for Gloucestershire firemen with a performance at the Fire Service College, Moreton in Marsh. Frankie's wit and wisdom spirals through silly jokes, audience commentary and knowing looks. Most enjoyable of all is the fireman's pole, resplendent on the stage, designed for Frankie to slide down – 'That pole is for your entrance! I beg your pardon?' Some cheeky audience comments about age, longevity, retirement and even suicide add an extra dimension to the laughter. Frankie sidesteps the mock insults, insisting on considering the future when 'I get to 55!' and seriously dismissing the notion of being

a hero with a reflection on the greats of his trade – Max Miller, Tommy Cooper, Eric and Ernie. Perhaps the most touching instalment of the series, Frankie seems genuinely moved to be performing for a roomful of real heroes and his comic style shines all the brighter for it.

Frankie's On... Call!

Frankie's very last television assignment took him to the Nottingham Queen's Medical Centre. A list of Frankie's professional career in corny medical comedy (*Carry On Matron*, *Carry On Nurse*, the so-called 'Carry On Bed Pans', none of which the great man was actually involved in) sets things up for the final montage of Frankie getting up to medical antics with a nurse and a stethoscope, a doctor's white coat and a bony skeleton. One young lady, asked where she comes from and answering Malaya, clearly tickles Frankie and

prompts his classic 'Marvellous bus service…' remark. Suggestions from the floor that he have a face-lift or a sex change, a resurrection of the 'Take the dress off, take the panties off … and never wear them again!' chestnut and an uncomfortably accurate 'I think you're overweight!' observation from a straightfaced medical man, make this totally awesome television.

Frankie's health was clearly not of the best, but his response to the 'overweight' observation is therapeutic rather than uncomfortable. Tongue firmly planted in cheek and pleading 'I try and keep in shape', Frankie launches into his very last joke – the whistling bottom which makes a noise every time he walks. Dismissing his final stage appearance as 'Some silly arse whistling!', Frankie salutes his final audience, shouts 'Up the National Health Service!' and happily takes the applause for the last time. ●

The final gig: Frankie with nurses Sue Burns and Fiona Stratton at the Queen's Medical Centre in Nottingham for the posthumously broadcast *Frankie's On... Call*.

Titter no more

FAREWELL TO **FRANKIE**

'I want to live forever … for years and years and donkey's years. Why? Because I want to find out who did it in the end…' **Frankie Howerd**

Frankie Howerd was a workaholic who never seemed to find the true happiness that he all too effortlessly spread among his fellow men. He was the ultimate mournful droll – a funny man who was constantly shocked by what his audience read into his harmless mutterings.

A rollercoaster of a career had been on the rise from the late 1980s with a seemingly endless line of public appearances only coming to a halt for an ill-fated trip to South America in late 1991. Upon his return, Frankie succumbed to an illness that plagued him for the remainder of his life. In and out of care throughout the early part of 1992, by April he was fighting for his life in a Harley Street clinic. It seemed the entire nation was waiting for news with bated breath and Frankie, ever the trooper, kept spirits high with his final public appearance. Emerging with a beautiful nurse on his arm and clutching a chocolate Easter bunny, Frankie looked frail but cheerful as he was photographed by the press. In effect, he then went home to die.

On Good Friday he dined with his sister Betty at his favourite restaurant, Al Gallo d'Oro. Though desperately wishing to end his days at his Somerset retreat, he was too poorly to make the journey and passed away at his Kensington home on Easter Sunday, 19 April 1992. With him were Betty and his manager Dennis Heymer, a loyal friend for over 30 years. Frankie was 75 years old but all the papers fell for his final joke and printed his 'professional' age of 70. One can imagine the glee on those gloriously crumpled features and the improbably bushy eyebrows shooting skywards in mock indignation.

Before the illness took its final turn for the worse, Frankie was cheerfully making plans for the future and enjoying the applause from fans old and young. Ever keen to carry on working, Frankie had already mapped out a very busy 1992 with at least one lip-smacking diversion from his usual performance area and at least one welcome return to a filmic genre upon which he had left an indelible mark over 20 years earlier. One of his burning ambitions, which looked likely to be fulfilled in 1992, was to star in his own crime detective series. Obsessed with the crime genre all his life, he would buy every book he could get hold of. Indeed, it was a form of prose which prompted the poignant quote at the top of this chapter.

Frankie's desire was not so laughable as one may think. He wasn't the greatest actor in the world but he had a bewitching screen presence which would have slipped into a big-budget

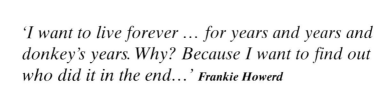

Don't blame me, I didn't write the stuff! Frankie rehearses his contribution to the Royal Command Performance, 14 November 1966.

'eccentric crimebuster' format with ease. A great admirer of *Inspector Morse* and, in particular, the 'Sins of the Fathers' episode which featured his old pal Lionel Jeffries, Frankie made a move to contact the writer. Jeremy Burnham, whose only Morse credit this was, was commissioned to write a treatment which would cast Frankie as a bumbling country vicar with a penchant for cracking fiendishly tricky crimes. The result was a sort of *Father Brown* with music hall overtones, casting the comedian as the charming Father Jocelyn Oscar Spottiswood. Nicknamed Holy JO, this character would live with his dominating sister-cum-housekeeper to add bucketloads of semi-domestic sitcom to the show, while murderous plots would be thrown at the character for brain-teasing deduction. Although a script was completed and Frankie was delighted with the project, even having tramped through Somerset with the writer and Dennis Heymer on the look-out for the right church location, Frankie died before the dialogue was completely Howerded up to his specifications.

More immediately, Frankie was all set to create the brief but potent role of the King of Spain in the 31st Peter Rogers and Gerald Thomas Carry On film, *Carry On Columbus*. The cast may have been awash with new faces, thanks in the main to producer John Goldstone, but Frankie was one of the hottest talents in the country and a veteran of the original series. A double that only the *Ab Fab* June Whitfield could match at the time. Frankie was very keen to get back into the series. He had even been halfheartedly discussing 'Carry On Pompeii' with Barbara Windsor and Joan Sims for television.

Shooting started on *Carry On Columbus* just two days after Frankie's death, although his role had already been recast because of his ill health. The silky charm of Leslie Phillips replaced the lugubrious dismay of Frankie Howerd. Screenwriter Dave Freeman, who had scripted *Carry On Behind*, several television Carry Ons and many *Bless This House* episodes for Sid James, suggests, however, that Frankie had had his eye on a different role.

'Frank wanted to play the opening scene of *Carry On Columbus* but was too ill. Rik Mayall played his scenes.'

Whichever was the case, leading cast member, Jim Dale, was devastated by the news. 'The Dave Freeman script had been sent to my home in America but I had been talking to Gerry Thomas on the phone at regular intervals. He had told me that Frankie had been confirmed as the King and, as I had a number of scenes with the character, I had already started rehearsing them with him in my mind's eye. You could easily imagine that wonderful face and sluggish comic style of his. It would have made my job of trying to be funny very easy indeed! It was only when I arrived in England to start filming that Gerry told me Frankie couldn't be in the film. I was very upset because I had been looking forward to working with him – having not really done a lot with him in *Carry On Doctor*. I was absolutely shattered when I heard he had died. He was a great loss to our cast and the country in general.'

Fellow Carry On cast member and longtime friend of Frankie, Joan Sims, remembers him with fondness. 'He personified my very favourite type of comedian. There wasn't an ounce of malice or nastiness in Frank's delivery. Like Norman Wisdom and Sid Field he came out wanting to be loved and caught the admiration and affection of his audience immediately.' Alan Simpson, who, for over 20 years, wrote frequently for the comedian, believes 'He was unlike anybody else. He really was unique. There is simply nobody like him. Frankie Howerd was a true one-off.'

Frankie was buried at St Gregory's, Weare in Somerset. Overseen by the Reverend George Williams, it was a quiet funeral with just a handful of friends from show business in attendance, including Cilla Black and June Whitfield. Both were mentioned in Frankie's will, being invited to take one personal item from his home as a keepsake. The memorial service was an altogether more star-studded affair. Held at St Martin's in the Fields on Wednesday 8 July 1992, the music and songs were selected from Frankie's personal favourites – from 'Autumn Leaves' to 'Send in the Clowns' – while the Reverend Martin Henwood injected just the right amount of celebration into the thoughtfulness of the occasion.

Cilla Black remembered the many invitations to Sunday lunch that Frankie would launch into, while pianist Vanessa Latarche played Chopin's Third Ballade in A Flat. Barry Cryer recited a wickedly inspired poem while June Whitfield and Griff Rhys Jones recalled working with Frankie with rare charm and humour. Perhaps the most poignant moment of all was Russ Conway's piano medley of numbers close to Frankie's heart – 'Comedy Tonight', 'Three Little Fishes' and 'When You're Smiling'. Accompanied by the Graveney School Choir, an embarrassed and uncertain smattering of applause trickled through the silence – applause which was heartily encouraged by Bruce Forsyth, stepping up to speak and proclaiming that you should clap at a memorial service. It was a moment to bring a tear to the coldest eye.

The first anniversary of Frankie's death was marked by an open-air comedy festival in his home town of York. On 18 October 1992, the Dead Comics' Society erected a commemorative plaque on Frankie's London home at 27 Edwardes Square, Kensington with friends and fans such as Jonathan Ross, Cilla Black, June Whitfield and Max Bygraves in attendance. 1993 saw Frankie's close friend and frequent writer, Barry Took, round up an impressive array of Howerd pen-pushers for a video repackaging of the legendary 1991 Birmingham Hippodrome performance under the title *Titter Ye Not!* Pinching the idea from the 1984 Woody Allen film, *Broadway Danny Rose*, Took gathered Barry Cryer, Johnny Speight, Peter Cook, Alan Simpson and Ian Hislop to contribute alcohol-fuelled memories of the great man interspersed with previously unavailable and unreleased footage from the concert. It remains the ultimate Frankie Howerd video and an essential addition to any self-respecting comedy fan's video library.

The following year, 1994, saw a collection of 40 years' worth of Frankie's scripts sold at

With Anna Neagle at the Variety Club's 15th Annual Awards ceremony, held at the Savoy on 14 March 1967.

Bonham's to a private collector. The same bidder also paid an additional £391 for Frankie's collection of letters, autographs, programmes and photographs. (If only I hadn't been struggling on a student grant at the time!) Having been well and truly inducted into the Comedy Hall of Fame, Frankie's image and legacy was included in Terry Johnson's dramatic investigation of fan obsession, *Dead Funny*. More interestingly, Frankie became a mainstay of the documentary makers who plundered the life and times of every clown worth his salt. Indeed, Frankie Howerd OBE was the very first subject of John Fisher's excellent *Heroes of Comedy* series. The Howerd effort, using extensive interview footage from the 1990 *Omnibus* show as well as extracts from the 1991 Birmingham concert, *Up Pompeii, Up the Chastity Belt* and *The Ladykillers*, wallowed in heartfelt superlatives from an

impressive line-up of interviewees. Clive
Anderson, Barry Cryer, Craig Ferguson, Eric
Sykes and Ned Sherrin all made interesting
contributions but it was Cilla Black,
desperately wishing that Frankie could have
got a knighthood if only to 'make him happy',
who stole the honours. Directed by Iain
McLean for broadcast on Channel 4, the show

first aired on New Year's Day 1995.

There was still a real sense of lost
opportunities and lost titters in the mid-1990s.
There was a gaping hole in British comedy
akin to when Eric Morecambe and Tommy
Cooper died. The programme-planners were
keen to plug the gap with archive footage and,
on 17 December 1996, ITV gave over an entire

evening to the master innuendo-monger. This featured the television début of Frankie's recorded 1991 concert from the Birmingham Hippodrome, as well as a screening of the feature film version of *Up Pompeii* and Howerd's intellectual highpoint, *Frankie On Campus*.

It was a celebration of a legendary career but not the opening of the floodgates. Every impersonator in the country still managed to toss in a quick Frankie when the laugh quota was low and the most skilled of them all, Rory Bremner, resurrected Frankie's elongated growl as the highlight of his inspired 'Jurassic Park for Comedians' routine. Even music channel the Box ran a saucy trailer with the strained Howerd-style rant of: 'Now for music with a touch of ooh … turn on the box. Yeeesss!'

But Frankie's reputation was not as solid or fêted as those other immortals of Britcom, Hancock, Hill or Cook. And what scant attention he received in the late 1990s was neither warranted nor wanted. For Channel 4's lacklustre Carry On Weekend the grubby documentary, *Carry On Darkly*, chose Frankie as one of the four key Carry On figures to investigate. He formed part of MOMI's Carry On exhibition, however, and was also remembered in ITV's *What's A Carry On?* celebration. And, as classic British comedy became a cheap time-filler on television and a pretty much guaranteed minor audience-grabber, the various ITV franchises began dishing out countless variations on the same theme.

In 2000, the usual suspects plus Jeanne Mockford were lined up for the Frankie instalment of the *London Legends* series, while on 19 December *The Unforgettable – Frankie Howerd* squeezed some priceless memories from Cilla Black, Bruce Forsyth, Eric Sykes, June Whitfield, Ray Galton, Alan Simpson, Dora Bryan and even his *Runaway Bus* co-star Petula Clark. Radio 2's *There'll Never Be Another* allowed host Graeme Garden to link classic Frankie clips with contributions from Eric Idle, Barry Took, Eric Sykes and Michael Grade. Meanwhile, the BBC2 investigative

documentary production team for *Reputations* were setting their sights on the private life and public times of the great man.

A decade after his death and over 50 years since the gangly, stuttering streak of confused babble stormed into a BBC studio and reinvented stand-up comedy, Frankie Howerd's legacy is as potent as ever. Performers like Larry Grayson and Kenneth Williams, who gladly and gayly plundered the wealth of Howerdisms, may have gone but they have been replaced by a fresh batch of camp performers like Dale Winton, Julian Clary and Graham Norton who happily propagate the warm and intimate patter of Frankie. You can also guarantee that a dubious gag can be followed by a high-pitched 'Missus!' or forced-out 'Ooh no!' for maximum pleasure. The patter, persona and prowling pun-pounding of Frankie Howerd is as much a part of the British way of life as fish 'n' chips and rain on a Bank Holiday Monday. He is a colossus of British comedy, an acute observer of our own faults and follies. If he was consumed by uncertain feelings and introspective gloom, he was also fully aware of his position in the great scheme of things. He was a mere player, like us all, but a player who had the opportunity to address an audience and enter their hearts and souls.

Speaking in 1978 he openly explained his feelings about the profession. 'Actors are like gypsies. You have to travel. We're really travelling salesmen and commercial travellers. We have to go out and sell our goods to make a living so it all involves a great amount of travelling. Very few actors can sit in the middle of where they are or stay at home. They have to travel because that is what acting is all about, meeting people all over the world. But I enjoy that. It's fine. That's why I joined the profession and that's what I do!'

Writ large on the canvas of the variety stage or the cinema screen, Frankie's style continues to inform, entertain and bewitch each new generation. Truly there is absolutely no one to compare to him. There was only one Frankie Howerd and we're all the richer for having known him. ●

Appendix

Books

On the Way I Lost It by Frankie Howerd
  (W H Allen, 1976)
By Royal Command by Bill Pertwee
Stars In Battledress by Bill Pertwee
  (Hodder & Stoughton, 1992)
*Star Turns – The Life and Work of Benny Hill and
  Frankie Howerd* by Barry Took
  (Weidenfeld & Nicolson, 1992)
Titter Ye Not! – The Life of Frankie Howerd
  by William Hall (HarperCollins, 1992:
  (David & Charles, 1989)
Frankie Howerd – the Illustrated Biography
  by Mick Middles (Headline Hardbacks, 2000)

Recordings

The Frankie Howerd Show, includes episodes
  broadcast 7 August 1966, 17 June 1973,
  10 November 1974 and 2 November 1975
  (BBC Radio Collection, ZBBC 1398, 1992:
  reissue BBC Gold ISBN 0563389648, 1996)
*Carrying On – Entertainment from the Carry On
  Team*, includes 'Lovely', 'Up Je t'aime',
  'Up Pompeii' and 'Salute!'
  (EMI Records Ltd, 0777 7 89596 4 9, 1993)
The Laughing Box, includes 'Up Je t'aime'
  (Castle Communications, MAT MC 269, 1993)
Frankie's On…, includes two episodes
  (Laughing Stock, ISBN: 1897774613, 1994)
The Frankie Howerd Show 2, includes episodes
  broadcast 10 June 1973, 1 July 1973,
  27 October 1974 and 8 December 1974
  (BBC Radio Collection, ZBBC 1730, 1995)
The Clown Jewels, includes an extract from
  The Frankie Howerd Show
  (BBC World-Wide, 1995)
Frankie Howerd: Frankie's On…,
  includes all four episodes
  (Laughing Stock, ISBN: 1897774753, 1996)
The Frankie Howerd Song and Dance Collection
  (QED 282, MCPS, 1998)
You Are Awful … But We Like You!: Showbiz
  Comedy Titbits of the 60s and 70s, includes
  'Up Je t'aime' (Sequel Records Castle Music
  Ltd, NEMCD 477, 2000)
Having A Laugh, four-CD Box set including
  'Up Je t'aime' (Castle Pulse X454, 2000)

Videos

An Alligator Named Daisy
  (Rank Video Library 5457)
BBC Comedy Greats 9: Frankie Howerd (BBCV 6935)

Best of British Cinema
  (Screen Entertainment SE9100)
Carry On Doctor (Cinema Club CC1068)
Carry On…Laughing: Hysterical History
  (Cinema Club CC7003)
Carry On Up the Jungle (Cinema Club CC1071)
Comedy Classics of the 60s, includes an extract
  from *East of Howerd*
  (Castle Vision CVB 1054)
Comedy Classics of the 70s, includes an extract
  from *The Russell Harty Show*
  (Castle Vision CVB 1055)
The Cool Mikado, British Classic Cinema
  (Fabulous, Polygram Video BCC 04041)
The Fast Lady (Rank Strand)
Frankie On Campus (LWT VC6145)
Further Up Pompeii (1991)
  (LWT International/Castle Vision, CVI 1423;
  reissued Granada Media GV0310)
The Golden Years of TV Comedy – 1966, includes
  Frankie Howerd series 2, episode 3 (BBCV 5783)
The Great St Trinian's Train Robbery
  (Warner Home Video PES38079)
The House in Nightmare Park
  (Lumiere LUM 2044)
Jumping For Joy (The Rank Collection, Carlton
  Home Entertainment, 30370 60063)
Let It Be Alright On the Night
  (Wiener World WWR2025)
The Plank (Thames Video Collection/The Video
  Collection, TV 9950)
Then Churchill Said To Me: Operation Panic,
  also includes *A Mole in the Hole* and
  Nanny By Searchlight (BBCV 5279)
*Then Churchill Said To Me: Those Who Loot We
  Shoot*, also includes *Blow Out* and *The Goose
  Has Landed* (BBCV 5280)
A Touch of the Sun
  (4Front Video, Polygram: 046 614 3)
Up Pompeii!: Vestal Virgins, also includes
  The Love Potion and *James (sic) Bondus*
  (BBCV 4458)
Up Pompeii!: The Legacy, also includes
  Roman Holiday and *Exodus* (BBCV 4465)
Up Pompeii (Warner Home Video WTB38107)
Up the Chastity Belt
  (Warner Home Video PES38181)
Up the Front (Warner Home Video PES38151)
The Very Best of Up Pompeii!
  (Second Sight 2TV2013; double video
  re-release of episodes previously
  available on BBCV)

Author, author
– Frankie
promoting his
1982 book
Trumps.

Index